IPython Interactive Computing and Visualization Cookbook

To Nick & Darbie

Over 100 hands-on recipes to sharpen your skills in high-performance numerical computing and data science with Python

Thank you for the painstaking proofreading!

Cyrille Rossant

Cyrille

11/7/14

[PACKT] open source*
PUBLISHING   community experience distilled

BIRMINGHAM - MUMBAI

IPython Interactive Computing and Visualization Cookbook

Copyright © 2014 Packt Publishing

First published: September 2014

Production reference: 1190914

Published by Packt Publishing Ltd.
Livery Place
35 Livery Street
Birmingham B3 2PB, UK.

ISBN 978-1-78328-481-8

www.packtpub.com

Cover image by Aniket Sawant (aniket_sawant_photography@hotmail.com)

Credits

Author
Cyrille Rossant

Reviewers
Chetan Giridhar
Robert Johansson
Maurice HT Ling
Jose Unpingco

Commissioning Editor
Kartikey Pandey

Acquisition Editor
Greg Wild

Content Development Editor
Sriram Neelakantan

Technical Editors
Madhuri Das
Taabish Khan
Pratik More

Copy Editors
Janbal Dharmaraj
Deepa Nambiar
Karuna Narayanan

Project Coordinator
Judie Jose

Proofreaders
Simran Bhogal
Martin Diver
Maria Gould
Ameesha Green
Paul Hindle
Lucy Rowland

Indexer
Tejal Soni

Graphics
Sheetal Aute
Ronak Dhruv
Disha Haria

Production Coordinators
Melwyn D'sa
Adonia Jones
Manu Joseph
Saiprasad Kadam
Nilesh R. Mohite
Komal Ramchandani
Alwin Roy
Nitesh Thakur

Cover Work
Alwin Roy

About the Author

Cyrille Rossant is a researcher in neuroinformatics, and is a graduate of Ecole Normale Supérieure, Paris, where he studied mathematics and computer science. He has worked at Princeton University, University College London, and Collège de France.

As part of his data science and software engineering projects, he gained experience in machine learning, high-performance computing, parallel computing, and big data visualization. He is one of the developers of Vispy, a high-performance visualization package in Python. He is the author of *Learning IPython for Interactive Computing and Data Visualization, Packt Publishing*, a beginner-level introduction to data analysis in Python, and the prequel of this book.

I would like to thank the IPython development team for their support. I am also deeply grateful to Nick Fiorentini and his partner Darbie Whitman for their invaluable help during the later stages of editing.

Finally, I would like to thank my relatives and notably my wife Claire.

About the Reviewers

Chetan Giridhar is an open source evangelist and Python enthusiast. He has been invited to talk at international Python conferences on topics such as filesystems, search engines, and real-time communication. He is also working as an associate editor at Python editorial, *The Python Papers Anthology*.

Chetan works as a lead engineer and evangelist at BlueJeans Network (`http://bluejeans.com/`), a leading video conferencing site on Cloud Company.

He has co-authored an e-book, *Design Patterns in Python*, *Testing Perspective*, and has reviewed books on Python programming at Packt Publishing.

> I'd like to thank my parents (Jayant and Jyotsana Giridhar), my wife Deepti, and my friends/colleagues for supporting and inspiring me.

Robert Johansson has a PhD in Theoretical Physics from Chalmers University of Technology, Sweden. He is currently working as a researcher at the Interdisciplinary Theoretical Science Research Group at RIKEN, Japan, focusing on computational condensed-matter physics and quantum mechanics.

Maurice HT Ling completed his PhD in Bioinformatics and BSc (Hons) in Molecular and Cell Biology from The University of Melbourne, Australia. He is currently a research fellow in Nanyang Technological University, Singapore, and an honorary fellow in The University of Melbourne, Australia. Maurice coedits *The Python Papers* and cofounded the Python User Group (Singapore), where he has served as an executive committee member since 2010. His research interests lies in life—biological and artificial life, and artificial intelligence—using computer science and statistics as tools to understand life and its numerous aspects. His personal website is `http://maurice.vodien.com`.

Jose Unpingco is the author of the *Python for Signal Processing* blog and the corresponding book. A graduate from University of California, San Diego, he has spent almost 20 years in the industry as an analyst, instructor, engineer, consultant, and technical director in the area of signal processing. His interests include time-series analysis, statistical signal processing, random processes, and large-scale interactive computing.

Unpingco has been an active member of the scientific Python community for over a decade, and developed some of the first video tutorials on IPython and scientific Python. He has also helped fund a number of scientific Python efforts in a wide variety of disciplines.

www.PacktPub.com

Support files, eBooks, discount offers, and more

You might want to visit www.PacktPub.com for support files and downloads related to your book.

Did you know that Packt offers eBook versions of every book published, with PDF and ePub files available? You can upgrade to the eBook version at www.PacktPub.com and as a print book customer, you are entitled to a discount on the eBook copy. Get in touch with us at service@packtpub.com for more details.

At www.PacktPub.com, you can also read a collection of free technical articles, sign up for a range of free newsletters and receive exclusive discounts and offers on Packt books and eBooks.

http://PacktLib.PacktPub.com

Do you need instant solutions to your IT questions? PacktLib is Packt's online digital book library. Here, you can access, read and search across Packt's entire library of books.

Why Subscribe?

- Fully searchable across every book published by Packt
- Copy and paste, print and bookmark content
- On demand and accessible via web browser

Free Access for Packt account holders

If you have an account with Packt at www.PacktPub.com, you can use this to access PacktLib today and view nine entirely free books. Simply use your login credentials for immediate access.

Table of Contents

Table of Contents ───

Preface

We are becoming awash in the flood of digital data from scientific research, engineering, economics, politics, journalism, business, and many other domains. As a result, analyzing, visualizing, and harnessing data is the occupation of an increasingly large and diverse set of people. Quantitative skills such as programming, numerical computing, mathematics, statistics, and data mining, which form the core of data science, are more and more appreciated in a seemingly endless plethora of fields.

My previous book, *Learning IPython for Interactive Computing and Data Visualization*, *Packt Publishing*, published in 2013, was a beginner-level introduction to data science and numerical computing with Python. This widely-used programming language is also one of the most popular platforms for these disciplines.

This book continues that journey by presenting more than 100 advanced recipes for data science and mathematical modeling. These recipes not only cover programming and computing topics such as interactive computing, numerical computing, high-performance computing, parallel computing, and interactive visualization, but also data analysis topics such as statistics, data mining, machine learning, signal processing, and many others.

All of this book's code has been written in the IPython notebook. IPython is at the heart of the Python data analysis platform. Originally created to enhance the default Python console, IPython is now mostly known for its widely acclaimed notebook. This web-based interactive computational environment combines code, rich text, images, mathematical equations, and plots into a single document. It is an ideal gateway to data analysis and high-performance numerical computing in Python.

What this book is

This cookbook contains in *excess* of a hundred focused recipes, answering specific questions in numerical computing and data analysis with IPython on:

- ▶ How to explore a public dataset with pandas, PyMC, and SciPy
- ▶ How to create interactive plots, widgets, and Graphical User Interfaces in the IPython notebook
- ▶ How to create a configurable IPython extension with custom magic commands
- ▶ How to distribute asynchronous tasks in parallel with IPython
- ▶ How to accelerate code with OpenMP, MPI, Numba, Cython, OpenCL, CUDA, and the Julia programming language
- ▶ How to estimate a probability density from a dataset
- ▶ How to get started using the R statistical programming language in the notebook
- ▶ How to train a classifier or a regressor with scikit-learn
- ▶ How to find interesting projections in a high-dimensional dataset
- ▶ How to detect faces in an image
- ▶ How to simulate a reaction-diffusion system
- ▶ How to compute an itinerary in a road network

The choice made in this book was to introduce a wide range of different topics instead of delving into the details of a few methods. The goal is to give you a taste of the incredibly rich capabilities of Python for data science. All methods are applied on diverse real-world examples.

Every recipe of this book demonstrates not only how to apply a method, but also how and why it works. It is important to understand the mathematical concepts and ideas underlying the methods instead of merely applying them blindly.

Additionally, each recipe comes with many references for the interested reader who wants to know more. As online references change frequently, they will be kept up to date on the book's website (http://ipython-books.github.io).

What this book covers

This book is split into two parts:

Part 1 (chapters 1 to 6) covers advanced methods in interactive numerical computing, high-performance computing, and data visualization.

Part 2 (chapters 7 to 15) introduces standard methods in data science and mathematical modeling. All of these methods are applied to real-world data.

Part 1 – Advanced High-Performance Interactive Computing

Chapter 1, A Tour of Interactive Computing with IPython, contains a brief but intense introduction to data analysis and numerical computing with IPython. It not only covers common packages such as Python, NumPy, pandas, and matplotlib, but also advanced IPython topics such as interactive widgets in the notebook, custom magic commands, configurable IPython extensions, and new language kernels.

Chapter 2, Best Practices in Interactive Computing, details best practices to write reproducible, high-quality code: task automation, version control with Git, workflows with IPython, unit testing with nose, continuous integration, debugging, and other related topics. The importance of these subjects in computational research and data analysis cannot be overstated.

Chapter 3, Mastering the Notebook, covers advanced topics related to the IPython notebook, notably the notebook format, notebook conversions, and CSS/JavaScript customization. The new interactive widgets available since IPython 2.0 are also extensively covered. These techniques make data analysis in the notebook more interactive than ever.

Chapter 4, Profiling and Optimization, covers methods to make your code faster and more efficient: CPU and memory profiling in Python, advanced optimization techniques with NumPy (including large array manipulations), and memory mapping of huge arrays with the HDF5 file format and the PyTables library. These techniques are essential for big data analysis.

Chapter 5, High-performance Computing, covers advanced techniques to make your code *much* faster: code acceleration with Numba and Cython, wrapping C libraries in Python with ctypes, parallel computing with IPython, OpenMP, and MPI, and General-Purpose Computing on Graphics Processing Units (GPGPU) with CUDA and OpenCL. The chapter ends with an introduction to the recent Julia language, which was designed for high-performance numerical computing and can be easily used in the IPython notebook.

Chapter 6, Advanced Visualization, introduces a few data visualization libraries that go beyond matplotlib in terms of styling or programming interfaces. It also covers interactive visualization in the notebook with Bokeh, mpld3, and D3.js. The chapter ends with an introduction to Vispy, a library that leverages the power of Graphics Processing Units for high-performance interactive visualization of big data.

Part 2 – Standard Methods in Data Science and Applied Mathematics

Chapter 7, Statistical Data Analysis, covers methods for getting insight into data. It introduces classic frequentist and Bayesian methods for hypothesis testing, parametric and nonparametric estimation, and model inference. The chapter leverages Python libraries such as pandas, SciPy, statsmodels, and PyMC. The last recipe introduces the statistical language R, which can be easily used in the IPython notebook.

Chapter 8, Machine Learning, covers methods to learn and make predictions from data. Using the scikit-learn Python package, this chapter illustrates fundamental data mining and machine learning concepts such as supervised and unsupervised learning, classification, regression, feature selection, feature extraction, overfitting, regularization, cross-validation, and grid search. Algorithms addressed in this chapter include logistic regression, Naive Bayes, K-nearest neighbors, Support Vector Machines, random forests, and others. These methods are applied to various types of datasets: numerical data, images, and text.

Chapter 9, Numerical Optimization, is about minimizing or maximizing mathematical functions. This topic is pervasive in data science, notably in statistics, machine learning, and signal processing. This chapter illustrates a few root-finding, minimization, and curve fitting routines with SciPy.

Chapter 10, Signal Processing, is about extracting relevant information from complex and noisy data. These steps are sometimes required prior to running statistical and data mining algorithms. This chapter introduces standard signal processing methods such as Fourier transforms and digital filters.

Chapter 11, Image and Audio Processing, covers signal processing methods for images and sounds. It introduces image filtering, segmentation, computer vision, and face detection with scikit-image and OpenCV. It also presents methods for audio processing and synthesis.

Chapter 12, Deterministic Dynamical Systems, describes dynamical processes underlying particular types of data. It illustrates simulation techniques for discrete-time dynamical systems as well as for ordinary differential equations and partial differential equations.

Chapter 13, Stochastic Dynamical Systems, describes dynamical random processes underlying particular types of data. It illustrates simulation techniques for discrete-time Markov chains, point processes, and stochastic differential equations.

Chapter 14, Graphs, Geometry, and Geographic Information Systems, covers analysis and visualization methods for graphs, social networks, road networks, maps, and geographic data.

Chapter 15, Symbolic and Numerical Mathematics, introduces SymPy, a computer algebra system that brings symbolic computing to Python. The chapter ends with an introduction to Sage, another Python-based system for computational mathematics.

What you need for this book

You need to know the content of this book's prequel, *Learning IPython for Interactive Computing and Data Visualization*: Python programming, the IPython console and notebook, numerical computing with NumPy, basic data analysis with pandas as well as plotting with matplotlib. This book tackles advanced scientific programming topics that require you to be familiar with the scientific Python ecosystem.

In Part 2, you need to know the basics of calculus, linear algebra, and probability theory. These chapters introduce different topics in data science and applied mathematics (statistics, machine learning, numerical optimization, signal processing, dynamical systems, graph theory, and others). You will understand these recipes better if you know fundamental concepts such as real-valued functions, integrals, matrices, vector spaces, probabilities, and so on.

Installing Python

There are many ways to install Python. We highly recommend the free Anaconda distribution (http://store.continuum.io/cshop/anaconda/). This Python distribution contains most of the packages that we will be using in this book. It also includes a powerful packaging system named conda. The book's website contains all the instructions to install Anaconda and run the code examples. You should learn how to install packages (conda install packagename) and how to create multiple Python environments with conda.

The code of this book has been written for Python 3 (more precisely, the code has been tested on Python 3.4.1, Anaconda 2.0.1, Windows 8.1 64-bit, although it definitely works on Linux and Mac OS X), but it also works with Python 2.7. We mention any compatibility issue when required. These issues are rare in this book, because NumPy does the heavy lifting in most cases. NumPy's interface hasn't changed between Python 2 and Python 3.

If you're unsure about which Python version you should use, pick Python 3. You should only pick Python 2 if you really need to (for example, if you absolutely need a Python package that doesn't support Python 3, or if part of your user base is stuck with Python 2). We cover this question in greater detail in *Chapter 2, Best Practices in Interactive Computing*.

With Anaconda, you can install Python 2 and Python 3 side-by-side using conda environments. This is how you can easily run the couple of recipes in this book that require Python 2.

GitHub repositories

A home page and two GitHub repositories accompany this book:

- ▶ The main webpage at http://ipython-books.github.io
- ▶ The main GitHub repository, with the codes and references of all recipes, at https://github.com/ipython-books/cookbook-code
- ▶ Datasets used in certain recipes at https://github.com/ipython-books/cookbook-data

The main GitHub repository is where you can:

- ▶ Find all code examples as IPython notebooks
- ▶ Find all up-to-date references
- ▶ Find up-to-date installation instructions
- ▶ Report errata, inaccuracies, or mistakes via the issue tracker

- ▶ Propose fixes via Pull Requests
- ▶ Add notes, comments, or further references via Pull Requests
- ▶ Add new recipes via Pull Requests

The online list of references is a particularly important resource. It contains many links to tutorials, courses, books, and videos about the topics covered in this book.

You can also follow updates about the book on my website (`http://cyrille.rossant.net`) and on my Twitter account (`@cyrillerossant`).

Who this book is for

This book targets students, researchers, teachers, engineers, data scientists, analysts, journalists, economists, and hobbyists interested in data analysis and numerical computing.

Readers familiar with the scientific Python ecosystem will find many resources to sharpen their skills in high-performance interactive computing with IPython.

Readers who need to implement algorithms for domain-specific applications will appreciate the introductions to a wide variety of topics in data analysis and applied mathematics.

Readers who are new to numerical computing with Python should start with the prequel of this book, *Learning IPython for Interactive Computing and Data Visualization*, *Cyrille Rossant*, *Packt Publishing, 2013*. A second edition is planned for 2015.

Conventions

In this book, you will find a number of styles of text that distinguish between different kinds of information. Here are some examples of these styles and an explanation of their meaning.

Code words in text, database table names, folder names, filenames, file extensions, pathnames, dummy URLs, user input, and Twitter handles are shown as follows: "Notebooks can be run in an interactive session via `%run notebook.ipynb`."

A block of code is set as follows:

```
def do_complete(self, code, cursor_pos):
    return {'status': 'ok',
            'cursor_start': ...,
            'cursor_end': ...,
            'matches': [...]}
```

Any command-line input or output is written as follows:

```
from IPython import embed
embed()
```

New terms and **important words** are shown in bold. Words that you see on the screen, in menus or dialog boxes for example, appear in the text like this: "The simplest option is to launch them from the **Clusters** tab in the notebook dashboard."

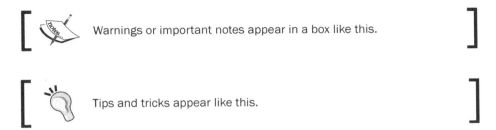

Warnings or important notes appear in a box like this.

Tips and tricks appear like this.

Reader feedback

Feedback from our readers is always welcome. Let us know what you think about this book—what you liked or may have disliked. Reader feedback is important for us to develop titles that you really get the most out of.

To send us general feedback, simply send an e-mail to feedback@packtpub.com, and mention the book title via the subject of your message.

If there is a topic that you have expertise in and you are interested in either writing or contributing to a book, see our author guide on www.packtpub.com/authors.

Customer support

Now that you are the proud owner of a Packt book, we have a number of things to help you to get the most from your purchase.

Downloading the example code

You can download the example code files for all Packt books you have purchased from your account at http://www.packtpub.com. If you purchased this book elsewhere, you can visit http://www.packtpub.com/support and register to have the files e-mailed directly to you.

Downloading the color images

We also provide you with a PDF file that has color images of the screenshots/diagrams used in this book. The color images will help you better understand the changes in the output. You can download this file from the following link: https://www.packtpub.com/sites/default/files/downloads/4818OS_ColoredImages.pdf.

Errata

Although we have taken every care to ensure the accuracy of our content, mistakes do happen. If you find a mistake in one of our books—maybe a mistake in the text or the code—we would be grateful if you would report this to us. By doing so, you can save other readers from frustration and help us improve subsequent versions of this book. If you find any errata, please report them by visiting http://www.packtpub.com/submit-errata, selecting your book, clicking on the **errata submission form** link, and entering the details of your errata. Once your errata are verified, your submission will be accepted and the errata will be uploaded on our website, or added to any list of existing errata, under the Errata section of that title. Any existing errata can be viewed by selecting your title from http://www.packtpub.com/support.

Piracy

Piracy of copyright material on the Internet is an ongoing problem across all media. At Packt, we take the protection of our copyright and licenses very seriously. If you come across any illegal copies of our works, in any form, on the Internet, please provide us with the location address or website name immediately so that we can pursue a remedy.

Please contact us at copyright@packtpub.com with a link to the suspected pirated material.

We appreciate your help in protecting our authors, and our ability to bring you valuable content.

Questions

You can contact us at questions@packtpub.com if you are having a problem with any aspect of the book, and we will do our best to address it.

1

A Tour of Interactive Computing with IPython

In this chapter, we will cover the following topics:

- ▶ Introducing the IPython notebook
- ▶ Getting started with exploratory data analysis in IPython
- ▶ Introducing the multidimensional array in NumPy for fast array computations
- ▶ Creating an IPython extension with custom magic commands
- ▶ Mastering IPython's configuration system
- ▶ Creating a simple kernel for IPython

Introduction

This book targets intermediate to advanced users who are familiar with Python, IPython, and scientific computing. In this chapter, we will give a brief recap on the fundamental tools we will be using throughout this book: IPython, the notebook, pandas, NumPy, and matplotlib.

In this introduction, we will give a broad overview of IPython and the Python scientific stack for high-performance computing and data science.

What is IPython?

IPython is an open source platform for interactive and parallel computing. It offers powerful interactive shells and a browser-based notebook. The **notebook** combines code, text, mathematical expressions, inline plots, interactive plots, and other rich media within a sharable web document. This platform provides an ideal framework for interactive scientific computing and data analysis. IPython has become essential to researchers, data scientists, and teachers.

IPython can be used with the Python programming language, but the platform also supports many other languages such as R, Julia, Haskell, or Ruby. The architecture of the project is indeed language-agnostic, consisting of messaging protocols and interactive clients (including the browser-based notebook). The clients are connected to **kernels** that implement the core interactive computing facilities. Therefore, the platform can be useful to technical and scientific communities that use languages other than Python.

In July 2014, **Project Jupyter** was announced by the IPython developers. This project will focus on the language-independent parts of IPython (including the notebook architecture), whereas the name IPython will be reserved to the Python kernel. In this book, for the sake of simplicity, we will just use the term IPython to refer to either the platform or the Python kernel.

A brief historical retrospective on Python as a scientific environment

Python is a high-level general-purpose language originally conceived by Guido van Rossum in the late 1980s (the name was inspired by the British comedy *Monty Python's Flying Circus*). This easy-to-use language is the basis of many scripting programs that glue different software components (**glue language**) together. In addition, Python comes with an extremely rich standard library (the *batteries included* philosophy), which covers string processing, Internet Protocols, operating system interfaces, and many other domains.

In the late 1990s, Travis Oliphant and others started to build efficient tools to deal with numerical data in Python: Numeric, Numarray, and finally, **NumPy**. **SciPy**, which implements many numerical computing algorithms, was also created on top of NumPy. In the early 2000s, John Hunter created **matplotlib** to bring scientific graphics to Python. At the same time, Fernando Perez created IPython to improve interactivity and productivity in Python. All the fundamental tools were here to turn Python into a great open source high-performance framework for scientific computing and data analysis.

It is worth noting that Python as a platform for scientific computing was built slowly, step-by-step, on top of a programming language that was not originally designed for this purpose. This fact might explain a few minor inconsistencies or weaknesses of the platform, which do not preclude it from being one of the most popular open frameworks for scientific computing at this time. (You can also refer to `http://cyrille.rossant.net/whats-wrong-with-scientific-python/`.)

Notable competing open source platforms for numerical computing and data analysis include R (which focuses on statistics) and Julia (a young, high-level language that focuses on high performance and parallel computing). We will see these two languages very briefly in this book, as they can be used from the IPython notebook.

In the late 2000s, Wes McKinney created **pandas** for the manipulation and analysis of numerical tables and time series. At the same time, the IPython developers started to work on a notebook client inspired by mathematical software such as **Sage**, **Maple**, and **Mathematica**. Finally, IPython 0.12, released in December 2011, introduced the HTML-based notebook that has now gone mainstream.

In 2013, the IPython team received a grant from the Sloan Foundation and a donation from Microsoft to support the development of the notebook. IPython 2.0, released in early 2014, brought many improvements and long-awaited features.

What's new in IPython 2.0?

Here is a short summary of the changes brought by IPython 2.0 (succeeding v1.1):

- The notebook comes with a new **modal user interface**:
    - In the **edit mode**, we can edit a cell by entering code or text.
    - In the **command mode**, we can edit the notebook by moving cells around, duplicating or deleting them, changing their types, and so on. In this mode, the keyboard is mapped to a set of shortcuts that let us perform notebook and cell actions efficiently.
- **Notebook widgets** are JavaScript-based GUI widgets that interact dynamically with Python objects. This major feature considerably expands the possibilities of the IPython notebook. Writing Python code in the notebook is no longer the only possible interaction with the kernel. JavaScript widgets and, more generally, any JavaScript-based interactive element, can now interact with the kernel in real-time.

▸ We can now open notebooks in different subfolders with the dashboard, using the same server. A REST API maps local URIs to the filesystem.

▸ Notebooks are now signed to prevent untrusted code from executing when notebooks are opened.

▸ The dashboard now contains a **Running** tab with the list of running kernels.

▸ The tooltip now appears when pressing *Shift + Tab* instead of *Tab*.

▸ Notebooks can be run in an interactive session via `%run notebook.ipynb`.

▸ The `%pylab` magic is discouraged in favor of `%matplotlib inline` (to embed figures in the notebook) and `import matplotlib.pyplot as plt`. The main reason is that `%pylab` clutters the interactive namespace by importing a huge number of variables. Also, it might harm the reproducibility and reusability of notebooks.

▸ Python 2.6 and 3.2 are no longer supported. IPython now requires Python 2.7 or >= 3.3.

Roadmap for IPython 3.0 and 4.0

IPython 3.0 and 4.0, planned for late 2014/early 2015, should facilitate the use of non-Python kernels and provide multiuser capabilities to the notebook.

References

Here are a few references:

▸ The Python webpage at `www.python.org`

▸ Python on Wikipedia at `http://en.wikipedia.org/wiki/Python_%28programming_language%29`

▸ Python's standard library present at `https://docs.python.org/2/library/`

▸ Guido van Rossum on Wikipedia at `http://en.wikipedia.org/wiki/Guido_van_Rossum`

▸ Conversation with Guido van Rossum on the birth of Python available at `www.artima.com/intv/pythonP.html`

▸ History of scientific Python available at `http://fr.slideshare.net/shoheihido/sci-pyhistory`

▸ What's new in IPython 2.0 at `http://ipython.org/ipython-doc/2/whatsnew/version2.0.html`

▸ IPython on Wikipedia at `http://en.wikipedia.org/wiki/IPython`

▸ History of the IPython notebook at `http://blog.fperez.org/2012/01/ipython-notebook-historical.html`

Introducing the IPython notebook

The notebook is the flagship feature of IPython. This web-based interactive environment combines code, rich text, images, videos, animations, mathematics, and plots into a single document. This modern tool is an ideal gateway to high-performance numerical computing and data science in Python. This entire book has been written in the notebook, and the code of every recipe is available as a notebook on the book's GitHub repository at `https://github.com/ipython-books/cookbook-code`.

In this recipe, we give an introduction to IPython and its notebook. In *Getting ready*, we also give general instructions on installing IPython and the Python scientific stack.

Getting ready

You will need Python, IPython, NumPy, pandas, and matplotlib in this chapter. Together with SciPy and SymPy, these libraries form the core of the Python scientific stack (`www.scipy.org/about.html`).

> You will find full detailed installation instructions on the book's GitHub repository at `https://github.com/ipython-books/cookbook-code`.
>
> We only give a summary of these instructions here; please refer to the link above for more up-to-date details.

If you're just getting started with scientific computing in Python, the simplest option is to install an all-in-one Python distribution. The most common distributions are:

- **Anaconda** (free or commercial license) available at `http://store.continuum.io/cshop/anaconda/`
- **Canopy** (free or commercial license) available at `www.enthought.com/products/canopy/`
- **Python(x,y)**, a free distribution only for Windows, available at `https://code.google.com/p/pythonxy/`

We *highly* recommend Anaconda. These distributions contain everything you need to get started. You can also install additional packages as needed. You will find all the installation instructions in the links mentioned previously.

> Throughout the book, we assume that you have installed Anaconda. We may not be able to offer support to readers who use another distribution.

Alternatively, if you feel brave, you can install Python, IPython, NumPy, pandas, and matplotlib manually. You will find all the instructions on the following websites:

- **Python** is the programming language underlying the ecosystem. The instructions are available at www.python.org/.

- **IPython** provides tools for interactive computing in Python. The instructions for installation are available at http://ipython.org/install.html.

- **NumPy/SciPy** are used for numerical computing in Python. The instructions for installation are available at www.scipy.org/install.html.

- **pandas** provides data structures and tools for data analysis in Python. The instructions for installation are available at http://pandas.pydata.org/getpandas.html.

- **matplotlib** helps in creating scientific figures in Python. The instructions for installation are available at http://matplotlib.org/index.html.

Python 2 or Python 3?

Though Python 3 is the latest version at this date, many people are still using Python 2. Python 3 has brought backward-incompatible changes that have slowed down its adoption. If you are just getting started with Python for scientific computing, you might as well choose Python 3. In this book, all the code has been written for Python 3, but it also works with Python 2. We will give more details about this question in *Chapter 2, Best Practices in Interactive Computing*.

Once you have installed either an all-in-one Python distribution (again, we *highly* recommend Anaconda), or Python and the required packages, you can get started! In this book, the IPython notebook is used in almost all recipes. This tool gives you access to Python from your web browser. We covered the essentials of the notebook in the *Learning IPython for Interactive Computing and Data Visualization* book. You can also find more information on IPython's website (http://ipython.org/ipython-doc/stable/notebook/index.html).

To run the IPython notebook server, type ipython notebook in a terminal (also called the **command prompt**). Your default web browser should open automatically and load the 127.0.0.1:8888 address. Then, you can create a new notebook in the dashboard or open an existing notebook. By default, the notebook server opens in the current directory (the directory you launched the command from). It lists all the notebooks present in this directory (files with the .ipynb extension).

On Windows, you can open a command prompt by pressing the Windows key and *R*, then typing cmd in the prompt, and finally by pressing *Enter*.

How to do it...

1. We assume that a Python distribution is installed with IPython and that we are now in an IPython notebook. We type the following command in a cell, and press *Shift + Enter* to evaluate it:

```
In [1]: print("Hello world!")
Hello world!
```

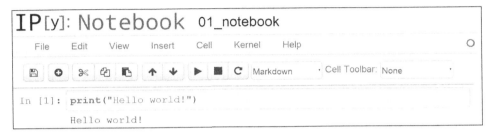

Screenshot of the IPython notebook

A notebook contains a linear succession of **cells** and **output areas**. A cell contains Python code, in one or multiple lines. The output of the code is shown in the corresponding output area.

2. Now, we do a simple arithmetic operation:

```
In [2]: 2+2
Out[2]: 4
```

The result of the operation is shown in the output area. Let's be more precise. The output area not only displays the text that is printed by any command in the cell, but it also displays a text representation of the last returned object. Here, the last returned object is the result of 2+2, that is, 4.

3. In the next cell, we can recover the value of the last returned object with the _ (underscore) special variable. In practice, it might be more convenient to assign objects to named variables such as in myresult = 2+2.

```
In [3]: _ * 3
Out[3]: 12
```

4. IPython not only accepts Python code, but also shell commands. These commands are defined by the operating system (mainly Windows, Linux, and Mac OS X). We first type ! in a cell before typing the shell command. Here, assuming a Linux or Mac OS X system, we get the list of all the notebooks in the current directory:

```
In [4]: !ls *.ipynb
notebook1.ipynb  ...
```

On Windows, you should replace ls with dir.

5. IPython comes with a library of **magic commands**. These commands are convenient shortcuts to common actions. They all start with % (the percent character). We can get the list of all magic commands with %lsmagic:

```
In [5]: %lsmagic
Out[5]: Available line magics:
%alias  %alias_magic  %autocall  %automagic  %autosave  %bookmark
%cd  %clear  %cls  %colors  %config  %connect_info  %copy  %ddir
%debug  %dhist  %dirs  %doctest_mode  %echo  %ed  %edit  %env
%gui  %hist  %history  %install_default_config  %install_ext
%install_profiles  %killbgscripts  %ldir  %less  %load  %load_ext
%loadpy  %logoff  %logon  %logstart  %logstate  %logstop  %ls
%lsmagic  %macro  %magic  %matplotlib  %mkdir  %more  %notebook
%page  %pastebin  %pdb  %pdef  %pdoc  %pfile  %pinfo  %pinfo2
%popd  %pprint  %precision  %profile  %prun  %psearch  %psource
%pushd  %pwd  %pycat  %pylab  %qtconsole  %quickref  %recall
%rehashx  %reload_ext  %ren  %rep  %rerun  %reset  %reset_
selective  %rmdir  %run  %save  %sc  %store  %sx  %system  %tb
%time  %timeit  %unalias  %unload_ext  %who  %who_ls  %whos  %xdel
%xmode

Available cell magics:
%%!  %%HTML  %%SVG  %%bash  %%capture  %%cmd  %%debug  %%file
%%html  %%javascript  %%latex  %%perl  %%powershell  %%prun
%%pypy  %%python  %%python3  %%ruby  %%script  %%sh  %%svg  %%sx
%%system  %%time  %%timeit  %%writefile
```

Cell magics have a %% prefix; they concern entire code cells.

6. For example, the %%writefile cell magic lets us create a text file easily. This magic command accepts a filename as an argument. All the remaining lines in the cell are directly written to this text file. Here, we create a file test.txt and write Hello world! in it:

```
In [6]: %%writefile test.txt
        Hello world!
Writing test.txt
In [7]: # Let's check what this file contains.
        with open('test.txt', 'r') as f:
            print(f.read())
Hello world!
```

7. As we can see in the output of %lsmagic, there are many magic commands in IPython. We can find more information about any command by adding ? after it. For example, to get some help about the %run magic command, we type %run? as shown here:

```
In [9]: %run?
Type:       Magic function
Namespace:  IPython internal
```

```
...
Docstring:
Run the named file inside IPython as a program.
[full documentation of the magic command...]
```

8. We covered the basics of IPython and the notebook. Let's now turn to the rich display and interactive features of the notebook. Until now, we have only created **code cells** (containing code). IPython supports other types of cells. In the notebook toolbar, there is a drop-down menu to select the cell's type. The most common cell type after the code cell is the **Markdown cell**.

    Markdown cells contain rich text formatted with **Markdown**, a popular plain text-formatting syntax. This format supports normal text, headers, bold, italics, hypertext links, images, mathematical equations in **LaTeX** (a typesetting system adapted to mathematics), code, HTML elements, and other features, as shown here:

    ```
    ### New paragraph
    This is *rich* **text** with [links](http://ipython.org),
    equations:

    $$\hat{f}(\xi) = \int_{-\infty}^{+\infty} f(x)\,
                    \mathrm{e}^{-i \xi x}$$

    code with syntax highlighting:
    ```python
    print("Hello world!")
    ```

    and images:
    ![This is an image](http://ipython.org/_static/IPy_header.png)
    ```

    Running a Markdown cell (by pressing *Shift + Enter*, for example) displays the output, as shown in the following screenshot:

New paragraph

This is *rich* **text** with links, equations:

$$\hat{f}(\xi) = \int_{-\infty}^{+\infty} f(x)\, e^{-i\xi x}$$

code with syntax highlighting:

```
print("Hello world!")
```

and images:

Rich text formatting with Markdown in the IPython notebook

LaTeX equations are rendered with the `MathJax` library. We can enter inline equations with `$...$` and displayed equations with `$$...$$`. We can also use environments such as `equation`, `eqnarray`, or `align`. These features are very useful to scientific users.

By combining code cells and Markdown cells, we can create a standalone interactive document that combines computations (code), text, and graphics.

9. IPython also comes with a sophisticated display system that lets us insert rich web elements in the notebook. Here, we show how to add HTML, **SVG (Scalable Vector Graphics)**, and even YouTube videos in a notebook.

First, we need to import some classes:

```
In [11]: from IPython.display import HTML, SVG, YouTubeVideo
```

We create an HTML table dynamically with Python, and we display it in the notebook:

```
In [12]: HTML('''
         <table style="border: 2px solid black;">
         ''' +
         ''.join(['<tr>' +
                 ''.join(['<td>{row},{col}</td>'.format(
                             row=row, col=col
                             ) for col in range(5)]) +
                 '</tr>' for row in range(5)]) +
         '''
         </table>
         ''')
```

0,0	0,1	0,2	0,3	0,4
1,0	1,1	1,2	1,3	1,4
2,0	2,1	2,2	2,3	2,4
3,0	3,1	3,2	3,3	3,4
4,0	4,1	4,2	4,3	4,4

An HTML table in the notebook

Similarly, we can create SVG graphics dynamically:

```
In [13]: SVG('''<svg width="600" height="80">''' +
         ''.join(['''<circle cx="{x}" cy="{y}" r="{r}"
                             fill="red"
```

```
                       stroke-width="2"
                       stroke="black">
            </circle>'''.format(x=(30+3*i)*(10-i),
                                 y=30,
                                 r=3.*float(i)
                                 ) for i in range(10)]) +
      '''</svg>''')
```

SVG in the notebook

Finally, we display a YouTube video by giving its identifier to `YoutubeVideo`:

```
In [14]: YouTubeVideo('j9YpkSX7NNM')
```

YouTube in the notebook

10. Now, we illustrate the latest interactive features in IPython 2.0+, namely JavaScript
    widgets. Here, we create a drop-down menu to select videos:

```
In [15]: from collections import OrderedDict
         from IPython.display import (display,
                                      clear_output,
                                      YouTubeVideo)
         from IPython.html.widgets import DropdownWidget
In [16]: # We create a DropdownWidget, with a dictionary
         # containing the keys (video name) and the values
         # (Youtube identifier) of every menu item.
         dw = DropdownWidget(values=OrderedDict([
```

```
                                    ('SciPy 2012', 'iwVvqwLDsJo'),
                                    ('PyCon 2012', '2G5YTlheCbw'),
                                    ('SciPy 2013', 'j9YpkSX7NNM')]
                                                            )
                                )

    # We create a callback function that displays the
    # requested Youtube video.
    def on_value_change(name, val):
        clear_output()
        display(YouTubeVideo(val))

    # Every time the user selects an item, the
    # function `on_value_change` is called, and the
    # `val` argument contains the value of the selected
    # item.
    dw.on_trait_change(on_value_change, 'value')

    # We choose a default value.
    dw.value = dw.values['SciPy 2013']

    # Finally, we display the widget.
    display(dw)
```

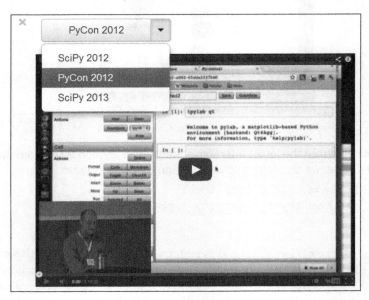

An interactive widget in the notebook

The interactive features of IPython 2.0 bring a whole new dimension to the notebook, and we can expect many developments in the future.

There's more...

Notebooks are saved as structured text files (JSON format), which makes them easily shareable. Here are the contents of a simple notebook:

```
{
 "metadata": {
  "name": ""
 },
 "nbformat": 3,
 "nbformat_minor": 0,
 "worksheets": [
  {
   "cells": [
    {
     "cell_type": "code",
     "collapsed": false,
     "input": [
      "print(\"Hello World!\")"
     ],
     "language": "python",
     "metadata": {},
     "outputs": [
      {
       "output_type": "stream",
       "stream": "stdout",
       "text": [
        "Hello World!\n"
       ]
      }
     ],
     "prompt_number": 1
    }
   ],
   "metadata": {}
  }
 ]
}
```

IPython comes with a special tool, **nbconvert**, which converts notebooks to other formats such as HTML and PDF (http://ipython.org/ipython-doc/stable/notebook/index.html).

Another online tool, **nbviewer**, allows us to render a publicly available notebook directly in the browser and is available at `http://nbviewer.ipython.org`.

We will cover many of these possibilities in the subsequent chapters, notably in *Chapter 3, Mastering the Notebook*.

Here are a few references about the notebook:

- Official page of the notebook available at `http://ipython.org/notebook`
- Documentation of the notebook available at `http://ipython.org/ipython-doc/dev/notebook/index.html`
- Official notebook examples present at `https://github.com/ipython/ipython/tree/master/examples/Notebook`
- User-curated gallery of interesting notebooks available at `https://github.com/ipython/ipython/wiki/A-gallery-of-interesting-IPython-Notebooks`
- Official tutorial on the interactive widgets present at `http://nbviewer.ipython.org/github/ipython/ipython/tree/master/examples/Interactive%20Widgets/`

See also

- The *Getting started with data exploratory analysis in IPython* recipe

Getting started with exploratory data analysis in IPython

In this recipe, we will give an introduction to IPython for data analysis. Most of the subject has been covered in the *Learning IPython for Interactive Computing and Data Visualization* book, but we will review the basics here.

We will download and analyze a dataset about attendance on Montreal's bicycle tracks. This example is largely inspired by a presentation from Julia Evans (available at `http://nbviewer.ipython.org/github/jvns/talks/blob/master/mtlpy35/pistes-cyclables.ipynb`). Specifically, we will introduce the following:

- Data manipulation with pandas
- Data visualization with matplotlib
- Interactive widgets with IPython 2.0+

How to do it...

1. The very first step is to import the scientific packages we will be using in this recipe, namely NumPy, pandas, and matplotlib. We also instruct matplotlib to render the figures as inline images in the notebook:

```
In [1]: import numpy as np
        import pandas as pd
        import matplotlib.pyplot as plt
        %matplotlib inline
```

2. Now, we create a new Python variable called `url` that contains the address to a **CSV (Comma-separated values)** data file. This standard text-based file format is used to store tabular data:

```
In [2]: url = "http://donnees.ville.montreal.qc.ca/storage/f/
2014-01-20T20%3A48%3A50.296Z/2013.csv"
```

3. pandas defines a `read_csv()` function that can read any CSV file. Here, we pass the URL to the file. pandas will automatically download and parse the file, and return a `DataFrame` object. We need to specify a few options to make sure that the dates are parsed correctly:

```
In [3]: df = pd.read_csv(url, index_col='Date',
                       parse_dates=True, dayfirst=True)
```

4. The `df` variable contains a `DataFrame` object, a specific pandas data structure that contains 2D tabular data. The `head(n)` method displays the first *n* rows of this table. In the notebook, pandas displays a `DataFrame` object in an HTML table, as shown in the following screenshot:

```
In [4]: df.head(2)
```

	Unnamed: 1	Berri1	CSC	Mais1	Mais2	Parc	PierDup	Rachel1	Totem_Laurier
Date									
2013-01-01	00:00	0	0	1	0	6	0	1	0
2013-01-02	00:00	69	0	13	0	18	0	2	0

First rows of the DataFrame

Here, every row contains the number of bicycles on every track of the city, for every day of the year.

5. We can get some summary statistics of the table with the `describe()` method:

```
In [5]: df.describe()
```

	Berri1	CSC	Mais1	Mais2	Parc	PierDup	Rachel1	Totem_Laurier
count	261.000000	261.000000	261.000000	261.000000	261.000000	261.000000	261.000000	261.000000
mean	2743.390805	1221.858238	1757.590038	3224.130268	1669.425287	1152.885057	3084.425287	1858.793103
std	2247.957848	1070.037364	1458.793882	2589.514354	1363.738862	1208.848429	2380.255540	1434.899574
min	0.000000	0.000000	1.000000	0.000000	6.000000	0.000000	0.000000	0.000000
25%	392.000000	12.000000	236.000000	516.000000	222.000000	12.000000	451.000000	340.000000
50%	2771.000000	1184.000000	1706.000000	3178.000000	1584.000000	818.000000	3111.000000	2087.000000
75%	4767.000000	2168.000000	3158.000000	5812.000000	3068.000000	2104.000000	5338.000000	3168.000000
max	6803.000000	3330.000000	4716.000000	7684.000000	4103.000000	4841.000000	8555.000000	4293.000000

Summary statistics of the DataFrame

6. Let's display some figures. We will plot the daily attendance of two tracks. First, we select the two columns, `Berri1` and `PierDup`. Then, we call the `plot()` method:

```
In [6]: df[['Berri1', 'PierDup']].plot()
```

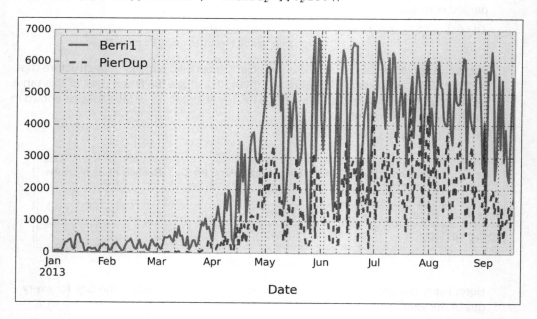

7. Now, we move to a slightly more advanced analysis. We will look at the attendance of all tracks as a function of the weekday. We can get the weekday easily with pandas: the `index` attribute of the `DataFrame` object contains the dates of all rows in the table. This index has a few date-related attributes, including `weekday`:

```
In [7]: df.index.weekday
Out[7]: array([1, 2, 3, 4, 5, 6, 0, 1, 2, ..., 0, 1, 2])
```

However, we would like to have names (Monday, Tuesday, and so on) instead of numbers between 0 and 6. This can be done easily. First, we create a `days` array with all the weekday names. Then, we index it by `df.index.weekday`. This operation replaces every integer in the index by the corresponding name in `days`. The first element, `Monday`, has the index 0, so every 0 in `df.index.weekday` is replaced by `Monday` and so on. We assign this new index to a new column, `Weekday`, in `DataFrame`:

```
In [8]: days = np.array(['Monday', 'Tuesday', 'Wednesday',
                         'Thursday', 'Friday', 'Saturday',
                         'Sunday'])
        df['Weekday'] = days[df.index.weekday]
```

8. To get the attendance as a function of the weekday, we need to group the table elements by the weekday. The `groupby()` method lets us do just that. Once grouped, we can sum all the rows in every group:

```
In [9]: df_week = df.groupby('Weekday').sum()
In [10]: df_week
```

	Berri1	CSC	Mais1	Mais2	Parc	PierDup	Rachel1	Totem_Laurier
Weekday								
Friday	105701	44252	71605	127526	64385	36850	118556	71426
Monday	106826	51646	68087	129982	69767	44500	119211	72883
Saturday	75754	27226	45947	79743	35544	46149	97143	56438
Sunday	74873	29181	40812	75746	37620	53812	100735	53798
Thursday	115193	52340	76273	141424	73668	36349	120684	74540
Tuesday	117244	54656	76974	141217	74299	40679	123533	76559
Wednesday	120434	59604	79033	145860	80437	42564	125173	79501

Grouped data with pandas

9. We can now display this information in a figure. We first need to reorder the table by the weekday using `ix` (indexing operation). Then, we plot the table, specifying the line width:

```
In [11]: df_week.ix[days].plot(lw=3)
         plt.ylim(0);  # Set the bottom axis to 0.
```

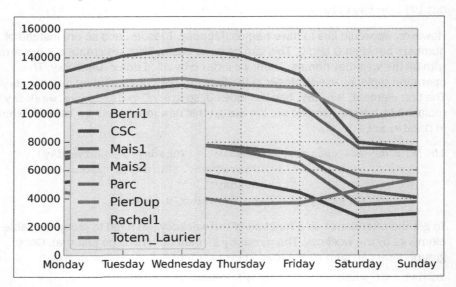

10. Finally, let's illustrate the new interactive capabilities of the notebook in IPython 2.0. We will plot a *smoothed* version of the track attendance as a function of time (**rolling mean**). The idea is to compute the mean value in the neighborhood of any day. The larger the neighborhood, the smoother the curve. We will create an interactive slider in the notebook to vary this parameter in real time in the plot. All we have to do is add the `@interact` decorator above our plotting function:

```
In [12]: from IPython.html.widgets import interact
         @interact
         def plot(n=(1, 30)):
             pd.rolling_mean(df['Berri1'], n).dropna().plot()
             plt.ylim(0, 8000)
             plt.show()
```

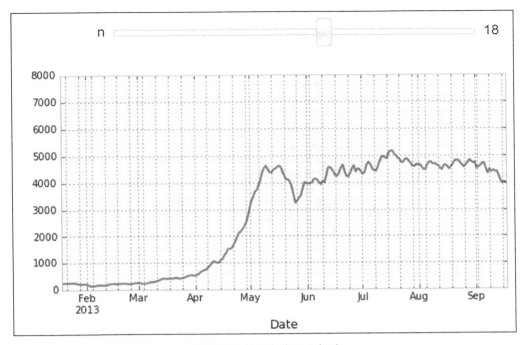

Interactive widget in the notebook

There's more...

pandas is the right tool to load and manipulate a dataset. Other tools and methods are generally required for more advanced analyses (signal processing, statistics, and mathematical modeling). We will cover these steps in the second part of this book, starting with *Chapter 7, Statistical Data Analysis*.

Here are some more references about data manipulation with pandas:

- *Learning IPython for Interactive Computing and Data Visualization, Packt Publishing*, our previous book
- *Python for Data Analysis, O'Reilly Media*, by Wes McKinney, the creator of pandas
- The documentation of pandas available at `http://pandas.pydata.org/pandas-docs/stable/`

See also

- The *Introducing the multidimensional array in NumPy for fast array computations* recipe

Introducing the multidimensional array in NumPy for fast array computations

NumPy is the main foundation of the scientific Python ecosystem. This library offers a specific data structure for high-performance numerical computing: the **multidimensional array**. The rationale behind NumPy is the following: Python being a high-level dynamic language, it is easier to use but slower than a low-level language such as C. NumPy implements the multidimensional array structure in C and provides a convenient Python interface, thus bringing together high performance and ease of use. NumPy is used by many Python libraries. For example, pandas is built on top of NumPy.

In this recipe, we will illustrate the basic concepts of the multidimensional array. A more comprehensive coverage of the topic can be found in the *Learning IPython for Interactive Computing and Data Visualization* book.

How to do it...

1. Let's import the built-in `random` Python module and NumPy:

   ```
   In [1]: import random
           import numpy as np
   ```

   We use the `%precision` magic (defined in IPython) to show only three decimals in the Python output. This is just to reduce the number of digits in the output's text.

   ```
   In [2]: %precision 3
   Out[2]: u'%.3f'
   ```

2. We generate two Python lists, `x` and `y`, each one containing 1 million random numbers between 0 and 1:

   ```
   In [3]: n = 1000000
           x = [random.random() for _ in range(n)]
           y = [random.random() for _ in range(n)]
   In [4]: x[:3], y[:3]
   Out[4]: ([0.996, 0.846, 0.202], [0.352, 0.435, 0.531])
   ```

3. Let's compute the element-wise sum of all these numbers: the first element of `x` plus the first element of `y`, and so on. We use a `for` loop in a list comprehension:

   ```
   In [5]: z = [x[i] + y[i] for i in range(n)]
           z[:3]
   Out[5]: [1.349, 1.282, 0.733]
   ```

4. How long does this computation take? IPython defines a handy `%timeit` magic command to quickly evaluate the time taken by a single statement:

```
In [6]: %timeit [x[i] + y[i] for i in range(n)]
1 loops, best of 3: 273 ms per loop
```

5. Now, we will perform the same operation with NumPy. NumPy works on multidimensional arrays, so we need to convert our lists to arrays. The `np.array()` function does just that:

```
In [7]: xa = np.array(x)
        ya = np.array(y)
In [8]: xa[:3]
Out[8]: array([ 0.996,  0.846,  0.202])
```

The `xa` and `ya` arrays contain the exact same numbers that our original lists, `x` and `y`, contained. Those lists were instances of the `list` built-in class, while our arrays are instances of the `ndarray` NumPy class. These types are implemented very differently in Python and NumPy. In this example, we will see that using arrays instead of lists leads to drastic performance improvements.

6. Now, to compute the element-wise sum of these arrays, we don't need to do a `for` loop anymore. In NumPy, adding two arrays means adding the elements of the arrays component-by-component. This is the standard mathematical notation in linear algebra (operations on vectors and matrices):

```
In [9]: za = xa + ya
        za[:3]
Out[9]: array([ 1.349,  1.282,  0.733])
```

We see that the `z` list and the `za` array contain the same elements (the sum of the numbers in `x` and `y`).

7. Let's compare the performance of this NumPy operation with the native Python loop:

```
In [10]: %timeit xa + ya
100 loops, best of 3: 10.7 ms per loop
```

We observe that this operation is more than one order of magnitude faster in NumPy than in pure Python!

8. Now, we will compute something else: the sum of all elements in `x` or `xa`. Although this is not an element-wise operation, NumPy is still highly efficient here. The pure Python version uses the built-in `sum()` function on an iterable. The NumPy version uses the `np.sum()` function on a NumPy array:

```
In [11]: %timeit sum(x)   # pure Python
         %timeit np.sum(xa)   # NumPy
100 loops, best of 3: 17.1 ms per loop
1000 loops, best of 3: 2.01 ms per loop
```

We also observe an impressive speedup here also.

9. Finally, let's perform one last operation: computing the arithmetic distance between any pair of numbers in our two lists (we only consider the first 1000 elements to keep computing times reasonable). First, we implement this in pure Python with two nested `for` loops:

```
In [12]: d = [abs(x[i] - y[j])
                 for i in range(1000) for j in range(1000)]
In [13]: d[:3]
Out[13]: [0.230, 0.037, 0.549]
```

10. Now, we use a NumPy implementation, bringing out two slightly more advanced notions. First, we consider a **two-dimensional array** (or matrix). This is how we deal with the two indices, *i* and *j*. Second, we use **broadcasting** to perform an operation between a 2D array and 1D array. We will give more details in the *How it works...* section.

```
In [14]: da = np.abs(xa[:1000,None] - ya[:1000])
In [15]: da
Out[15]: array([[ 0.23 ,   0.037,   ...,   0.542,   0.323,   0.473],
                   ...,
                 [ 0.511,   0.319,   ...,   0.261,   0.042,   0.192]])
In [16]: %timeit [abs(x[i] - y[j])
                    for i in range(1000) for j in range(1000)]
         %timeit np.abs(xa[:1000,None] - ya[:1000])
1 loops, best of 3: 292 ms per loop
100 loops, best of 3: 18.4 ms per loop
```

Here again, we observe significant speedups.

How it works...

A NumPy array is a homogeneous block of data organized in a multidimensional finite grid. All elements of the array share the same **data type**, also called **dtype** (integer, floating-point number, and so on). The **shape** of the array is an *n*-tuple that gives the size of each axis.

A 1D array is a **vector**; its shape is just the number of components.

A 2D array is a **matrix**; its shape is *(number of rows, number of columns)*.

The following figure illustrates the structure of a 3D (3, 4, 2) array that contains 24 elements:

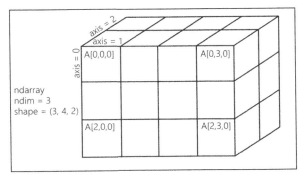

A NumPy array

The slicing syntax in Python nicely translates to array indexing in NumPy. Also, we can add an extra dimension to an existing array, using `None` or `np.newaxis` in the index. We used this trick in our previous example.

Element-wise arithmetic operations can be performed on NumPy arrays that have the *same shape*. However, broadcasting relaxes this condition by allowing operations on arrays with different shapes in certain conditions. Notably, when one array has fewer dimensions than the other, it can be virtually stretched to match the other array's dimension. This is how we computed the pairwise distance between any pair of elements in `xa` and `ya`.

How can array operations be so much faster than Python loops? There are several reasons, and we will review them in detail in *Chapter 4, Profiling and Optimization*. We can already say here that:

▸ In NumPy, array operations are implemented internally with C loops rather than Python loops. Python is typically slower than C because of its interpreted and dynamically-typed nature.

▸ The data in a NumPy array is stored in a **contiguous** block of memory in RAM. This property leads to more efficient use of CPU cycles and cache.

There's more...

There's obviously much more to say about this subject. Our previous book, *Learning IPython for Interactive Computing and Data Visualization*, contains more details about basic array operations. We will use the array data structure routinely throughout this book. Notably, *Chapter 4, Profiling and Optimization*, covers advanced techniques of using NumPy arrays.

Here are some more references:

- ▸ Introduction to the `ndarray` on NumPy's documentation available at
  `http://docs.scipy.org/doc/numpy/reference/arrays.ndarray.html`
- ▸ Tutorial on the NumPy array available at `http://wiki.scipy.org/Tentative_NumPy_Tutorial`
- ▸ The NumPy array in the SciPy lectures notes present at `http://scipy-lectures.github.io/intro/numpy/array_object.html`

See also

- ▸ The *Getting started with exploratory data analysis in IPython* recipe
- ▸ The *Understanding the internals of NumPy to avoid unnecessary array copying* recipe in *Chapter 4, Profiling and Optimization*

Creating an IPython extension with custom magic commands

Although IPython comes with a wide variety of magic commands, there are cases where we need to implement custom functionality in a new magic command. In this recipe, we will show how to create line and magic cells, and how to integrate them in an IPython extension.

How to do it...

1. Let's import a few functions from the IPython magic system:

   ```
   In [1]: from IPython.core.magic import (register_line_magic,
                                            register_cell_magic)
   ```

2. Defining a new line magic is particularly simple. First, we create a function that accepts the contents of the line (except the initial %-prefixed name). The name of this function is the name of the magic. Then, we decorate this function with `@register_line_magic`:

   ```
   In [2]: @register_line_magic
           def hello(line):
               if line == 'french':
                   print("Salut tout le monde!")
               else:
                   print("Hello world!")
   In [3]: %hello
   Hello world!
   In [4]: %hello french
   Salut tout le monde!
   ```

3. Let's create a slightly more useful `%%csv` cell magic that parses a CSV string and returns a pandas `DataFrame` object. This time, the arguments of the function are the characters that follow `%%csv` in the first line and the contents of the cell (from the cell's second line to the last).

```
In [5]: import pandas as pd
        #from StringIO import StringIO  # Python 2
        from io import StringIO  # Python 3

        @register_cell_magic
        def csv(line, cell):
            # We create a string buffer containing the
            # contents of the cell.
            sio = StringIO(cell)
            # We use pandas' read_csv function to parse
            # the CSV string.
            return pd.read_csv(sio)
In [6]: %%csv
        col1,col2,col3
        0,1,2
        3,4,5
        7,8,9
Out[6]:
     col1  col2  col3
0     0     1     2
1     3     4     5
2     7     8     9
```

We can access the returned object with `_`.

```
In [7]: df = _
        df.describe()
Out[7]:
             col1       col2       col3
count    3.000000   3.000000   3.000000
mean     3.333333   4.333333   5.333333
...
min      0.000000   1.000000   2.000000
max      7.000000   8.000000   9.000000
```

4. The method we described is useful in an interactive session. If we want to use the same magic in multiple notebooks or if we want to distribute it, then we need to create an **IPython extension** that implements our custom magic command. The first step is to create a Python script (`csvmagic.py` here) that implements the magic. We also need to define a special function `load_ipython_extension(ipython)`:

```
In [8]: %%writefile csvmagic.py
        import pandas as pd
        #from StringIO import StringIO  # Python 2
        from io import StringIO  # Python 3
```

```
            def csv(line, cell):
                sio = StringIO(cell)
                return pd.read_csv(sio)

        def load_ipython_extension(ipython):
            """This function is called when the extension
            is loaded. It accepts an
            IPython InteractiveShell instance.
            We can register the magic with the
            `register_magic_function` method."""
            ipython.register_magic_function(csv, 'cell')
Overwriting csvmagic.py
```

5. Once the extension module is created, we need to import it into the IPython session. We can do this with the `%load_ext` magic command. Here, loading our extension immediately registers our `%%csv` magic function in the interactive shell:

```
In [9]: %load_ext csvmagic
In [10]: %%csv
         col1,col2,col3
         0,1,2
         3,4,5
         7,8,9
Out[10]:
    col1  col2  col3
0      0     1     2
1      3     4     5
2      7     8     9
```

How it works...

An IPython extension is a Python module that implements the top-level `load_ipython_extension(ipython)` function. When the `%load_ext` magic command is called, the module is loaded and the `load_ipython_extension(ipython)` function is called. This function is passed the current `InteractiveShell` instance as an argument. This object implements several methods we can use to interact with the current IPython session.

The InteractiveShell class

An interactive IPython session is represented by a (singleton) instance of the `InteractiveShell` class. This object handles the history, interactive namespace, and most features available in the session.

Within an interactive shell, we can get the current `InteractiveShell` instance with the `get_ipython()` function.

The list of all methods of `InteractiveShell` can be found in the reference API (see link at the end of this recipe). The following are the most important attributes and methods:

- ▶ `user_ns`: The **user namespace** (a dictionary).
- ▶ `push()`: **Push** (or inject) Python variables in the interactive namespace.
- ▶ `ev()`: **Evaluate** a Python expression in the user namespace.
- ▶ `ex()`: **Execute** a Python statement in the user namespace.
- ▶ `run_cell()`: **Run a cell** (given as a string), possibly containing IPython magic commands.
- ▶ `safe_execfile()`: **Safely execute** a Python script.
- ▶ `system()`: Execute a **system** command.
- ▶ `write()`: **Write** a string to the default output.
- ▶ `write_err()`: **Write** a string to the default **error** output.
- ▶ `register_magic_function()`: **Register** a standalone function as an IPython **magic function**. We used this method in this recipe.

Loading an extension

The Python extension module needs to be importable when using `%load_ext`. Here, our module is in the current directory. In other situations, it has to be in the Python path. It can also be stored in `~\.ipython\extensions`, which is automatically put in the Python path.

To ensure that our magic is automatically defined in our IPython profile, we can instruct IPython to load our extension automatically when a new interactive shell is launched. To do this, we have to open the `~/.ipython/profile_default/ipython_config.py` file and put `'csvmagic'` in the `c.InteractiveShellApp.extensions` list. The `csvmagic` module needs to be importable. It is common to create a **Python package** that implements an IPython extension, which itself defines custom magic commands.

There's more...

Many third-party extensions and magic commands exist, notably `cythonmagic`, `octavemagic`, and `rmagic`, which all allow us to insert non-Python code in a cell. For example, with `cythonmagic`, we can create a Cython function in a cell and import it in the rest of the notebook.

Here are a few references:

- ▶ Documentation of IPython's extension system available at `http://ipython.org/ipython-doc/dev/config/extensions/`
- ▶ Defining new magic commands explained at `http://ipython.org/ipython-doc/dev/interactive/reference.html#defining-magics`

> ► Index of IPython extensions at `https://github.com/ipython/ipython/wiki/Extensions-Index`

> ► API reference of `InteractiveShell` available at `http://ipython.org/ipython-doc/dev/api/generated/IPython.core.interactiveshell.html`

See also

> ► The *Mastering IPython's configuration system* recipe

Mastering IPython's configuration system

IPython implements a truly powerful configuration system. This system is used throughout the project, but it can also be used by IPython extensions. It could even be used in entirely new applications.

In this recipe, we show how to use this system to write a configurable IPython extension. We will create a simple magic command that displays random numbers. This magic command comes with configurable parameters that can be set by the user in their IPython configuration file.

How to do it...

1. We create an IPython extension in a `random_magics.py` file. Let's start by importing a few objects.

    Be sure to put the code in steps 1-5 in an external text file named `random_magics.py`, rather than in the notebook's input!

   ```
   from IPython.utils.traitlets import Int, Float, Unicode, Bool
   from IPython.core.magic import (Magics, magics_class, line_magic)
   import numpy as np
   ```

2. We create a `RandomMagics` class deriving from `Magics`. This class contains a few configurable parameters:

   ```
   @magics_class
   class RandomMagics(Magics):
       text = Unicode(u'{n}', config=True)
       max = Int(1000, config=True)
       seed = Int(0, config=True)
   ```

3. We need to call the parent's constructor. Then, we initialize a random number generator with a seed:

```
def __init__(self, shell):
    super(RandomMagics, self).__init__(shell)
    self._rng = np.random.RandomState(self.seed or None)
```

4. We create a `%random` line magic that displays a random number:

```
@line_magic
def random(self, line):
    return self.text.format(n=self._rng.randint(self.max))
```

5. Finally, we register that magic when the extension is loaded:

```
def load_ipython_extension(ipython):
    ipython.register_magics(RandomMagics)
```

6. Let's test our extension in the notebook:

```
In [1]: %load_ext random_magics
In [2]: %random
Out[2]: '635'
In [3]: %random
Out[3]: '47'
```

7. Our magic command has a few configurable parameters. These variables are meant to be configured by the user in the IPython configuration file or in the console when starting IPython. To configure these variables in the terminal, we can type the following command in a system shell:

```
ipython --RandomMagics.text='Your number is {n}.' --RandomMagics.
max=10 --RandomMagics.seed=1
```

In this session, we get the following behavior:

```
In [1]: %load_ext random_magics
In [2]: %random
Out[2]: u'Your number is 5.'
In [3]: %random
Out[3]: u'Your number is 8.'
```

8. To configure the variables in the IPython configuration file, we have to open the `~/.ipython/profile_default/ipython_config.py` file and add the following line:

```
c.RandomMagics.text = 'random {n}'
```

After launching IPython, we get the following behavior:

```
In [4]: %random
Out[4]: 'random 652'
```

How it works...

IPython's configuration system defines several concepts:

- A **user profile** is a set of parameters, logs, and command history, which are specific to a user. A user can have different profiles when working on different projects. A xxx profile is stored in `~/.ipython/profile_xxx`, where `~` is the user's home directory.
    - On Linux, the path is generally `/home/yourname/.ipython/profile_xxx`
    - On Windows, the path is generally `C:\Users\YourName\.ipython\profile_xxx`

- A **configuration object**, or `Config`, is a special Python dictionary that contains key-value pairs. The `Config` class derives from Python's `dict`.

- The `HasTraits` class is a class that can have special `trait` attributes. **Traits** are sophisticated Python attributes that have a specific type and a default value. Additionally, when a trait's value changes, a callback function is automatically and transparently called. This mechanism allows a class to be notified whenever a trait attribute is changed.

- A `Configurable` class is the base class of all classes that want to benefit from the configuration system. A `Configurable` class can have configurable attributes. These attributes have default values specified directly in the class definition. The main feature of `Configurable` classes is that the default values of the traits can be overridden by configuration files on a class-by-class basis. Then, instances of `Configurables` can change these values at leisure.

- A **configuration file** is a Python or JSON file that contains the parameters of `Configurable` classes.

The `Configurable` classes and configuration files support an inheritance model. A `Configurable` class can derive from another `Configurable` class and override its parameters. Similarly, a configuration file can be included in another file.

Configurables

Here is a simple example of a `Configurable` class:

```
from IPython.config.configurable import Configurable
from IPython.utils.traitlets import Float

class MyConfigurable(Configurable):
    myvariable = Float(100.0, config=True)
```

By default, an instance of the `MyConfigurable` class will have its `myvariable` attribute equal to `100`. Now, let's assume that our IPython configuration file contains the following lines:

```
c = get_config()
c.MyConfigurable.myvariable = 123.
```

Then, the `myvariable` attribute will default to `123`. Instances are free to change this default value after they are instantiated.

The `get_config()` function is a special function that is available in any configuration file.

Additionally, `Configurable` parameters can be specified in the command-line interface, as we saw in this recipe.

This configuration system is used by all IPython applications (notably `console`, `qtconsole`, and `notebook`). These applications have many configurable attributes. You will find the list of these attributes in your profile's configuration files.

Magics

The **Magics** class derives from `Configurable` and can contain configurable attributes. Moreover, magic commands can be defined by methods decorated by `@line_magic` or `@cell_magic`. The advantage of defining class magics instead of function magics (as in the previous recipe) is that we can keep a state between multiple magic calls (because we are using a class instead of a function).

There's more...

Here are a few references:

- Configuring and customizing IPython at `http://ipython.org/ipython-doc/dev/config/index.html`
- Detailed overview of the configuration system at `http://ipython.org/ipython-doc/dev/development/config.html`
- Defining custom magics available at `http://ipython.org/ipython-doc/dev/interactive/reference.html#defining-magics`
- The traitlets module available at `http://ipython.org/ipython-doc/dev/api/generated/IPython.utils.traitlets.html`

See also

- The *Creating an IPython extension with custom magic commands* recipe

Creating a simple kernel for IPython

The architecture that has been developed for IPython and that will be the core of Project Jupyter is becoming increasingly language independent. The decoupling between the client and kernel makes it possible to write kernels in any language. The client communicates with the kernel via socket-based messaging protocols. Thus, a kernel can be written in any language that supports sockets.

However, the messaging protocols are complex. Writing a new kernel from scratch is not straightforward. Fortunately, IPython 3.0 brings a lightweight interface for kernel languages that can be wrapped in Python.

This interface can also be used to create an entirely customized experience in the IPython notebook (or another client application such as the console). Normally, Python code has to be written in every code cell; however, we can write a kernel for any domain-specific language. We just have to write a Python function that accepts a code string as input (the contents of the code cell), and sends text or rich data as output. We can also easily implement code completion and code inspection.

We can imagine many interesting interactive applications that go far beyond the original use cases of IPython. These applications might be particularly useful for nonprogrammer end users such as high school students.

In this recipe, we will create a simple graphing calculator. The calculator is transparently backed by NumPy and matplotlib. We just have to write functions as `y = f(x)` in a code cell to get a graph of these functions.

Getting ready

This recipe has been tested on the development version of IPython 3.0. It should work on the final version of IPython 3.0 with no or minimal changes. We give all references about wrapper kernels and messaging protocols at the end of this recipe.

How to do it...

 Warning: This recipe works only on IPython >= 3.0!

1. First, we create a `plotkernel.py` file. This file will contain the implementation of our custom kernel. Let's import a few modules:

    Be sure to put the code in steps 1-6 in an external text file named `plotkernel.py`, rather than in the notebook's input!

   ```python
   from IPython.kernel.zmq.kernelbase import Kernel
   import numpy as np
   import matplotlib.pyplot as plt
   from io import BytesIO
   import urllib, base64
   ```

2. We write a function that returns a base64-encoded PNG representation of a matplotlib figure:

```
def _to_png(fig):
    """Return a base64-encoded PNG from a
    matplotlib figure."""
    imgdata = BytesIO()
    fig.savefig(imgdata, format='png')
    imgdata.seek(0)
    return urllib.parse.quote(
        base64.b64encode(imgdata.getvalue()))
```

3. Now, we write a function that parses a code string, which has the form `y = f(x)`, and returns a NumPy function. Here, `f` is an arbitrary Python expression that can use NumPy functions:

```
_numpy_namespace = {n: getattr(np, n)
                    for n in dir(np)}
def _parse_function(code):
    """Return a NumPy function from a string 'y=f(x)'."""
    return lambda x: eval(code.split('=')[1].strip(),
                          _numpy_namespace, {'x': x})
```

4. For our new wrapper kernel, we create a class that derives from `Kernel`. There are a few metadata fields we need to provide:

```
class PlotKernel(Kernel):
    implementation = 'Plot'
    implementation_version = '1.0'
    language = 'python'  # will be used for
                         # syntax highlighting
    language_version = ''
    banner = "Simple plotting"
```

5. In this class, we implement a `do_execute()` method that takes code as input and sends responses to the client:

```
def do_execute(self, code, silent,
               store_history=True,
               user_expressions=None,
               allow_stdin=False):

    # We create the plot with matplotlib.
    fig = plt.figure(figsize=(6,4), dpi=100)
    x = np.linspace(-5., 5., 200)
    functions = code.split('\n')
    for fun in functions:
        f = _parse_function(fun)
        y = f(x)
        plt.plot(x, y)
    plt.xlim(-5, 5)
```

```
        # We create a PNG out of this plot.
        png = _to_png(fig)

        if not silent:
            # We send the standard output to the client.
            self.send_response(self.iopub_socket,
                'stream', {
                    'name': 'stdout',
                    'data': 'Plotting {n} function(s)'. \
                            format(n=len(functions))})

        # We prepare the response with our rich data
        # (the plot).
        content = {
            'source': 'kernel',

            # This dictionary may contain different
            # MIME representations of the output.
            'data': {
                'image/png': png
            },

            # We can specify the image size
            # in the metadata field.
            'metadata' : {
                    'image/png' : {
                        'width': 600,
                        'height': 400
                    }
                }
        }

        # We send the display_data message with the
        # contents.
        self.send_response(self.iopub_socket,
            'display_data', content)

    # We return the execution results.
    return {'status': 'ok',
            'execution_count': self.execution_count,
            'payload': [],
            'user_expressions': {},
            }
```

6. Finally, we add the following lines at the end of the file:

```
if __name__ == '__main__':
    from IPython.kernel.zmq.kernelapp import IPKernelApp
    IPKernelApp.launch_instance(kernel_class=PlotKernel)
```

7. Our kernel is ready! The next step is to indicate to IPython that this new kernel is available. To do this, we need to create a **kernel spec** `kernel.json` file and put it in `~/.ipython/kernels/plot/`. This file contains the following lines:

```
{
  "argv": ["python", "-m",
          "plotkernel", "-f",
          "{connection_file}"],
  "display_name": "Plot",
  "language": "python"
}
```

The `plotkernel.py` file needs to be importable by Python. For example, we could simply put it in the current directory.

8. In IPython 3.0, we can launch a notebook with this kernel from the IPython notebook dashboard. There is a drop-down menu at the top right of the notebook interface that contains the list of available kernels. Select the Plot kernel to use it.

9. Finally, in a new notebook backed by our custom plot kernel, we can simply write the mathematical equation, `y = f(x)`. The corresponding graph appears in the output area. Here is an example:

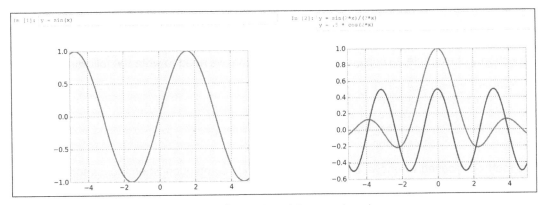

Example of our custom plot wrapper kernel

How it works...

We will give more details about the architecture of IPython and the notebook in *Chapter 3, Mastering the Notebook*. We will just give a summary here. Note that these details might change in future versions of IPython.

The kernel and client live in different processes. They communicate via messaging protocols implemented on top of network sockets. Currently, these messages are encoded in JSON, a structured, text-based document format.

Our kernel receives code from the client (the notebook, for example). The `do_execute()` function is called whenever the user sends a cell's code.

The kernel can send messages back to the client with the `self.send_response()` method:

▶ The first argument is the socket, here, the **IOPub** socket

▶ The second argument is the **message type**, here, `stream`, to send back standard output or a standard error, or `display_data` to send back rich data

▶ The third argument is the contents of the message, represented as a Python dictionary

The data can contain multiple MIME representations: text, HTML, SVG, images, and others. It is up to the client to handle these data types. In particular, the HTML notebook client knows how to represent all these types in the browser.

The function returns execution results in a dictionary.

In this toy example, we always return an `ok` status. In production code, it would be a good idea to detect errors (syntax errors in the function definitions, for example) and return an error status instead.

All messaging protocol details can be found at the links given at the end of this recipe.

There's more...

Wrapper kernels can implement optional methods, notably for code completion and code inspection. For example, to implement code completion, we need to write the following method:

```
def do_complete(self, code, cursor_pos):
    return {'status': 'ok',
            'cursor_start': ...,
            'cursor_end': ...,
            'matches': [...]}
```

This method is called whenever the user requests code completion when the cursor is at a given `cursor_pos` location in the code cell. In the method's response, the `cursor_start` and `cursor_end` fields represent the interval that code completion should overwrite in the output. The `matches` field contains the list of suggestions.

These details might have changed by the time IPython 3.0 is released. You will find all up-to-date information in the following references:

▶ Wrapper kernels, available at `http://ipython.org/ipython-doc/dev/development/wrapperkernels.html`

▶ Messaging protocols, available at `http://ipython.org/ipython-doc/dev/development/messaging.html`

▶ KernelBase API reference, available at `http://ipython.org/ipython-doc/dev/api/generated/IPython.kernel.zmq.kernelbase.html`

2
Best Practices in Interactive Computing

In this chapter, we will cover the following topics:

- ▶ Choosing (or not) between Python 2 and Python 3
- ▶ Efficient interactive computing workflows with IPython
- ▶ Learning the basics of the distributed version control system Git
- ▶ A typical workflow with Git branching
- ▶ Ten tips for conducting reproducible interactive computing experiments
- ▶ Writing high-quality Python code
- ▶ Writing unit tests with nose
- ▶ Debugging your code with IPython

Introduction

This is a special chapter about good practices in interactive computing. If the rest of the book is about the content, then this chapter is about the form. It describes how to work efficiently and properly with the tools this book is about. We will cover the essentials of the version control system Git before tackling reproducible computing experiments (notably with the IPython notebook).

We will also cover more general topics in software development, such as code quality, debugging, and testing. Attention to these subjects can greatly improve the quality of our end products (for example, software, research, and publications). We will only scratch the surface here, but you will find many references to learn more about these important topics.

Choosing (or not) between Python 2 and Python 3

In this first recipe, we will briefly cover a transverse and kind of a prosaic subject: Python 2 or Python 3?

Python 3 has been available since 2008, but many Python users are still stuck with Python 2. By improving many aspects of Python 2, Python 3 has broken compatibility with the previous branch. Migrating to Python 3 may therefore require a significant investment.

Even if there aren't that many compatibility-breaking changes, a program that works perfectly fine in Python 2 may not work at all in Python 3. For example, your very first `Hello World` Python 2 program doesn't work anymore in Python 3; `print "Hello World!"` raises a `SyntaxError` in Python 3. Indeed, `print` is now a function rather than a statement. You should write `print("Hello World!")`, which also works fine in Python 2.

Whether you start a new project or need to maintain an old Python library, the question of choosing between Python 2 and Python 3 arises. Here, we give some arguments and pointers that should let you make an informed decision.

> When we refer to Python 2, we especially mean Python 2.6 or Python 2.7, as these last versions of the Python 2.x branch are closer to Python 3 than Python 2.5 and earlier versions. It is more complicated to support Python 2.5+ and Python 3.x at the same time.
>
> Similarly, when we refer to Python 3 or Python 3.x, we especially mean Python 3.3 or above.

How to do it...

First, what are the differences between Python 2 and Python 3?

Main differences in Python 3 compared to Python 2

Here is a partial list of differences:

- Instead of a statement, `print` is a function (parentheses are compulsory).
- Division of integers yields floating-point numbers and not integers.
- Several built-in functions return iterators or views instead of lists. For example, `range` behaves in Python 3 like `xrange` in Python 2, and the latter no longer exists in Python 3.
- Dictionaries do not have the `iterkeys()`, `iteritems()`, and `itervalues()` methods anymore. You should use the `keys()`, `items()`, and `values()` functions instead.

- ▶ The following is a quote from the official Python documentation:

  "Everything you thought you knew about binary data and Unicode has changed."

- ▶ String formatting with `%` is deprecated; use `str.format` instead.

- ▶ Instead of a statement, `exec` is a function.

Python 3 brings many other improvements and new features regarding syntax and standard library content. You will find more details in the references at the end of this recipe.

Now, you have basically two options for your project: stick with a single branch (Python 2 or Python 3), or maintain compatibility with both branches.

Python 2 or Python 3?

It is natural to have a preference for Python 3; it is the future, whereas Python 2 is the past. Why bother supporting a deprecated version of Python? Here are a few situations where you might want to keep compatibility with Python 2:

- ▶ You need to maintain a large project written in Python 2, and it would be too costly to update it to Python 3 (even if semiautomatic updating tools exist).

- ▶ Your project has dependencies that do not work with Python 3.

 Most libraries we will be using in this book support both Python 2 and Python 3. This book's code is also compatible with both branches.

- ▶ Your end users work on environments that do not support Python 3 well. For example, they may work in a large institution where deploying a new version of Python on many servers would be too costly.

In these situations, you may choose to stick with Python 2, with the risk that your code becomes obsolete in the near future. Otherwise, you could pick Python 3 and its shiny new features, with the risk of leaving behind Python 2 users. You could also write your code in Python 2 and make it ready for Python 3. Thus, you can reduce the number of changes that will be required during a subsequent port to Python 3.

Fortunately, you don't necessarily have to choose between Python 2 and Python 3. There are ways to support both versions at the same time. Even if this involves slightly more work than just sticking to a single branch, it can be quite interesting in certain cases. Note, however, that you may miss many Python 3-only features if you go down this road.

Supporting both Python 2 and Python 3

There are basically two ways to support both branches in your code: use the **2to3** tool, or write code that *just works* in both branches.

Using 2to3

2to3 is a program in the standard library that automatically converts Python 2 code to Python 3. For example, run `2to3 -w example.py` to migrate a single Python 2 module to Python 3. You can find more information on the 2to3 tool at `https://docs.python.org/2/library/2to3.html`.

You can configure your installation script so that 2to3 runs automatically when users install your package. Python 3 users will get the automatically-converted Python 3 version of your package.

This solution requires your program to be well-covered by a solid testing suite and a continuous integration system that tests both Python 2 and Python 3 (see the recipes about unit testing later in this chapter). This is how you can ensure that your code works fine in both versions.

Writing code that works in Python 2 and Python 3

You can also write code that works in Python 2 and Python 3. This solution is simpler if you start a new project from scratch. A widely-used method is to rely on a lightweight and mature module called **six**, developed by Benjamin Petersons. This module is only a single file, so you can easily distribute it with your package. Wherever you would use a function or feature that is only supported in one Python branch, you need to use a specific function implemented in six. This function either wraps or emulates the corresponding functionality, thus it can work in both branches. You can find more information on six at `http://pythonhosted.org/six/`.

This method requires you to change some habits. For example, to iterate over all items of a dictionary in Python 2, you would write the following code:

```
for k, v in d.iteritems():
    # ...
```

Now, instead of the preceding code, you write the following code with six:

```
from six import iteritems
for k, v in iteritems(d):
    # ...
```

The `iteritems()` method of dictionaries in Python 2 is replaced by `items()` in Python 3. The six module's `iteritems` function internally calls one method or the other, depending on the Python version.

Downloading the example code

There's more...

As we have seen, there are many options you can choose regarding the Python 2 or Python 3 question. In brief, you should consider the following options:

- Decide very carefully whether you absolutely need to support Python 2 or not:
  - If so, prepare your code for Python 3 by avoiding Python 2-only syntax or features. You can use six, 2to3, or similar tools.
  - If not, stick to Python 3.
- In all cases, make sure your project has a solid testing suite, an excellent code coverage (approaching 100 percent), and a continuous integration system that tests your code against all versions of Python that you officially support

Here are several references on the subject:

- An excellent free book about porting code to Python 3, by Lennart Regebro, available at `http://python3porting.com/`
- Official recommendations on porting code to Python 3, available at `https://docs.python.org/3/howto/pyporting.html`
- Official wiki page about the Python 2/Python 3 question, available at `https://wiki.python.org/moin/Python2orPython3`
- Python 3 questions and answers, by Nick Coghlan, available at `http://python-notes.curiousefficiency.org/en/latest/python3/questions_and_answers.html`
- *What's new in Python 3*, available at `https://docs.python.org/3.3/whatsnew/3.0.html`
- *Ten awesome features of Python that you can't use because you refuse to upgrade to Python 3*, a presentation by Aaron Meurer, available at `http://asmeurer.github.io/python3-presentation/slides.html`
- Using the `__future__` module when writing the compatibility code, available at `https://docs.python.org/2/library/__future__.html`
- Key differences between Python 2 and Python 3, available at `https://sebastianraschka.com/Articles/2014_python_2_3_key_diff.html`

See also

- The *Writing high-quality Python code* recipe
- The *Writing unit tests with nose* recipe

Efficient interactive computing workflows with IPython

There are multiple ways of using IPython for interactive computing. Some of them are better in terms of flexibility, modularity, reusability, and reproducibility. We will review and discuss them in this recipe.

Any interactive computing workflow is based on the following cycle:

► Write some code
► Execute it
► Interpret the results
► Repeat

This fundamental loop (also known as **Read-Eval-Print Loop** or **REPL**) is particularly useful when doing exploratory research on data or model simulations, or when building a complex algorithm step by step. A more classical workflow (the edit-compile-run-debug loop) would consist of writing a full-blown program, and then performing a complete analysis. This is generally more tedious. It is more common to build an algorithmic solution iteratively, by doing small-scale experiments and tweaking the parameters, and this is precisely what interactive computing is about.

Integrated Development Environments (**IDEs**), providing comprehensive facilities for software development (such as a source code editor, compiler, and debugger), are widely used for classical workflows. However, when it comes to interactive computing, alternatives to IDEs exist. We will review them here.

How to do it...

Here are a few possible workflows for interactive computing, by increasing order of complexity. Of course, IPython is at the core of all of these methods.

The IPython terminal

IPython is the *de facto* standard for interactive computing in Python. The IPython terminal (the `ipython` command) offers a command-line interface specifically designed for REPLs. It is a much more powerful tool than the native Python interpreter (the `python` command). The IPython terminal is a convenient tool for quick experiments, simple shell interactions, and to find help. Forgot the input arguments of NumPy's `savetxt` function? Just type in `numpy.savetxt?` in IPython (you will first need to use `import numpy`, of course). Some people even use the IPython terminal as a (sophisticated) calculator!

Yet, the terminal quickly becomes limited when it is used alone. The main issue is that the terminal is not a code editor, and thus entering more than a few lines of code can be inconvenient. Fortunately, there are various ways of solving this problem, as detailed in the following sections.

IPython and text editor

The simplest solution to the *not-a-text-editor* problem is, perhaps unsurprisingly, to use IPython along with a text editor. The `%run` magic command then becomes the central tool in this workflow:

▸ Write some code in your favorite text editor and save it in a `myscript.py` Python script file.

▸ In IPython, assuming you are in the right directory, type in `%run myscript.py`.

▸ The script is executed. The standard output is displayed in real time in the IPython terminal along with possible errors. Top-level variables defined in the script are accessible in the IPython terminal at the end of the script's execution.

▸ If code changes are required in the script, repeat the process.

> The IPython-text editor workflow can be made yet more efficient with adequate keyboard shortcuts. You can, for instance, automate your text editor such that, when pressing *F8*, the following command is executed in the running IPython interpreter:
>
> `%run <CURRENT_FILE_NAME>`
>
> This approach is described here (on Windows, with Notepad++ and AutoHotKey):
>
> `http://cyrille.rossant.net/python-ide-windows/`

With a good text editor, this workflow can be quite efficient. As the script is reloaded when you execute `%run`, your changes will be taken into account automatically. Things become more complicated when your script imports other Python modules that you modify, as these won't be reloaded with `%run`. You can use a deep reload to solve this problem:

```
import myscript
from IPython.lib.deepreload import reload as dreload
dreload(myscript)
```

Modules imported in `myscript` will then be reloaded. A related IPython magic command is `%autoreload` (you first need to execute `%load_ext autoreload`). This command tries to automatically reload the modules imported in the interactive namespace, but it is not always successful. You may need to reload the changed modules explicitly with `reload(module)` (in Python 2) or `imp.reload(module)` (Python 3).

The IPython notebook

The IPython notebook plays a central role in efficient interactive workflows. It is a well-designed mix between a code editor and a terminal, bringing the best of both worlds within a unified environment.

You can start writing all your code in your notebook's cells. You write, execute, and test your code at the same place, thereby improving your productivity. You can put long comments in Markdown cells and structure your notebook with Markdown headers.

Once portions of your code become mature enough and do not require further changes, you can (and should) refactor them into reusable Python components (functions, classes, and modules). This will clean up your notebooks and facilitate future reuse of your code. Let's emphasize the fact that it is very important to refactor your code constantly into reusable components. IPython notebooks are currently not easily reusable by third-party code, and they are not designed for this. Notebooks are convenient for preliminary analyses and exploratory research, but they should not preclude you from regularly cleaning and refactoring your code into Python components.

A major advantage of notebooks is that they give you documents retracing everything you did with your code. They are extremely useful for reproducible research. Notebooks are saved in human-readable JSON documents, thus they work relatively well with version control systems such as Git.

Integrated Development Environments

IDEs are particularly well-adapted for classic software development, but they can also be used for interactive computing. A good Python IDE combines a powerful text editor (for example, one that includes features such as syntax highlighting and tab completion), an IPython terminal, and a debugger within a unified environment.

There are multiple commercial and open-source IDEs for most platforms. **Eclipse/PyDev** is a popular (although slightly heavy) open source cross-platform environment. **Spyder** is another open source IDE with good integration of IPython and matplotlib. **PyCharm** is one of many commercial environments that support IPython.

Microsoft's IDE for Windows, Visual Studio, has an open source plugin named **Python Tools for Visual Studio** (**PTVS**). This tool brings Python support to Visual Studio. PTVS natively supports IPython. You don't necessarily need a paid version of Visual Studio; you can download a free package bundling PTVS with Visual Studio.

There's more...

Here are a few links to various IDEs for Python:

▸ `http://pydev.org` for PyDev for Eclipse
▸ `http://code.google.com/p/spyderlib/` for Spyder, an open source IDE

- ▶ www.jetbrains.com/pycharm/ for PyCharm
- ▶ http://pytools.codeplex.com for PyTools for Microsoft Visual Studio on Windows
- ▶ http://code.google.com/p/pyscripter/ for PyScripter
- ▶ www.iep-project.org for IEP, the Interactive Editor for Python

See also

- ▶ The *Learning the basics of the distributed version control system Git* recipe
- ▶ The *Debugging your code with IPython* recipe

Learning the basics of the distributed version control system Git

Using a **distributed version control system** is so natural nowadays that if you are reading this book, you are probably already using one. However, if you aren't, read this recipe carefully. You should always use a version control system for your code.

Getting ready

Notable distributed version control systems include **Git**, **Mercurial**, and **Bazaar**. In this chapter, we chose the popular Git system. You can download the Git program and Git GUI clients from http://git-scm.com. On Windows, you can also install **msysGit** (http://msysgit.github.io) and **TortoiseGit** (https://code.google.com/p/tortoisegit/).

 Distributed systems tend to be more popular than centralized systems such as SVN or CVS. Distributed systems allow local (offline) changes and offer more flexible collaboration systems.

Online providers supporting Git include **GitHub** (https://github.com), **Bitbucket** (https://bitbucket.org), **Google code** (https://code.google.com), **Gitorious** (https://gitorious.org), and **SourceForge** (https://sourceforge.net). At the time of writing this book, creating an account is free on all these websites. GitHub offers free unlimited public repositories, while Bitbucket offers free unlimited public and private repositories. GitHub offers special features and discounts to academics (https://github.com/edu). Synchronizing your Git repositories on such a website is particularly convenient when you work on multiple computers.

You need to install Git (and possibly a GUI) for this recipe (see `http://git-scm.com/downloads`). We also suggest that you create an account on one of these websites. GitHub is a popular choice, notably for its user-friendly web interface and its well-developed social features. GitHub also provides a very good GUI on Windows (`https://windows.github.com`) and Mac OS X (`https://mac.github.com`). Most Python libraries we will be using in this book are being developed on GitHub.

How to do it...

We will show two methods to initialize a repository.

Creating a local repository

This method is best when starting to work locally. This can be with using the following steps:

1. The very first thing to do when starting a new project or computing experiment is create a new folder locally:

   ```
   $ mkdir myproject
   $ cd myproject
   ```

2. We initialize a Git repository:

   ```
   $ git init
   ```

3. Let's set our name and e-mail address:

   ```
   $ git config --global user.name "My Name"
   $ git config --global user.email "me@home"
   ```

4. We create a new file, and tell Git to track it:

   ```
   $ touch __init__.py
   $ git add __init__.py
   ```

5. Finally, let's create our first commit:

   ```
   $ git commit -m "Initial commit."
   ```

Cloning a remote repository

This method is best when the repository is to be synchronized with an online provider such as GitHub. Let's perform the following steps:

1. We create a new repository on the web interface of our online provider.
2. On the main webpage of the newly created project, we click on the **Clone** button with the repository URL and we type in a terminal:

   ```
   $ git clone /path/to/myproject.git
   ```

3. We set our name and e-mail address:

```
$ git config --global user.name "My Name"
$ git config --global user.email "me@home"
```

4. Let's create a new file and tell Git to track it:

```
$ touch __init__.py
$ git add __init__.py
```

5. We create our first commit:

```
$ git commit -m "Initial commit."
```

6. We push our local changes to the remote server:

```
$ git push origin
```

When we have a local repository (created with the first method), we can synchronize it with a remote server using a `git remote add` command.

How it works...

When you start a new project or a new computing experiment, create a new folder on your computer. You will eventually add code, text files, datasets, and other resources in this folder. The distributed version control system keeps track of the changes you make to your files as your project evolves. It is more than a simple backup, as every change you make on any file can be saved along with the corresponding timestamp. You can even revert to a previous state at any time; never be afraid of breaking your code anymore!

Specifically, you can take a snapshot of your project at any time by doing a **commit**. The snapshot includes all staged (or tracked) files. You are in total control of which files and changes will be tracked. With Git, you specify a file as staged for your next commit with `git add`, before committing your changes with `git commit`. The `git commit -a` command allows you to commit all changes in the files that are already being tracked.

When committing, you need to provide a message describing the changes you made. This makes the repository's history considerably more informative.

How often should you commit?

The answer is very often. Git only takes responsibility of your work when you commit changes. What happens between two commits may be lost, so you'd better commit very regularly. Besides, commits are quick and cheap as they are local; that is, they do not involve any remote communication with an external server.

Git is a distributed version control system; your local repository does not need to synchronize with an external server. However, you should synchronize if you need to work on several computers, or if you prefer to have a remote backup. Synchronization with a remote repository can be done with `git push` (send your local commits on the remote server), `git fetch` (download remote branches and objects), or `git pull` (synchronize the remote changes on your local repository).

There's more...

The simplistic workflow shown in this recipe is linear. In practice though, workflows with Git are typically nonlinear; this is the concept of branching. We will describe this idea in the next recipe, *A typical workflow with Git branching*.

Here are some excellent references on Git:

> ▸ Hands-on tutorial, available at `https://try.github.io`
>
> ▸ Git Guided Tour, at `http://gitimmersion.com`
>
> ▸ Atlassian Git tutorial, available at `www.atlassian.com/git`
>
> ▸ Online course, available at `www.codeschool.com/courses/try-git`
>
> ▸ Git tutorial by Lars Vogel, available at `www.vogella.com/tutorials/Git/article.html`
>
> ▸ GitHub Git tutorial, available at `http://git-lectures.github.io`
>
> ▸ Git tutorial for scientists, available at `http://nyuccl.org/pages/GitTutorial/`
>
> ▸ GitHub help, available at `https://help.github.com`
>
> ▸ *Pro Git* by Scott Chacon, available at `http://git-scm.com`

See also

> ▸ The *A typical workflow with Git branching* recipe

A typical workflow with Git branching

A distributed version control system such as Git is designed for complex and nonlinear workflows typical in interactive computing and exploratory research. A central concept is **branching**, which we will discuss in this recipe.

Getting ready

You need to work in a local Git repository for this recipe (see the previous recipe, *Learning the basics of the distributed version control system Git*).

How to do it...

1. We create a new branch named `newidea`:

   ```
   $ git branch newidea
   ```

2. We switch to this branch:

   ```
   $ git checkout newidea
   ```

3. We make changes to the code, for instance, by creating a new file:

   ```
   $ touch newfile.py
   ```

4. We add this file and commit our changes:

   ```
   $ git add newfile.py
   $ git commit -m "Testing new idea."
   ```

5. If we are happy with the changes, we merge the branch to the *master* branch (the default):

   ```
   $ git checkout master
   $ git merge newidea
   ```

   Otherwise, we delete the branch:

   ```
   $ git checkout master
   $ git branch -d newidea
   ```

Other commands of interest include:

- `git status`: Find the current **status** of the repository
- `git log`: Show the commit logs
- `git branch`: Show the existing **branches** and highlight the current one
- `git diff`: Show the **differences** between commits or branches

Stashing

It may happen that while we are halfway through some work, we need to make some other change in another commit or another branch. We could commit our half-done work, but this is not ideal. A better idea is to **stash** our working copy in a secured location so that we can recover all of our uncommitted changes later. Here is how it works:

1. We save our uncommitted changes with the following command:

   ```
   $ git stash
   ```

2.   We can do anything we want with the repository: checkout a branch, commit changes, pull or push from a remote repository, and so on.

3.   When we want to recover our uncommitted changes, we type the following command:

```
$ git stash pop
```

We can have several stashed states in the repository. More information about stashing can be found with `git stash --help`.

How it works...

Let's imagine that in order to test a new idea, you need to make non-trivial changes to your code in multiple files. You create a new branch, test your idea, and end up with a modified version of your code. If this idea was a dead end, you switch back to the original branch of your code. However, if you are happy with the changes, you **merge** it into the main branch.

The strength of this workflow is that the main branch can evolve independently from the branch with the new idea. This is particularly useful when multiple collaborators are working on the same repository. However, it is also a good habit to have, especially when there is a single contributor.

Merging is not always a trivial operation, as it can involve two divergent branches with potential conflicts. Git tries to resolve conflicts automatically, but it is not always successful. In this case, you need to resolve the conflicts manually.

An alternative to merging is **rebasing**, which is useful when the main branch has changed while you were working on your branch. Rebasing your branch on the main branch allows you to move your branching point to a more recent point. This process may require you to resolve conflicts.

Git branches are lightweight objects. Creating and manipulating them is cheap. They are meant to be used frequently. It is important to perfectly grasp all related notions and `git` commands (notably `checkout`, `merge`, and `rebase`). The previous recipe contains many excellent references.

There's more...

Many people have thought about effective workflows. For example, a common but complex workflow, called git-flow, is described at `http://nvie.com/posts/a-successful-git-branching-model/`. However, it may be preferable to use a simpler workflow in small and mid-size projects, such as the one described at `http://scottchacon.com/2011/08/31/github-flow.html`. The latter workflow elaborates on the simplistic example shown in this recipe.

A related notion to branching is **forking**. There can be multiple copies of the same repository on different servers. Imagine that you want to contribute to IPython's code stored on GitHub. You probably don't have the permission to modify their repository, but you can make a copy into your personal account—this is called forking. In this copy, you can create a branch and propose a new feature or a bug fix. Then, you can propose the IPython developers to merge your branch into their master branch with a **pull request**. They can review your changes, propose suggestions, and eventually merge your work (or not). GitHub is built around this idea and thereby offers a clean, modern way to collaborate on open source projects.

Performing code reviews before merging pull requests leads to higher code quality in a collaborative project. When at least two people review any piece of code, the probability of merging bad or wrong code is reduced.

There is, of course, much more to say about Git. Version control systems are complex and quite powerful in general, and Git is no exception. Mastering Git requires time and experimentation. The previous recipe contains many excellent references.

Here are a few further references about branches and workflows:

▶ Git workflows available at `www.atlassian.com/git/workflows`

▶ Learn Git branching at `http://pcottle.github.io/learnGitBranching/`

▶ The Git workflow recommended on the NumPy project (and others), described at `http://docs.scipy.org/doc/numpy/dev/gitwash/development_workflow.html`

▶ A post on the IPython mailing list about an efficient Git workflow, by Fernando Perez, available at `http://mail.scipy.org/pipermail/ipython-dev/2010-October/006746.html`

See also

▶ The *Learning the basics of the distributed version control system Git* recipe

Ten tips for conducting reproducible interactive computing experiments

In this recipe, we present ten tips that can help you conduct efficient and **reproducible** interactive computing experiments. These are more guidelines than absolute rules.

First, we will show how you can improve your productivity by minimizing the time spent doing repetitive tasks and maximizing the time spent thinking about your core work.

Second, we will demonstrate how you can achieve more reproducibility in your computing work. Notably, academic research requires experiments to be reproducible so that any result or conclusion can be verified independently by other researchers. It is not uncommon for errors or manipulations in methods to result in erroneous conclusions that can have damaging consequences. For example, in the 2010 research paper in economics *Growth in a Time of Debt*, by Carmen Reinhart and Kenneth Rogoff, computational errors were partly responsible for a flawed study with global ramifications for policy makers (see `http://en.wikipedia.org/wiki/Growth_in_a_Time_of_Debt`).

How to do it...

1. Organize your directory structure carefully and coherently. The specific structure does not matter. What matters is to be consistent throughout your projects regarding file-naming conventions, folders, subfolders, and so on. Here is a simple example:

   - `my_project/`
     - `data/`
     - `code/`
       - `common.py`
       - `idea1.ipynb`
       - `idea2.ipynb`
     - `figures/`
     - `notes/`
     - `README.md`

2. Write notes in text files using a lightweight markup language such as **Markdown** (`http://daringfireball.net/projects/markdown/`) or **reStructuredText** (**reST**). All meta-information related to your project, files, data sets, code, figures, lab notebooks, and so on, should be written down in text files.

3. Relatedly, document everything non-trivial in your code with comments, docstrings, and so on. You can use a documentation tool such as **Sphinx** (`http://sphinx-doc.org`). However, do not spend too much time documenting unstable and bleeding-edge code while you are working on it; it might change frequently and your documentation may soon be out of date. Write your code in such a way that it's easily understandable without comments (name your variables and functions well, use Pythonic patterns, and so on). See also the next recipe, *Write high-quality Python code*.

4. Use a distributed version control system such as Git for all text-based files, but not binary files (except maybe for very small ones when you really need to). You should use one repository per project. Synchronize the repositories on a remote server, using a free or paid hosting provider (such as GitHub or Bitbucket) or your own server (your host institution might be able to set up one for you). Use a specific system to store and share binary data files, such as `figshare.com` or `datadryad.org`.

5. Write all your interactive computing code in IPython notebooks first and refactor it into standalone Python components only when it is sufficiently mature and stable.

6. For full reproducibility, make sure that you record the exact versions of all components in your entire software stack (operating system, Python distribution, modules, and so on). A possibility is to use virtual environments with **virtualenv** or **conda**.

7. Cache long-to-compute intermediary results using Python's native **pickle** module, **dill** (`https://pypi.python.org/pypi/dill`), or **Joblib** (`http://pythonhosted.org/joblib/`). Joblib notably implements a NumPy-aware **memoize** pattern (not to be confused with memorize), which allows you to cache the results of computationally intensive functions. See also the **ipycache** IPython extension (`https://github.com/rossant/ipycache`); it implements a `%%cache` cell magic in the notebook.

Saving persistent data in Python

For purely internal purposes, you can use Joblib, NumPy's `save` and `savez` functions for arrays, and pickle for any other Python object (prefer native types such as lists and dictionaries rather than custom classes). For sharing purposes, prefer text files for small datasets (less than 10k points), for example, CSV for arrays, and JSON or YAML for highly structured data. For larger datasets, you can use HDF5 (see the *Manipulating large arrays with HDF5 and PyTables* and *Manipulating large heterogeneous tables with HDF5 and PyTables* recipes of *Chapter 4, Profiling and Optimization*).

8. When developing and trying out algorithms on large data sets, run them and compare them on small portions of your data first, before moving to the full sets.

9. When running jobs in a batch, use parallel computing to take advantage of your multicore processing units, for example, with `IPython.parallel`, Joblib, Python's multiprocessing package, or any other parallel computing library.

10. Automate your work as much as possible with Python functions or scripts. Use command-line arguments for user-exposed scripts, but prefer Python functions over scripts when possible. On Unix systems, learn terminal commands to improve your productivity. For repetitive tasks on Windows or GUI-based systems, use automation tools such as AutoIt (`www.autoitscript.com/site/autoit/`) or AutoHotKey (`www.autohotkey.com`). Learn keyboard shortcuts in the programs you use a lot, or create your own shortcuts.

For example, you can create a keyboard shortcut to launch an IPython notebook server in the current directory. The following link contains an AutoHotKey script, which does this in Windows Explorer:

`http://cyrille.rossant.net/start-an-ipython-notebook-server-in-windows-explorer/`

How it works...

The tips given in this recipe ultimately aim to optimize your workflows, in terms of human time, computer time, and quality. Using coherent conventions and structure for your code makes it easier for you to organize your work. Documenting everything saves everyone's time, including (eventually) yours! Should you be hit by a bus tomorrow, which I really hope you are not, you should ensure that your substitute can take over quickly, thanks to your conscientiously-written documentation. (You can find more information about the bus factor at `http://en.wikipedia.org/wiki/Bus_factor`.)

Using a distributed version control system with an online hosting service makes it easy for you to work on the same code base from multiple locations, without ever worrying about backups. As you can go back in time in your code, you have very little chance of unintentionally breaking it.

The IPython notebook is an excellent tool for reproducible interactive computing. It lets you keep a detailed record of your work. Also, the IPython notebook's ease of use means that you don't have to worry about reproducibility; just do all of your interactive work in notebooks, put them under version control, and commit regularly. Don't forget to refactor your code into independent reusable components.

Be sure to optimize the time you spend in front of your computer. When working on an algorithm, this cycle frequently happens: you do a slight modification, you launch the code, get the results, make another change, and so on and so forth. If you need to try out a lot of changes, you should ensure that the execution time is fast enough (no more than a few seconds). Using advanced optimization techniques is not necessarily the best option at this stage of experimentation. You should cache your results, try out your algorithms on data subsets, and run your simulations with shorter durations. You can also launch batch jobs in parallel when you want to test different parameter values.

Finally, desperately try to avoid doing repetitive tasks. It is worth spending time automating such tasks when they occur frequently in your day-to-day work. It is more difficult to automate tasks that involve GUIs, but it is feasible thanks to free tools such as AutoIt or AutoHotKey.

There's more...

Here are a few references about reproducibility in computing:

▶ *An efficient workflow for reproducible science*, a talk by Trevor Bekolay, available at `http://bekolay.org/scipy2013-workflow/`.

▶ *Ten Simple Rules for Reproducible Computational Research*, *Sandve et al.*, *PLoS Computational Biology*, *2013*, available at `http://dx.doi.org/10.1371/journal.pcbi.1003285`.

▶ Konrad Hinsen's blog at `http://khinsen.wordpress.com`.

▶ Software Carpentry, a volunteer organization running workshops for scientists; the workshops cover scientific programming, interactive computing, version control, testing, reproducibility, and task automation. You can find more information at `http://software-carpentry.org`.

See also

▶ The *Efficient interactive computing workflows with IPython* recipe

▶ The *Writing high-quality Python code* recipe

Writing high-quality Python code

Writing code is easy. Writing high-quality code is much harder. Quality is to be understood both in terms of actual code (variable names, comments, docstrings, and so on) and architecture (functions, modules, and classes). In general, coming up with a well-designed code architecture is much more challenging than the implementation itself.

In this recipe, we will give a few tips about how to write high-quality code. This is a particularly important topic in academia, as more and more scientists without prior experience in software development need to program.

The references given at the end of this recipe contain much more details than what we could mention here.

How to do it...

1. Take the time to learn the Python language seriously. Review the list of all modules in the standard library—you may discover that functions you implemented already exist. Learn to write *Pythonic* code, and do not translate programming idioms from other languages such as Java or C++ to Python.

2. Learn common **design patterns**; these are general reusable solutions to commonly occurring problems in software engineering.

3. Use assertions throughout your code (the `assert` keyword) to prevent future bugs (**defensive programming**).

4. Start writing your code with a bottom-up approach; write independent Python functions that implement focused tasks.

5. Do not hesitate to refactor your code regularly. If your code is becoming too complicated, think about how you can simplify it.

6. Avoid classes when you can. If you can use a function instead of a class, choose the function. A class is only useful when you need to store persistent state between function calls. Make your functions as *pure* as possible (no side effects).

7. In general, prefer Python native types (lists, tuples, dictionaries, and types from Python's collections module) over custom types (classes). Native types lead to more efficient, readable, and portable code.

8. Choose keyword arguments over positional arguments in your functions. Argument names are easier to remember than argument ordering. They make your functions self-documenting.

9. Name your variables carefully. Names of functions and methods should start with a verb. A variable name should describe what it is. A function name should describe what it does. The importance of naming things well cannot be overstated.

10. Every function should have a docstring describing its purpose, arguments, and return values, as shown in the following example. You can also look at the conventions chosen in popular libraries such as NumPy. The important thing is to be consistent within your code. You can use a markup language such as Markdown or reST:

```
def power(x, n):
    """Compute the power of a number.

    Arguments:
      * x: a number.
      * n: the exponent.

    Returns:
      * c: the number x to the power of n.

    """
    return x ** n
```

11. Follow (at least partly) Guido van Rossum's Style Guide for Python, also known as **Python Enhancement Proposal number 8 (PEP8)**, available at `www.python.org/dev/peps/pep-0008/`. It is a long read, but it will help you write well-readable Python code. It covers many little things such as spacing between operators, naming conventions, comments, and docstrings. For instance, you will learn that it is considered a good practice to limit any line of your code to 79 characters (or 99 exceptionally if that improves readability). This way, your code can be correctly displayed in most situations (such as in a command-line interface or on a mobile device) or side by side with another file. Alternatively, you can decide to ignore certain rules. In general, following common guidelines is beneficial on projects involving many developers.

12. You can check your code automatically against most of the style conventions in PEP8 with the **pep8** Python package. Install it with `pip install pep8` and execute it with `pep8 myscript.py`.

13. Use a tool for static code analysis such as Pylint (`www.pylint.org`). It lets you find potential errors or low-quality code *statically*, that is, without running your code.

14. Use blank lines to avoid cluttering your code (see PEP8). You can also demarcate sections in a long Python module with salient comments like this:

```
# Imports
# -------
import numpy


# Utility functions
# ----------------
def fun():
    pass
```

15. A Python module should not contain more than a few hundreds lines of code. Having too many lines of code in a module may be a sign that you need to split it into several modules.

16. Organize important projects (with tens of modules) into subpackages, for example:

   ❑ `core/`

   ❑ `io/`

   ❑ `utils/`

   ❑ `__init__.py`

17. Take a look at how major Python projects are organized. For example, IPython's code is well-organized into a hierarchy of subpackages with focused roles. Reading the code itself is also quite instructive.

18. Learn best practices to create and distribute a new Python package. Make sure that you know setuptools, pip, wheels, virtualenv, PyPI, and so on. Also, you are highly encouraged to take a serious look at conda (`http://conda.pydata.org`), a powerful and generic packaging system created by Continuum Analytics. Packaging is a chaotic and rapidly evolving topic in Python, so read only the most recent references. There are a few references in the *There's more...* section.

How it works...

Writing readable code means that other people (or you in a few months or years) will understand it quicker and will be more willing to use it. It also facilitates bug tracking.

Modular code is also easier to understand and to reuse. Implementing your program's functionality in independent functions that are organized as a hierarchy of packages and modules is an excellent way of achieving high code quality.

It is easier to keep your code loosely coupled when you use functions instead of classes. Spaghetti code is really hard to understand, debug, and reuse.

Iterate between bottom-up and top-down approaches while working on a new project. Starting with a bottom-up approach lets you gain experience with the code before you start thinking about the overall architecture of your program. Still, make sure you know where you're going by thinking about how your components will work together.

There's more...

Much has been written on how to write beautiful code—see the following references. You can find many books on the subject. In the next recipe, we will cover standard techniques to make sure that our code not only looks nice but also works as expected: unit testing, code coverage, and continuous integration.

Here are a few references:

- *Python Cookbook*, by David Beazley and Brian K. Jones, with many Python 3 advanced recipes, available at `http://shop.oreilly.com/product/0636920027072.do`
- *The Hitchhiker's Guide to Python!*, available at `http://docs.python-guide.org/en/latest/`
- Design patterns on Wikipedia, available at `http://en.wikipedia.org/wiki/Software_design_pattern`
- Design patterns in Python, described at `https://github.com/faif/python-patterns`
- Coding standards of Tahoe-LAFS, available at `https://tahoe-lafs.org/trac/tahoe-lafs/wiki/CodingStandards`

- ▸ *How to be a great software developer*, by Peter Nixey, available at `http://peternixey.com/post/83510597580/how-to-be-a-great-software-developer`
- ▸ *Why you should write buggy software with as few features as possible*, a talk by Brian Granger, available at `www.youtube.com/watch?v=OrpPDkZef5I`
- ▸ *The Hitchhiker's Guide to Packaging*, available at `http://guide.python-distribute.org`
- ▸ *Python Packaging User Guide*, available at `http://python-packaging-user-guide.readthedocs.org`

See also

- ▸ The *Ten tips for conducting reproducible interactive computing experiments* recipe
- ▸ The *Writing unit tests with nose* recipe

Writing unit tests with nose

Manual testing is essential to ensuring that our software works as expected and does not contain critical bugs. However, manual testing is severely limited because bugs may be introduced every time a change is made in the code. We can't possibly expect to manually test our entire program at every commit.

Nowadays, automated testing is a standard practice in software engineering. In this recipe, we will briefly cover important aspects of automated testing: unit tests, test-driven development, test coverage, and continuous integration. Following these practices is absolutely necessary in order to produce high-quality software.

Getting ready

Python has a native unit-testing module that you can readily use (`unittest`). Other third-party unit testing packages exist, such as py.test or nose, which we have chosen here. nose makes it a bit easier to write a test suite, and it has a library of external plugins. Your users don't need that extra dependency unless they want to run the test suite themselves. You can install nose with `pip install nose`.

How to do it...

In this example, we will write a unit test for a function that downloads a file from a URL. A testing suite should run and successfully pass even in the absence of a network connection. We take care of that by fooling Python's `urllib` module with a mock HTTP server.

> The code snippets used in this recipe have been written for Python 3. A few changes are required to make them work with Python 2, and we have indicated these changes in the code. The versions for Python 2 and Python 3 are both available on the book's website.
>
> You may also be interested in the `requests` module; it provides a much simpler API for HTTP requests (`http://docs.python-requests.org/en/latest/`).

1. We create a file named `datautils.py` with the following code:

```
In [1]: %%writefile datautils.py
# Version 1.
import os
from urllib.request import urlopen  # Python 2: use urllib2

def download(url):
    """Download a file and save it in the current folder.
    Return the name of the downloaded file."""
    # Get the filename.
    file = os.path.basename(url)
    # Download the file unless it already exists.
    if not os.path.exists(file):
        with open(file, 'w') as f:
            f.write(urlopen(url).read())
    return file
Writing datautils.py
```

2. We create a file named `test_datautils.py` with the following code:

```
In [2]: %%writefile test_datautils.py
# Python 2: use urllib2
from urllib.request import (HTTPHandler, install_opener,
                            build_opener, addinfourl)
import os
import shutil
import tempfile
from io import StringIO  # Python 2: use StringIO
from datautils import download

TEST_FOLDER = tempfile.mkdtemp()
ORIGINAL_FOLDER = os.getcwd()

class TestHTTPHandler(HTTPHandler):
```

```
    """Mock HTTP handler."""
    def http_open(self, req):
        resp = addinfourl(StringIO('test'), '',
                          req.get_full_url(), 200)
        resp.msg = 'OK'
        return resp

def setup():
    """Install the mock HTTP handler for unit tests."""
    install_opener(build_opener(TestHTTPHandler))
    os.chdir(TEST_FOLDER)

def teardown():
    """Restore the normal HTTP handler."""
    install_opener(build_opener(HTTPHandler))
    # Go back to the original folder.
    os.chdir(ORIGINAL_FOLDER)
    # Delete the test folder.
    shutil.rmtree(TEST_FOLDER)

def test_download1():
    file = download("http://example.com/file.txt")
    # Check that the file has been downloaded.
    assert os.path.exists(file)
    # Check that the file contains the contents of
    # the remote file.
    with open(file, 'r') as f:
        contents = f.read()
    print(contents)
    assert contents == 'test'
Writing test_datautils.py
```

3. Now, to launch the tests, we execute the following command in a terminal:

```
$ nosetests
.

Ran 1 test in 0.042s

OK
```

4. Our first unit test passes! Now, let's add a new test. We add some code at the end of test_datautils.py:

```
In [4]: %%writefile test_datautils.py -a

        def test_download2():
```

```
            file = download("http://example.com/")
            assert os.path.exists(file)
    Appending to test_datautils.py
```

5. We launch the tests again with the `nosetests` command:

   $ nosetests
   .E
   ERROR: test_datautils.test_download2
   Traceback (most recent call last):
     File "datautils.py", line 12, in download
       with open(file, 'wb') as f:
   IOError: [Errno 22] invalid mode ('wb') or filename: ''
   Ran 2 tests in 0.032s
   FAILED (errors=1)

6. The second test fails. In a real-world scenario, we might need to debug the program. This should be easy because the bug is isolated in a single test function. Here, by inspecting the traceback error and the code, we find that the bug results from the requested URL not ending with a proper file name. Thus, the inferred file name, `os.path.basename(url)`, is empty. Let's fix this by replacing the `download` function in `datautils.py` with the following function:

```
In [6]: %%file datautils.py
# Version 2.
import os
from urllib.request import urlopen  # Python 2: use urllib2


def download(url):
    """Download a file and save it in the current folder.
    Return the name of the downloaded file."""
    # Get the filename.
    file = os.path.basename(url)
    # Fix the bug, by specifying a fixed filename if the
    # URL does not contain one.
    if not file:
        file = 'downloaded'
    # Download the file unless it already exists.
    if not os.path.exists(file):
        with open(file, 'w') as f:
            f.write(urlopen(url).read())
    return file
Overwriting datautils.py
```

7. Finally, let's run the tests again:

```
$ nosetests
..
Ran 2 tests in 0.036s
OK
```

 By default, `nosetests` hides the standard output (unless errors occur). If you want the standard output to show up, use `nosetests --nocapture`.

How it works...

A `test_xxx.py` module should accompany every Python module named `xxx.py`. This testing module contains functions (unit tests) that execute and test functionality implemented in the `xxx.py` module.

By definition, a given unit test must focus on one very specific functionality. All unit tests should be completely independent. Writing a program as a collection of well-tested, mostly decoupled units forces you to write modular code that is more easily maintainable.

However, sometimes your module's functions require preliminary work to run (for example, setting up the environment, creating data files, or setting up a web server). The unit testing framework can handle this; just write `setup()` and `teardown()` functions (called **fixtures**), and they will be called at the beginning and at the end of the test module, respectively. Note that the state of the system environment should be exactly the same before and after a testing module runs (for example, temporarily created files should be deleted in `teardown`).

Here, the `datautils.py` module contains a single function, `download`, that accepts a URL as an argument, downloads the file, and saves it locally. This module comes with a testing module named `test_datautils.py`. You should choose the same convention in your program (`test_<modulename>` for the testing module of `modulename`). This testing module contains one or several functions prefixed with `test_`. This is how nose automatically discovers the unit tests across your project. nose also accepts other similar conventions.

 nose runs all tests it can find in your project, but you can, of course, have more fine-grained control over the tests to run. Type `nosetests --help` to get the list of all options. You can also check out the documentation at `http://nose.readthedocs.org/en/latest/testing.html`.

The testing module also contains the `setup` and `teardown` functions, which are automatically detected as fixtures by nose. A custom HTTP handler object is created within the `setup` function. This object captures all HTTP requests, even those with fictional URLs. The `setup` function then moves into a test folder (created with the `tempfile` module) to avoid potential conflicts between downloaded files and existing files. In general, unit tests should not leave any trace; this is how we ensure that they are fully reproducible. Likewise, the `teardown` function deletes the test folder.

In Python 3.2 and higher versions, you can also use `tempfile.TemporaryDirectory` to create a temporary directory.

The first unit test downloads a file from a mock URL and checks whether it contains the expected contents. By default, a unit test passes if it does not raise an exception. This is where `assert` statements, which raise exceptions if the statement is `False`, are useful. nose also comes with convenient routines and decorators for precisely determining the conditions under which a particular unit test is expected to pass or fail (for example, it should raise a particular exception to pass, or it should run in less than *X* seconds, and so on).

Further convenient assert-like functions are provided by NumPy (see `http://docs.scipy.org/doc/numpy/reference/routines.testing.html`). They are especially useful when working with arrays. For example, `np.testing.assert_allclose(x, y)` asserts that the x and y arrays are almost equal, up to a given precision that can be specified.

Writing a full testing suite takes time. It imposes strong (but good) constraints on your code's architecture. It's a real investment, but it is always profitable in the long run. Also, knowing that your project is backed by a full testing suite is a real load off your mind.

First, thinking about unit tests from the beginning forces you to think about a modular architecture. It is really difficult to write unit tests for a monolithic program full of interdependencies.

Second, unit tests make it easier for you to find and fix bugs. If a unit test fails after introducing a change in the program, isolating and reproducing the bugs becomes trivial.

Third, unit tests help you avoid **regressions**, that is, fixed bugs that silently reappear in a later version. When you discover a new bug, you should write a specific failing unit test for it. To fix it, make this test pass. Now, if the bug reappears later, this unit test will fail and you will immediately be able to address it.

Let's say that you write a complex program in several layers, with an *n+1* layer based on an *n* layer. Having a battery of successful unit tests for the *n* layer makes you confident that it works as expected. When working on the *n+1* layer, you can focus on this layer instead of constantly worrying whether the layer below works or not.

Unit testing is not the whole story, as it just concerns independent components. Further levels of testing are required in order to ensure good integration of the components within the program.

There's more...

Unit testing is a wide topic, and we only scratched the surface in this recipe. We give some further information here.

Test coverage

Using unit tests is good. However, measuring **test coverage** is even better: it quantifies how much of our code is being covered by your testing suite. Ned Batchelder's **coverage** module (http://nedbatchelder.com/code/coverage/) does precisely this. It integrates very well with nose.

First, install coverage with `pip install coverage`. Then run your testing suite with the following command:

```
$ nosetests --with-cov --cover-package datautils
```

This command instructs nose to launch your testing suite with coverage measurement for the `datautils` package only.

The `coveralls.io` service brings test-coverage features to a continuous integration server (refer to the *Unit testing and continuous integration* section). It works seamlessly with GitHub.

Workflows with unit testing

Note the particular workflow we have used in this example. After writing our `download` function, we created a first unit test that passed. Then we created a second test that failed. We investigated the issue and fixed the function. The second test passed. We could continue writing more and more complex unit tests, until we are confident that the function works as expected in most situations.

 Run `nosetests --pdb` to drop into the Python debugger on failures. This is quite convenient to find out quickly why a unit test fails.

This is **test-driven development**, which consists of writing unit tests *before* writing the actual code. This workflow forces us to think about what our code does and how one uses it, instead of how it is implemented.

Unit testing and continuous integration

A good habit to get into is running the full testing suite of our project at every commit. In fact, it is even possible to do this completely transparently and automatically through **continuous integration**. We can set up a server that automatically runs our testing suite in the cloud at every commit. If a test fails, we get an automatic e-mail telling us what the problem is so that we can fix it.

There are many continuous integration systems and services: Jenkins/Hudson, `https://drone.io`, `http://stridercd.com`, `https://travis-ci.org`, and many others. Some of them play well with GitHub projects. For example, to use Travis CI with a GitHub project, create an account on Travis CI, link your GitHub project to this account, and then add a `.travis.yml` file with various settings in your repository (see the additional details in the following references).

In conclusion, unit testing, code coverage, and continuous integration are standard practices that should be used for all significant projects.

Here are a few references:

▸ Test-driven development, available at `http://en.wikipedia.org/wiki/Test-driven_development`

▸ *Untested code is broken code: test automation in enterprise software delivery*, by Martin Aspeli, available at `www.deloittedigital.com/eu/blog/untested-code-is-broken-code-test-automation-in-enterprise-software-deliver`

▸ Documentation of Travis CI in Python, at `http://about.travis-ci.org/docs/user/languages/python/`

Debugging your code with IPython

Debugging is an integral part of software development and interactive computing. A widespread debugging technique consists of placing `print` statements in various places in the code. Who hasn't done this? It is probably the simplest solution, but it is certainly not the most efficient (it's the poor man's debugger).

IPython is perfectly adapted for debugging, and the integrated debugger is quite easy to use (actually, IPython merely offers a nice interface to the native Python debugger `pdb`). In particular, tab completion works in the IPython debugger. This recipe describes how to debug code with IPython.

Earlier versions of the IPython notebook did not support the debugger, that is, the debugger could be used in the IPython terminal and Qt console, but not in the notebook. This issue was fixed in IPython 1.0.

How to do it...

There are two not-mutually exclusive ways of debugging code in Python. In the post-mortem mode, the debugger steps into the code as soon as an exception is raised so that we can investigate what caused it. In the step-by-step mode, we can stop the interpreter at a breakpoint and resume its execution step by step. This process allows us to check carefully the state of our variables as our code is executed.

Both methods can actually be used simultaneously; we can do step-by-step debugging in the post-mortem mode.

The post-mortem mode

When an exception is raised within IPython, execute the `%debug` magic command to launch the debugger and step into the code. Also, the `%pdb on` command tells IPython to launch the debugger automatically as soon as an exception is raised.

Once you are in the debugger, you have access to several special commands, the most important ones being listed here:

- `p varname` **prints** the value of a variable
- `w` shows your current location within the stack
- `u` goes **up** in the stack
- `d` goes **down** in the stack
- `l` shows the **lines** of code around your current location
- `a` shows the **arguments** of the current function

The call stack contains the list of all active functions at a given location in the code's execution. You can easily navigate up and down the stack to inspect the values of the function arguments. Although quite simple to use, this mode should let you resolve most of your bugs. For more complex problems, you may need to do step-by-step debugging.

Step-by-step debugging

You have several options to start the step-by-step debugging mode. First, in order to put a breakpoint somewhere in your code, insert the following commands:

```
import pdb; pdb.set_trace()
```

Second, you can run a script from IPython with the following command:

```
%run -d -b extscript.py:20 script
```

This command runs the `script.py` file under the control of the debugger with a breakpoint on line 20 in `extscript.py` (which is imported at some point by `script.py`). Finally, you can do step-by-step debugging as soon as you are in the debugger.

Step-by-step debugging consists of precisely controlling the course of the interpreter. Starting from the beginning of a script or from a breakpoint, you can resume the execution of the interpreter with the following commands:

- ▶ `s` executes the current line and stops as soon as possible afterwards (**step-by-step** debugging, that is, the most fine-grained execution pattern)
- ▶ `n` continues the execution until the **next** line in the current function is reached
- ▶ `r` continues the execution until the current function **returns**
- ▶ `c` **continues** the execution until the next breakpoint is reached
- ▶ `j 30` brings you to line 30 in the current file

You can add breakpoints dynamically from within the debugger using the `b` command or with `tbreak` (temporary breakpoint). You can also clear all or some of the breakpoints, enable or disable them, and so on. You can find the full details of the debugger at `https://docs.python.org/3/library/pdb.html`.

There's more...

To debug your code with IPython, you typically need to execute it first with IPython, for example, with `%run`. However, you may not always have an easy way of doing this. For instance, your program may run with a custom command-line Python script, it may be launched by a complex bash script, or it may be integrated within a GUI. In these cases, you can embed an IPython interpreter at any point in your code (launched by Python), instead of running your whole program with IPython (which may be overkill if you just need to debug a small portion of your code).

To embed IPython within your program, simply insert the following commands somewhere in your code:

```
from IPython import embed
embed()
```

When your Python program reaches this code, it will pause and launch an interactive IPython terminal at this specific point. You will then be able to inspect all local variables, run any code you want, and possibly debug your code before resuming normal execution.

 rfoo, available at `https://code.google.com/p/rfoo/`, lets you inspect and modify the namespace of a running Python script remotely.

GUI debuggers

Most Python IDEs offer graphical debugging features (see the *Efficient interactive computing workflows with IPython* recipe). A GUI can sometimes be more convenient than a command-line debugger. Let's also mention Winpdb (`winpdb.org`), a graphical platform-independent Python debugger.

3
Mastering the Notebook

In this chapter, we will cover the following topics:

- ▶ Teaching programming in the notebook with IPython blocks
- ▶ Converting an IPython notebook to other formats with nbconvert
- ▶ Adding custom controls in the notebook toolbar
- ▶ Customizing the CSS style in the notebook
- ▶ Using interactive widgets – a piano in the notebook
- ▶ Creating a custom JavaScript widget in the notebook – a spreadsheet editor for pandas
- ▶ Processing webcam images in real time from the notebook

Introduction

In this chapter, we will see many features of the notebook, including the interactive widgets that have been brought by IPython 2.0. As we have only seen basic features in the previous chapters, we will dive deeper into the architecture of the notebook here.

What is the notebook?

The notebook was released in 2011, ten years after the creation of IPython. Its development has a long and complex history that is nicely summarized by Fernando Perez on his blog, `http://blog.fperez.org/2012/01/ipython-notebook-historical.html`. Inspired by mathematical software such as Maple, Mathematica, or Sage, the notebook really fostered the popularity of IPython.

By mixing together code, text, images, plots, hypertext links, and mathematical equations in a single document, the notebook brings reproducibility to interactive computing. The notebook, when used correctly, can radically change workflows in scientific computing. Prior to the notebook, one had to juggle between a text editor and an interactive prompt; now, one can stay focused within a single unified environment.

The notebook is not only a tool but also a powerful and robust architecture. Furthermore, this architecture is mostly language independent, so it's no longer tied to Python. The notebook defines a set of messaging protocols, APIs, and JavaScript code that can be used by other languages. In effect, we are now seeing non-Python kernels that can interact with the notebook such as IJulia, IHaskell, IRuby, and others.

At the SciPy conference in July 2014, the IPython developers even announced their decision to split the project into the following two parts:

 ▸ The new **Project Jupyter** will implement all language-independent parts: the notebook, the messaging protocol, and the overall architecture. For more details, visit `http://jupyter.org`.

 ▸ IPython will be the name of the Python kernel.

In this book, we do not make that semantic distinction, and we will use the term IPython to refer to the project as a whole (language-independent parts and Python kernel).

The notebook ecosystem

Notebooks are represented as **JavaScript Object Notation** (**JSON**) documents. JSON is a language-independent, text-based file format for representing structured documents. As such, notebooks can be processed by any programming language, and they can be converted to other formats such as Markdown, HTML, LaTeX/PDF, and others.

An ecosystem is being built around the notebook, and we can expect to see more and more usage in the near future. For example, Google is working on bringing the IPython notebook to Google Drive for collaborative data analytics. Also, notebooks are being used to create slides, teaching materials, blog posts, research papers, and even books. In fact, this very book is entirely written in the notebook.

IPython 2.0 introduced interactive widgets in the notebook. These widgets bring Python and the browser even closer. We can now create applications that implement bidirectional communication between the IPython kernel and the browser. Also, any JavaScript interactive library can be, in principle, integrated within the notebook. For example, the D3.js JavaScript visualization library is now being used by several Python projects to enable interactive visualization capabilities to the notebook. We are probably going to see many interesting uses of these interactive features in the near future.

Architecture of the IPython notebook

IPython implements a two-process model, with a **kernel** and a **client**. The client is the interface offering the user the ability to send Python code to the kernel. The kernel executes the code and returns the result to the client for display. In the **Read-Evaluate-Print Loop** (**REPL**) terminology, the kernel implements the *Evaluate*, whereas the client implements the *Read* and the *Print* of the process.

The client can be a Qt widget if we run the Qt console, or a browser if we run the notebook. In the notebook, the kernel receives entire cells at once, and thus has no notion of a notebook. There is a strong decoupling between the linear document containing the notebook, and the underlying kernel. This is a very strong constraint that may limit the possibilities, but that nevertheless leads to great simplicity and flexibility.

Another fundamental assumption in the whole architecture is that there can be at most one kernel connected to a notebook. However, IPython 3.0 offers the possibility of choosing the language kernel for any notebook.

It is important to keep these points in mind when thinking about new use-case scenarios for the notebook.

In the notebook, in addition to the Python kernel and the browser client, there is a Python server based on **Tornado** (www.tornadoweb.org). This process serves the HTML-based notebook interface.

All communication procedures between the different processes are implemented on top of the **ZeroMQ** (or **ZMQ**) messaging protocol (http://zeromq.org). The notebook communicates with the underlying kernel using **WebSocket**, a TCP-based protocol implemented in modern web browsers.

The browsers that officially support the notebook in IPython 2.x are as follows:

- Chrome ≥ 13
- Safari ≥ 5
- Firefox ≥ 6

The notebook should also work on Internet Explorer ≥ 10. These requirements are essentially those for WebSocket.

Connecting multiple clients to one kernel

In a notebook, typing `%connect_info` in a cell gives the information we need to connect a new client (such as a Qt console) to the underlying kernel:

```
In [1]: %connect_info
{
    "stdin_port": 53978,
    "ip": "127.0.0.1",
    "control_port": 53979,
    "hb_port": 53980,
    "signature_scheme": "hmac-sha256",
    "key": "053...349",
    "shell_port": 53976,
    "transport": "tcp",
    "iopub_port": 53977
}
Paste the above JSON code into a file, and connect with:
    $> ipython <app> --existing <file>
or, if you are local, you can connect with just:
    $> ipython <app> --existing kernel-6e0...b92.json
or even just:
    $> ipython <app> --existing
if this is the most recent IPython session you have started.
```

Here, `<app>` is `console`, `qtconsole`, or `notebook`.

It is even possible to have the kernel and the client running on different machines. You will find the instructions to run a public notebook server in the IPython documentation, available at `http://ipython.org/ipython-doc/dev/notebook/public_server.html#running-a-public-notebook-server`.

Security in notebooks

It is possible for someone to put malicious code in an IPython notebook. Since notebooks may contain hidden JavaScript code in a cell output, it is theoretically possible for malicious code to execute surreptitiously when the user opens a notebook.

For this reason, IPython 2.0 introduced a security model where HTML and JavaScript code in a notebook can be either trusted or untrusted. Outputs generated by the user are always trusted. However, outputs that were already there when the user first opened an existing notebook are untrusted.

The security model is based on a cryptographic signature present in every notebook. This signature is generated using a secret key owned by every user.

You can find further references on the security model in the following section.

References

The following are some references about the notebook architecture:

- The IPython two-process model, explained at `http://ipython.org/ipython-doc/stable/overview.html#decoupled-two-process-model`
- Documentation of the notebook, available at `http://ipython.org/ipython-doc/stable/interactive/notebook.html`
- Security in the notebook, described at `http://ipython.org/ipython-doc/dev/notebook/security.html`
- The notebook server, described at `http://ipython.org/ipython-doc/dev/interactive/public_server.html`
- The IPython messaging protocol, at `http://ipython.org/ipython-doc/dev/development/messaging.html`
- Tutorial about how to write a custom kernel for the notebook, at `http://andrew.gibiansky.com/blog/ipython/ipython-kernels/`

Here are a few (mostly experimental) kernels in non-Python languages for the notebook:

- IJulia, available at `https://github.com/JuliaLang/IJulia.jl`
- IRuby, available at `https://github.com/isotope11/iruby`
- IHaskell, available at `https://github.com/gibiansky/IHaskell`
- IGo, available at `https://github.com/takluyver/igo`
- IScala, available at `https://github.com/mattpap/IScala`

Teaching programming in the notebook with IPython blocks

The IPython notebook is not only a tool for scientific research and data analysis but also a great tool for teaching. In this recipe, we show a simple and fun Python library for teaching programming notions: **IPython Blocks** (available at http://ipythonblocks.org). This library allows you or your students to create grids of colorful blocks. You can change the color and size of individual blocks, and you can even animate your grids. There are many basic technical notions you can illustrate with this tool. The visual aspect of this tool makes the learning process more effective and engaging.

In this recipe, we will notably perform the following tasks:

 ▸ Illustrate matrix multiplication with an animation
 ▸ Display an image as a block grid

This recipe is partly inspired by the example at http://nbviewer.ipython.org/gist/picken19/b0034ba7ec690e89ea79.

Getting ready

You need to install IPython Blocks for this recipe. You can just type in a terminal pip install ipythonblocks. Note that you can also execute this shell command from the IPython notebook by prefixing this command with !.

```
In [1]: !pip install ipythonblocks
```

For the last part of this recipe, you also need to install Pillow, available at http://pillow.readthedocs.org/en/latest/; you will find more instructions in *Chapter 11, Image and Audio Processing*. With Anaconda, you can execute conda install pillow in a terminal.

Finally, you need to download the *Portrait* dataset from the book's website (https://github.com/ipython-books/cookbook-data) and extract it in the current directory. You can also play with your own images!

How to do it...

1. First, we import some modules as follows:

```
In [1]: import time
        from IPython.display import clear_output
        from ipythonblocks import BlockGrid, colors
```

2. Now, we create a block grid with five columns and five rows, and we fill each block in purple:

```
In [2]: grid = BlockGrid(width=5, height=5,
                          fill=colors['Purple'])
        grid.show()
```

3. We can access individual blocks with 2D indexing. This illustrates the indexing syntax in Python. We can also access an entire row or line with a : (colon). Each block is represented by an RGB color. The library comes with a handy dictionary of colors, assigning RGB tuples to standard color names as follows:

```
In [3]: grid[0,0] = colors['Lime']
        grid[-1,0] = colors['Lime']
        grid[:,-1] = colors['Lime']
        grid.show()
```

4. Now, we are going to illustrate matrix multiplication, a fundamental notion in linear algebra. We will represent two (n,n) matrices, A (in cyan) and B (lime) aligned with C = A B (yellow). To do this, we use a small trick of creating a big white grid of size (2n+1, 2n+1). The matrices A, B, and C are just views on parts of the grid.

```
In [4]: n = 5
        grid = BlockGrid(width=2*n+1,
                         height=2*n+1,
                         fill=colors['White'])
        A = grid[n+1:,:n]
        B = grid[:n,n+1:]
        C = grid[n+1:,n+1:]
        A[:,:] = colors['Cyan']
        B[:,:] = colors['Lime']
        C[:,:] = colors['Yellow']
        grid.show()
```

5. Let's turn to matrix multiplication itself. We perform a loop over all rows and columns, and we highlight the corresponding rows and columns in A and B that are multiplied together during the matrix product. We combine IPython's `clear_output()` method with `grid.show()` and `time.sleep()` (pause) to implement the animation as follows:

```
In [5]: for i in range(n):
            for j in range(n):
                # We reset the matrix colors.
                A[:,:] = colors['Cyan']
                B[:,:] = colors['Lime']
                C[:,:] = colors['Yellow']
                # We highlight the adequate rows
                # and columns in red.
                A[i,:] = colors['Red']
                B[:,j] = colors['Red']
                C[i,j] = colors['Red']
                # We animate the grid in the loop.
                clear_output()
                grid.show()
                time.sleep(0.25)
```

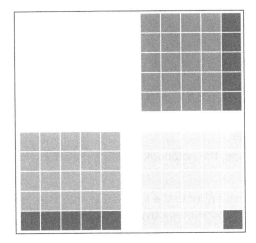

6. Finally, we will display an image with IPython Blocks. We import the JPG image with `Image.open()` and we retrieve the data with `getdata()` as follows:

```
In [6]: from PIL import Image
        imdata = Image.open('data/photo.jpg').getdata()
```

7. Now, we create a `BlockGrid` instance with the appropriate number of rows and columns, and we set each block's color to the corresponding pixel's color in the image. We use a small block size, and we remove the lines between the blocks as follows:

```
In [7]: rows, cols = imdata.size
        grid = BlockGrid(width=rows, height=cols,
                          block_size=4, lines_on=False)
        for block, rgb in zip(grid, imdata):
            block.rgb = rgb
        grid.show()
```

There's more...

As demonstrated in this recipe, the notebook is an ideal platform for education activities at all levels.

This library has been developed prior to the interactive notebook features brought by IPython 2.0. We can now expect even more interactive developments.

Converting an IPython notebook to other formats with nbconvert

An IPython notebook is saved in a JSON text file. This file contains the entire contents of the notebook: text, code, and outputs. The matplotlib figures are encoded as base64 strings within the notebooks, resulting in standalone, but sometimes big, notebook files.

> JSON is a human-readable, text-based, open standard format that can represent structured data. Although derived from JavaScript, it is language independent. Its syntax bears some resemblance with Python dictionaries. JSON can be parsed in many languages including JavaScript and Python (the `json` module in Python's standard library).

IPython comes with a tool called **nbconvert** that can convert notebooks to other formats: raw text, Markdown, HTML, LaTeX/PDF, and even slides with the `reveal.js` library. You will find more information about the different supported formats on the nbconvert documentation.

In this recipe, we will see how to manipulate the contents of a notebook and how to convert it to other formats.

Getting ready

You need to install pandoc, available at `http://johnmacfarlane.net/pandoc/`, which is a tool for converting files from one markup language to another.

To convert a notebook to PDF, you need a LaTeX distribution, which is available at `http://latex-project.org/ftp.html`. You also need to download the *Notebook* dataset from the book's website (`https://github.com/ipython-books/cookbook-data`), and extract it in the current directory.

On Windows, you may need the `pywin32` package. If you use Anaconda, you can install it with `conda install pywin32`.

How to do it...

1. Let's open the `test` notebook in the `data` folder. A notebook is just a plain text file (JSON), so we open it in the text mode (`r` mode) as follows:

```
In [1]: with open('data/test.ipynb', 'r') as f:
            contents = f.read()
        print(len(contents))
3787
```

Here is an excerpt of the `test.ipynb` file:

```
{
  "metadata": {
   "celltoolbar": "Edit Metadata",
   "name": "",
   "signature": "sha256:50db..."
  },
  "nbformat": 3,
  "nbformat_minor": 0,
  "worksheets": [
   {
...
      "source": [
       "# First chapter"
      ]
     },
...
   ],
   "metadata": {}
  }
 ]
}
```

2. Now that we have loaded the notebook in a string, let's parse it with the `json` module as follows:

    ```
    In [3]: import json
            nb = json.loads(contents)
    ```

3. Let's have a look at the keys in the notebook dictionary:

    ```
    In [4]: print(nb.keys())
            print('nbformat ' + str(nb['nbformat']) +
                  '.' + str(nb['nbformat_minor']))
    [u'nbformat', u'nbformat_minor', u'worksheets', u'metadata']
    nbformat 3.0
    ```

> The version of the notebook format is indicated in `nbformat` and `nbformat_minor`. Backwards-incompatible changes in the notebook format are to be expected in future versions of IPython. This recipe has been tested with the IPython 2.x branch and the notebook format v3.

4. The main field is `worksheets`; there is only one by default. A worksheet contains a list of cells and some metadata. The `worksheets` field may disappear in a future version of the notebook format. Let's have a look at the contents of a worksheet:

```
In [5]: nb['worksheets'][0].keys()
Out[5]: [u'cells', u'metadata']
```

5. Each cell has a type, optional metadata, some contents (text or code), possibly one or several outputs, and other information. Let's look at a Markdown cell and a code cell:

```
In [6]: nb['worksheets'][0]['cells'][1]
Out[6]: {u'cell_type': u'markdown',
 u'metadata': {u'my_field': [u'value1', u'2405']},
              u'source': [u"Let's write ...:\n", ...]}
In [7]: nb['worksheets'][0]['cells'][2]
Out[7]: {u'cell_type': u'code',
         u'collapsed': False,
         u'input': [u'import numpy as np\n', ...],
         u'language': u'python',
         u'metadata': {},
         u'outputs': [
                       {u'metadata': {},
                        u'output_type': u'display_data',
                        u'png': u'iVB...mCC\n',
                        u'prompt_number': 1}]}
```

6. Once parsed, the notebook is represented as a Python dictionary. Manipulating it is therefore quite convenient in Python. Here, we count the number of Markdown and code cells as follows:

```
In [8]: cells = nb['worksheets'][0]['cells']
        nm = len([cell for cell in cells
                 if cell['cell_type'] == 'markdown'])
        nc = len([cell for cell in cells
                 if cell['cell_type'] == 'code'])
        print(("There are {nm} Markdown cells and "
              "{nc} code cells.").format(nm=nm, nc=nc))
There are 2 Markdown cells and 1 code cells.
```

7. Let's have a closer look at the image output of the cell with the matplotlib figure:

```
In [9]: png = cells[2]['outputs'][0]['png']
        cells[2]['outputs'][0]
Out[9]: {u'metadata': {},
         u'output_type': u'display_data',
         u'png': u'iVBORwoAAAANSUhE...ErAAAElTkQmCC\n'}
```

8. In general, there can be zero, one, or multiple outputs. Additionally, each output can have multiple representations. Here, the matplotlib figure has a PNG representation (the base64-encoded image) and a text representation (the internal representation of the figure).

9. Now, we are going to use nbconvert to convert our text notebook to other formats. This tool can be used from the command line. Note that the API of nbconvert may change in future versions. Here, we convert the notebook to an HTML document as follows:

```
In [10]: !ipython nbconvert --to html data/test.ipynb
[NbConvertApp] Writing 187617 bytes to test.html
```

10. Let's display this document in an `<iframe>` (a small window showing an external HTML document within the notebook):

```
In [11]: from IPython.display import IFrame
         IFrame('test.html', 600, 200)
```

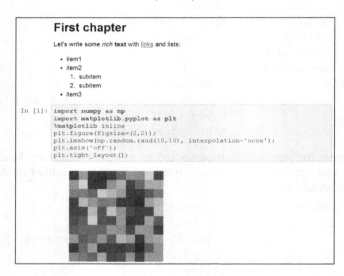

11. We can also convert the notebook to LaTeX and PDF. In order to specify the title and author of the document, we need to extend the default LaTeX template. First, we create a file called `mytemplate.tplx` that extends the default `article.tplx` template provided by nbconvert. We specify the contents of the author and title blocks as follows:

```
In [12]: %%writefile mytemplate.tplx
         ((*- extends 'article.tplx' -*))

         ((* block author *))
         \author{Cyrille Rossant}
         ((* endblock author *))
```

```
            ((* block title *))
            \title{My document}
            ((* endblock title *))
    Writing mytemplate.tplx
```

12. Then, we can run nbconvert by specifying our custom template as follows:

```
In [13]: !ipython nbconvert --to latex --template mytemplate data/
test.ipynb
          !pdflatex test.tex
[NbConvertApp] PDF successfully created
```

We used nbconvert to convert the notebook to LaTeX, and `pdflatex` (coming with our LaTeX distribution) to compile the LaTeX document to PDF. The following screenshot shows the PDF version of the notebook:

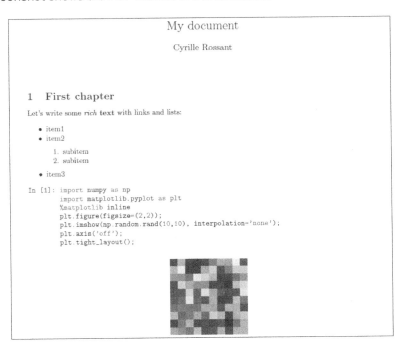

How it works...

As we have seen in this recipe, an `.ipynb` file contains a structured representation of the notebook. This JSON file can be easily parsed and manipulated in Python.

nbconvert is a tool for converting a notebook to another format. The conversion can be customized in several ways. Here, we extended an existing template using `jinja2`, a templating package. You will find more information in the documentation of nbconvert.

There's more...

There is a free online service, **nbviewer**, that lets us render IPython notebooks in HTML dynamically in the cloud. The idea is that we provide to nbviewer a URL to a raw notebook (in JSON), and we get a rendered HTML output. The main page of nbviewer (`http://nbviewer.ipython.org`) contains a few examples.

This service is maintained by the IPython developers and is hosted on Rackspace (`www.rackspace.com`).

Here are some more references:

- Documentation of nbconvert, at `http://ipython.org/ipython-doc/dev/interactive/nbconvert.html`
- A list of conversion examples with nbconvert, at `https://github.com/ipython/nbconvert-examples`
- JSON on Wikipedia, available at `http://en.wikipedia.org/wiki/JSON`

Adding custom controls in the notebook toolbar

The CSS and JavaScript of the HTML notebook can be customized through the files in `~/.ipython/profile_default/static/custom`, where ~ is your home directory, and `default` is your IPython profile.

In this recipe, we will use these customization options to add a new button in the notebook toolbar that linearly renumbers all code cells.

How to do it...

1. First, we are going to inject JavaScript code directly in the notebook. This is useful for testing purposes, or if we don't want the changes to be permanent. The JavaScript code will be loaded with that notebook only. To do this, we can just use the `%%javascript` cell magic as follows:

```
In [1]: %%javascript
        // This function allows us to add buttons
        // to the notebook toolbar.
        IPython.toolbar.add_buttons_group([
        {
            // The button's label.
            'label': 'renumber all code cells',
```

```
// The button's icon.
// See a list of Font-Awesome icons here:
// http://fortawesome.github.io/Font-
//                      Awesome/icons/
'icon': 'icon-list-ol',

// The callback function.
'callback': function () {

    // We retrieve the lists of all cells.
    var cells = IPython.notebook.get_cells();

    // We only keep the code cells.
    cells = cells.filter(function(c)
      {
          return c instanceof IPython.CodeCell;
      })

    // We set the input prompt of all code
    // cells.
    for (var i = 0; i < cells.length; i++) {
        cells[i].set_input_prompt(i + 1);
    }
}
}]);
```

2. Running the preceding code cell adds a button in the toolbar as shown in the following screenshot. Clicking on this button automatically updates the prompt numbers of all code cells.

Adding a Renumber toolbar button

3. To make these changes permanent, that is, to add this button on every notebook in the current profile, we can open the `~/.ipython/profile_default/static/custom/custom.js` file and add the following lines of code:

```
$([IPython.events]).on('app_initialized.NotebookApp',
    function(){
        // Copy the JavaScript code (in step 1) here.
    });
```

The preceding code will be automatically loaded in the notebook, and the renumber button will appear on top of every notebook in the current profile.

There's more...

The IPython notebook JavaScript API that allowed us to add a button to the notebook toolbar is still unstable at the time of writing. It may change at any time, and it is not well documented. This recipe has only been tested with IPython 2.0. You may nevertheless find a not-so-official and partial API documentation on this page: http://ipjsdoc.herokuapp.com.

We should expect a more stable API in the future.

See also

▶ The *Customizing the CSS style in the notebook* recipe

Customizing the CSS style in the notebook

In this recipe, we show how to customize the CSS in the notebook interface and in an exported HTML notebook.

Getting ready

You are expected to know a bit of CSS3 for this recipe. You can find many tutorials online (see the references at the end of this recipe).

You also need to download the *Notebook* dataset from the book's website (http://ipython-books.github.io), and extract it in the current directory.

How to do it...

1. First, we create a new IPython profile to avoid cluttering our default profile as follows:

```
In [1]: !ipython profile create custom_css
```

2. In Python, we retrieve the path to this profile (~/.ipython) and to the custom.css file (empty by default).

```
In [2]: dir = !ipython locate profile custom_css
        dir = dir[0]
In [3]: import os
        csspath = os.path.realpath(os.path.join(
                dir, 'static/custom/custom.css'))
In [4]: csspath
Out[4]: '~\.ipython\profile_custom_css\static\
                                    custom\custom.css'
```

3. We can now edit this file here. We change the background color, the font size of code cells, the border of some cells, and we highlight the selected cells in edit mode.

```
In [5]: %%writefile {csspath}

        body {
            /* Background color for the whole notebook. */
            background-color: #f0f0f0;
        }

        /* Level 1 headers. */
        h1 {
            text-align: right;
            color: red;
        }

        /* Code cells. */
        div.input_area > div.highlight > pre {
            font-size: 10px;
        }

        /* Output images. */
        div.output_area img {
            border: 3px #ababab solid;
            border-radius: 8px;
        }

        /* Selected cells. */
        div.cell.selected {
            border: 3px #ababab solid;
            background-color: #ddd;
        }

        /* Code cells in edit mode. */
        div.cell.edit_mode {
            border: 3px red solid;
            background-color: #faa;
        }
Overwriting C:\Users\Cyrille\.ipython\profile_custom_css\static\
custom\custom.css
```

Opening a notebook with the `custom_css` profile (with the `ipython notebook --profile=custom_css` command) leads to a custom style as follows:

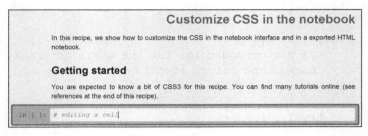

Custom CSS in the interactive notebook interface

4. We can also use this style sheet with nbconvert. We just have to convert a notebook to a static HTML document, and copy the `custom.css` file in the current directory. Here, we use a test notebook that has been downloaded from the book's website (see *Getting ready*):

```
In [6]: !cp {csspath} custom.css
        !ipython nbconvert --to html data/test.ipynb
[NbConvertApp] Writing 187617 bytes to test.html
```

5. Here is what this HTML document looks like:

```
In [7]: from IPython.display import IFrame
        IFrame('test.html', 600, 650)
```

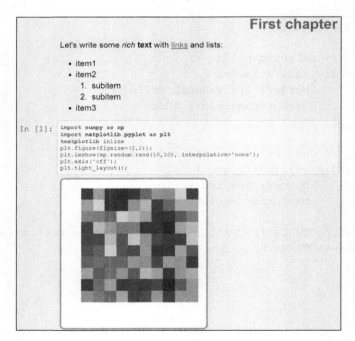

There's more...

Here are a few tutorials and references about CSS:

► CSS tutorial on w3schools, at `www.w3schools.com/css/DEFAULT.asp`

► CSS tutorial on Mozilla Developer Network, at `https://developer.mozilla.org/en-US/docs/Web/Guide/CSS/Getting_started`

► Blog post by Matthias Bussonnier about how to customize the notebook CSS, at `http://nbviewer.ipython.org/github/Carreau/posts/blob/master/Blog1.ipynb`

See also

► The *Adding custom controls in the notebook toolbar* recipe

Using interactive widgets – a piano in the notebook

Starting with IPython 2.0, we can put interactive widgets in notebooks to create rich GUI applications that interact with our Python kernel. IPython comes with a rich set of graphical controls such as buttons, sliders, and drop-down menus. We have full control of their placement and appearance. We can combine different widgets to form complex layouts. We can even create our own interactive widgets from scratch as we will see in the next recipe, *Creating a custom Javascript widget in the notebook – a spreadsheet editor for pandas*.

In this recipe, we will show many possibilities offered by the interactive widget API in IPython 2.0+. We will create a very basic piano in the notebook.

Getting ready

You need to download the *Piano* dataset from the book's website (http://ipython-books.github.io). This dataset contains synthetic sounds of piano notes obtained on `archive.org` (CC0 1.0 Universal license). It is available at `https://archive.org/details/SynthesizedPianoNotes`.

How to do it...

1. Let's import a few modules as follows:

```
In [1]: import numpy as np
        import os
        from IPython.display import (Audio, display,
                                        clear_output)
        from IPython.html import widgets
        from functools import partial
```

2. To create a piano, we will draw one button per note. The corresponding note plays when the user clicks on the button. This is implemented by displaying an `<audio>` element as follows:

```
In [2]: dir = 'data/synth'
In [3]: # This is the list of notes.
        notes = 'C,C#,D,D#,E,F,F#,G,G#,A,A#,B,C'.split(',')
In [4]: def play(note, octave=0):
            """This function displays an HTML Audio element
            that plays automatically when it appears."""
            f = os.path.join(dir,
                "piano_{i}.mp3".format(i=note+12*octave))
            clear_output()
            display(Audio(filename=f, autoplay=True))
```

3. We are going to place all buttons within a container widget. In IPython 2.0, widgets can be organized hierarchically. One common use case is to organize several widgets in a given layout. Here, `piano` will contain 12 buttons for the 12 notes:

```
In [5]: piano = widgets.ContainerWidget()
```

 The API for creating container widgets such as horizontal or vertical boxes has changed in IPython 3.0. Refer to IPython's documentation for more details.

4. We create our first widget: a slider control that specifies the octave (0 or 1 here):

```
In [6]: octave_slider = widgets.IntSliderWidget()
        octave_slider.max = 1
        octave_slider
```

```
octave_slider = widgets.IntSliderWidget()
octave_slider.max = 1
octave_slider
```

```
                                                    0
```

5. Now, we create the buttons. There are several steps. First, we instantiate a `ButtonWidget` object for each note. Then, we specify a `callback()` function that plays the corresponding note (given by an index) at a given octave (given by the current value of the octave slider). Finally, we set the CSS of each button, notably the white or black color.

```
In [7]: buttons = []
        for i, note in enumerate(notes):
            button = widgets.ButtonWidget(description=note)

            def on_button_clicked(i, _):
                play(i+1, octave_slider.value)

            button.on_click(partial(on_button_clicked, i))

            button.set_css({
                    'width': '30px',
                    'height': '60px',
                    'padding': '0',
                    'color':
                        ('black', 'white')['#' in note],
                    'background':
                        ('white', 'black')['#' in note],
                     'border': '1px solid black',
                     'float': 'left'})

            buttons.append(button)
```

6. Finally, we arrange all widgets within the containers. The `piano` container contains the buttons, and the main container (`container`) contains the slider and the piano. This can be implemented:

```
In [8]: piano.children = buttons
In [9]: container = widgets.ContainerWidget()
        container.children = [octave_slider,
                              piano]
```

7. By default, widgets are organized vertically within a container. Here, the octave slider will be above the piano. Within the piano, we want all notes to be arranged horizontally. We do this by replacing the default `vbox` CSS class by the `hbox` class. The following screenshot shows the piano in the IPython notebook:

```
In [10]: display(container)
         piano.remove_class('vbox')
         piano.add_class('hbox')
```

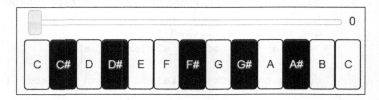

How it works...

The IPython widgets are represented by rich objects that are shared between the Python kernel and the browser. A widget contains special attributes called **trait attributes**. For example, the `value` trait attribute of `SliderWidget` is dynamically and automatically linked to the value that is selected by the user in the notebook's slider.

This link is bidirectional. Changing this attribute in Python updates the slider in the notebook.

The placement of the widgets is controlled by container widgets and with CSS classes. You will find more information in the documentation.

This architecture enables the creation of rich graphical applications in the notebook that are backed by Python code.

There's more...

▶ Widget examples at `http://nbviewer.ipython.org/github/ipython/ipython/blob/master/examples/Interactive%20Widgets/Index.ipynb`

See also

▶ The *Creating a custom JavaScript widget in the notebook – a spreadsheet editor for pandas* recipe

Creating a custom JavaScript widget in the notebook – a spreadsheet editor for pandas

We have previously introduced the new interactive features of the IPython notebook 2.0. In this recipe, we dive deeper into the subject by showing how to go beyond the existing widgets provided by IPython 2.0. Specifically, we will create a custom JavaScript-based widget that communicates with the Python kernel.

Specifically, we will create a basic interactive Excel-like data grid editor in the IPython notebook, compatible with pandas' `DataFrame`. Starting from a `DataFrame` object, we will be able to edit it within a GUI in the notebook. The editor is based on the `Handsontable` JavaScript library (`http://handsontable.com`). Other JavaScript data grid editors could be used as well.

Getting ready

You will need both IPython 2.0+ and the Handsontable JavaScript library for this recipe. The following are the instructions to load this Javascript library in the IPython notebook:

1. First, go to `https://github.com/handsontable/jquery-handsontable/tree/master/dist`.

2. Then, download `jquery.handsontable.full.css` and `jquery.handsontable.full.js`, and put these two files in `~\.ipython\profile_default\static\custom\`.

3. In this folder, add the following line in `custom.js`:

   ```
   require(['/static/custom/jquery.handsontable.full.js']);
   ```

4. In this folder, add the following line in `custom.css`:

   ```
   @import "/static/custom/jquery.handsontable.full.css"
   ```

5. Now, refresh the notebook!

How to do it...

1. Let's import a few functions and classes as follows:

   ```
   In [1]: from IPython.html import widgets
           from IPython.display import display
           from IPython.utils.traitlets import Unicode
   ```

2. We create a new widget. The `value` trait will contain the JSON representation of the entire table. This trait will be synchronized between Python and JavaScript, thanks to the IPython 2.0's widget machinery.

```
In [2]: class HandsonTableWidget(widgets.DOMWidget):
            _view_name = Unicode('HandsonTableView',
                                        sync=True)
            value = Unicode(sync=True)
```

3. Now, we write the JavaScript code for the widget. The three important functions that are responsible for the synchronization are as follows:

   - `render` is for the widget initialization
   - `update` is for Python to JavaScript update
   - `handle_table_change` is for JavaScript to Python update

```
In [3]: %%javascript
var table_id = 0;
require(["widgets/js/widget"], function(WidgetManager){
    // Define the HandsonTableView
    var HandsonTableView = IPython.DOMWidgetView.extend({

        render: function(){
            // Initialization: creation of the HTML elements
            // for our widget.

            // Add a <div> in the widget area.
            this.$table = $('<div />')
                .attr('id', 'table_' + (table_id++))
                .appendTo(this.$el);

            // Create the Handsontable table.
            this.$table.handsontable({
            });

        },

        update: function() {
            // Python --> Javascript update.

            // Get the model's JSON string, and parse it.
            var data = $.parseJSON(this.model.get('value'));
```

```
            // Give it to the Handsontable widget.
            this.$table.handsontable({data: data});

            return HandsonTableView.__super__.
                                    update.apply(this);
        },

        // Tell Backbone to listen to the change event
        // of input controls.
        events: {"change": "handle_table_change"},

        handle_table_change: function(event) {
            // Javascript --> Python update.

            // Get the table instance.
            var ht = this.$table.handsontable('getInstance');

            // Get the data, and serialize it in JSON.
            var json = JSON.stringify(ht.getData());

            // Update the model with the JSON string.
            this.model.set('value', json);

            this.touch();
        },
    });

    // Register the HandsonTableView with the widget manager.
    WidgetManager.register_widget_view(
        'HandsonTableView', HandsonTableView);
});
```

4. Now, we have a synchronized table widget that we can already use. However, we would like to integrate it with pandas. To do this, we create a light wrapper around a `DataFrame` instance. We create two callback functions for synchronizing the pandas object with the IPython widget. Changes in the GUI will automatically trigger a change in `DataFrame`, but the converse is not true. We'll need to re-display the widget if we change the `DataFrame` instance in Python:

```
In [4]: from io import StringIO
        import numpy as np
        import pandas as pd
In [5]: class HandsonDataFrame(object):
            def __init__(self, df):
                self._df = df
```

```
                        self._widget = HandsonTableWidget()
                        self._widget.on_trait_change(
                                self._on_data_changed, 'value')
                        self._widget.on_displayed(self._on_displayed)

                    def _on_displayed(self, e):
                        # DataFrame ==> Widget (upon initialization)
                        json = self._df.to_json(orient='values')
                        self._widget.value = json

                    def _on_data_changed(self, e, val):
                        # Widget ==> DataFrame (called every time the
                        # user changes a value in the widget)
                        buf = StringIO(val)
                        self._df = pd.read_json(buf, orient='values')

                    def to_dataframe(self):
                        return self._df

                    def show(self):
                        display(self._widget)
```

5. Now, let's test all that! We first create a random `DataFrame` instance:

```
In [6]: data = np.random.randint(size=(3, 5),
                                  low=100, high=900)
        df = pd.DataFrame(data)
        df
Out[6]:
352   201   859   322   352
326   519   848   802   642
171   480   213   619   192
```

6. We wrap it in `HandsonDataFrame` and show it as follows:

```
In [7]: ht = HandsonDataFrame(df)
        ht.show()
```

```
In [14]:  ht = HandsonDataFrame(df)
          ht.show()

    ✕   352   201   859   322    352
        326   519   848   1024   42
        171   480   213   619    192
```

7. We can now change the values interactively, and they will be changed in Python accordingly:

```
In [8]: ht.to_dataframe()
Out[8]:
352   201   859    322   352
326   519   848   1024   642
171   480   213    619   192
```

How it works...

Let's explain briefly the architecture underlying the interactive Python-JavaScript communication in IPython 2.0+.

The implementation follows the **Model-View-Controller** (**MVC**) design pattern, which is popular in GUI applications. There is a model in the backend (Python kernel) that holds some data. In the frontend (browser), there are one or several views of that model. Those views are dynamically synchronized with the model. When an attribute of the model changes on Python's side, it also changes on JavaScript's side, and vice versa. We can implement Python and JavaScript functions to respond to model changes. These changes are generally triggered by a user action.

In Python, dynamic attributes are implemented as traits. These special class attributes automatically trigger callback functions when they are updated. In JavaScript, the `Backbone. js` MVC library is used. The communication between Python and the browser is done via **Comms**, a special communication protocol in IPython.

To create a new widget, we need to create a class deriving from `DOMWidget`. Then, we define trait attributes that can be synchronized between Python and JavaScript if `sync=True` is passed to the trait constructors. We can register callback functions that react to trait changes (from either Python or JavaScript), using `widget.on_trait_change(callback, trait_name)`. The `callback()` function can have one of the following signatures:

*   `callback()`
*   `callback(trait_name)`
*   `callback(trait_name, new_value)`
*   `callback(trait_name, old_value, new_value)`

In JavaScript, the `render()` function creates the HTML elements in the cell's widget area upon initialization. The `update()` method allows us to react to changes in the model in the backend side (Python). In addition, we can use `Backbone.js` to react to changes in the frontend (browser). By extending the widget with the `{"change": "callback"}` events, we tell `Backbone.js` to call the `callback()` JavaScript function as soon as the HTML input controls change. This is how we react to user-triggered actions here.

There's more...

The following are the ways this proof-of-concept could be improved:

- ▶ Synchronizing only changes instead of synchronizing the whole array every time (the method used here would be slow on large tables)
- ▶ Avoiding recreating a new `DataFrame` instance upon every change, but updating the same `DataFrame` instance in-place
- ▶ Supporting named columns
- ▶ Hiding the wrapper, that is, make it so that the default rich representation of `DataFrame` in the notebook is `HandsonDataFrame`
- ▶ Implementing everything in an easy-to-use extension

Here are a few references about the widget architecture in the IPython notebook 2.0+:

- ▶ Official example about custom widgets, available at `http://nbviewer.ipython.org/github/ipython/ipython/tree/master/examples/Interactive%20Widgets`
- ▶ MVC pattern in Wikipedia, at `https://en.wikipedia.org/wiki/Model%E2%80%93view%E2%80%93controller`
- ▶ Backbone.js, available at `http://backbonejs.org/`
- ▶ Course on `Backbone.js`, available at `www.codeschool.com/courses/anatomy-of-backbonejs`
- ▶ IPEP 21: Widget Messages (comms), available at `https://github.com/ipython/ipython/wiki/IPEP-21%3A-Widget-Messages`
- ▶ IPEP 23: IPython widgets, available at `https://github.com/ipython/ipython/wiki/IPEP-23%3A-Backbone.js-Widgets`

See also

- ▶ The *Processing webcam images in real time from the notebook* recipe

Processing webcam images in real time from the notebook

In this recipe, we show how to let the notebook and the Python kernel communicate in both directions.

Specifically, we will retrieve the webcam feed from the browser using HTML5's `<video>` element, and pass it to Python in real time using the interactive capabilities of the IPython notebook 2.0+. Then, we will process the image in Python with an edge detector (implemented in scikit-image), and display it in the notebook in real time.

Most of the code for this recipe comes from Jason Grout's example, available at `https://github.com/jasongrout/ipywidgets`.

Getting ready

You need Pillow and scikit-image for this recipe. (For more information, refer to *Chapter 11, Image and Audio Processing*.)

You also need a recent browser supporting the HTML5 capture API. You can find the specification at `http://dev.w3.org/2011/webrtc/editor/getusermedia.html`.

How to do it...

1. We need to import several modules as follows:

```
In [1]: from IPython.html.widgets import DOMWidget
        from IPython.utils.traitlets import (Unicode, Bytes,
                                                    Instance)
        from IPython.display import display

        from skimage import io, filter, color
        import urllib
        import base64
        from PIL import Image
        from io import BytesIO # to change in Python 2
        import numpy as np
        from numpy import array, ndarray
        import matplotlib.pyplot as plt
```

2. We define two functions to convert images from and to base64 strings. This conversion is a common way to pass binary data between processes (in our case, the browser and Python):

```
In [2]: def to_b64(img):
            imgdata = BytesIO()
            pil = Image.fromarray(img)
            pil.save(imgdata, format='PNG')
            imgdata.seek(0)
            return urllib.parse.quote(
                    base64.b64encode(
                        imgdata.getvalue()))
```

```
In [3]: def from_b64(b64):
            im = Image.open(BytesIO(
                            base64.b64decode(b64)))
            return array(im)
```

3. We define a Python function that will process the webcam image in real time. It accepts and returns a NumPy array. This function applies an edge detector with the `roberts()` function in scikit-image as follows:

```
In [4]: def process_image(image):
            img = filter.roberts(image[:,:,0]/255.)
            return (255-img*255).astype(np.uint8)
```

4. Now, we create a custom widget to handle the bidirectional communication of the video flow between the browser and Python:

```
In [5]:
class Camera(DOMWidget):
    _view_name = Unicode('CameraView', sync=True)

    # This string contains the base64-encoded raw
    # webcam image (browser -> Python).
    imageurl = Unicode('', sync=True)

    # This string contains the base64-encoded processed
    # webcam image (Python -> browser).
    imageurl2 = Unicode('', sync=True)

    # This function is called whenever the raw webcam
    # image is changed.
    def _imageurl_changed(self, name, new):
        head, data = new.split(',', 1)
        if not data:
            return

        # We convert the base64-encoded string
        # to a NumPy array.
        image = from_b64(data)

        # We process the image.
        image = process_image(image)

        # We convert the processed image
        # to a base64-encoded string.
        b64 = to_b64(image)

        self.imageurl2 = 'data:image/png;base64,' + b64
```

5. The next step is to write the JavaScript code for the widget. The code is long, so we just highlight the important parts here. The full code is on the book's website:

```
In [6]: %%javascript

var video        = $('<video>')[0];
var canvas       = $('<canvas>')[0];
var canvas2       = $('<img>')[0];
[...]

require(["widgets/js/widget"], function(WidgetManager){
    var CameraView = IPython.DOMWidgetView.extend({
        render: function(){
            var that = this;

            // We append the HTML elements.
            setTimeout(function() {
                that.$el.append(video).
                        append(canvas).
                        append(canvas2);}, 200);

            // We initialize the webcam.
            [...]

            // We initialize the size of the canvas.
            video.addEventListener('canplay', function(ev){
                if (!streaming) {
                  height = video.videoHeight / (
                      video.videoWidth/width);
                  video.setAttribute('width', width);
                  video.setAttribute('height', height);
                  [...]
                  streaming = true;
                }
            }, false);

            // Play/Pause functionality.
            var interval;
            video.addEventListener('play', function(ev){
                // We get the picture every 100ms.
                interval = setInterval(takepicture, 100);
            })
            video.addEventListener('pause', function(ev){
                clearInterval(interval);
            })
```

```
        // This function is called at each time step.
        // It takes a picture and sends it to the model.
        function takepicture() {
            canvas.width = width; canvas.height = height;
            canvas2.width = width; canvas2.height = height;

            video.style.display = 'none';
            canvas.style.display = 'none';

            // We take a screenshot from the webcam feed and
            // we put the image in the first canvas.
            canvas.getContext('2d').drawImage(video,
                0, 0, width, height);

            // We export the canvas image to the model.
            that.model.set('imageurl',
                            canvas.toDataURL('image/png'));
            that.touch();
        }
    },

    update: function(){
        // This function is called whenever Python modifies
        // the second (processed) image. We retrieve it and
        // we display it in the second canvas.
        var img = this.model.get('imageurl2');
        canvas2.src = img;
        return CameraView.__super__.update.apply(this);
    }
});

// Register the view with the widget manager.
WidgetManager.register_widget_view('CameraView',
                                CameraView);
});
```

6. Finally, we create and display the widget as follows:

```
In [7]: c = Camera()
        display(c)
```

How it works...

Let's explain the principle of this implementation. The model has two attributes: the incoming (raw) image from the browser and the outgoing (processed) image from Python. Every 100 milliseconds, JavaScript makes a capture of the webcam feed (in the `<video>` HTML element) by copying it to a first canvas. The canvas image is serialized in base64 and assigned to the first model attribute. Then, the Python function `_imageurl_changed()` is called. The image is deserialized, processed by scikit-image, and reserialized. The second attribute is then modified by Python, and is set to the serialized processed image. Finally, the `update()` function in JavaScript deserializes the processed image and displays it in a second canvas.

There's more...

The speed of this example could be greatly improved by capturing the webcam image from Python rather than from the browser. Here, the bottleneck probably stems from the two transfers that occur at every time step from the browser to Python and conversely.

It would be more efficient to capture the webcam's image from Python using a library such as `OpenCV` or `SimpleCV`. However, since these libraries may be difficult to install, it is much simpler to let the browser access the webcam device.

See also

  ▶ The *Creating a custom JavaScript widget in the notebook – a spreadsheet editor for pandas* recipe

4
Profiling and Optimization

In this chapter, we will cover the following topics:

- ▶ Evaluating the time taken by a statement in IPython
- ▶ Profiling your code easily with cProfile and IPython
- ▶ Profiling your code line-by-line with line_profiler
- ▶ Profiling the memory usage of your code with memory_profiler
- ▶ Understanding the internals of NumPy to avoid unnecessary array copying
- ▶ Using stride tricks with NumPy
- ▶ Implementing an efficient rolling average algorithm with stride tricks
- ▶ Making efficient array selections in NumPy
- ▶ Processing huge NumPy arrays with memory mapping
- ▶ Manipulating large arrays with HDF5 and PyTables
- ▶ Manipulating large heterogeneous tables with HDF5 and PyTables

Introduction

Although Python is generally known (a bit unfairly) as a *slow* language, it is possible to achieve very good performance with the right methods. This is the objective of this chapter and the next. This chapter describes how to evaluate (**profile**) what makes a program slow, and how this information can be used to **optimize** the code and make it more efficient. The next chapter will deal with more advanced high-performance computing methods that should only be tackled when the methods described here are not sufficient.

The recipes of this chapter are organized into three parts:

▸ **Time and memory profiling**: Evaluating the performance of code

▸ **NumPy optimization**: Using NumPy more efficiently, particularly with large arrays

▸ **Memory mapping with arrays**: Implementing memory mapping techniques for out-of-core computations on huge arrays, notably with the HDF5 file format

Evaluating the time taken by a statement in IPython

The `%timeit` magic and the `%%timeit` cell magic (that applies to an entire code cell) allow you to quickly evaluate the time taken by one or several Python statements. For more extensive profiling, you may need to use more advanced methods presented in the next recipes.

How to do it...

We are going to estimate the time taken to calculate the sum of the inverse squares of all positive integer numbers up to a given n:

1. Let's define n:

   ```
   In [1]: n = 100000
   ```

2. Let's time this computation in pure Python:

   ```
   In [2]: %timeit sum([1. / i**2 for i in range(1, n)])
   10 loops, best of 3: 131 ms per loop
   ```

3. Now, let's use the `%%timeit` cell magic to time the same computation written on two lines:

   ```
   In [3]: %%timeit s = 0.
           for i in range(1, n):
               s += 1. / i**2
   10 loops, best of 3: 137 ms per loop
   ```

4. Finally, let's time the NumPy version of this computation:

   ```
   In [4]: import numpy as np
   In [5]: %timeit np.sum(1. / np.arange(1., n) ** 2)
   1000 loops, best of 3: 1.71 ms per loop
   ```

How it works...

The `%timeit` command accepts several optional parameters. One such parameter is the number of statement evaluations. By default, this number is chosen automatically so that the `%timeit` command returns within a few seconds. However, this number can be specified directly with the `-r` and `-n` parameters. Type `%timeit?` in IPython to get more information.

The `%%timeit` cell magic also accepts an optional setup statement in the first line (on the same line as `%%timeit`), which is executed but not timed. All variables created in this statement are available inside the cell.

There's more...

If you are not in an IPython interactive session, you can use `timeit.timeit()`. This function, defined in Python's `timeit` module, benchmarks a Python statement stored in a string. IPython's `%timeit` magic command is a convenient wrapper around `timeit()`, useful in an interactive session. For more information on the `timeit` module, refer to `https://docs.python.org/3/library/timeit.html`.

See also

- The *Profiling your code easily with cProfile and IPython* recipe
- The *Profiling your code line-by-line with line_profiler* recipe

Profiling your code easily with cProfile and IPython

The `%timeit` magic command is often helpful, yet a bit limited when you need detailed information about what takes most of the execution time in your code. This magic command is meant for **benchmarking** (comparing the execution times of different versions of a function) rather than **profiling** (getting a detailed report of the execution time, function by function).

Python includes a profiler named `cProfile` that breaks down the execution time into the contributions of all called functions. IPython provides convenient ways to leverage this tool in an interactive session.

How to do it...

IPython offers the `%prun` line magic and the `%%prun` cell magic to easily profile one or multiple lines of code. The `%run` magic command also accepts a `-p` flag to run a Python script under the control of the profiler. These commands accept a lot of options, and you may want to take a look at their documentation with `%prun?` and `%run?`.

In this example, we will profile a numerical simulation of random walks starting at the origin. We will cover these kinds of simulations in more detail in *Chapter 13, Stochastic Dynamical Systems*.

1. Let's import NumPy and matplotlib:

```
In [1]: import numpy as np
        import matplotlib.pyplot as plt
In [2]: %matplotlib inline
```

2. Let's create a function generating random +1 and -1 values in an array:

```
In [3]: def step(*shape):
            # Create a random n-vector with +1 or -1
            # values.
            return 2 * (np.random.random_sample(shape)
                        < .5) - 1
```

3. Now, let's write the simulation code in a cell starting with `%%prun` in order to profile the entire simulation. The various options allow us to save the report in a file and to sort the first 10 results by cumulative time. We will explain these options in more detail in the *How it works...* section.

```
In [4]: %%prun -s cumulative -q -l 10 -T prun0
        n = 10000
        iterations = 50
        x = np.cumsum(step(iterations, n), axis=0)
        bins = np.arange(-30, 30, 1)
        y = np.vstack([np.histogram(x[i,:], bins)[0]
                       for i in range(iterations)])
```

4. The profiling report has been saved in a text file named `prun0`. Let's display it (the following output is a stripped down version that fits on this page):

```
In [5]: print(open('prun0', 'r').read())
            2960 function calls in 0.075 seconds
Ordered by: cumulative time
ncalls  cumtime  percall function
    50    0.037    0.001 histogram
     1    0.031    0.031 step
    50    0.024    0.000 sort
```

```
    1    0.019    0.019 rand
    1    0.005    0.005 cumsum
```

Here, we observe the time taken by the different functions involved, directly or indirectly, in our code.

5. If we run the exact same simulation with 500 iterations instead of 50, we obtain the following results:

```
29510 function calls in 1.359 seconds
ncalls   cumtime  percall function
  500     0.566    0.001 histogram
    1     0.388    0.388 cumsum
    1     0.383    0.383 step
  500     0.339    0.001 sort
    1     0.241    0.241 rand
```

We can observe that the number of iterations has a big influence on the relative performance cost of the involved functions (notably cumsum here).

How it works...

Python's profiler creates a detailed report of the execution time of our code, function by function. Here, we can observe the number of calls of the functions histogram, cumsum, step, sort, and rand, and the total time spent in those functions during the code's execution. Internal functions are also profiled. For each function, we get the total number of calls, the total and cumulative times, and their per-call counterparts (division by ncalls). The **total time** represents how long the interpreter stays in a given function, *excluding* the time spent in calls to subfunctions. The **cumulative time** is similar but *includes* the time spent in calls to subfunctions. The filename, function name, and line number are displayed in the last column.

The %prun and %%prun magic commands accept multiple optional options (type %prun? for more details). In the example, -s allows us to **sort** the report by a particular column, -q to suppress (**quell**) the pager output (which is useful when we want to integrate the output in a notebook), -l to **limit** the number of lines displayed or to filter the results by function name (which is useful when we are interested in a particular function), and -T to save the report in a **text** file. In addition, we can choose to save (**dump**) the binary report in a file with -D, or to **return** it in IPython with -r. This database-like object contains all information about the profiling and can be analyzed through Python's pstats module.

 Every profiler brings its own overhead that can bias the profiling results (**probe effect**). In other words, a profiled program may run significantly slower than a non-profiled program. That's a point to keep in mind.

"Premature optimization is the root of all evil"

As Donald Knuth's well-known quote suggests, optimizing code prematurely is generally considered a bad practice. Code optimization should only be conducted when it's really needed, that is, when the code is really too slow in normal situations. Additionally, we should know exactly where we need to optimize your code; typically, the vast majority of the execution time comprises a relatively small part of the code. The only way to find out is by profiling your code; optimization should never be done without preliminary profiling.

I was once dealing with some fairly complicated code that was slower than expected. I thought I had a pretty good idea of what was causing the problem and how I could resolve it. The solution would involve significant changes in the code. Fortunately, I first profiled my code, just to be sure. My diagnostic appeared to be utterly wrong; I had written somewhere `max(x)` instead of `np.max(x)` by mistake, where x was a very large vector. It was Python's built-in function that was called, instead of NumPy's heavily optimized routine for arrays. If I hadn't profiled my code, I would probably have missed this mistake forever. The program was working perfectly fine, only 150 times slower!

For more general advice on programming optimization, see `http://en.wikipedia.org/wiki/Program_optimization`.

There's more...

Profiling code in IPython is particularly simple (especially in the notebook), as we have seen in this recipe. However, it may be undesirable or difficult to execute the code that we need to profile from IPython (GUIs, for example). In this case, we can use `cProfile` directly. It is slightly less straightforward than with IPython.

1. First, we call the following command:

   ```
   $ python -m cProfile -o profresults myscript.py
   ```

   The file `profresults` will contain the dump of the profiling results of `myscript.py`.

2. Then, we execute the following code from Python or IPython to display the profiling results in a human-readable form:

   ```
   import pstats
   p = pstats.Stats('profresults')
   p.strip_dirs().sort_stats("cumulative").print_stats()
   ```

Explore the documentation of the `cProfile` and `pstats` modules to discover all of the analyses that you can perform on the profiling reports.

 The repository at `https://github.com/rossant/easy_profiler` contains a simple command-line tool that facilitates the profiling of Python scripts.

There are a few GUI tools for exploring and visualizing the output of a profiling session. For example, **RunSnakeRun** allows you to view profile dumps in a GUI program.

Here are a few references:

> ▶ Documentation of `cProfile` and `pstats`, available at `https://docs.python.org/3/library/profile.html`

> ▶ RunSnakeRun, at `www.vrplumber.com/programming/runsnakerun/`

> ▶ Python profiling tools, available at `http://blog.ionelmc.ro/2013/06/08/python-profiling-tools/`

See also

> ▶ The *Profiling your code line-by-line with line_profiler* recipe

Profiling your code line-by-line with line_profiler

Python's native `cProfile` module and the corresponding `%prun` magic break down the execution time of code *function by function*. Sometimes, we may need an even more fine-grained analysis of code performance with a *line-by-line* report. Such reports can be easier to read than the reports of `cProfile`.

To profile code line-by-line, we need an external Python module named `line_profiler` created by Robert Kern, available at `http://pythonhosted.org/line_profiler/`. In this recipe, we will demonstrate how to use this module within IPython.

Getting ready

To install `line_profiler`, type `pip install line_profiler` in a terminal, or type `!pip install line_profiler` in IPython (you need a C compiler).

On Windows, you can use Chris Gohlke's unofficial package available at `www.lfd.uci.edu/~gohlke/pythonlibs/#line_profiler`.

How do to it...

We will profile the same simulation code as in the previous recipe, line-by-line:

1. First, let's import NumPy and the `line_profiler` IPython extension module that comes with the package:

```
In [1]: import numpy as np
In [2]: %load_ext line_profiler
```

2. This IPython extension module provides a `%lprun` magic command to profile a Python function line-by-line. It works best when the function is defined in a file and not in the interactive namespace or in the notebook. Therefore, here we write our code in a Python script using the `%%writefile` cell magic:

```
In [3]: %%writefile simulation.py
        import numpy as np
        def step(*shape):
            # Create a random n-vector with +1 or -1
            # values.
            return (2 * (np.random.random_sample(shape)
                        < .5) - 1)
        def simulate(iterations, n=10000):
            s = step(iterations, n)
            x = np.cumsum(s, axis=0)
            bins = np.arange(-30, 30, 1)
            y = np.vstack([np.histogram(x[i,:], bins)[0]
                          for i in range(iterations)])
            return y
```

3. Now, let's import this script into the interactive namespace so that we can execute and profile our code:

```
In [4]: import simulation
```

4. We execute the function under the control of the line profiler. The functions to be profiled need to be explicitly specified in the `%lprun` magic command. We also save the report in a file, `lprof0`:

```
In [5]: %lprun -T lprof0 -f simulation.simulate simulation.
simulate(50)
```

5. Let's display the report (the following output is a stripped-down version that fits in the page):

```
In [6]: print(open('lprof0', 'r').read())
File: simulation.py
Function: simulate at line 7
Total time: 0.114508 s
Line #   % Time  Line Contents
```

```
 7                    def simulate(iterations, n=10000):
 8      36.3              s = step(iterations, n)
 9       5.6              x = np.cumsum(s, axis=0)
10       0.1              bins = np.arange(-30, 30, 1)
11      58.1              y = np.vstack([np.histogram(...)])
12       0.0              return y
```

6. If we perform the same analysis with 10 times the previous number of iterations (`simulation.simulate(500)`), we get the following report:

```
Total time: 1.28704 s
 7                    def simulate(iterations, n=10000):
 8      29.2              s = step(iterations, n)
 9      30.9              x = np.cumsum(s, axis=0)
10       0.0              bins = np.arange(-30, 30, 1)
11      39.9              y = np.vstack([np.histogram(...)])
12       0.0              return y
```

How it works...

The `%lprun` command accepts a Python statement as its main argument. The functions to profile need to be explicitly specified with `-f`. Other optional arguments include `-D`, `-T`, and `-r`, and they work in a similar way to their `%prun` magic command counterparts.

The `line_profiler` module displays the time spent on each line of the profiled functions, either in timer units or as a fraction of the total execution time. These details are essential when we are looking for hotspots in our code.

There's more...

As in the previous recipe, there may be a need to run the line-by-line profiler on a standalone Python program that cannot be launched easily from IPython. The procedure is a bit convoluted.

1. We download the `kernprof` file from `https://github.com/rkern/line_profiler/blob/master/kernprof.py`, and save it in your code's directory.

2. In the code, we decorate the functions we wish to profile with `@profile`. We need to remove these decorators at the end of the profiling session, as they will raise `NameError` exceptions if the code is executed normally (that is, not under the control of the line profiler):

```
@profile
def thisfunctionneedstobeprofiled():
    pass
```

See also the `http://stackoverflow.com/ questions/18229628/python-profiling- using-line-profiler-clever-way-to- remove-profile-statements` link for a clever way to remove profile statements.

3. We execute the following command in a terminal:

```
python -m kernprof -l -v myscript.py > lprof.txt
```

The `myscript.py` script will be executed, and the report will be saved in `lprof.txt`.

 The repository at `https://github.com/rossant/ easy_profiler` offers a slightly simpler way of using the line-by-line profiler.

Tracing the step-by-step execution of a Python program

Let's also talk about **tracing** tools for Python, which can be useful for profiling or debugging a program, or for educational purposes.

Python's `trace` module allows us to trace program execution of Python code. That's extremely useful during in-depth debugging and profiling sessions. We can follow the entire sequence of instructions executed by the Python interpreter. More information on the trace module is available at `https://docs.python.org/3/library/trace.html`.

In addition, the **Online Python Tutor** is an online interactive educational tool that can help us understand what the Python interpreter is doing step-by-step as it executes a program's source code. The Online Python Tutor is available at `http://pythontutor.com/`.

See also

▸ The *Profiling your code easily with cProfile and IPython* recipe
▸ The *Profiling the memory usage of your code with memory_profiler* recipe

Profiling the memory usage of your code with memory_profiler

The methods described in the previous recipe were about CPU time profiling. That may be the most obvious factor when it comes to code profiling. However, memory is also a critical factor. For instance, running `np.zeros(500000000)` is likely to instantaneously crash your computer! This command may allocate more memory than is available on your system; your computer will then reach a nonresponsive state within seconds.

Writing memory-optimized code is not trivial and can really make your program faster. This is particularly important when dealing with large NumPy arrays, as we will see later in this chapter.

In this recipe, we will look at a simple memory profiler. This library, unsurprisingly called `memory_profiler`, was created by Fabian Pedregosa. Its usage is very similar to `line_profiler`, and it can be conveniently used from IPython. You can download it from `https://pypi.python.org/pypi/memory_profiler`.

Getting ready

You can install `memory_profiler` with `pip install memory_profiler`.

On Windows, you also need `psutil`, which is available at `https://pypi.python.org/pypi/psutil`. You can install it with `pip install psutil`, or by downloading the package from `https://code.google.com/p/psutil/`. You can also download an installer from Chris Gohlke's webpage at `www.lfd.uci.edu/~gohlke/pythonlibs/`.

The example in this recipe is the continuation of the previous recipe.

How to do it...

1. Assuming that the simulation code has been loaded as shown in the previous recipe, we load the memory profiler IPython extension:

   ```
   In [9]: %load_ext memory_profiler
   ```

2. Now, let's run the code under the control of the memory profiler:

   ```
   In [10]: %mprun -T mprof0 -f simulation.simulate simulation.simulate(50)
   ```

3. Let's show the results:

   ```
   In [11]: print(open('mprof0', 'r').read())
   Filename: simulation.py
   Line #    Mem usage    Increment    Line Contents
        7    39.672 MB    0.000 MB     def simulate(...):
        8    41.977 MB    2.305 MB         s = step(iterations, n)
        9    43.887 MB    1.910 MB         x = np.cumsum(...)
       10    43.887 MB    0.000 MB         bins = np.arange(...)
       11    43.887 MB    0.000 MB         y = np.vstack(...)
       12    43.887 MB    0.000 MB         return y
   ```

4. Finally, here is the report with 500 iterations:

   ```
   Line #    Mem usage   Increment    Line Contents
        7    40.078 MB   0.000 MB     def simulate(...):
        8    59.191 MB   19.113 MB        s = step(iterations, n)
   ```

```
 9    78.301 MB  19.109 MB       x = np.cumsum(...)
10    78.301 MB   0.000 MB       bins = np.arange(...)
11    78.301 MB   0.000 MB       y = np.vstack(...)
12    78.301 MB   0.000 MB       return y
```

How it works...

The `memory_profiler` package checks the memory usage of the interpreter at every line. The **increment** column allows us to spot those places in the code where large amounts of memory are allocated. This is especially important when working with arrays. Unnecessary array creations and copies can considerably slow down a program. We will tackle this issue in the next few recipes.

There's more...

We can use `memory_profiler` without IPython, and we can also use a quick memory benchmark in IPython for single commands.

Using memory_profiler for standalone Python programs

Using the memory profiler with standalone Python programs is similar but slightly simpler than with `line_profiler`.

1. First, in our Python scripts, we decorate the functions we wish to profile with `@profile`.

2. Then, we run:

   ```
   $ python -m memory_profiler myscript.py > mprof.txt
   ```

   The profiling report will be saved in `myprof.txt`.

Using the %memit magic command in IPython

The `memory_profiler` IPython extension also comes with a `%memit` magic command that lets us benchmark the memory used by a single Python statement. Here is a simple example:

```
In [14]: %memit np.random.randn(1000, 1000)
maximum of 1: 46.199219 MB per loop
```

Other tools

There are other tools to monitor the memory usage of a Python program, notably Guppy-PE (http://guppy-pe.sourceforge.net/), PySizer (http://pysizer.8325.org/), and Pympler (https://code.google.com/p/pympler/). Used in conjunction with IPython and Python's introspection capabilities, these tools allow you to analyze the memory usage of a namespace or a particular object.

See also

▸ The *Profiling your code line-by-line with line_profiler* recipe

▸ The *Understanding the internals of NumPy to avoid unnecessary array copying* recipe

Understanding the internals of NumPy to avoid unnecessary array copying

We can achieve significant performance speedups with NumPy over native Python code, particularly when our computations follow the **Single Instruction, Multiple Data** (**SIMD**) paradigm. However, it is also possible to unintentionally write non-optimized code with NumPy.

In the next few recipes, we will see some tricks that can help us write optimized NumPy code. In this recipe, we will see how to avoid unnecessary array copies in order to save memory. In that respect, we will need to dig into the internals of NumPy.

Getting ready

First, we need a way to check whether two arrays share the same underlying data buffer in memory. Let's define a function `id()` that returns the memory location of the underlying data buffer:

```
def id(x):
    # This function returns the memory
    # block address of an array.
    return x.__array_interface__['data'][0]
```

Two arrays with the same data location (as returned by `id`) share the same underlying data buffer. However, the opposite is true only if the arrays have the same **offset** (meaning that they have the same first element). Two shared arrays with different offsets will have slightly different memory locations, as shown in the following example:

```
In [1]: id(a), id(a[1:])
Out[1]: (71211328, 71211336)
```

In the next few recipes, we'll make sure to use this method with arrays that have the same offset. Here is a more general and reliable solution for finding out whether two arrays share the same data:

```
In [2]: def get_data_base(arr):
            """For a given Numpy array, finds the
            base array that "owns" the actual data."""
            base = arr
            while isinstance(base.base, np.ndarray):
```

```
            base = base.base
        return base

    def arrays_share_data(x, y):
        return get_data_base(x) is get_data_base(y)

In [3]: print(arrays_share_data(a,a.copy()),
              arrays_share_data(a,a[1:]))
False True
```

Thanks to Michael Droettboom for pointing this out and proposing this alternative solution.

How to do it...

Computations with NumPy arrays may involve internal copies between blocks of memory. These copies are not always necessary, in which case they should be avoided, as we will see in the following tips:

1. We may sometimes need to make a copy of an array; for instance, if we need to manipulate an array while keeping an original copy in memory:

```
In [3]: a = np.zeros(10); aid = id(a); aid
Out[3]: 65527008L
In [4]: b = a.copy(); id(b) == aid
Out[4]: False
```

2. Array computations can involve in-place operations (the first example in the following code: the array is modified) or implicit-copy operations (the second example: a new array is created):

```
In [5]: a *= 2; id(a) == aid
Out[5]: True
In [6]: a = a*2; id(a) == aid
Out[6]: False
```

Be sure to choose the type of operation you actually need. Implicit-copy operations are significantly slower, as shown here:

```
In [7]: %%timeit a = np.zeros(10000000)
        a *= 2
10 loops, best of 3: 23.9 ms per loop
In [8]: %%timeit a = np.zeros(10000000)
        a = a*2
10 loops, best of 3: 77.9 ms per loop
```

3. Reshaping an array may or may not involve a copy. The reasons will be explained in the *How it works...* section. For instance, reshaping a 2D matrix does not involve a copy, unless it is transposed (or more generally, **non-contiguous**):

```
In [9]: a = np.zeros((10, 10)); aid = id(a)
In [10]: b = a.reshape((1, -1)); id(b) == aid
Out[10]: True
In [11]: c = a.T.reshape((1, -1)); id(c) == aid
Out[11]: False
```

Therefore, the latter instruction will be significantly slower than the former.

4. Both the `flatten` and the `ravel` methods of an array reshape it into a 1D vector (a flattened array). However, the `flatten` method always returns a copy, and the `ravel` method returns a copy only if necessary (thus it's faster, especially with large arrays).

```
In [12]: d = a.flatten(); id(d) == aid
Out[12]: False
In [13]: e = a.ravel(); id(e) == aid
Out[13]: True
In [14]: %timeit a.flatten()
1000000 loops, best of 3: 1.65 µs per loop
In [15]: %timeit a.ravel()
1000000 loops, best of 3: 566 ns per loop
```

5. **Broadcasting rules** allow us to make computations on arrays with different but compatible shapes. In other words, we don't always need to reshape or tile our arrays to make their shapes match. The following example illustrates two ways of doing an **outer product** between two vectors: the first method involves array tiling, the second one (faster) involves broadcasting:

```
In [16]: n = 1000
In [17]: a = np.arange(n)
         ac = a[:, np.newaxis]  # Column vector.
         ar = a[np.newaxis, :]  # Row vector.
In [18]: %timeit np.tile(ac, (1, n)) * np.tile(ar, (n, 1))
10 loops, best of 3: 25 ms per loop
In [19]: %timeit ar * ac
100 loops, best of 3: 4.63 ms per loop
```

How it works...

In this section, we will see what happens under the hood when using NumPy, and how this knowledge allows us to understand the tricks given in this recipe.

Why are NumPy arrays efficient?

A NumPy array is basically described by metadata (notably the number of dimensions, the shape, and the data type) and the actual data. The data is stored in a homogeneous and contiguous block of memory, at a particular address in system memory (**Random Access Memory**, or **RAM**). This block of memory is called the **data buffer**. This is the main difference when compared to a pure Python structure, such as a list, where the items are scattered across the system memory. This aspect is the critical feature that makes NumPy arrays so efficient.

Why is this so important? Here are the main reasons:

- Computations on arrays can be written very efficiently in a low-level language such as C (and a large part of NumPy is actually written in C). Knowing the address of the memory block and the data type, it is just simple arithmetic to loop over all items, for example. There would be a significant overhead to do that in Python with a list.

- **Spatial locality** in memory access patterns results in performance gains notably due to the CPU cache. Indeed, the cache loads bytes in chunks from RAM to the CPU registers. Adjacent items are then loaded very efficiently (**sequential locality**, or **locality of reference**).

- Finally, the fact that items are stored contiguously in memory allows NumPy to take advantage of **vectorized instructions** of modern CPUs, such as Intel's **SSE** and **AVX**, AMD's XOP, and so on. For example, multiple consecutive floating point numbers can be loaded in 128, 256, or 512 bits registers for vectorized arithmetical computations implemented as CPU instructions.

 Additionally, NumPy can be linked to highly optimized linear algebra libraries such as **BLAS** and **LAPACK** through **ATLAS** or the **Intel Math Kernel Library** (**MKL**). A few specific matrix computations may also be multithreaded, taking advantage of the power of modern multicore processors.

In conclusion, storing data in a contiguous block of memory ensures that the architecture of modern CPUs is used optimally, in terms of memory access patterns, CPU cache, and vectorized instructions.

What is the difference between in-place and implicit-copy operations?

Let's explain the example in step 2. An expression such as a `*=` 2 corresponds to an in-place operation, where all values of the array are multiplied by two. By contrast, a `=` a`*`2 means that a new array containing the values of a`*`2 is created, and the variable a now points to this new array. The old array becomes unreferenced and will be deleted by the garbage collector. No memory allocation happens in the first case, contrary to the second case.

More generally, expressions such as a[i:j] are **views** to parts of an array; they point to the memory buffer containing the data. Modifying them with in-place operations changes the original array. Hence, a[:] = a*2 results in an in-place operation, unlike a = a*2.

Knowing this subtlety of NumPy can help you fix some bugs (where an array is implicitly and unintentionally modified because of an operation on a view), and optimize the speed and memory consumption of your code by reducing the number of unnecessary copies.

Why can't some arrays be reshaped without a copy?

We explain the example in step 3 here, where a transposed 2D matrix cannot be flattened without a copy. A 2D matrix contains items indexed by two numbers (row and column), but it is stored internally as a 1D contiguous block of memory, accessible with a single number. There is more than one way of storing matrix items in a 1D block of memory: we can put the elements of the first row first, then the second row, and so on, or the elements of the first column first, then the second column, and so on. The first method is called **row-major order**, whereas the latter is called **column-major order**. Choosing between the two methods is only a matter of internal convention: NumPy uses the row-major order, like C, but unlike FORTRAN.

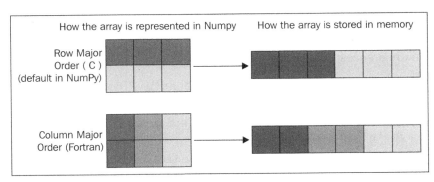

Internal array layouts: row-major and column-major orders

More generally, NumPy uses the notion of strides to convert between a multidimensional index and the memory location of the underlying (1D) sequence of elements. The specific mapping between array[i1, i2] and the relevant byte address of the internal data is given by:

```
offset = array.strides[0] * i1 + array.strides[1] * i2
```

When reshaping an array, NumPy avoids copies when possible by modifying the strides attribute. For example, when transposing a matrix, the order of strides is reversed, but the underlying data remains identical. However, flattening a transposed array cannot be accomplished simply by modifying strides (try it!), so a copy is needed (thanks to Chris Beaumont for clarifying an earlier version of this paragraph).

Internal array layout can also explain some unexpected performance discrepancies between very similar NumPy operations. As a small exercise, can you explain the following benchmarks?

```
In [20]: a = np.random.rand(5000, 5000)
In [21]: %timeit a[0,:].sum()
100000 loops, best of 3: 17.9 µs per loop
In [22]: %timeit a[:,0].sum()
10000 loops, best of 3: 60.6 µs per loop
```

What are NumPy broadcasting rules?

Broadcasting rules describe how arrays with different dimensions and/or shapes can be used for computations. The general rule is that *two dimensions are compatible when they are equal, or when one of them is 1*. NumPy uses this rule to compare the shapes of the two arrays element-wise, starting with the trailing dimensions and working its way forward. The smallest dimension is internally stretched to match the other dimension, but this operation does not involve any memory copy.

There's more...

Here are a few references:

▶ Broadcasting rules and examples, available at `http://docs.scipy.org/doc/numpy/user/basics.broadcasting.html`

▶ Array interface in NumPy, at `http://docs.scipy.org/doc/numpy/reference/arrays.interface.html`

▶ Locality of reference, at `http://en.wikipedia.org/wiki/Locality_of_reference`

▶ Internals of NumPy in the SciPy lectures notes, available at `http://scipy-lectures.github.io/advanced/advanced_numpy/`

▶ 100 NumPy exercises by Nicolas Rougier, available at `www.loria.fr/~rougier/teaching/numpy.100/index.html`

See also

▶ The *Using stride tricks with NumPy* recipe

Using stride tricks with NumPy

In this recipe, we will dig deeper into the internals of NumPy arrays, by generalizing the notion of row-major and column-major orders to multidimensional arrays. The general notion is that of **strides**, which describe how the items of a multidimensional array are organized within a one-dimensional data buffer. Strides are mostly an implementation detail, but they can also be used in specific situations to optimize some algorithms.

Getting ready

We suppose that NumPy has been imported and that the `id` function has been defined (see the previous recipe, *Understanding the internals of NumPy to avoid unnecessary array copying*).

How to do it...

1. Strides are integer numbers describing the byte step in the contiguous block of memory for each dimension.

   ```
   In [3]: x = np.zeros(10); x.strides
   Out[3]: (8,)
   ```

   This vector x contains double-precision floating point numbers (float64, 8 bytes); one needs to go *8 bytes forward* to go from one item to the next.

2. Now, let's look at the strides of a 2D array:

   ```
   In [4]: y = np.zeros((10, 10)); y.strides
   Out[4]: (80, 8)
   ```

   In the first dimension (vertical), one needs to go *80 bytes* (10 float64 items) *forward* to go from one item to the next, because the items are internally stored in row-major order. In the second dimension (horizontal), one needs to go *8 bytes forward* to go from one item to the next.

3. Let's show how we can revisit the broadcasting rules from the previous recipe using strides:

   ```
   In [5]: n = 1000; a = np.arange(n)
   ```

   We will create a new array, b, pointing to the same memory block as a, but with a different shape and different strides. This new array will look like a vertically-tiled version of a. We use a special function in NumPy to change the strides of an array:

   ```
   In [6]: b = np.lib.stride_tricks.as_strided(a, (n, n),
                                              (0, 4))
   ```

```
Out[7]: array([[  0,  1,  2, ..., 997, 998, 999],
                ...,
               [  0,  1,  2, ..., 997, 998, 999]])
In [8]: b.size, b.shape, b.nbytes
Out[8]: (1000000, (1000, 1000), 4000000)
```

NumPy believes that this array contains one million different elements, whereas the data buffer actually contains the same 1000 elements as a.

4. We can now perform an efficient outer product using the same principle as with broadcasting rules:

```
In [9]: %timeit b * b.T
100 loops, best of 3: 5.03 ms per loop
In [10]: %timeit np.tile(a, (n, 1)) \
                 * np.tile(a[:, np.newaxis], (1, n))
10 loops, best of 3: 28 ms per loop
```

How it works...

Every array has a number of dimensions, a shape, a data type, and strides. Strides describe how the items of a multidimensional array are organized in the data buffer. There are many different schemes for arranging the items of a multidimensional array in a one-dimensional block. NumPy implements a **strided indexing scheme**, where the position of any element is a **linear combination** of the dimensions, the coefficients being the strides. In other words, strides describe, in any dimension, how many bytes we need to jump over in the data buffer to go from one item to the next.

The position of any element in a multidimensional array is given by a linear combination of its indices, as follows:

$$\text{an array} \qquad\qquad \text{one item}$$

$$\text{ndim} = N \qquad\qquad \text{indices} = \left(i_0, ..., i_{N-1}\right)$$

$$\text{shape} = \left(d_0, ..., d_{N-1}\right) \qquad\qquad \text{position} = \sum_{k=0}^{N-1} s_k i_k$$

$$\text{strides} = \left(s_0, ..., s_{N-1}\right)$$

$$\text{itemsize} = \alpha$$

$$\text{examples: column-major and row-major orders}$$

$$s_k^{column} = \prod_{j=0}^{k-1} \alpha d_j, \qquad\qquad s_k^{row} = \prod_{j=k+1}^{N-1} \alpha d_j$$

Artificially changing the strides allows us to make some array operations more efficient than with standard methods, which may involve array copies. Internally, that's how broadcasting works in NumPy.

The `as_strided` method takes an array, a shape, and strides as arguments. It creates a new array, but uses the same data buffer as the original array. The only thing that changes is the metadata. This trick lets us manipulate NumPy arrays as usual, except that they may take much less memory than what NumPy thinks. Here, using 0 in the strides implies that any array item can be addressed by many multidimensional indices, resulting in memory savings.

> Be careful with strided arrays! The `as_strided` function does not check whether you stay inside the memory block bounds. This means that you need to handle edge effects manually; otherwise, you may end up with garbage values in your arrays.

We will see a more useful application of stride tricks in the next recipe.

See also

▶ The *Implementing an efficient rolling average algorithm with stride tricks* recipe

Implementing an efficient rolling average algorithm with stride tricks

Stride tricks can be useful for local computations on arrays, when the computed value at a given position depends on the neighboring values. Examples include dynamical systems, digital filters, and cellular automata.

In this recipe, we will implement an efficient **rolling average** algorithm (a particular type of convolution-based linear filter) with NumPy stride tricks. A rolling average of a 1D vector contains, at each position, the average of the elements around this position in the original vector. Roughly speaking, this process filters out the noisy components of a signal so as to keep only the slower components.

Getting ready

Make sure to reuse the `id()` function from the *Understanding the internals of NumPy to avoid unnecessary array copying* recipe. This function returns the memory address of the internal data buffer of a NumPy array.

How to do it...

The idea is to start from a 1D vector, and make a *virtual* 2D array where each line is a shifted version of the previous line. When using stride tricks, this process is very efficient as it does not involve any copy.

1. Let's generate a 1D vector:

```
In [1]: import numpy as np
        from numpy.lib.stride_tricks import as_strided
In [2]: n = 5; k = 2
In [3]: a = np.linspace(1, n, n); aid = id(a)
```

2. Let's change the strides of a to add shifted rows:

```
In [4]: as_strided(a, (k, n), (8, 8))
Out[4]: array([[ 1e+00,   2e+00,   3e+00,   4e+00,   5e+00],
               [ 2e+00,   3e+00,   4e+00,   5e+00,  -1e-23]])
```

The last value indicates an out-of-bounds problem: stride tricks can be dangerous as memory access is not checked. Here, we should take edge effects into account by limiting the shape of the array.

```
In [5]: as_strided(a, (k, n-k+1), (8, 8))
Out[5]: array([[ 1.,   2.,   3.,   4.],
               [ 2.,   3.,   4.,   5.]])
```

3. Now, let's implement the computation of the rolling average. The first version (standard method) involves explicit array copies, whereas the second version uses stride tricks:

```
In [6]: def shift1(x, k):
            return np.vstack([x[i:n-k+i+1] for i in
                                  range(k)])
In [7]: def shift2(x, k):
            return as_strided(x, (k, n-k+1),
                                  (x.itemsize,)*2)
```

4. These two functions return the same result, except that the array returned by the second function refers to the original data buffer:

```
In [8]: b = shift1(a, k); b, id(b) == aid
Out[8]: (array([[ 1.,   2.,   3.,   4.],
                [ 2.,   3.,   4.,   5.]]), False)
In [9]: c = shift2(a, k); c, id(c) == aid
Out[9]: (array([[ 1.,   2.,   3.,   4.],
                [ 2.,   3.,   4.,   5.]]), True)
```

5. Let's generate a signal:

```
In [10]: n, k = 100, 10
         t = np.linspace(0., 1., n)
         x = t + .1 * np.random.randn(n)
```

6. We compute the signal rolling average by creating the shifted version of the signal, and averaging along the vertical dimension. The result is shown in the next figure:

```
In [11]: y = shift2(x, k)
         x_avg = y.mean(axis=0)
```

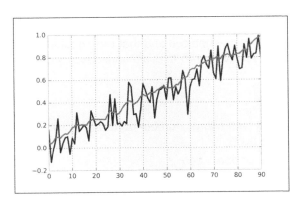

A signal and its rolling average

7. Let's evaluate the time taken by the first method:

```
In [15]: %timeit shift1(x, k)
10000 loops, best of 3: 163 µs per loop
In [16]: %%timeit y = shift1(x, k)
         z = y.mean(axis=0)
10000 loops, best of 3: 63.8 µs per loop
```

8. And by the second method:

```
In [17]: %timeit shift2(x, k)
10000 loops, best of 3: 23.3 µs per loop
In [18]: %%timeit y = shift2(x, k)
         z = y.mean(axis=0)
10000 loops, best of 3: 35.8 µs per loop
```

In the first version, most of the time is spent in the array copy, whereas in the stride trick version, most of the time is instead spent in the computation of the average.

See also

▸   The *Using stride tricks with NumPy* recipe

Making efficient array selections in NumPy

NumPy offers several ways of selecting slices of arrays. **Array views** refer to the original data buffer of an array, but with different offsets, shapes, and strides. They only permit strided selections (that is, with linearly spaced indices). NumPy also offers specific functions to make arbitrary selections along one axis. Finally, fancy indexing is the most general selection method, but it is also the slowest as we will see in this recipe. Faster alternatives should be chosen when possible.

Getting ready

We suppose that NumPy has been imported and that the id function has been defined (see the *Understanding the internals of NumPy to avoid unnecessary array copying* recipe).

How to do it...

1. Let's create an array with a large number of rows. We will select slices of this array along the first dimension:

    ```
    In [3]: n, d = 100000, 100
    In [4]: a = np.random.random_sample((n, d)); aid = id(a)
    ```

2. Let's select one row from every 10 rows, using two different methods (array view and fancy indexing):

    ```
    In [5]: b1 = a[::10]
            b2 = a[np.arange(0, n, 10)]
    In [6]: np.array_equal(b1, b2)
    Out[6]: True
    ```

3. The view refers to the original data buffer, whereas fancy indexing yields a copy:

    ```
    In [7]: id(b1) == aid, id(b2) == aid
    Out[7]: (True, False)
    ```

4. Let's compare the performance of both methods:

    ```
    In [8]: %timeit a[::10]
    100000 loops, best of 3: 2.03 µs per loop
    In [9]: %timeit a[np.arange(0, n, 10)]
    10 loops, best of 3: 46.3 ms per loop
    ```

    Fancy indexing is several orders of magnitude slower as it involves copying a large array.

5. When nonstrided selections need to be done along one dimension, array views are
    not an option. However, alternatives to fancy indexing still exist in this case. Given a
    list of indices, NumPy's `take()` function performs a selection along one axis:

```
In [10]: i = np.arange(0, n, 10)
In [11]: b1 = a[i]
         b2 = np.take(a, i, axis=0)
In [12]: np.array_equal(b1, b2)
Out[12]: True
```

The second method is faster:

```
In [13]: %timeit a[i]
10 loops, best of 3: 50.2 ms per loop
In [14]: %timeit np.take(a, i, axis=0)
100 loops, best of 3: 11.1 ms per loop
```

 Performance of fancy indexing has been improved in recent
versions of NumPy; this trick is especially useful on older
versions of NumPy.

6. When the indices to select along one axis are specified by a vector of Boolean masks,
    the `compress()` function is an alternative to fancy indexing:

```
In [15]: i = np.random.random_sample(n) < .5
In [16]: b1 = a[i]
         b2 = np.compress(i, a, axis=0)
In [17]: np.array_equal(b1, b2)
Out[17]: True
In [18]: %timeit a[i]
1 loops, best of 3: 286 ms per loop
In [19]: %timeit np.compress(i, a, axis=0)
10 loops, best of 3: 41.3 ms per loop
```

The second method is also faster than fancy indexing.

How it works...

Fancy indexing is the most general way of making completely arbitrary selections of an array.
However, more specific and faster methods often exist and should be preferred when possible.

Array views should be used whenever strided selections have to be done, but we need to be
careful about the fact that views refer to the original data buffer.

There's more...

Here are a few references:

- ▶ The complete list of NumPy routines is available in the NumPy Reference Guide, at `http://docs.scipy.org/doc/numpy/reference/`

- ▶ The list of indexing routines is available at `http://docs.scipy.org/doc/numpy/reference/routines.indexing.html`

Processing huge NumPy arrays with memory mapping

Sometimes, we need to deal with NumPy arrays that are too big to fit in the system memory. A common solution is to use **memory mapping** and implement **out-of-core computations**. The array is stored in a file on the hard drive, and we create a memory-mapped object to this file that can be used as a regular NumPy array. Accessing a portion of the array results in the corresponding data being automatically fetched from the hard drive. Therefore, we only consume what we use.

How to do it...

1. Let's create a memory-mapped array:

```
In [1]: import numpy as np
In [2]: nrows, ncols = 1000000, 100
In [3]: f = np.memmap('memmapped.dat', dtype=np.float32,
                      mode='w+', shape=(nrows, ncols))
```

2. Let's feed the array with random values, one column at a time because our system's memory is limited!

```
In [4]: for i in range(ncols):
            f[:,i] = np.random.rand(nrows)
```

We save the last column of the array:

```
In [5]: x = f[:,-1]
```

3. Now, we flush memory changes to disk by deleting the object:

```
In [6]: del f
```

4. Reading a memory-mapped array from disk involves the same `memmap` function. The data type and the shape need to be specified again, as this information is not stored in the file:

```
In [7]: f = np.memmap('memmapped.dat', dtype=np.float32,
                       shape=(nrows, ncols))
In [8]: np.array_equal(f[:,-1], x)
Out[8]: True
In [9]: del f
```

 This method is not the most adapted for long-term storage of data and data sharing. The following recipes in this chapter will show a better way based on the HDF5 file format.

How it works...

Memory mapping lets you work with huge arrays almost as if they were regular arrays. Python code that accepts a NumPy array as input will also accept a `memmap` array. However, we need to ensure that the array is used efficiently. That is, the array is never loaded as a whole (otherwise, it would waste system memory and would dismiss any advantage of the technique).

Memory mapping is also useful when you have a huge file containing raw data in a homogeneous binary format with a known data type and shape. In this case, an alternative solution is to use NumPy's `fromfile()` function with a file handle created with Python's native `open()` function. Using `f.seek()` lets you position the cursor at any location and load a given number of bytes into a NumPy array.

There's more...

Another way of dealing with huge NumPy matrices is to use **sparse matrices** through SciPy's **sparse** subpackage. It is adapted when our matrices contain mostly zeros, as is often the case with simulations of partial differential equations, graph algorithms, or specific machine learning applications. Representing matrices as dense structures can be a waste of memory, and sparse matrices offer a more efficient compressed representation.

Using sparse matrices in SciPy is not straightforward as multiple implementations exist. Each implementation is best for a particular kind of application. Here are a few references:

- SciPy lecture notes about sparse matrices, available at `http://scipy-lectures.github.io/advanced/scipy_sparse/index.html`
- Reference documentation on sparse matrices, at `http://docs.scipy.org/doc/scipy/reference/sparse.html`
- Documentation of memmap, at `http://docs.scipy.org/doc/numpy/reference/generated/numpy.memmap.html`

See also

▸ The *Manipulating large arrays with HDF5 and PyTables* recipe

▸ The *Manipulating large heterogeneous tables with HDF5 and PyTables* recipe

Manipulating large arrays with HDF5 and PyTables

NumPy arrays can be persistently saved on disk using built-in functions in NumPy such as `np.savetxt`, `np.save`, or `np.savez`, and loaded in memory using analogous functions. These methods are best when the arrays contain less than a few million points. For larger arrays, these methods suffer from two major problems: they become too slow, and they require the arrays to be fully loaded in memory. Arrays containing billions of points can be too big to fit in system memory, and alternative methods are required.

These alternative methods rely on **memory mapping**: the array resides on the hard drive, and chunks of the array are selectively loaded in memory as soon as the CPU needs them. This technique is memory-efficient, at the expense of a slight overhead due to hard drive access. Cache mechanisms and optimizations can mitigate this issue.

The previous recipe showed a basic memory mapping technique using NumPy. In this recipe, we will use a package named **PyTables**, which is specifically designed to deal with very large datasets. It implements fast memory-mapping techniques via a widely-used and open file format specification called **Hierarchical Data Format**, or **HDF5**. An HDF5 file contains one or several datasets (arrays or heterogeneous tables) organized into a POSIX-like hierarchy. Any part of the datasets can be accessed efficiently and easily without unnecessarily wasting the system memory.

As we will see later in this recipe, an alternative for PyTables is **h5py**. It is more lightweight and more adapted than PyTables in some situations.

In this recipe, we will see how to manipulate large arrays using HDF5 and PyTables. The next recipe will be about pandas-like heterogeneous tables.

Getting ready

You need PyTables 3.0+ for this recipe and the next one. With Anaconda, you can install PyTables using `conda install tables`. You will also find binary installers at `http://pytables.github.io/usersguide/installation.html`. Windows users can find installers on `www.lfd.uci.edu/~gohlke/pythonlibs/#pytables`.

Prior to version 3.0, PyTables used a camel case convention for the names of attributes and methods. The latest versions use the more standard Python convention using underscores. So, for example, `tb.open_file` is `tb.openFile` in versions prior to 3.0.

How to do it...

1. First, we need to import NumPy and PyTables (the package's name is `tables`):

   ```
   In [1]: import numpy as np
           import tables as tb
   ```

2. Let's create a new empty HDF5 file:

   ```
   In [2]: f = tb.open_file('myfile.h5', 'w')
   ```

3. We create a new top-level group named `experiment1`:

   ```
   In [3]: f.create_group('/', 'experiment1')
   Out[3]: /experiment1 (Group) u''
     children := []
   ```

4. Let's also add some metadata to this group:

   ```
   In [4]: f.set_node_attr('/experiment1', 'date', '2014-09-01')
   ```

5. In this group, we create a 1000*1000 array named `array1`:

   ```
   In [5]: x = np.random.rand(1000, 1000)
           f.create_array('/experiment1', 'array1', x)
   Out[5]: /experiment1/array1 (Array(1000L, 1000L))
   ```

6. Finally, we need to close the file to commit the changes on disk:

   ```
   In [6]: f.close()
   ```

7. Now, let's open this file. We could have done this in another Python session since the array has been saved in the HDF5 file.

   ```
   In [7]: f = tb.open_file('myfile.h5', 'r')
   ```

8. We can retrieve an attribute by giving the group path and the attribute name:

   ```
   In [8]: f.get_node_attr('/experiment1', 'date')
   Out[8]: '2014-09-01'
   ```

9. We can access any item in the file using attributes, replacing slashes with dots in the paths, and starting with `root` (corresponding to the path /). IPython's tab completion is particularly useful in this respect when exploring a file interactively.

```
In [9]: y = f.root.experiment1.array1
        # /experiment1/array1
        type(y)
Out[9]: tables.array.Array
```

10. The array can be used as a NumPy array, but an important distinction is that it is stored on disk instead of system memory. Performing a computation on this array automatically loads the requested section of the array into memory, thus it is more efficient to access only the array's views.

```
In [10]: np.array_equal(x[0,:], y[0,:])
Out[10]: True
```

11. It is also possible to get a node from its absolute path, which is useful when the path is only known at runtime:

```
In [11]: f.get_node('/experiment1/array1')
Out[11]: /experiment1/array1 (Array(1000, 1000))
```

12. We're done for this recipe, so let's do some clean-up:

```
In [12]: f.close()
In [13]: import os
         os.remove('myfile.h5')
```

How it works...

In this recipe, we stored a single array in the file, but HDF5 is especially useful when many arrays need to be saved in a single file. HDF5 is generally used in big projects, when large arrays have to be organized within a hierarchical structure. For example, it is largely used at NASA, NOAA, and many other scientific institutions (see `www.hdfgroup.org/users.html`). Researchers can store recorded data across multiple devices, multiple trials, and multiple experiments.

In HDF5, the data is organized within a tree. Nodes are either **groups** (analogous to folders in a file system) or **datasets** (analogous to files). A group can contain subgroups and datasets, whereas datasets only contain data. Both groups and datasets can contain attributes (metadata) that have a basic data type (integer or floating point number, string, and so on). HDF5 also supports internal and external links; a given path can refer to another group or dataset within the same file, or within another file. This feature may be useful if you need different files for the same experiment or project.

Being able to access a chunk of a single array without loading the rest of the array and the file in memory is quite convenient. Moreover, a loaded array can be polymorphically accessed using standard NumPy's slicing syntax. Code that accepts a NumPy array as an argument can, in principle, accept a PyTables array object as an argument as well.

There's more...

In this recipe, we created a PyTables `Array` object to store our NumPy array. Other similar types of objects include `CArrays` that store large arrays in chunks and support lossless compression. Also, an `EArray` object is extendable in at most one dimension, which is useful when the dimensions of the array are not known when creating the array in the file. A common use case is recording data during an online experiment.

The other main type of HDF5 object is `Table`, which stores tabular data in a two-dimensional table with heterogeneous data types. In PyTables, a `Table` is to an `Array` what a pandas `DataFrame` is to a NumPy `ndarray`. We will see those in the next recipe.

An interesting feature of HDF5 files is that they are not tied to PyTables. As HDF5 is an open format specification, libraries exist in most languages (C, FORTRAN, MATLAB, and many others), so it's easy to open an HDF5 file in these languages.

In HDF5, a dataset may be stored in a **contiguous** block of memory, or in chunks. **Chunks** are atomic objects and HDF5/PyTables can only read and write entire chunks. Chunks are internally organized within a tree data structure called a **B-tree**. When we create a new array or table, we can specify the **chunk shape**. It is an internal detail, but it can greatly affect performance when writing and reading parts of the dataset.

The optimal chunk shape depends on how we plan to access the data. There is a trade-off between many small chunks (large overhead due to managing lots of chunks) and a few large chunks (inefficient disk I/O). In general, the chunk size is recommended to be smaller than 1 MB. The chunk cache is also an important parameter that may affect performance.

Relatedly, we should specify as an optional argument the expected number of rows when we create an `EArray` or a `Table` object so as to optimize the internal structure of the file. You can find more information in the PyTables users guide section on optimization (see the link mentioned in the following references), which is a must-read if you plan to do anything slightly complex on large HDF5 files (more than 100 MB).

Finally, we should mention another HDF5 library in Python named **h5py**. This lightweight library offers an easy interface to HDF5 files, with emphasis on arrays rather than tables. It provides very natural access to HDF5 arrays from NumPy, and may be sufficient if you do not need the database-like features of PyTables. For more information on h5py, refer to `www.h5py.org`.

Here are a few references:

▸ HDF5 chunking, at `www.hdfgroup.org/HDF5/doc/Advanced/Chunking/`

▸ PyTables optimization guide, available at `http://pytables.github.io/usersguide/optimization.html`

▸ Difference between PyTables and h5py, from the perspective of h5py, at `https://github.com/h5py/h5py/wiki/FAQ#whats-the-difference-between-h5py-and-pytables`

▸ Difference between PyTables and h5py, from the perspective of PyTables, at `www.pytables.org/moin/FAQ#HowdoesPyTablescomparewiththeh5pyproject.3F`

See also

▸ The *Processing huge NumPy arrays with memory mapping* recipe

▸ The *Manipulating large heterogeneous tables with HDF5 and PyTables* recipe

▸ The *Ten tips for conducting reproducible interactive computing experiments* recipe in *Chapter 2, Best Practices in Interactive Computing*

Manipulating large heterogeneous tables with HDF5 and PyTables

PyTables can store homogeneous blocks of data as NumPy-like arrays in HDF5 files. It can also store heterogeneous tables, as we will see in this recipe.

Getting ready

You need PyTables for this recipe (see the previous recipe for installation instructions).

How to do it...

1. Let's import NumPy and PyTables:

```
In [1]: import numpy as np
        import tables as tb
```

2. Let's create a new HDF5 file:

```
In [2]: f = tb.open_file('myfile.h5', 'w')
```

3. We will create an HDF5 table with two columns: the name of a city (a string with 64 characters at most), and its population (a 32-bit integer). We can specify the columns by creating a complex data type with NumPy:

```
In [3]: dtype = np.dtype([('city','S64'),
                          ('population', 'i4')])
```

4. Now, we create the table in /table1:

```
In [4]: table = f.create_table('/', 'table1', dtype)
```

5. Let's add a few rows:

```
In [5]: table.append([('Brussels', 1138854),
                      ('London',   8308369),
                      ('Paris',    2243833)])
```

6. After adding rows, we need to flush the table to commit the changes on disk:

```
In [6]: table.flush()
```

7. There are many ways to access the data from a table. The easiest but not particularly efficient way is to load the entire table in memory, which returns a NumPy array:

```
In [7]: table[:]
Out[7]: array([('Brussels', 1138854),
               ('London', 8308369),
               ('Paris', 2243833)],
              dtype=[('city', 'S64'),
                     ('population', '<i4')])
```

8. It is also possible to load a particular column (with all rows):

```
In [8]: table.col('city')
Out[8]: array(['Brussels', 'London', 'Paris'],
              dtype='|S64')
```

9. When dealing with a large number of rows, we can make a SQL-like query in the table to load all rows that satisfy particular conditions:

```
In [9]: [row['city'] for row in
         table.where('population>2e6')]
Out[9]: ['London', 'Paris']
```

10. Finally, if their indices are known, we can access specific rows:

```
In [10]: table[1]
Out[10]: ('London', 8308369)
```

How it works...

A table can be created from scratch like in this recipe, or from either an existing NumPy array or a pandas `DataFrame`. In the first case, the description of the columns can be given with a NumPy data type as shown here, with a dictionary, or with a class deriving from `IsDescription`. In the second case, the table description will be automatically inferred from the given array or table.

Rows can be added efficiently at the end of the table using `table.append()`. To add a single row, first get a new row instance with `row = table.row`, set the fields of the row as if it were a dictionary, and then call `row.append()` to add the new row at the end of the table. Calling `flush()` after a set of writing operations ensures that these changes are synchronized on disk. PyTables uses complex cache mechanisms to ensure maximum performance when writing and reading data in a table; thus, new rows are not immediately written to the disk.

PyTables supports highly efficient SQL-like queries called **in-kernel queries**. The string containing the query expression is compiled and evaluated on all rows. A less-efficient method consists of iterating over all rows with `table.iterrows()` and using an `if` statement on the rows' fields.

There's more...

Here are a few references:

▸ In-kernel queries, at `http://pytables.github.io/usersguide/condition_syntax.html`.

▸ An alternative to PyTables and HDF5 might come from the Blaze project, still in early development at the time of writing. For more information on Blaze, refer to `http://blaze.pydata.org`.

See also

▸ The *Manipulating large arrays with HDF5 and PyTables* recipe

5
High-performance Computing

In this chapter, we will cover the following topics:

- ► Accelerating pure Python code with Numba and Just-In-Time compilation
- ► Accelerating array computations with Numexpr
- ► Wrapping a C library in Python with ctypes
- ► Accelerating Python code with Cython
- ► Optimizing Cython code by writing less Python and more C
- ► Releasing the GIL to take advantage of multi-core processors with Cython and OpenMP
- ► Writing massively parallel code for NVIDIA graphics cards (GPUs) with CUDA
- ► Writing massively parallel code for heterogeneous platforms with OpenCL
- ► Distributing Python code across multiple cores with IPython
- ► Interacting with asynchronous parallel tasks in IPython
- ► Parallelizing code with MPI in IPython
- ► Trying the Julia language in the notebook

Introduction

The previous chapter presented techniques for code optimization. Sometimes, these methods are not sufficient, and we need to resort to advanced high-performance computing techniques.

In this chapter, we will see three broad, but not mutually exclusive categories of methods:

- **Just-In-Time compilation** (**JIT**) of Python code
- Resorting to a lower-level language, such as C, from Python
- Dispatching tasks across multiple computing units using parallel computing

With Just-In-Time compilation, Python code is dynamically compiled into a lower-level language. Compilation occurs at runtime rather than ahead of execution. The translated code runs faster since it is compiled rather that interpreted. JIT compilation is a popular technique as it can lead to fast *and* high-level languages, whereas these two characteristics used to be mutually exclusive in general.

JIT compilation techniques are implemented in packages such as **Numba**, **Numexpr**, **Blaze**, and others. In this chapter, we will cover the first two packages. Blaze is a promising project but it is still in its infancy at the time of writing this book.

We will also introduce a new high-level language, **Julia**, which uses JIT compilation to achieve high performance. This language can be used effectively in the IPython notebook, thanks to the **IJulia** package.

 PyPy (http://pypy.org), successor of Psyco, is another related project. This alternative implementation of Python (the reference implementation being CPython) integrates a JIT compiler. Thus, it is typically much faster than CPython. However, at the time of writing this book, PyPy does not fully support NumPy yet. Additionally, PyPy and SciPy tend to form distinct communities.

Resorting to a lower-level language such as C is another interesting method. Popular libraries include **ctypes**, **SWIG**, or **Cython**. Using ctypes requires writing C code and having access to a C compiler, or using a compiled C library. By contrast, Cython lets us write code in a superset of Python, which is translated to C with various performance results. Unfortunately, it is not always easy to write efficient Cython code. In this chapter, we will cover ctypes and Cython, and we will see how to achieve interesting speedups on complex examples.

Finally, we will cover two classes of parallel computing techniques: using multiple CPU cores with IPython and using massively parallel architectures such as **Graphics Processing Units** (**GPUs**).

Here are a few references:

- A blog post on PyPy and NumPy by Travis Oliphant available at http://technicaldiscovery.blogspot.com/2011/10/thoughts-on-porting-numpy-to-pypy.html
- Interfacing Python with C, a tutorial in the scikit lectures notes available at http://scipy-lectures.github.io/advanced/interfacing_with_c/interfacing_with_c.html

CPython and concurrent programming

Python is sometimes criticized for its poor native support of multi-core processors. Let's explain why.

The mainstream implementation of the Python language is **CPython**, written in C. CPython integrates a mechanism called the **Global Interpreter Lock** (**GIL**). As mentioned at `http://wiki.python.org/moin/GlobalInterpreterLock`:

> *The GIL facilitates memory management by preventing multiple native threads from executing Python bytecodes at once.*

In other words, by disabling concurrent threads within one Python process, the GIL considerably simplifies the memory management system. Memory management is therefore not thread-safe in CPython.

An important implication is that with CPython, a pure Python program cannot be easily executed in parallel over multiple cores. This is an important issue as modern processors contain more and more cores.

What possible solutions do we have in order to take advantage of multi-core processors?

- Removing the GIL in CPython. This solution has been tried but has never made it into CPython. It would bring too much complexity in the implementation of CPython, and it would degrade the performance of single-threaded programs.

- Using multiple processes instead of multiple threads. This is a popular solution; it can be done with the native **multiprocessing** module or with IPython. We will cover the latter in this chapter.

- Rewriting specific portions of your code in Cython and replacing all Python variables with C variables. This allows you to remove the GIL temporarily in a loop, thereby enabling use of multi-core processors. We will cover this solution in the *Releasing the GIL to take advantage of multi-core processors with Cython and OpenMP* recipe.

- Implementing a specific portion of your code in a language that offers better support for multi-core processors and calling it from your Python program.

- Making your code use the NumPy functions that benefit from multi-core processors, such as `numpy.dot()`. NumPy needs to be compiled with BLAS/LAPACK/ATLAS/MKL.

A must-read reference on the GIL can be found at `http://www.dabeaz.com/GIL/`.

Compiler-related installation instructions

In this section, we will give a few instructions for using compilers with Python. Use-cases include using ctypes, using Cython, and building C extensions for Python.

Linux

On Linux, you can install the **GCC** (**GNU Compiler Collection**) compiler. On Ubuntu or Debian, you can install GCC with the `sudo apt-get install build-essential` command.

Mac OS X

On Mac OS X, you can install Apple XCode. Starting with XCode 4.3, you must manually install command-line tools from XCode's menu through **Preferences | Downloads | Command Line Tools**.

Windows

On Windows, using compilers with Python is notoriously tedious. It is generally difficult to find all the necessary instructions online. We detail these instructions here (you'll also find them on the book's GitHub repository):

The instructions differ according to whether you use a 32-bit or 64-bit version of Python, and whether you use Python 2.x or Python 3.x. To quickly find out this information in a Python terminal, type the following:

```
import sys
print(sys.version)
print(64 if sys.maxsize > 2**32 else 32)
```

Python 32-bit

1. First, you need to install a C compiler. With Python 32-bit, you can download and install MinGW from `http://www.mingw.org`, which is an open source distribution of GCC.

2. Depending on your version of the `distutils` library, you may need to manually fix a bug in its source code. Open `C:\Python27\Lib\distutils\cygwinccompiler.py` in a text editor (or a similar path depending on your specific configuration), and replace all occurrences of `-mno-cygwin` with an empty string.

3. Open or create a text file named `distutils.cfg` in `C:\Python27\Lib\distutils\` and add the following lines:

    ```
    [build]
    compiler = mingw32
    ```

Python 64-bit

1. With Python 2.x, you need Visual Studio 2008 Express. With Python 3.x, you need Visual Studio 2010 Express.

2. You also need the Microsoft Windows SDK (2008 or 2010 according to your Python version):

   ❑ **Python 2.x**: Microsoft Windows SDK for Windows 7 and .NET Framework 3.5 available at `http://www.microsoft.com/en-us/download/details.aspx?id=3138`

   ❑ **Python 3.x**: Microsoft Windows SDK for Windows 7 and .NET Framework 4 available at `http://www.microsoft.com/en-us/download/details.aspx?id=8279`

3. Make sure that the path to the folder containing `cl.exe` is in the system's `PATH` environment variable. This path should look like `C:\Program Files (x86)\Microsoft Visual Studio 9.0\VC\bin\amd64` (using Visual Studio 2008's C compiler available with the Microsoft Windows SDK for Windows 7 and .NET Framework 3.5).

4. You need to execute a few commands in Windows' command-line terminal every time you want to use the compiler with Python (for example, before typing `ipython notebook`):

```
call "C:\Program Files\Microsoft SDKs\Windows\v7.0\Bin\SetEnv.Cmd"
/x64 /release

set DISTUTILS_USE_SDK=1
```

DLL hell

When using compiled packages, particularly those obtained on Chris Gohlke's webpage at `http://www.lfd.uci.edu/~gohlke/pythonlibs/`, you may get obscure DLL-related errors. To fix those problems, you can open the spurious DLLs in Dependency Walker available at `http://www.dependencywalker.com`. This program can tell you that a DLL is missing. You can search for it in your computer and add its location to the `PATH` environment variable.

References

Here are a few references:

► Installing Cython on Windows, at `http://wiki.cython.org/InstallingOnWindows`

► Cython on Windows 64-bit, at `https://github.com/cython/cython/wiki/64BitCythonExtensionsOnWindows`

► Building Python wheels for Windows, at `http://cowboyprogrammer.org/building-python-wheels-for-windows/`

Accelerating pure Python code with Numba and just-in-time compilation

Numba (`http://numba.pydata.org`) is a package created by Continuum Analytics (`http://www.continuum.io`). At the time of writing, Numba is still a young and relatively experimental package, but its technology is promising. Numba takes pure Python code and translates it automatically (just-in-time) into optimized machine code. In practice, this means that we can write a non-vectorized function in pure Python, using `for` loops, and have this function vectorized automatically by using a single decorator. Performance speedups when compared to pure Python code can reach several orders of magnitude and may even outmatch manually-vectorized NumPy code.

In this section, we will show how to accelerate pure Python code generating the Mandelbrot fractal.

Getting ready

The easiest way to install Numba is to use the Anaconda distribution (also maintained by Continuum Analytics), and type in a terminal `conda install numba`. On Windows, an alternative is to download a binary installer from Chris Gohlke's webpage at `http://www.lfd.uci.edu/~gohlke/pythonlibs/#numba`. In this case, there are dependencies (Numpy-MKL, LLVMPy, llvmmath, and Meta), all available on the same page.

How to do it...

1. Let's import NumPy and define a few variables:

   ```
   In [1]: import numpy as np
   In [2]: size = 200
           iterations = 100
   ```

2. The following function generates the fractal in pure Python. It accepts an empty array m as argument.

   ```
   In [3]: def mandelbrot_python(m, size, iterations):
               for i in range(size):
                   for j in range(size):
                       c = -2 + 3./size*j + 1j*(1.5-3./size*i)
                       z = 0
                       for n in range(iterations):
                           if np.abs(z) <= 10:
   ```

```
                     z = z*z + c
                     m[i, j] = n
              else:
                     break
```

3. Let's run the simulation and display the fractal:

    ```
    In [4]: m = np.zeros((size, size))
            mandelbrot_python(m, size, iterations)
    In [5]: import matplotlib.pyplot as plt
            %matplotlib inline
            plt.imshow(np.log(m), cmap=plt.cm.hot)
            plt.xticks([]); plt.yticks([])
    ```

    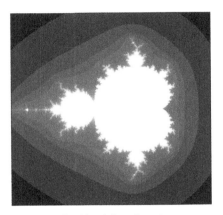

    The Mandelbrot fractal

4. Now, we evaluate the time taken by this function:

    ```
    In [6]: %%timeit m = np.zeros((size, size))
            mandelbrot_python(m, size, iterations)
    1 loops, best of 1: 6.18 s per loop
    ```

5. Let's try to accelerate this function using Numba. First, we import the package:

    ```
    In [7]: import numba
            from numba import jit, complex128
    ```

6. Next, we add the @jit decorator right above the function definition. Numba tries to automatically infer the type of the local variables, but we can also specify the types explicitly:

    ```
    In [8]: @jit(locals=dict(c=complex128, z=complex128))
            def mandelbrot_numba(m, size, iterations):
                for i in range(size):
                    for j in range(size):
                        c = -2 + 3./size*j + 1j*(1.5-3./size*i)
                        z = 0
    ```

```
                    for n in range(iterations):
                        if np.abs(z) <= 10:
                            z = z*z + c
                            m[i, j] = n
                        else:
                            break
```

7. This function works just like the pure Python version. How much faster is it?

```
In [10]: %%timeit m = np.zeros((size, size))
         mandelbrot_numba(m, size, iterations)
1 loops, best of 10: 44.8 ms per loop
```

The Numba version is more than 100 times faster than the pure Python version here!

How it works...

Python bytecode is normally interpreted at runtime by the Python interpreter (for example, CPython). By contrast, a Numba function is parsed and translated directly to machine code ahead of execution, using a powerful compiler architecture named **LLVM** (**Low Level Virtual Machine**). Citing the official documentation:

> *Numba is aware of NumPy arrays as typed memory regions and so can speedup code using NumPy arrays. Other, less well-typed code will be translated to Python C-API calls effectively removing the "interpreter" but not removing the dynamic indirection.*

Numba is not able to compile any Python functions. There are also some subtle restrictions on the type of local variables. Numba tries to infer the type of the function's variables automatically, but it is not always successful. In this case, we can specify the types explicitly.

Numba generally gives the most impressive speedups on functions that involve tight loops on NumPy arrays (such as in this recipe).

Blaze, another project from Continuum Analytics, is the next generation of NumPy. It will offer data structures with much more flexibility than NumPy arrays, and it will support out-of-core computations. Together with Numba, Blaze will form a highly efficient compiler-like infrastructure for big data algorithms and complex numerical simulations. We can expect Blaze to play an important role in the future, as it should combine the nice and easy syntax of Python with the performance of native code and parallel processing techniques (notably multi-core processors and Graphical Processing Units). Other worthwhile related projects, but slightly older than Blaze and Numba, include **Theano** and **Numexpr** (which we will see in the next recipe).

There's more...

Let's compare the performance of Numba with manually-vectorized code using NumPy, which is the standard way of accelerating pure Python code such as the code given in this recipe. In practice, it means replacing the code inside the two loops over i and j with array computations. This is relatively easy here as the operations closely follow the **Single Instruction, Multiple Data** (**SIMD**) paradigm:

```
In [1]: import numpy as np
        import matplotlib.pyplot as plt
        %matplotlib inline
In [2]: def initialize(size):
            x, y = np.meshgrid(np.linspace(-2, 1, size),
                        np.linspace(-1.5, 1.5, size))
            c = x + 1j*y
            z = c.copy()
            m = np.zeros((size, size))
            return c, z, m
In [3]: size = 200
        iterations = 100

        def mandelbrot_numpy(c, z, m, iterations):
            for n in range(iterations):
                indices = np.abs(z) <= 10
                z[indices] = z[indices]**2 + c[indices]
                m[indices] = n
In [4]: %%timeit -n1 -r10 c, z, m = initialize(size)
        mandelbrot_numpy(c, z, m, iterations)
1 loops, best of 10: 245 ms per loop
```

Here, Numba beats NumPy. However, we cannot draw any firm conclusion from this single experiment. Whether Numba or NumPy is faster depends on the particular implementation of the algorithm, simulation parameters, machine characteristics, and so on.

Here are a few references:

- ▶ Documentation of Numba available at `http://numba.pydata.org/doc.html`
- ▶ Types supported by Numba available at `http://numba.pydata.org/numba-doc/dev/types.html`
- ▶ Numba examples available at `http://numba.pydata.org/numba-doc/dev/examples.html`
- ▶ Blaze available at `http://blaze.pydata.org`
- ▶ Theano available at `http://deeplearning.net/software/theano/`

▶ The *Accelerating array computations with Numexpr* recipe

Accelerating array computations with Numexpr

Numexpr is a package that improves upon a weakness of NumPy; the evaluation of complex array expressions is sometimes slow. The reason is that multiple temporary arrays are created for the intermediate steps, which is suboptimal with large arrays. Numexpr evaluates algebraic expressions involving arrays, parses them, compiles them, and finally executes them faster than NumPy.

This principle is somewhat similar to Numba, in that normal Python code is compiled dynamically by a JIT compiler. However, Numexpr only tackles algebraic array expressions rather than arbitrary Python code. We will see how that works in this recipe.

Getting ready

You will find the instructions to install Numexpr in the documentation available at
`http://github.com/pydata/numexpr`.

How to do it...

1. Let's import NumPy and Numexpr:

   ```
   In [1]: import numpy as np
           import numexpr as ne
   ```

2. Then, we generate three large vectors:

   ```
   In [2]: x, y, z = np.random.rand(3, 1000000)
   ```

3. Now, we evaluate the time taken by NumPy to calculate a complex algebraic expression involving our vectors:

   ```
   In [3]: %timeit x + (y**2 + (z*x + 1)*3)
   10 loops, best of 3: 48.1 ms per loop
   ```

4. Let's perform the same calculation with Numexpr. We need to give the expression as a string:

   ```
   In [4]: %timeit ne.evaluate('x + (y**2 + (z*x + 1)*3)')
   100 loops, best of 3: 11.5 ms per loop
   ```

5. Numexpr can use multiple cores. Here, we have 2 physical cores and 4 virtual threads with Intel's Hyper-Threading Technology. We can specify how many cores we want Numexpr to use using the `set_num_threads()` function:

```
In [5]: ne.ncores
Out[5]: 4
In [6]: for i in range(1, 5):
            ne.set_num_threads(i)
            %timeit ne.evaluate('x + (y**2 + (z*x + 1)*3)')
10 loops, best of 3: 19.4 ms per loop
10 loops, best of 3: 14 ms per loop
10 loops, best of 3: 12.8 ms per loop
10 loops, best of 3: 11.5 ms per loop
```

How it works...

Numexpr analyzes the array expression, parses it, and compiles it into a lower-level language. Numexpr is aware of CPU-vectorized instructions as well as CPU cache characteristics. As such, Numexpr can optimize vectorized computations dynamically.

There is some overlap between Numexpr, Numba, and Blaze. We can probably expect some crosstalk between these projects in the future.

See also

▸ The *Accelerating pure Python code with Numba and just-in-time compilation* recipe

Wrapping a C library in Python with ctypes

Wrapping a C library in Python allows us to leverage existing C code or to implement a critical part of the code in a fast language such as C.

It is relatively easy to use externally-compiled libraries with Python. The first possibility is to call a command-line executable with an `os.system` command, but this method does not extend to compiled libraries (on Windows, **Dynamically Linked Libraries**, or **DLLs**). A more powerful method consists of using a native Python module called **ctypes**. This module allows us to call functions defined in a compiled library (written in C) from Python. The `ctypes` module takes care of the data type conversions between C and Python. In addition, the `numpy.ctypeslib` module provides facilities to use NumPy arrays wherever data buffers are used in the external library.

In this example, we will rewrite the code of the Mandelbrot fractal in C, compile it in a shared library, and call it from Python.

Getting ready

The code of this recipe is written for Windows. It can be adapted to other systems with minor changes.

A C compiler is required. You will find all compiler-related instructions in this chapter's introduction. In particular, for the C compiler to work on Windows, you need to execute a sequence of instructions in the Windows terminal before launching the IPython notebook. You will find a batch script with the appropriate instructions on the book's repository (in the folder containing the code for this chapter).

How to do it...

The first step is to write and compile the Mandelbrot example in C. The second step is to access the library from Python using ctypes. If you are only interested in discovering how to access an existing compiled library, you can go straight to step 3, assuming that `mandelbrot.dll` is a compiled library defining a function named `mandelbrot()`.

1. Let's write the code of the Mandelbrot fractal in C:

```
In [1]: %%writefile mandelbrot.c

        // Needed when creating a DLL.
        #define EXPORT __declspec(dllexport)

        #include "stdio.h"
        #include "stdlib.h"

        // This function will be available in the DLL.
        EXPORT void __stdcall mandelbrot(int size,
                                         int iterations,
                                         int *col)
        {
            // Variable declarations.
            int i, j, n, index;
            double cx, cy;
            double z0, z1, z0_tmp, z0_2, z1_2;

            // Loop within the grid.
            for (i = 0; i < size; i++)
            {
                cy = -1.5 + (double)i / size * 3;
                for (j = 0; j < size; j++)
                {
                    // We initialize the loop of the
```

```
        // system.
        cx = -2.0 + (double)j / size * 3;
        index = i * size + j;
        // Let's run the system.
        z0 = 0.0;
        z1 = 0.0;
        for (n = 0; n < iterations; n++)
        {
            z0_2 = z0 * z0;
            z1_2 = z1 * z1;
            if (z0_2 + z1_2 <= 100)
            {
                // Update the system.
                z0_tmp = z0_2 - z1_2 + cx;
                z1 = 2 * z0 * z1 + cy;
                z0 = z0_tmp;
                col[index] = n;
            }
            else
            {
                break;
            }
        }
    }
  }
}
```

2. Now, let's build this C source file into a DLL with Microsoft Visual Studio's `cl.exe`. The `/LD` option specifies that a DLL is to be created:

```
In [2]: !cl /LD mandelbrot.c
/out:mandelbrot.dll
Creating library mandelbrot.lib and object mandelbrot.exp
```

3. Let's access the library with ctypes:

```
In [3]: import ctypes
In [4]: # Load the DLL file in Python.
        lb = ctypes.CDLL('mandelbrot.dll')
        lib = ctypes.WinDLL(None, handle=lb._handle)
        # Access the mandelbrot function.
        mandelbrot = lib.mandelbrot
```

4. NumPy and ctypes allow us to wrap the C function defined in the DLL:

```
In [5]: from numpy.ctypeslib import ndpointer
In [6]: # Define the types of the output and arguments.
```

```
                 mandelbrot.restype = None
                 mandelbrot.argtypes = [ctypes.c_int, ctypes.c_int,
                                        ndpointer(ctypes.c_int)]
```

5. To use this function, we first need to initialize an empty array and pass it as an argument to the `mandelbrot()` wrapper function:

```
In [7]: import numpy as np
        # We initialize an empty array.
        size = 200
        iterations = 100
        col = np.empty((size, size), dtype=np.int32)
        # We execute the C function.
        mandelbrot(size, iterations, col)
In [8]: %timeit mandelbrot(size, iterations, col)
100 loops, best of 3: 12.5 ms per loop
```

6. We free the library at the end of the script:

```
In [9]: from ctypes.wintypes import HMODULE
        ctypes.windll.kernel32.FreeLibrary.argtypes = [HMODULE]
        ctypes.windll.kernel32.FreeLibrary(lb._handle)
```

How it works...

In the C code, the `__declspec(dllexport)` command declares the function visible in the DLL. The `__stdcall` keyword declares the standard calling convention on Windows.

As arguments, the `mandelbrot()` function accepts:

▶ The **size** of the `col` buffer (the `col` value is the last iteration where the corresponding point is within a disc around the origin)

▶ The number of **iterations**

▶ A **pointer** to the buffer of integers

`mandelbrot()` does not return any value; rather, it updates the buffer that was passed by reference to the function (it is a pointer).

To wrap this function in Python, we need to declare the types of the input arguments. The ctypes module defines constants for the different data types. In addition, the `numpy.ctypeslib.ndpointer()` function lets us use a NumPy array wherever a pointer is expected in the C function. The data type given as argument to `ndpointer()` needs to correspond to the NumPy data type of the array passed to the function.

Once the function has been correctly wrapped, it can be called as if it was a standard Python function. Here, the initially-empty NumPy array is filled with the Mandelbrot fractal after the call to `mandelbrot()`.

There's more...

SciPy contains a module called **weave** that provides similar functionality. We can write C code in a Python string and let weave compile and execute it at runtime using a C compiler. This module does not seem well-maintained and appears to be incompatible with Python 3. Cython or ctypes are probably better options.

A more recent alternative to ctypes is cffi (`http://cffi.readthedocs.org`), which may be a bit faster and more convenient to use. You can also refer to `http://eli.thegreenplace.net/2013/03/09/python-ffi-with-ctypes-and-cffi/`.

Accelerating Python code with Cython

Cython is both a language (a superset of Python) and a Python library. With Cython, we start from a regular Python program and we add annotations about the type of the variables. Then, Cython translates that code to C and compiles the result to a Python extension module. Finally, we can use this compiled module in any Python program.

While dynamic typing comes with a performance cost in Python, statically-typed variables in Cython generally lead to faster code execution.

Performance gains are most significant in CPU-bound programs, notably in tight Python loops. By contrast, I/O-bound programs are not expected to benefit much from a Cython implementation.

In this recipe, we will see how to accelerate the Mandelbrot code example with Cython.

Getting ready

A C compiler is required. You will find all compiler-related instructions in the introduction of this chapter.

You also need to install Cython from `http://www.cython.org`. With Anaconda, you can type `conda install cython` in a terminal.

How to do it...

We assume that the variables `size` and `iterations` have been defined as in the previous recipes.

1. To use Cython in the IPython notebook, we first need to import the `cythonmagic` extension provided by IPython:

   ```
   In [6]: %load_ext cythonmagic
   ```

2. As a first try, let's just add the `%%cython` magic before the definition of the `mandelbrot()` function. Internally, this cell magic compiles the cell into a standalone Cython module, hence the need for all required imports to occur within the same cell. This cell does not have access to any variable or function defined in the interactive namespace:

```
In [6]: %%cython
        import numpy as np
        def mandelbrot_cython(m, size, iterations):
            # The exact same content as in
            # mandelbrot_python (first recipe of
            # this chapter).
```

3. How fast is this version?

```
In [7]: %%timeit -n1 -r1 m = np.zeros((size, size),
                                        dtype=np.int32)
        mandelbrot_cython(m, size, iterations)
1 loops, best of 1: 5.7 s per loop
```

We get virtually no speedup here. We need to specify the type of our Python variables.

4. Let's add type information using typed memory views for NumPy arrays (we explain these in the *How it works...* section). We also use a slightly different way to test whether particles have escaped from the domain (`if` test):

```
In [8]: %%cython
        import numpy as np
        def mandelbrot_cython(int[:,::1] m,
                              int size,
                              int iterations):
            cdef int i, j, n
            cdef complex z, c
            for i in range(size):
                for j in range(size):
                    c = -2 + 3./size*j + 1j*(1.5-3./size*i)
                    z = 0
                    for n in range(iterations):
                        if z.real**2 + z.imag**2 <= 100:
                            z = z*z + c
                            m[i, j] = n
                        else:
                            break
```

5. How fast is this new version?

```
In [9]: %%timeit -n1 -r1 m = np.zeros((size, size),
                                        dtype=np.int32)
        mandelbrot_cython(m, size, iterations)
1 loops, best of 1: 230 ms per loop
```

All we have done is specified the type of the local variables and function arguments and bypassed NumPy's `np.abs()` function when computing the absolute value of z. These changes have helped Cython to generate more optimized C code from Python code.

How it works...

The `cdef` keyword declares a variable as a statically-typed C variable. C variables lead to faster code execution because the overhead from Python's dynamic typing is mitigated. Function arguments can also be declared as statically-typed C variables.

In general, variables used inside tight loops should be declared with `cdef`. To ensure that our code is well-optimized, we can use **annotations**. We just add the `-a` flag after the `%%cython` magic and the non-optimized lines will be shown in a gradient of yellow (white lines are faster, yellow lines are slower). This is shown in the following screenshot. The color depends on the relative number of Python API calls at each line.

```
1:  import numpy as np
2:
3:  def mandelbrot_cython(int[:,::1] m,
4:                        int size,
5:                        int iterations):
6:      cdef int i, j, n
7:      cdef complex z, c
8:      for i in range(size):
9:          for j in range(size):
10:             c = -2 + 3./size*j + 1j*(1.5-3./size*i)
11:             z = 0
12:             for n in range(iterations):
13:                 if z.real**2 + z.imag**2 <= 100:
14:                     z = z*z + c
15:                     m[i, j] = n
16:                 else:
17:                     break
```

Annotations in Cython

There are two ways of declaring NumPy arrays as C variables with Cython: using **array buffers** or using **typed memory views**. In this recipe, we used typed memory views. We will cover array buffers in the next recipe.

Typed memory views allow efficient access to data buffers with a NumPy-like indexing syntax. For example, we can use `int[:,::1]` to declare a C-ordered 2D NumPy array with integer values, with `::1` meaning a contiguous layout in this dimension. Typed memory views can be indexed just like NumPy arrays.

However, memory views do not implement element-wise operations like NumPy. Thus, memory views act as convenient data containers within tight `for` loops. For element-wise NumPy-like operations, array buffers should be used instead.

We could achieve a significant performance speedup by replacing the call to `np.abs` with a faster expression. The reason is that `np.abs` is a NumPy function with a slight call overhead. It is designed to work with relatively large arrays, not scalar values. This overhead results in a significant performance hit in a tight loop such as here. This bottleneck can be spotted with Cython annotations.

There's more...

Using Cython from IPython is very convenient with the `%%cython` cell magic. However, it is sometimes necessary to create a reusable C extension module with Cython. This is actually what IPython's `%%cython` cell magic does under the hood.

1. The first step is to write a standalone Cython script in a `.pyx` file. This should correspond exactly to the entire contents of a `%%cython` cell magic.

2. The second step is to create a `setup.py` file that we will use to compile the Cython module. Here is a basic `setup.py` file, assuming a `mandelbrot.pyx` file:

```python
from distutils.core import setup
from distutils.extension import Extension
from Cython.Distutils import build_ext

setup(
    cmdclass = {'build_ext': build_ext},
    ext_modules = [Extension("mandelbrot",
                             ["mandelbrot.pyx"])]
)
```

3. The third step is to execute this setup script with Python:

```
In [3]: !python setup.py build_ext --inplace
running build_ext
cythoning mandelbrot.pyx to mandelbrot.c
building 'mandelbrot' extension
```

4. Two files have been created during the build process: the C source file and a compiled Python extension. The file extension is `.pyd` on Windows (DLL files) and `.so` on UNIX:

```
In [4]: !dir mandelbrot.*
mandelbrot.c
mandelbrot.pyd
mandelbrot.pyx
```

5. Finally, we can load the compiled module as usual (using `from mandelbrot import mandelbrot`).

With this technique, Cython code can also be integrated within a Python package. Here are a few references:

- ▸ Distributing Cython modules, explained at `http://docs.cython.org/src/userguide/source_files_and_compilation.html`
- ▸ Compilation with Cython, explained at `http://docs.cython.org/src/reference/compilation.html`

See also

- ▸ The *Optimizing Cython code by writing less Python and more C* recipe
- ▸ The *Releasing the GIL to take advantage of multicore processors with Cython and OpenMP* recipe

Optimizing Cython code by writing less Python and more C

In this recipe, we will consider a more complicated Cython example. Starting from a slow implementation in pure Python, we will use different Cython features to speed it up progressively.

We will implement a very simple ray tracing engine. **Ray tracing** consists of rendering a scene by simulating the physical properties of light propagation. This rendering method leads to photorealistic scenes, but it is computationally intensive.

Here, we will render a single sphere with diffuse and specular lighting. First we'll give the example's code in pure Python. Then, we will accelerate it incrementally with Cython.

 The code is long and contains many functions. We will first give the full code of the pure Python version. Then, we will just describe the changes required to accelerate the code with Cython. The entire scripts are available on the book's website.

How to do it...

1. First, let's implement the pure Python version:

```
In [1]: import numpy as np
        import matplotlib.pyplot as plt
In [2]: %matplotlib inline
In [3]: w, h = 200, 200  # Size of the window in pixels.
```

We create a normalization function for vectors:

```
def normalize(x):
    # This function normalizes a vector.
    x /= np.linalg.norm(x)
    return x
```

Now, we create a function that computes the intersection of a ray with a sphere:

```
def intersect_sphere(O, D, S, R):
    # Return the distance from O to the intersection
    # of the ray (O, D) and the sphere (S, R), or
    # +inf if there is no intersection.
    # O and S are 3D points, D (direction) is a
    # normalized vector, R is a scalar.
    a = np.dot(D, D)
    OS = O - S
    b = 2 * np.dot(D, OS)
    c = np.dot(OS, OS) - R*R
    disc = b*b - 4*a*c
    if disc > 0:
        distSqrt = np.sqrt(disc)
        q = (-b - distSqrt) / 2.0 if b < 0 \
            else (-b + distSqrt) / 2.0
        t0 = q / a
        t1 = c / q
        t0, t1 = min(t0, t1), max(t0, t1)
        if t1 >= 0:
            return t1 if t0 < 0 else t0
    return np.inf
```

The following function traces a ray:

```
def trace_ray(rayO, rayD):
    # Find first point of intersection with the scene.
    t = intersect_sphere(rayO, rayD, position, radius)
    # No intersection?
    if t == np.inf:
        return
    # Find the point of intersection on the object.
    M = rayO + rayD * t
    N = normalize(M - position)
    toL = normalize(L - M)
    toO = normalize(O - M)
    # Ambient color.
    col = ambient
    # Diffuse color.
```

```
col += diffuse * max(np.dot(N, toL), 0) * color
# Specular color.
col += specular_c * color_light * \
    max(np.dot(N, normalize(toL + toO)), 0) \
        ** specular_k
return col
```

Finally, the main loop is implemented in the following function:

```
def run():
    img = np.zeros((h, w, 3))
    # Loop through all pixels.
    for i, x in enumerate(np.linspace(-1.,1.,w)):
        for j, y in enumerate(np.linspace(-1.,1.,h)):
            # Position of the pixel.
            Q[0], Q[1] = x, y
            # Direction of the ray going through the
            # optical center.
            D = normalize(Q - O)
            depth = 0
            rayO, rayD = O, D
            # Launch the ray and get the
            # color of the pixel.
            col = trace_ray(rayO, rayD)
            if col is None:
                continue
            img[h - j - 1, i, :] = np.clip(col, 0, 1)
    return img
```

Now, we initialize the scene and define a few parameters:

```
In [4]: # Sphere properties.
        position = np.array([0., 0., 1.])
        radius = 1.
        color = np.array([0., 0., 1.])
        diffuse = 1.
        specular_c = 1.
        specular_k = 50

        # Light position and color.
        L = np.array([5., 5., -10.])
        color_light = np.ones(3)
        ambient = .05

        # Camera.
        O = np.array([0., 0., -1.])  # Position.
        Q = np.array([0., 0., 0.])   # Pointing to.
```

Let's render the scene:

```
In [5]: img = run()
In [6]: plt.imshow(img)
        plt.xticks([]); plt.yticks([])
```

Ray tracing with Python and Cython. Left: the outcome of this recipe. Right: outcome of an extended version.

2. How slow is this implementation?

```
In [7]: %timeit run()
1 loops, best of 1: 3.58 s per loop
```

3. If we just use the `%%cython` magic with the adequate `import numpy as np` and `cimport numpy as np` commands at the top of the cell, we only get a modest improvement, only a tenth of a second quicker.

4. We could do better by giving information about the type of the variables. Since we use vectorized computations on NumPy arrays, we cannot easily use memory views. Rather, we will use array buffers. First, at the very beginning of the Cython module (or `%%cython` cell), we declare NumPy data types as follows:

```
import numpy as np
cimport numpy as np
DBL = np.double
ctypedef np.double_t DBL_C
```

Then, we declare a NumPy array with `cdef np.ndarray[DBL_C, ndim=1]` (in this example, a 1D array of double precision floating point numbers). There is a difficulty here because NumPy arrays can only be declared inside functions, not at the top level. Thus, we need to slightly tweak the overall architecture of the code by passing some arrays as function arguments instead of using global variables. However, even by declaring the type of all variables, we gain virtually no speedup at all.

5. In the current implementation, we incur a performance hit because of the large number of NumPy function calls on tiny arrays (three elements). NumPy is designed to deal with large arrays, and it does not make much sense to use it for arrays that small.

    In this specific situation, we can try to bypass NumPy by rewriting some functions using the C standard library. We use the `cdef` keyword to declare a C-style function. These functions can yield significant performance speedups. Here, we get a 2-3x speedup by replacing the `normalize()` Python function with the following C function:

    ```
    from libc.math cimport sqrt
    cdef normalize(np.ndarray[DBL_C, ndim=1] x):
        cdef double n
        n = sqrt(x[0]*x[0] + x[1]*x[1] + x[2]*x[2])
        x[0] /= n
        x[1] /= n
        x[2] /= n
        return x
    ```

6. To get the most interesting speedups, we need to completely bypass NumPy. Where do we use NumPy precisely?

    ❑   Many variables are NumPy arrays (mostly one-dimensional vectors with three elements).

    ❑   Element-wise operations yield implicit NumPy API calls.

    ❑   We also use a few NumPy built-in functions such as `numpy.dot()`.

    In order to bypass NumPy in our example, we need to reimplement all these features for our specific needs. The first possibility is to use a native Python type for vectors (for example, tuples), and write C-style functions that implement operations on tuples (always assuming they have exactly three elements). For example, the addition between two tuples can be implemented as follows:

    ```
    cdef tuple add(tuple x, tuple y):
        return (x[0]+y[0], x[1]+y[1], x[2]+y[2])
    ```

    We get an interesting speedup (30x compared to pure Python), but we can do even better by using a pure C data type.

7. We are going to define a pure C structure instead of using a Python type for our vectors. In other words, we are not only bypassing NumPy, but we are also bypassing Python by moving to pure C code. To declare a C structure representing a 3D vector in Cython, we can use the following code:

    ```
    cdef struct Vec3:
        double x, y, z
    ```

To create a new `Vec3` variable, we can use the following function:

```
cdef Vec3 vec3(double x, double y, double z):
    cdef Vec3 v
    v.x = x
    v.y = y
    v.z = z
    return v
```

As an example, here is the function used to add two `Vec3` objects:

```
cdef Vec3 add(Vec3 u, Vec3 v):
    return vec3(u.x + v.x, u.y + v.y, u.z + v.z)
```

The code can be updated to make use of these fast C-style functions. Finally, the image can be declared as a 3D memory view. With all these changes, the Cython implementation runs in ~12 ms, 300 times faster than the pure Python version!

In summary, we have achieved a very interesting speedup by basically rewriting the entire implementation in C with an enhanced Python syntax.

How it works...

Let's explain briefly how the ray tracing code works. We model a three-dimensional scene with objects such as planes and spheres (here, there is only one sphere). There is also a camera and a plane representing the rendered image:

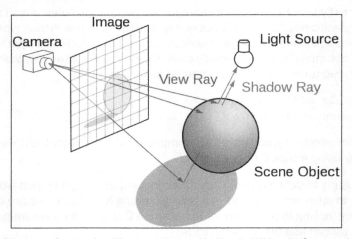

Principles of ray tracing ("Ray trace diagram" by Henrik, Wikimedia Commons)

There is a main loop over all pixels of the image. For each pixel, we launch a ray from the camera center to the scene through the current pixel and compute the first intersection point between that ray and an object from the scene. Then, we compute the pixel's color as a function of the object material's color, the position of the lights, the normal of the object at the intersection point, and so on. There are several physics-inspired lighting equations that describe how the color depends on these parameters. Here, we use the **Blinn-Phong shading model** with ambient, diffuse, and specular lighting components:

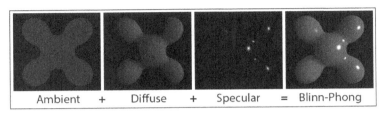

Blinn-Phong shading model ("Phong components", Wikimedia Commons)

Of course, a full ray tracing engine is far more complex than what we have implemented in this example. We can model other optic and lighting characteristics such as reflections, refractions, shadows, depth of field, and others. It is also possible to implement ray tracing algorithms on the graphics card for real-time photorealistic rendering. Here are a few references:

 ▶ Blinn-Phong shading model on Wikipedia, available at `http://en.wikipedia.org/wiki/Blinn-Phong_shading_model`

 ▶ Ray tracing on Wikipedia, available at `http://en.wikipedia.org/wiki/Ray_tracing_(graphics)`

There's more...

Although powerful, Cython requires a good understanding of Python, NumPy, and C. The most interesting performance speedups are achieved when dynamically-typed Python variables are converted to statically-typed C variables, notably within tight loops.

Here are a few references:

 ▶ Cython extension types available at `http://docs.cython.org/src/userguide/extension_types.html`

 ▶ Extended version of our ray tracing engine available at `http://gist.github.com/rossant/6046463`

See also

 ▶ The _Accelerating Python code with Cython_ recipe

 ▶ The _Releasing the GIL to take advantage of multicore processors with Cython and OpenMP_ recipe

Releasing the GIL to take advantage of multicore processors with Cython and OpenMP

As we have seen in this chapter's introduction, CPython's GIL prevents pure Python code from taking advantage of multi-core processors. With Cython, we have a way to release the GIL temporarily in a portion of the code in order to enable multi-core computing. This is done with **OpenMP**, a multiprocessing API that is supported by most C compilers.

In this recipe, we will see how to parallelize the previous recipe's code on multiple cores.

Getting ready

To enable OpenMP in Cython, you just need to specify some options to the compiler. There is nothing special to install on your computer besides a good C compiler. See the instructions in this chapter's introduction for more details.

In this recipe, we use Microsoft's Visual C++ compiler on Windows, but the code can be easily adapted to other systems.

How to do it...

Our simple ray tracing engine implementation is **embarrassingly parallel**; there is a main loop over all pixels, within which the exact same function is called repetitively. There is no crosstalk between loop iterations. Therefore, it would be theoretically possible to execute all iterations in parallel.

Here, we will execute one loop (over all columns in the image) in parallel with OpenMP.

You will find the entire code on the book's website. We will only show the most important steps here:

1. We add the following options to the `%%cython` magic command: `--compile-args=/openmp --link-args=/openmp`. The exact syntax may depend on your compiler and/or your system. For example, `/openmp` should be replaced by `-fopenmp` with GCC.

2. We import the `prange()` function:

   ```
   from cython.parallel import prange
   ```

3. We add `nogil` after each function definition in order to remove the GIL. We cannot use any Python variable or function inside a function annotated with `nogil`. For example:

   ```
   cdef Vec3 add(Vec3 x, Vec3 y) nogil:
       return vec3(x.x + y.x, x.y + y.y, x.z + y.z)
   ```

4. To run a loop in parallel over the cores with OpenMP, we use `prange()`:

```
with nogil:
    for i in prange(w):
        # ...
```

The GIL needs to be released before using any parallel computing feature such as `prange()`.

5. With these changes, we reach a 4x speedup on a quad-core processor.

How it works...

The GIL has been described in the introduction of this chapter. The `nogil` keyword tells Cython that a particular function or code section should be executed without the GIL. When the GIL is released, it is not possible to make any Python API calls, meaning that only C variables and C functions (declared with `cdef`) can be used.

See also

▸ The *Accelerating Python code with Cython* recipe

▸ The *Optimizing Cython code by writing less Python and more C* recipe

▸ The *Distributing Python code across multiple cores with IPython* recipe

Writing massively parallel code for NVIDIA graphics cards (GPUs) with CUDA

Graphics Processing Units (**GPUs**) are powerful processors specialized in real-time rendering. We find GPUs in virtually any computer, laptop, video game console, tablet, or smartphone. Their massively parallel architecture comprises tens to thousands of cores. The video game industry has been fostering the development of increasingly powerful GPUs over the last two decades.

GPUs are routinely used in modern supercomputers (for example in Cray's Titan at Oak Ridge National Laboratory, ~20 petaFLOPS, ~20,000 CPUs, and as many NVIDIA GPUs). A high-end $1000 GPU today is roughly as powerful as a $100 million supercomputer from 2000 (several teraFLOPS).

 FLOPS means FLoating-point Operations Per Second. A 1 teraFLOPS GPU can perform up to one trillion floating-point operations per second.

Since the mid-2000s, GPUs are no longer limited to graphics processing. We can now implement scientific algorithms on a GPU. The only condition is that the algorithm follows the **SIMD (Single Instruction, Multiple Data) paradigm**, where a sequence of instructions is executed in parallel with multiple data. This is called **General Purpose Programming on Graphics Processing Units** (**GPGPU**). GPGPU is used in many areas: meteorology, data mining, computer vision, image processing, finance, physics, bioinformatics, and many more. Writing code for GPUs can be challenging as it requires understanding the internal architecture of the hardware.

CUDA is a proprietary GPGPU framework created in 2007 by NVIDIA Corporation, one of the main GPU manufacturers. Programs written in CUDA only work on NVIDIA graphics cards. There is another competing GPGPU framework called **OpenCL**, an open standard supported by other major companies. OpenCL programs can work on GPUs and CPUs from most manufacturers (notably NVIDIA, AMD, and Intel).

In this recipe, we will show a very basic example of GPGPU. We'll implement the embarrassingly parallel computation of the Mandelbrot fractal in CUDA. In the next recipe, we will implement the exact same example in OpenCL.

> Should you choose OpenCL or CUDA for a new project? The answer depends most notably on the hardware of your user base. If you need the highest performance possible for a specific project in your lab where all computers have an NVIDIA card, and if releasing your program to the world is not a high priority, you could choose CUDA. If you envision distributing your program to many people running different platforms, you should probably choose OpenCL. Featurewise, these two platforms are very roughly equivalent.

We can use CUDA in Python thanks to PyCUDA, a Python package written by Andreas Klöckner (`http://documen.tician.de/pycuda/`).

Getting ready

Installing and configuring PyCUDA is not straightforward in general. First, you need an NVIDIA GPU. Then, you need to install the CUDA SDK. Finally, you have to install and configure PyCUDA. Note that PyCUDA depends on a few external packages, notably pytools.

On Windows, you should use Chris Gohlke's package. Make sure your version of CUDA matches the version used in the PyCUDA package. If you have DLL-related problems, use Dependency Walker on the `*.pyd` files in PyCUDA's installation folder (with Anaconda, it should look like `C:\anaconda\lib\site-packages\pycuda`). If you use Windows 64-bit, make sure that `C:\Windows\SysWOW64` is in your system PATH. Finally, make sure you have the version of Visual Studio that corresponds to your version of Python (see the instructions related to C compilers at the beginning of this chapter).

You will find more information at the following links:

- CUDA SDK available at `http://developer.nvidia.com/cuda-downloads`
- PyCUDA wiki available at `http://wiki.tiker.net`

How to do it...

1. Let's import PyCUDA:

   ```
   In [1]: import pycuda.driver as cuda
           import pycuda.autoinit
           from pycuda.compiler import SourceModule
           import numpy as np
   ```

2. We initialize the NumPy array that will contain the fractal:

   ```
   In [2]: size = 200
           iterations = 100
           col = np.empty((size, size), dtype=np.int32)
   ```

3. We allocate GPU memory for this array:

   ```
   In [3]: col_gpu = cuda.mem_alloc(col.nbytes)
   ```

4. We write the CUDA kernel in a string. Arguments to the `mandelbrot()` function are:

   - The figure **size**
   - The number of **iterations**
   - The **pointer** to the memory buffer

   This function executes on every single pixel. It updates the `col` buffer with the pixel's color:

   ```
   In [4]: code = """
           __global__ void mandelbrot(int size,
                                       int iterations,
                                       int *col) {
               // Get the row and column of the thread.
               int i = blockIdx.y * blockDim.y + threadIdx.y;
               int j = blockIdx.x * blockDim.x + threadIdx.x;
               int index = i * size + j;

               // Declare and initialize the variables.
               double cx, cy;
               double z0, z1, z0_tmp, z0_2, z1_2;
               cx = -2.0 + (double)j / size * 3;
               cy = -1.5 + (double)i / size * 3;

               // Main loop.
               z0 = z1 = 0.0;
   ```

```
            for (int n = 0; n < iterations; n++)
            {
                z0_2 = z0 * z0;
                z1_2 = z1 * z1;
                if (z0_2 + z1_2 <= 100)
                {
                    // Need to update both z0 and z1,
                    // hence the need for z0_tmp.
                    z0_tmp = z0_2 - z1_2 + cx;
                    z1 = 2 * z0 * z1 + cy;
                    z0 = z0_tmp;
                    col[index] = n;
                }
                else break;
            }
        }
        """
```

5. Now, we compile the CUDA program:

    ```
    In [5]: prg = SourceModule(code)
            mandelbrot = prg.get_function("mandelbrot")
    ```

6. We define the block size and the grid size, specifying how the threads will be parallelized with respect to the data:

    ```
    In [6]: block_size = 10
            block = (block_size, block_size, 1)
            grid = (size // block_size, size // block_size, 1)
    ```

7. We call the compiled function:

    ```
    In [7]: mandelbrot(np.int32(size),
                        np.int32(iterations),
                        col_gpu,
                        block=block, grid=grid)
    ```

8. Once the function has completed, we copy the contents of the CUDA buffer back to the NumPy array `col`:

    ```
    In [8]: cuda.memcpy_dtoh(col, col_gpu)
    ```

9. The `col` array now contains the Mandelbrot fractal. We find that this CUDA program is executed in 0.7 ms on a mobile GeForce GPU.

How it works...

GPU programming is a rich and highly technical topic, encompassing low-level architectural details of GPUs. Of course, we only scratched the surface here with the simplest paradigm possible (the "embarrassingly parallel" problem). We give further references in a later section.

A CUDA GPU has a number of **multiprocessors**, and each multiprocessor has multiple **stream processors** (also called **CUDA cores**). Each multiprocessor executes in parallel with the others. Within a multiprocessor, the stream processors execute the same instruction at the same time, but on multiple data bits (SIMD paradigm).

Central notions to the CUDA programming model are those of kernels, threads, blocks, and grids:

- A **kernel** is a program written in a C-like language that runs on the GPU.
- A **thread** represents one execution of a kernel on one *stream processor*.
- A **block** contains multiple threads executing on one *multiprocessor*.
- A **grid** contains a number of blocks.

The number of threads per block is limited by the size of the multiprocessors and depends on the graphics card model (1024 in recent models). However, a grid can contain an arbitrary number of blocks.

Within a block, threads are executed within **warps** of typically 32 threads. Better performance is achieved when conditional branching in a kernel is organized into groups of 32 threads.

Threads within a block can synchronize at synchronization barriers using the `__syncthreads()` function. This feature enables inter-thread communication within one block. However, blocks execute independently so that two threads from different blocks cannot synchronize.

Within a block, threads are organized into a 1D, 2D, or 3D structure, and similarly for blocks within a grid, as shown in the following figure. This structure is convenient as it matches most common multidimensional datasets encountered in real-world problems.

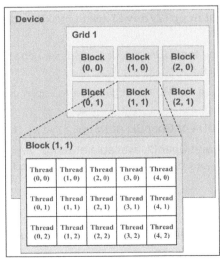

The CUDA programming model (showing threads, blocks, and grids — image by NVIDIA Corporation)

The kernel can retrieve the thread index within the block (`threadIdx`), as well as the block index within the grid (`blockIdx`) to determine which bit of data it should work on. In this recipe, the 2D image of the fractal is partitioned into 10 x 10 blocks, each block containing 100 pixels, with one thread per pixel. The kernel `mandelbrot` computes the color of a single pixel.

There are several levels of memory on the GPU, ranging from small, fast, and local memory shared by a few threads within a block; to large, slow, and global memory shared by all blocks. We need to tweak the memory access patterns in the code to match the hardware constraints and achieve higher performance. In particular, data access is more efficient when the threads within a warp access *consecutive* addresses in the global memory; the hardware **coalesces** all memory accesses into a single access to consecutive **DRAM** (**Dynamic Random Access Memory**) locations.

PyCUDA lets us upload/download data from NumPy arrays to buffers residing on the GPU. This operation is generally costly. Complex real-world problems frequently involve iterative steps happening on both the CPU and on the GPU, such that communication between the two is a common performance bottleneck. Higher performance is achieved when there are few of these exchanges.

There is some boilerplate code in (Py)CUDA on the C/Python side that consists of initializing the GPU, allocating data, uploading/downloading data to/from the GPU, compiling the kernel, executing the kernel, and so on. You can find all the details in the CUDA/PyCUDA documentation, but as a first approach, you can also just copy and paste code from this recipe or any tutorial.

There's more...

Here are a few references:

- Official CUDA portal at `http://developer.nvidia.com/category/zone/cuda-zone`
- Education and training for CUDA, at `http://developer.nvidia.com/cuda-education-training`
- Suggested books about CUDA, at `http://developer.nvidia.com/suggested-reading`
- Choosing between CUDA or OpenCL, at `http://wiki.tiker.net/CudaVsOpenCL`
- A blog post on CUDA and OpenCL available at `http://streamcomputing.eu/blog/2011-06-22/opencl-vs-cuda-misconceptions/`

See also

- The *Writing massively parallel code for heterogeneous platforms with OpenCL* recipe

Writing massively parallel code for heterogeneous platforms with OpenCL

In the previous recipe, we introduced CUDA, a *proprietary* GPGPU framework created by NVIDIA Corporation. In this recipe, we present OpenCL, an alternative *open* framework initiated by Apple in 2008. It is now adopted by mainstream companies including Intel, NVIDIA, AMD, Qualcomm, ARM, and others. These companies are regrouped within the non-profit technology consortium **Khronos Group** (which also maintains the OpenGL real-time rendering specification). Programs written in OpenCL can run on GPUs and CPUs (**heterogeneous computing**).

 CUDA and OpenCL are relatively similar in terms of concepts, syntax, and features. CUDA sometimes leads to slightly higher performance, since its API matches the hardware more closely than OpenCL's generic API.

We can use OpenCL in Python thanks to **PyOpenCL**, a Python package written by Andreas Klöckner (`http://documen.tician.de/pyopencl/`).

In this recipe, we will implement the Mandelbrot fractal in OpenCL. The OpenCL kernel is very similar to the CUDA kernel from the previous recipe. The Python API used to access OpenCL is somewhat different from PyCUDA, but the concepts are equivalent.

Getting ready

Installing PyOpenCL is generally not straightforward. The first step is to install the OpenCL SDK for your hardware (CPU and/or GPU). Then, you have to install and configure PyOpenCL. On Windows, you should use Chris Gohlke's package. Some installation instructions in the previous recipe apply here as well.

Here are a few references:

- The PyOpenCL Wiki available at `http://wiki.tiker.net`
- The documentation of PyOpenCL available at `http://documen.tician.de/pyopencl/`

Here are the links to the various OpenCL SDKs:

- Intel's SDK is available at `http://software.intel.com/en-us/vcsource/tools/opencl-sdk`
- AMD's SDK is available at `http://developer.amd.com/tools-and-sdks/heterogeneous-computing/`
- NVIDIA's SDK is available at `http://developer.nvidia.com/opencl`

How to do it...

1. Let's import PyOpenCL:

   ```
   In [1]: import pyopencl as cl
           import numpy as np
   ```

2. The following object defines some flags related to memory management on the device:

   ```
   In [2]: mf = cl.mem_flags
   ```

3. We create an OpenCL context and a command queue:

   ```
   In [3]: ctx = cl.create_some_context()
           queue = cl.CommandQueue(ctx)
   ```

4. Now, we initialize the NumPy array that will contain the fractal:

   ```
   In [4]: size = 200
           iterations = 100
           col = np.empty((size, size), dtype=np.int32)
   ```

5. We allocate GPU memory for this array:

   ```
   In [5]: col_buf = cl.Buffer(ctx,
                               mf.WRITE_ONLY,
                               col.nbytes)
   ```

6. We write the OpenCL kernel in a string:

   ```
   In [6]: code = """
           __kernel void mandelbrot(int size,
                                    int iterations,
                                    global int *col)
           {
               // Get the row and column index of the thread.
               int i = get_global_id(1);
               int j = get_global_id(0);
               int index = i * size + j;

               // Declare and initialize the variables.
               double cx, cy;
               double z0, z1, z0_tmp, z0_2, z1_2;
               cx = -2.0 + (double)j / size * 3;
               cy = -1.5 + (double)i / size * 3;

               // Main loop.
               z0 = z1 = 0.0;
               for (int n = 0; n < iterations; n++)
   ```

```
        {
            z0_2 = z0 * z0;
            z1_2 = z1 * z1;
            if (z0_2 + z1_2 <= 100)
            {
                // Need to update both z0 and z1.
                z0_tmp = z0_2 - z1_2 + cx;
                z1 = 2 * z0 * z1 + cy;
                z0 = z0_tmp;
                col[index] = n;
            }
            else break;
        }
    }
    """
```

7. Now, we compile the OpenCL program:

   ```
   In [7]: prg = cl.Program(ctx, code).build()
   Build on <pyopencl.Device 'Intel(R) Core(TM) i3-2365M CPU @
   1.40GHz' on 'Intel(R) OpenCL' at 0x765b188> succeeded.
   ```

8. We call the compiled function, passing the command queue, the grid size, and the buffers as arguments:

   ```
   In [8]: prg.mandelbrot(queue, col.shape, None, np.int32(size),
   np.int32(iterations), col_buf).wait()
   ```

9. Once the function has completed, we copy the contents of the OpenCL buffer back into the NumPy array col:

   ```
   In [9]: cl.enqueue_copy(queue, col, col_buf)
   ```

10. Finally, we can check that the function was successful by imshow()-ing the NumPy array col. We can also do a quick benchmark with %timeit, and we find that this function takes ~3.7 ms to complete on an Intel i3 dual-core CPU.

How it works...

The principles detailed in the previous recipe apply here as well. There is a change of terminology between CUDA and OpenCL:

- CUDA threads are equivalent to OpenCL **work items**.
- CUDA blocks are equivalent to OpenCL **work groups**.
- A CUDA grid is equivalent to an OpenCL **NDRange**.
- A CUDA streaming processor is equivalent to an OpenCL **compute unit**.

In the kernel, we can get a work item's index with `get_local_id(dim)`, `get_group_id(dim)`, and `get_global_id(dim)`. The `global` qualifier in the function's arguments specifies that a variable corresponds to an object in global memory.

An OpenCL context is the environment within which work items execute. It includes devices with their memories and command queues. The command queue is a queue used by the host application to submit work to a device.

This program works the same on a CPU or a GPU, depending on the installed OpenCL SDK and on the available OpenCL context. If multiple contexts exist, PyOpenGL may ask the user to choose the device. The context may also be specified programmatically (see `http://documen.tician.de/pyopencl/runtime.html#pyopencl.Context`). On a CPU, the code is parallelized and vectorized over multiple cores and with vector instructions such as SSE or AVX.

There's more...

OpenCL is a relatively young standard but we should expect it to have more and more importance in the future. It is supported by the biggest companies in the GPU industry. It supports interoperability with OpenGL, the industry standard for real-time, hardware-accelerated computer graphics (maintained by the very same Khronos Group). It is on its way to being supported on mobile platforms (smartphones and tablets), and in the browser as well with **WebCL** (which is still a draft at the time of writing).

Here are a few OpenCL resources:

▶ OpenCL tutorial available at `http://opencl.codeplex.com`
▶ Courses available at `http://developer.amd.com/partners/university-programs/opencl-university-course-listings/`
▶ Books on OpenCL, at `http://streamcomputing.eu/knowledge/for-developers/books/`

See also

▶ The *Writing massively parallel code for NVIDIA graphics cards (GPUs) with CUDA* recipe

Distributing Python code across multiple cores with IPython

Despite CPython's GIL, it is possible to execute several tasks in parallel on multi-core computers using multiple processes instead of multiple threads. Python offers a native **multiprocessing** module. IPython offers an even simpler interface that brings powerful parallel computing features in an interactive environment. We will describe this tool here.

How to do it...

1. First, we launch four IPython engines in separate processes. We have basically two options to do this:
    - Executing `ipcluster start -n 4` in a system shell
    - Using the web interface provided in the IPython notebook's main page by clicking on the **Clusters** tab and launching four engines

2. Then, we create a client that will act as a proxy to the IPython engines. The client automatically detects the running engines:

    ```
    In [2]: from IPython.parallel import Client
            rc = Client()
    ```

3. Let's check the number of running engines:

    ```
    In [3]: rc.ids
    Out[3]: [0, 1, 2, 3]
    ```

4. To run commands in parallel over the engines, we can use the `%px` line magic or the `%%px` cell magic:

    ```
    In [4]: %%px
            import os
            print("Process {0:d}.".format(os.getpid()))
    [stdout:0] Process 2988.
    [stdout:1] Process 5192.
    [stdout:2] Process 4484.
    [stdout:3] Process 1360.
    ```

5. We can specify which engines to run the commands on using the `--targets` or `-t` option:

    ```
    In [5]: %%px -t 1,2
            # The os module has already been imported in
            # the previous cell.
            print("Process {0:d}.".format(os.getpid()))
    [stdout:1] Process 5192.
    [stdout:2] Process 4484.
    ```

6. By default, the `%px` magic executes commands in **blocking mode**; the cell only returns when the commands have completed on all engines. It is possible to run non-blocking commands with the `--noblock` or `-a` option. In this case, the cell returns immediately, and the task's status and results can be polled asynchronously from IPython's interactive session:

```
In [6]: %%px -a
        import time
        time.sleep(5)
Out[6]: <AsyncResult: execute>
```

7. The previous command returned an `ASyncResult` instance that we can use to poll the task's status:

```
In [7]: print(_.elapsed, _.ready())
(0.061, False)
```

8. The `%pxresult` blocks until the task finishes:

```
In [8]: %pxresult
In [9]: print(_.elapsed, _.ready())
(5.019, True)
```

9. IPython provides convenient functions for common use cases, such as a parallel `map` function:

```
In [10]: v = rc[:]
         res = v.map(lambda x: x*x, range(10))
In [11]: print(res.get())
[0, 1, 4, 9, 16, 25, 36, 49, 64, 81]
```

How it works...

There are several steps to distribute code across multiple cores:

1. Launching several IPython **engines** (there is typically one process per core).
2. Creating a `Client` that acts as a proxy to these engines.
3. Using the client to launch tasks on the engines and retrieve the results.

Engines are Python processes that execute code on different computing units. They are very similar to IPython kernels.

There are two main interfaces for accessing the engines:

▶ With the **direct interface**, we access engines directly and explicitly with their identifiers.

▶ With the **load-balanced interface**, we access engines through an interface that automatically and dynamically assigns work to appropriate engines.

We can also create custom interfaces for alternative styles of parallelism.

In this recipe, we used the direct interface; we addressed individual engines explicitly by specifying their identifiers in the `%px` magics.

As we have seen in this recipe, tasks can be launched synchronously or asynchronously. The `%px*` magic commands are particularly convenient in the notebook, as they let us work seamlessly on multiple engines in parallel.

There's more...

The parallel computing capabilities of IPython offer an easy way to launch independent jobs in parallel over multiple cores. A more advanced use case is when jobs have **dependencies**.

Dependent parallel tasks

There are two types of dependencies:

- ▸ **Functional dependency**: It determines whether a given task can execute on a given engine, according to the engine's operating system, the presence or absence of specific Python modules, or other conditions. IPython provides a `@require` decorator for functions that need specific Python modules to run on the engines. Another decorator is `@depend`; it lets us define arbitrary conditions implemented in a Python function returning `True` or `False`.

- ▸ **Graph dependency**: It determines whether a given task can execute at a given time on a given engine. We may require a task to run only after one or several other tasks have finished. Additionally, we can impose this condition within any individual engine; an engine may need to execute a specific set of tasks before executing our task. For example, here is how to require tasks B and C (with asynchronous results `arB` and `arC`) to finish before task A starts:

```
with view.temp_flags(after=[arB, arC]):
    arA = view.apply_async(f)
```

IPython provides options to specify whether all or any of the dependencies should be met for the task to run. Additionally, we can specify whether success- and/or failure-dependent tasks should be considered as met or not.

When a task's dependency is unmet, the scheduler reassigns it to one engine, then to another engine, and so on until an appropriate engine is found. If the dependency cannot be met on any engine, an `ImpossibleDependency` error is raised for the task.

Passing data between dependent tasks is not particularly easy with IPython.parallel. A first possibility is to use blocking calls in the interactive session; wait for tasks to finish, retrieve the results, and send them back to the next tasks. Another possibility is to share data between engines via the filesystem, but this solution does not work well on multiple computers. An alternate solution is described at: `http://nbviewer.ipython.org/gist/minrk/11415238`.

Alternative parallel computing solutions

Besides IPython, there are numerous alternative parallel computing frameworks in Python, including **ParallelPython**, **joblib**, and many others.

There are also third-party (often commercial) services that provide Python-based clouds, such as **PythonAnywhere** or **Wakari**. They are generally used in two ways:

- ▶ **Distributing a large number of computational tasks across multiple nodes in parallel**: Instead of being limited to a few cores with one or several local computers, we can use hundreds or thousands of servers in parallel without worrying about the maintenance of the whole infrastructure (it is handled by the company).

- ▶ **Hosting Python applications online, typically with a web interface**: For example, with Wakari, IPython notebooks can run on the cloud. An interesting use case is teaching, where students can instantaneously use IPython from a web browser connected to the Internet without installing anything locally.

References

Here are a few references about IPython.parallel:

- ▶ Documentation of IPython.parallel available at `http://ipython.org/ipython-doc/dev/parallel/`

- ▶ IPython parallel tutorial by the IPython developers available at `http://nbviewer.ipython.org/github/minrk/IPython-parallel-tutorial/blob/master/Index.ipynb`

- ▶ Dependencies in IPython.parallel, explained at `http://ipython.org/ipython-doc/dev/parallel/parallel_task.html#dependencies`

- ▶ DAG dependencies, described at `http://ipython.org/ipython-doc/dev/parallel/dag_dependencies.html`

- ▶ Examples of advanced techniques with IPython.parallel available at `http://github.com/ipython/ipython/tree/master/examples/Parallel%20Computing`

Here are some references about alternative parallel computing solutions in Python:

- ▶ Parallel Python available at `http://www.parallelpython.com`

- ▶ Joblib available at `http://pythonhosted.org/joblib/parallel.html`

- ▶ List of parallel computing packages available at `http://wiki.python.org/moin/ParallelProcessing`

- ▶ Python Anywhere available at `http://www.pythonanywhere.com`

- ▶ Wakari available at `http://wakari.io`

- ▶ IPCluster on Wakari described at `http://continuum.io/blog/ipcluster-wakari-intro`

▸ Teaching with Wakari described at `http://continuum.io/blog/teaching-with-wakari`

See also

▸ The *Interacting with asynchronous parallel tasks in IPython* recipe
▸ The *Parallelizing code with MPI in IPython* recipe

Interacting with asynchronous parallel tasks in IPython

In this recipe, we will show how to interact with asynchronous tasks running in parallel with IPython.

Getting ready

You need to start the IPython engines (see the previous recipe). The simplest option is to launch them from the **Clusters** tab in the notebook dashboard. In this recipe, we use four engines.

How to do it...

1. Let's import a few modules:

```
In [1]: import time
        import sys
        from IPython import parallel
        from IPython.display import clear_output, display
        from IPython.html import widgets
```

2. We create a `Client`:

```
In [2]: rc = parallel.Client()
```

3. Now, we create a load-balanced view on the IPython engines:

```
In [3]: view = rc.load_balanced_view()
```

4. We define a simple function for our parallel tasks:

```
In [4]: def f(x):
            import time
            time.sleep(.1)
            return x*x
```

5. We will run this function on 100 integer numbers in parallel:

```
In [5]: numbers = list(range(100))
```

6. We execute `f()` on our list `numbers` in parallel across all of our engines, using `map_async()`. This function immediately returns an `AsyncResult` object that allows us to interactively retrieve information about the tasks:

```
In [6]: ar = view.map_async(f, numbers)
```

7. This object has a `metadata` attribute: a list of dictionaries for all engines. We can get the date of submission and completion, the status, the standard output and error, and other information:

```
In [7]: ar.metadata[0]
Out[7]: {
 'execute_result': None,
 'engine_id': None,
 ...
 'submitted': datetime.datetime(2014, 1, 1, 10, 30, 38, 9487),
 'follow': None}
```

8. Iterating over the `AsyncResult` instance works normally; the iteration progresses in real-time while the tasks are being completed:

```
In [8]: for _ in ar:
             print(_, end=', ')
0, 1, 4,..., 9409, 9604, 9801,
```

9. Now, we create a simple progress bar for our asynchronous tasks. The idea is to create a loop polling for the tasks' status at every second. An `IntProgressWidget` widget is updated in real-time and shows the progress of the tasks:

```
In [9]: def progress_bar(ar):
            # We create a progress bar.
            w = widgets.IntProgressWidget()
            # The maximum value is the number of tasks.
            w.max = len(ar.msg_ids)
            # We display the widget in the output area.
            display(w)
            # Repeat every second:
            while not ar.ready():
                # Update the widget's value with the
                # number of tasks that have finished
                # so far.
                w.value = ar.progress
                time.sleep(1)
            w.value = w.max
In [10]: ar = view.map_async(f, numbers)
In [11]: progress_bar(ar)
```

The progress bar is shown in the following screenshot:

```
progress_bar(ar)
```

10. Finally, it is easy to debug a parallel task on an engine. We can launch a Qt client on the remote kernel by calling `%qtconsole` within a `%%px` cell magic:

```
In [12]: %%px -t 1
         %qtconsole
```

The Qt console allows us to inspect the remote namespace for debugging or analysis purposes, as shown in the following screenshot:

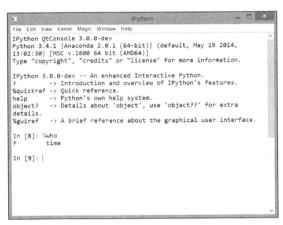

Qt console for debugging an IPython engine

How it works...

`AsyncResult` instances are returned by asynchronous parallel functions. They implement several useful attributes and methods, notably:

- `elapsed`: Elapsed time since submission
- `progress`: Number of tasks that have competed so far
- `serial_time`: Sum of the computation time of all of the tasks done in parallel
- `metadata`: Dictionary with further information about the task
- `ready()`: Returns whether the call has finished
- `successful()`: Returns whether the call has completed without raising an exception (an exception is raised if the task has not completed yet)

- ► `wait()`: Blocks until the tasks have completed (there is an optional timeout argument)
- ► `get()`: Blocks until the tasks have completed and returns the result (there is an optional timeout argument)

There's more...

Here are a few references:

- ► Documentation of the AsyncResult class available at `http://ipython.org/ipython-doc/dev/parallel/asyncresult.html`
- ► Documentation of the task interface available at `http://ipython.org/ipython-doc/dev/parallel/parallel_task.html`
- ► Printing engines output in real-time, demonstrated at `http://github.com/ipython/ipython/blob/master/examples/Parallel%20Computing/iopubwatcher.py`

See also

- ► The *Distributing Python code across multiple cores with IPython* recipe
- ► The *Parallelizing code with MPI in IPython* recipe

Parallelizing code with MPI in IPython

Message Passing Interface (**MPI**) is a standardized communication protocol for parallel systems. It is used in many parallel computing applications to exchange data between nodes. MPI has a high barrier to entry, but it is very efficient and powerful.

IPython's parallel computing system has been designed from the ground up to work with MPI. If you are new to MPI, it is a good idea to start using it from IPython. If you are an experienced MPI user, you will find that IPython integrates seamlessly with your parallel application.

In this recipe, we will see how to use MPI with IPython through a very simple example.

Getting ready

To use MPI with IPython, you need:

- ► A standard MPI implementation such as OpenMPI available at `http://www.open-mpi.org` or MPICH available at `http://www.mpich.org`
- ► The mpi4py package available at `http://mpi4py.scipy.org`

For example, here are the commands to install MPI for IPython on Ubuntu and Anaconda:

```
conda install mpich2
conda install mpi4py
```

You can also do `pip install mpi4py` for mpi4py. MPI can also be used on Windows. The website of *Python Tools for Visual Studio* available at `http://pytools.codeplex.com` contains the instructions to do this.

How to do it...

1. We first need to create a MPI profile with:

    ```
    In [1]: !ipython profile create --parallel --profile=mpi
    ```

2. Then, we open `~/.ipython/profile_mpi/ipcluster_config.py` and add the line `c.IPClusterEngines.engine_launcher_class = 'MPI'`.

3. Once the MPI profile has been created and configured, we can launch the engines by typing in a terminal: `ipcluster start -n 2 --engines MPI --profile=mpi`.

4. Now, to actually use the engines, we create a client in the notebook:

    ```
    In [2]: import numpy as np
            from IPython.parallel import Client
    In [3]: c = Client(profile='mpi')
    ```

5. Let's create a view on all engines:

    ```
    In [4]: view = c[:]
    ```

6. In this example, we compute the sum of all integers between 0 and 15 in parallel over two cores. We first distribute the array with the 16 values across the engines (each engine gets a subarray):

    ```
    In [5]: view.scatter('a', np.arange(16., dtype='float'))
    Out[5]: <AsyncResult: scatter>
    ```

7.   We compute the total sum in parallel using MPI's `allreduce()` function. Every node makes the same computation and returns the same result:

```
In [6]: %%px
        from mpi4py import MPI
        import numpy as np
        print MPI.COMM_WORLD.allreduce(np.sum(a), op=MPI.SUM)
[stdout:0] 120.0
[stdout:1] 120.0
```

If you get a different result, it means that the engines were not actually started with MPI (see `http://stackoverflow.com/a/20159018/1595060`).

How it works...

In this example, each node:

▶   Receives a subset of the integers

▶   Computes the local sum of those integers

▶   Sends this local sum to all other engines

▶   Receives the local sum of the other engines

▶   Computes the total sum of those local sums

This is how `allreduce()` works in MPI; the principle is to **scatter** data across engines first, then to **reduce** the local computations through a global operator (here, `MPI.SUM`).

IPython's direct interface also supports the scatter/gather paradigm natively, without resorting to MPI. However, these operations can only be launched from the interactive session, not from the engines themselves.

There are many other parallel computing paradigms in MPI. You can find more information here:

▶   MPI tutorials by Wes Kendall available at `http://mpitutorial.com`

▶   MPI tutorials by Blaise Barney, Lawrence Livermore National Laboratory, available at `http://computing.llnl.gov/tutorials/mpi/`

See also

▶   The *Distributing Python code across multiple cores with IPython* recipe

▶   The *Interacting with asynchronous parallel tasks in IPython* recipe

Trying the Julia language in the notebook

Julia (http://julialang.org) is a young, high-level, dynamic language for high-performance numerical computing. The first version was released in 2012 after three years of development at MIT. Julia borrows ideas from Python, R, MATLAB, Ruby, Lisp, C, and other languages. Its major strength is to combine the expressivity and ease of use of high-level, dynamic languages with the speed of C (almost). This is achieved via an LLVM-based Just-In-Time (JIT) compiler that targets machine code for x86-64 architectures.

In this recipe, we will try Julia in the IPython notebook using the **IJulia** package available at http://github.com/JuliaLang/IJulia.jl. We will also show how to use Python packages (such as NumPy and matplotlib) from Julia. Specifically, we will compute and display a Julia set.

This recipe is inspired by a Julia tutorial given by David P. Sanders at the SciPy 2014 conference (http://nbviewer.ipython.org/github/dpsanders/scipy_2014_julia/tree/master/).

Getting ready

You first need to install Julia. You will find packages for Windows, Mac OS X, and Linux on Julia's website at http://julialang.org/downloads/. On Ubuntu, you can type sudo apt-get install julia in a terminal. For IJulia, you also need a C++ compiler. On Ubuntu, you can type sudo apt-get install build-essential.

Then, open a Julia terminal with the julia command, and install IJulia by typing Pkg.add("IJulia") in the Julia terminal. This package should also create a julia profile in your IPython installation.

Finally, to launch a Julia notebook, run ipython notebook --profile=julia in a terminal. You'll recognize the dashboard of the IPython notebook. The only difference is that the Julia language is used in the notebook instead of Python.

This recipe has been tested on Ubuntu 14.04 with Julia 0.2.1.

How to do it...

1. We can't avoid the customary *Hello World* example. The println() function displays a string and adds a line break at the end:

```
In [1]: println("Hello world!")
Hello world!
```

2. We create a polymorphic function, f, that computes the expression z*z+c. We will evaluate this function on arrays, so we use element-wise operators with a dot (.) prefix:

    ```
    In [2]: f(z, c) = z.*z .+ c
    Out[2]: f (generic function with 1 method)
    ```

3. Let's evaluate f on scalar complex numbers (the imaginary number *i* is 1im).

    ```
    In [3]: f(2.0 + 1.0im, 1.0)
    Out[3]: 4.0 + 4.0im
    ```

4. Now, we create a (2, 2) matrix. Components are separated by a space and rows are separated by a semicolon (;). The type of this Array is automatically inferred from its components. The Array type is a built-in data type in Julia, similar, but not identical, to NumPy's ndarray type:

    ```
    In [4]: z = [-1.0 - 1.0im  1.0 - 1.0im;
                 -1.0 + 1.0im  1.0 + 1.0im]
    Out[4]: 2x2 Array{Complex{Float64},2}:
     -1.0-1.0im   1.0-1.0im
     -1.0+1.0im   1.0+1.0im
    ```

5. We can index arrays with brackets []. A notable difference with Python is that indexing starts from 1 instead of 0. MATLAB has the same convention. Furthermore, the keyword end refers to the last item in that dimension:

    ```
    In [5]: z[1,end]
    Out[5]: 1.0 - 1.0im
    ```

6. We can evaluate f on the matrix z and a scalar c (polymorphism):

    ```
    In [6]: f(z, 0)
    Out[6]: 2x2 Array{Complex{Float64},2}:
     0.0+2.0im   0.0-2.0im
     0.0-2.0im   0.0+2.0im
    ```

7. Now, we create a function, julia, that computes a Julia set. Optional named arguments are separated from positional arguments by a semicolon (;). Julia's syntax for flow control is close to that of Python's, except that colons are dropped, indentation doesn't count, and block end keywords are mandatory:

    ```
    In [7]: function julia(z, c; maxiter=200)
                for n = 1:maxiter
                    if abs2(z) > 4.0
                        return n-1
                    end
                    z = f(z, c)
                end
    ```

```
            return maxiter
        end
Out[7]: julia (generic function with 1 method)
```

8. We can use Python packages from Julia. First, we have to install the `PyCall` package by using Julia's built-in package manager (`Pkg`). Once the package is installed, we can use it in the interactive session with `using PyCall`:

```
In [8]: Pkg.add("PyCall")
        using PyCall
```

9. We can import Python packages with the `@pyimport` **macro** (a metaprogramming feature in Julia). This macro is the equivalent of Python's `import` command:

```
In [9]: @pyimport numpy as np
```

10. The `np` namespace is now available in the Julia interactive session. NumPy arrays are automatically converted to Julia `Array` objects:

```
In [10]: z = np.linspace(-1., 1., 100)
Out[10]: 100-element Array{Float64,1}:
 -1.0
 -0.979798
...
  0.979798
  1.0
```

11. We can use list comprehensions to evaluate the function `julia` on many arguments:

```
In [11]: m = [julia(z[i], 0.5) for i=1:100]
Out[11]: 100-element Array{Int64,1}:
 2
...
 2
```

12. Let's try the Gadfly plotting package. This library offers a high-level plotting interface inspired by Dr. Leland Wilkinson's textbook *The Grammar of Graphics*. In the notebook, plots are interactive thanks to the **D3.js** library:

```
In [12]: Pkg.add("Gadfly")
         using Gadfly
In [13]: plot(x=1:100, y=m, Geom.point, Geom.line)
Out[13]: Plot(...)
```

Here is a screenshot:

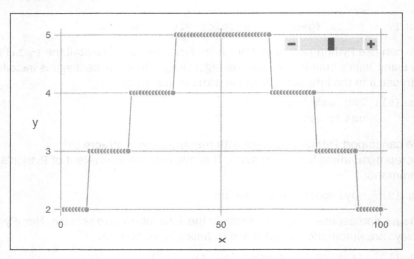

A Gadfly plot in the IPython notebook with Julia

13. Now, we compute a Julia set by using two nested loops. In general, and unlike Python, there is no significant performance penalty in using `for` loops instead of vectorized operations. High-performance code can be written either with vectorized operations or `for` loops:

```
In [14]: @time m = [julia(complex(r, i), complex(-0.06, 0.67))
                    for i = 1:-.001:-1,
                        r = -1.5:.001:1.5];
elapsed time: 0.881234749 seconds (48040248 bytes allocated)
```

14. Finally, we use the `PyPlot` package to draw matplotlib figures in Julia:

```
In [15]: Pkg.add("PyPlot")
         using PyPlot
In [16]: imshow(m, cmap="RdGy",
                extent=[-1.5, 1.5, -1, 1]);
```

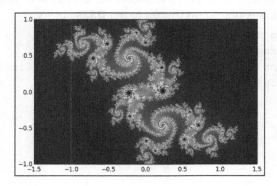

How it works...

Languages used to be either low-level, difficult to use, but fast (such as C); or high-level, easy to use, but slow (such as Python). In Python, solutions to this problem include NumPy and Cython, among others.

Julia developers chose to create a new high-level but fast language, bringing the best of both worlds together. This is essentially achieved through modern Just-In-Time compilation techniques implemented with LLVM.

Julia dynamically parses code and generates low-level code in the LLVM Intermediate Representation. This representation features a language-independent instruction set that is then compiled to machine code. Code written with explicit loops is directly compiled to machine code. This explains why the performance-motivated vectorization of code is generally not required with Julia.

There's more...

Strengths of Julia include:

- A powerful and flexible dynamic type system based on multiple dispatch for parametric polymorphism
- Facilities for metaprogramming
- A simple interface for calling C, FORTRAN, or Python code from Julia
- Built-in support for fine-grained parallel and distributed computing
- A built-in multidimensional array data type and numerical computing library
- A built-in package manager based on Git
- External packages for data analysis such as DataFrames (equivalent of pandas) and Gadfly (statistical plotting library)
- Integration in the IPython notebook

What are the strengths of Python over Julia? At the time of this writing, Julia is much younger and less mature than Python and SciPy. Therefore, there are fewer packages and less documentation in Julia than in Python. The syntax of the Julia language is still changing. Additionally, Python is much more commonly found in production environments than Julia. Thus, bringing numerical computing code to a production environment is easier when the code is in Python.

That being said, the Julia ecosystem and its community are growing fast. We can reasonably expect Julia to become increasingly popular in the future. Also, since both languages can be used in the IPython notebook, we don't necessarily have to *choose* between Python and Julia. We can call Python code and use Python modules from Julia and vice versa.

We have only scratched the surface of the Julia language in this recipe. Topics of interest we couldn't cover in details here include Julia's type system, the metaprogramming features, the support for parallel computing, and the package manager, among others.

Here are some references:

- The Julia language on Wikipedia available at
  `http://en.wikipedia.org/wiki/Julia_%28programming_language%29`
- Official documentation of Julia available at
  `http://docs.julialang.org/en/latest/`
- The *Why We Created Julia* blog post available at
  `http://julialang.org/blog/2012/02/why-we-created-julia/`
- PyCall.jl for calling Python from Julia available at
  `http://github.com/stevengj/PyCall.jl`
- PyPlot.jl for using matplotlib in Julia available at
  `http://github.com/stevengj/PyPlot.jl`
- Gadfly.jl, a Julia plotting library, available at
  `http://dcjones.github.io/Gadfly.jl/`
- DataFrames.jl, an equivalent of pandas for Julia, available at
  `http://juliastats.github.io/DataFrames.jl/`
- Julia Studio, an IDE for Julia, available at
  `http://forio.com/labs/julia-studio/`

6
Advanced Visualization

In this chapter, we will cover the following topics:

- ▸ Making nicer matplotlib figures with prettyplotlib
- ▸ Creating beautiful statistical plots with seaborn
- ▸ Creating interactive web visualizations with Bokeh
- ▸ Visualizing a NetworkX graph in the IPython notebook with D3.js
- ▸ Converting matplotlib figures to D3.js visualizations with mpld3
- ▸ Getting started with Vispy for high-performance interactive data visualizations

Introduction

Visualization is a central theme of this book. We create graphics in most recipes because that's the most efficient way to communicate quantitative information. In most cases, we use matplotlib to create plots. In this chapter, we will see more advanced visualization features in Python.

First, we will see a few packages that let us improve the default styling of matplotlib figures and the MATLAB-like pyplot interface. There are other high-level visualization programming interfaces that can be more convenient in some situations.

Also, the Web platform is getting closer and closer to Python. The IPython notebook is a good example of this trend. In this chapter, we will see a few techniques and libraries to create interactive Web visualizations in Python. These techniques will let us combine the power of Python for data analysis and the power of the Web for interactivity.

Finally, we will introduce Vispy, a new high-performance interactive visualization library for big data.

Making nicer matplotlib figures with prettyplotlib

matplotlib is sometimes criticized for the default appearance of its figures. For example, the default color maps are neither aesthetically appealing nor do they present perceptually clear information.

There are many attempts to circumvent this problem. In this recipe, we will present **prettyplotlib**, created by Olga Botvinnik. This lightweight Python library considerably improves the default styling of many kinds of matplotlib figures.

Getting ready

You will find the installation instructions of prettyplotlib on the project's page at `http://github.com/olgabot/prettyplotlib`. You can basically just do `pip install prettyplotlib` in a terminal.

How to do it...

1. Let's first import NumPy and matplotlib:

```
In [1]: import numpy as np
        import matplotlib.pyplot as plt
        import matplotlib as mpl
        %matplotlib inline
```

2. We then draw several curves with matplotlib:

```
In [2]: np.random.seed(12)
        for i in range(8):
            x = np.arange(1000)
            y = np.random.randn(1000).cumsum()
            plt.plot(x, y, label=str(i))
        plt.legend()
```

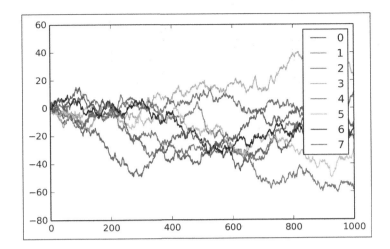

 If you're reading the printed version of this book, you won't see the colors. You can find the colored images on the book's website.

3. Now, we create the exact same plot with prettyplotlib. We just replace the `matplotlib.pyplot` namespace with `prettyplotlib`:

```
In [3]: import prettyplotlib as ppl
        np.random.seed(12)
        for i in range(8):
            x = np.arange(1000)
            y = np.random.randn(1000).cumsum()
            ppl.plot(x, y, label=str(i))
        ppl.legend()
```

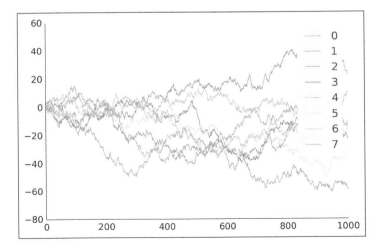

4. Let's show another example with an image. We first use matplotlib's `pcolormesh()` function to display a 2D array as an image:

```
In [4]: np.random.seed(12)
        plt.pcolormesh(np.random.rand(16, 16))
        plt.colorbar()
```

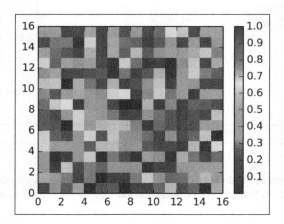

The default *rainbow* color map is known to cause visualized data to be misinterpreted.

5. Now, we use prettyplotlib to display the exact same image:

```
In [5]: np.random.seed(12)
        ppl.pcolormesh(np.random.rand(16, 16))
```

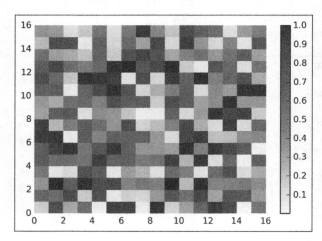

This visualization is much clearer, in that high or low values are more obvious than with the rainbow color map.

How it works...

prettyplotlib merely tweaks the default styling options of matplotlib. The plotting interface is basically the same as matplotlib. To understand how to modify matplotlib's styling, it is worthwhile looking at prettyplotlib's code.

There's more...

There are other ways to improve matplotlib's styling:

- A blog post by Randal Olson explains how to make clean and beautiful plots with matplotlib; this is available at `http://www.randalolson.com/2014/06/28/how-to-make-beautiful-data-visualizations-in-python-with-matplotlib/`

- There is some work in progress in matplotlib to add style sheet support; more information can be found at `http://github.com/matplotlib/matplotlib/blob/master/doc/users/style_sheets.rst`

- Information about why rainbow color maps are misleading, at `http://eagereyes.org/basics/rainbow-color-map`

See also

- The *Creating beautiful statistical plots with seaborn* recipe

Creating beautiful statistical plots with seaborn

matplotlib comes with a high-level plotting API called **pyplot**. Inspired by MATLAB (a widespread commercial software for numerical computing), this interface may be a bit too low-level for scientists, in that it can lead to boilerplate code that is difficult to read and maintain. Yet, it is probably one of the most widely used plotting interfaces in the scientific Python community.

There exist higher-level, more convenient plotting interfaces. In this recipe, we present **seaborn** created by Michael Waskom. This library exposes a high-level plotting API that is specifically adapted to statistical figures. It also integrates nicely with pandas.

Getting ready

You will find the installation instructions of seaborn on the project's page at `http://github.com/mwaskom/seaborn`. You can just type `pip install seaborn` in a terminal.

How to do it...

1. Let's import NumPy, matplotlib, and seaborn:

```
In [1]: import numpy as np
        import matplotlib.pyplot as plt
        import seaborn as sns
        %matplotlib inline
```

2. We generate a random dataset (following the example on seaborn's website at `http://nbviewer.ipython.org/github/mwaskom/seaborn/blob/master/examples/linear_models.ipynb`):

```
In [2]: x1 = np.random.randn(80)
        x2 = np.random.randn(80)
        x3 = x1 * x2
        y1 = .5 + 2 * x1 - x2 + 2.5 * x3 + \
             3 * np.random.randn(80)
        y2 = .5 + 2 * x1 - x2 + 2.5 * np.random.randn(80)
        y3 = y2 + np.random.randn(80)
```

3. Seaborn implements many easy-to-use statistical plotting functions. For example, here is how to create a **violin plot**. This type of plot allows us to show the detailed distribution of sets of points, instead of just quartiles like in box plots:

```
In [3]: sns.violinplot([x1,x2, x3])
```

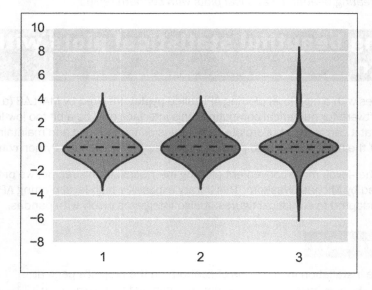

4. Seaborn also implements all-in-one statistical visualization functions. For example, we can use a single function (`regplot()`) to perform *and* display a linear regression between two variables:

    ```
    In [4]: sns.regplot(x2, y2)
    ```

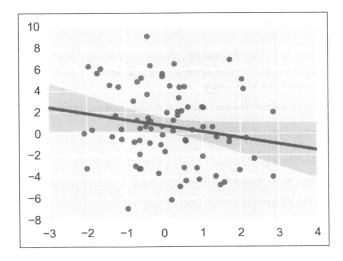

5. Seaborn has built-in support for pandas data structures. Here, we display the pairwise correlations between all variables defined in a `DataFrame` object:

    ```
    In [5]: df = pd.DataFrame(dict(x1=x1, x2=x2, x3=x3,
                                   y1=y1, y2=y2, y3=y3))
            sns.corrplot(df)
    ```

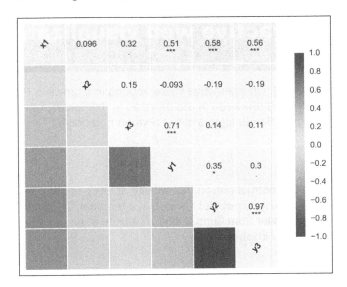

There's more...

Besides seaborn, there are other high-level plotting interfaces:

▶ *The Grammar of Graphics* is a book by Dr. Leland Wilkinson that has influenced many high-level plotting interfaces such as R's *ggplot2*, Python's *ggplot* by yhat, and others.

▶ **Vega**, by Trifacta, is a declarative visualization grammar that can be translated to D3.js (a JavaScript visualization library). Also, **Vincent** is a Python library that lets us create visualizations with Vega.

▶ Tableau's **VizQL** is a commercial database-oriented visualization language.

Here are some more references:

▶ Vega available at `http://trifacta.github.io/vega/`

▶ Vincent available at `http://vincent.readthedocs.org/en/latest/`

▶ ggplot2 available at `http://ggplot2.org/`

▶ ggplot for Python available at `http://blog.yhathq.com/posts/ggplot-for-python.html`

▶ VizQL available at `http://www.tableausoftware.com/fr-fr/products/technology`

See also

▶ The *Making nicer matplotlib figures with prettyplotlib* recipe

Creating interactive web visualizations with Bokeh

Bokeh is a library for creating rich interactive visualizations in a browser. Plots are designed in Python, and they are entirely rendered in the browser. In this recipe, we will learn how to create and render interactive Bokeh figures in the IPython notebook.

Getting ready

Install Bokeh by following the instructions on the website at `http://bokeh.pydata.org`. In principle, you can just type `pip install bokeh` in a terminal. On Windows, you can also download the binary installer from Chris Gohlke's website at `http://www.lfd.uci.edu/~gohlke/pythonlibs/#bokeh`.

How to do it...

1. Let's import NumPy and Bokeh. We need to call the `output_notebook()` function in order to tell Bokeh to render plots in the IPython notebook:

```
In [1]: import numpy as np
        import bokeh.plotting as bkh
        bkh.output_notebook()
```

2. We create some random data:

```
In [2]: x = np.linspace(0., 1., 100)
        y = np.cumsum(np.random.randn(100))
```

3. Let's draw a curve:

```
In [3]: bkh.line(x, y, line_width=5)
        bkh.show()
```

An interactive plot is rendered in the notebook. We can pan and zoom by clicking on the buttons above the plot:

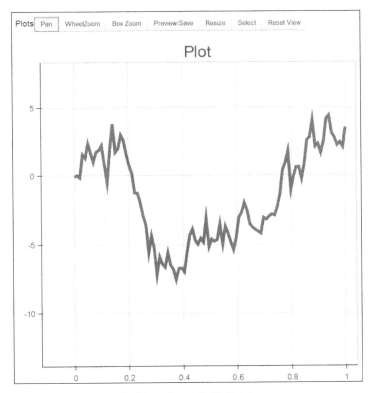

An interactive plot with Bokeh

4. Let's move on to another example. We first load a sample dataset (*Iris flowers*). We also generate some colors based on the species of the flowers:

```
In [4]: from bokeh.sampledata.iris import flowers
        colormap = {'setosa': 'red',
                    'versicolor': 'green',
                    'virginica': 'blue'}
        flowers['color'] = flowers['species'].map(
                                    lambda x: colormap[x])
```

5. Now, we render an interactive scatter plot:

```
In [5]: bkh.scatter(flowers["petal_length"],
                     flowers["petal_width"],
                     color=flowers["color"],
                     fill_alpha=0.25, size=10,)
        bkh.show()
```

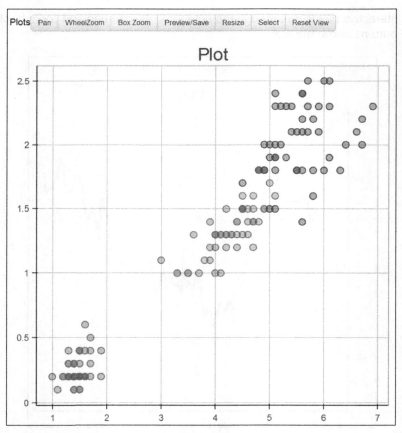

An interactive scatter plot with Bokeh

There's more...

Bokeh figures in the notebook are interactive even in the absence of a Python server. For example, our figures can be interactive in nbviewer. Bokeh can also generate standalone HTML/JavaScript documents from our plots. More examples can be found in the gallery at `http://bokeh.pydata.org/docs/gallery.html`.

There is an IPython extension in Bokeh that simplifies the integration of interactive plots in the notebook. This is available at `http://github.com/ContinuumIO/bokeh/tree/master/extensions`.

In the same vein, let's mention *plot.ly*, an online commercial service for interactive Web-based visualization that offers Python interfaces, available at `http://plot.ly`.

See also

► The *Converting matplotlib figures to D3.js visualizations with mpld3* recipe

Visualizing a NetworkX graph in the IPython notebook with D3.js

D3.js (`http://d3js.org`) is a popular interactive visualization framework for the Web. Written in JavaScript, it allows us to create data-driven visualizations based on Web technologies such as HTML, SVG, and CSS. There are many other JavaScript visualization and charting libraries, but we will focus on D3.js in this recipe.

Being a pure JavaScript library, D3.js has in principle nothing to do with Python. However, the HTML-based IPython notebook can integrate D3.js visualizations seamlessly.

In this recipe, we will create a graph in Python with NetworkX and visualize it in the IPython notebook with D3.js.

Getting ready

You need to know the basics of HTML, JavaScript, and D3.js for this recipe.

How to do it...

1. Let's import the packages:

```
In [1]: import json
        import numpy as np
        import networkx as nx
```

```
import matplotlib.pyplot as plt
%matplotlib inline
```

2. We load a famous social graph published in 1977 called **Zachary's Karate Club graph**. This graph represents the friendships between members of a Karate club. The club's president and the instructor were involved in a dispute, resulting in a split of this group. Here, we simply display the graph with matplotlib (using the `networkx.draw()` function):

```
In [2]: g = nx.karate_club_graph()
        nx.draw(g)
```

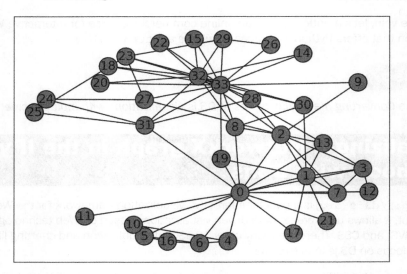

3. Now, we're going to display this graph in the notebook with D3.js. The first step is to bring this graph to JavaScript. Here, we choose to export the graph to JSON. D3.js generally expects each edge to be an object with a source and target. Also, we specify which side each member has taken (`club` attribute). NetworkX comes with a built-in export function that we can use here:

```
In [3]: from networkx.readwrite import json_graph
        data = json_graph.node_link_data(g)
        with open('graph.json', 'w') as f:
            json.dump(data, f, indent=4)
```

4. The next step is to create an HTML object that will contain the visualization. Here, we create a `<div>` element in the notebook. We also specify a few CSS styles for nodes and links (also called edges):

```
In [4]: %%html
        <div id="d3-example"></div>
```

```
<style>
.node {stroke: #fff; stroke-width: 1.5px;}
.link {stroke: #999; stroke-opacity: .6;}
</style>
```

5. The last step is trickier. We write the JavaScript code to load the graph from the JSON file and display it with D3.js. Knowing the basics of D3.js is required here (see the documentation of D3.js). The code is long, and you can find it on the book's website. Here, we highlight the most important steps:

```
In [5]: %%javascript
    // We load the d3.js library.
    require(["d3"], function(d3) {
        // The code in this block is executed when the
        // d3.js library has been loaded.
        [...]
        // We create a force-directed dynamic graph
        // layout.
        var force = d3.layout.force().charge(-120).
                linkDistance(30).size([width, height]);
        [...]
        // In the <div> element, we create a <svg> graphic
        // that will contain our interactive
        // visualization.
        var svg = d3.select("#d3-example").select("svg");
        [...]
        // We load the JSON file.
        d3.json("graph.json", function(error, graph) {
            // We create the graph here.
            force.nodes(graph.nodes).links(graph.links)
                .start();

            // We create a <line> SVG element for each
            // link in the graph.
            var link = svg.selectAll(".link")
                    .data(graph.links)
                    .enter().append("line")
                    .attr("class", "link");

            // We create <circle> SVG elements for the
            // nodes.
            var node = svg.selectAll(".node")
                .data(graph.nodes)
                .enter().append("circle")
```

```
    [...]
    .style("fill", function(d) {
        return color(d.club);
    })
    .call(force.drag);
    [...]
    });
  });
```

When we execute this cell, the HTML object created in the previous cell is updated. The graph is animated and interactive; we can click on nodes, see their labels, and move them within the canvas:

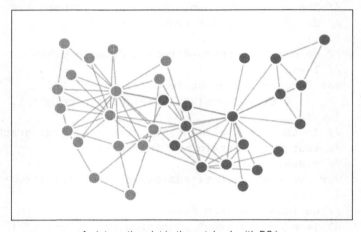

An interactive plot in the notebook with D3.js

There's more...

D3.js' gallery contains many more examples of beautiful, interactive visualizations for the Web. They are available at http://github.com/mbostock/d3/wiki/Gallery.

In this recipe, we created an HTML/JavaScript interactive visualization from a static dataset. With IPython 2.0 and above, we can also create dynamic, real-time visualizations that involve bi-directional communication between the browser and the Python kernel. There is an experimental implementation by Brian Granger available at http://nbviewer.ipython.org/github/ellisonbg/talk-2014-strata-sc/blob/master/Graph%20Widget.ipynb.

Let's also mention **Vincent**, a Python to Vega translator. Vega is a JSON-based visualization grammar that can be translated to D3.js. Vincent makes it possible to design an interactive visualization in Python and render it in the browser. More information can be found at http://vincent.readthedocs.org/en/latest/.

▸ The *Creating interactive web visualizations with Bokeh* recipe

▸ The *Converting matplotlib figures to D3.js visualizations with mpld3* recipe

Converting matplotlib figures to D3.js visualizations with mpld3

The **mpld3** library automatically converts matplotlib figures to interactive D3.js visualizations. In this recipe, we will see how to use this library in the notebook.

Getting ready

To install the mpld3 library, you can just type `pip install mpld3` in a terminal. See also the main website at `http://mpld3.github.io`.

How to do it...

1. First, we load NumPy and matplotlib as usual:

```
In [1]: import numpy as np
        import matplotlib.pyplot as plt
        %matplotlib inline
```

2. Then, we enable the mpld3 figures in the notebook with a single function call:

```
In [2]: from mpld3 import enable_notebook
        enable_notebook()
```

3. Now, let's create a scatter plot with matplotlib:

```
In [3]: X = np.random.normal(0, 1, (100, 3))
        color = np.random.random(100)
        size = 500 * np.random.random(100)
        plt.scatter(X[:,0], X[:,1], c=color,
                    s=size, alpha=0.5, linewidths=2)
        plt.grid(color='lightgray', alpha=0.7)
```

The matplotlib figure is rendered with D3.js instead of the standard matplotlib backend. In particular, the figure is interactive (we can pan and zoom in the figure):

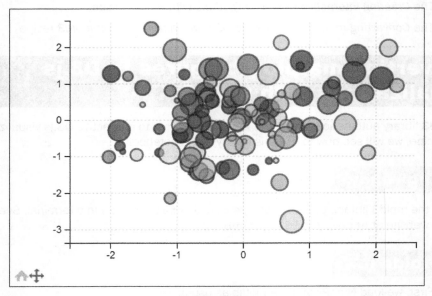

An interactive matplotlib figure with mpld3

4. Now, we create a more complex example with multiple subplots that represent different 2D projections of a 3D dataset. We use the `sharex` and `sharey` keywords in matplotlib's `subplots()` function to automatically bind the x and y axes of the different figures. Panning and zooming in any of the subplots automatically updates all the other subplots:

```
In [4]: fig, ax = plt.subplots(3, 3, figsize=(6, 6),
                               sharex=True, sharey=True)
        fig.subplots_adjust(hspace=0.3)
        X[::2,2] += 3
        for i in range(3):
            for j in range(3):
                ax[i,j].scatter(X[:,i], X[:,j], c=color,
                    s=.1*size, alpha=0.5, linewidths=2)
                ax[i,j].grid(color='lightgray', alpha=0.7)
```

This use case is perfectly handled by mpld3; the D3.js subplots are dynamically linked together:

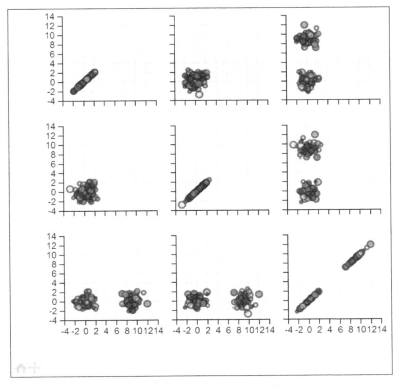

Interactive linked subplots in mpld3

How it works...

mpld3 works by first crawling and exporting a matplotlib figure to JSON (in the context of the **mplexporter** framework). Then, the library generates D3.js code from this JSON representation. This architecture can enable other matplotlib backends besides D3.js.

There's more...

Here are some references:

- ▶ mplexporter available at `http://github.com/mpld3/mplexporter`
- ▶ mpld3 on GitHub available at `https://github.com/jakevdp/mpld3`

▸ The *Creating interactive web visualizations with Bokeh* recipe

▸ The *Visualizing a NetworkX graph in the IPython notebook with D3.js* recipe

Getting started with Vispy for high-performance interactive data visualizations

Most existing plotting or visualization libraries in Python can display small or medium datasets (that contain no more than a few tens of thousands of points). In the *Big Data* era, it is sometimes necessary to display larger datasets.

Vispy (`http://vispy.org`) is a young 2D/3D high-performance visualization library that can display very large datasets. Vispy leverages the computational power of modern Graphics Processing Units (GPUs) through the OpenGL library.

The power of GPUs has been fostered by the video game industry in the last two decades. GPUs are specialized in high-performance, real-time rendering. As such, they are perfectly adapted to interactive scientific plotting.

Vispy offers a Pythonic object-oriented interface to OpenGL, useful to those who know OpenGL or who are willing to learn it. Higher-level graphical interfaces are also being developed at the time of this writing, and experimental versions are already available. These interfaces do not require any knowledge of OpenGL.

In this recipe, we will give a brief introduction to the fundamental concepts of OpenGL. There are two situations where you would need to know these concepts:

▸ If you want to use Vispy today, before the availability of the high-level plotting interfaces

▸ If you want to create custom, sophisticated, high-performance visualizations that are not yet implemented in Vispy

Here, we display a digital signal using Vispy's object-oriented interface to OpenGL.

Getting ready

Vispy depends on NumPy. A backend library is necessary (for example, PyQt4 or PySide).

This recipe has been tested with the development version of Vispy available at `http://github.com/vispy/vispy`. You should clone the GitHub repository and install Vispy with the following command:

```
python setup.py install
```

The API used in this recipe might change in future versions.

How to do it...

1. Let's import NumPy, `vispy.app` (to display a canvas), and `vispy.gloo` (object-oriented interface to OpenGL):

```
In [1]: import numpy as np
        from vispy import app
        from vispy import gloo
```

2. In order to display a window, we need to create a **Canvas**:

```
In [2]: c = app.Canvas(keys='interactive')
```

3. When using `vispy.gloo`, we need to write **shaders**. These programs, written in a C-like language, run on the GPU and give us full flexibility for our visualizations. Here, we create a trivial **vertex shader** that directly displays 2D data points (stored in the `a_position` variable) in the canvas. We will see more details in the next section:

```
In [3]: vertex = """
        attribute vec2 a_position;
        void main (void)
        {
            gl_Position = vec4(a_position, 0.0, 1.0);
        }
        """
```

4. The other shader we need to create is the **fragment shader**. It lets us control the pixels' color. Here, we display all data points in black:

```
In [4]: fragment = """
        void main()
        {
            gl_FragColor = vec4(0.0, 0.0, 0.0, 1.0);
        }
        """
```

5. Next, we create an **OpenGL** `Program`. This object contains shaders and links the shader variables to the NumPy data:

```
In [5]: program = gloo.Program(vertex, fragment)
```

6. We link the `a_position` variable to a *(1000, 2)* NumPy array that contains the coordinates of 1000 data points. In the default coordinate system, the coordinates of the four canvas corners are *(+/-1, +/-1)*:

```
In [6]: program['a_position'] = np.c_[
                np.linspace(-1.0, +1.0, 1000),
                np.random.uniform(-0.5, +0.5, 1000)]
```

7. We create a callback function when the window is being resized. Updating the **OpenGL viewport** lets us ensure that Vispy uses the entire canvas:

```
In [7]: @c.connect
        def on_resize(event):
            gloo.set_viewport(0, 0, *event.size)
```

8. We create a callback function when the canvas needs to be refreshed. This `on_draw()` function renders the entire scene. First, we clear the window in white (it is necessary to do this at every frame). Then, we draw a succession of line segments using our OpenGL program:

```
In [8]: @c.connect
        def on_draw(event):
            gloo.clear((1,1,1,1))
            program.draw('line_strip')
```

9. Finally, we show the canvas and run the application:

```
In [9]: c.show()
        app.run()
```

The following figure shows a screenshot:

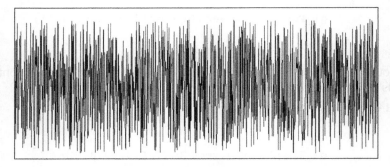

Basic visualization example with Vispy

How it works...

OpenGL is an open standard for hardware-accelerated interactive visualization. It is widely used in video games, industry (**Computer-Aided Design**, or **CAD**), virtual reality, and scientific applications (medical imaging, computer graphics, and so on).

OpenGL is a mature technology created in the early 1990s. In the early 2000s, OpenGL 2.0 brought a major new feature: the possibility to customize fundamental steps of the **rendering pipeline**. This pipeline defines the way data is processed on the GPU for real-time rendering. Many OpenGL courses and tutorials cover the old, fixed pipeline. However, Vispy exclusively supports the modern, programmable pipeline.

Here, we will introduce the fundamental concepts of the programmable pipeline used in this recipe. OpenGL is considerably more complex than what we can cover here. However, Vispy provides a vastly simplified API for the most common features of OpenGL.

 Vispy is based on **OpenGL ES 2.0**, a flavor of OpenGL that is supported on desktop computers, mobile devices, and modern web browsers (through **WebGL**). Modern graphics cards can support additional features. These features will be available in future versions of Vispy.

There are four major elements in the rendering pipeline of a given OpenGL program:

- **Data buffers** store numerical data on the GPU. The main types of buffers are **vertex buffers**, **index buffers**, and **textures**.

- **Variables** are available in the shaders. There are four major types of variables: **attributes**, **uniforms**, **varyings**, and **texture samplers**.

- **Shaders** are GPU programs written in a C-like language called **OpenGL Shading Language** (**GLSL**). The two main types of shaders are **vertex shaders** and **fragment shaders**.

- **The primitive type** defines the way data points are rendered. The main types are points, lines, and triangles.

Here is how the rendering pipeline works:

1. Data is sent to the GPU and stored in buffers.

2. The vertex shader processes the data in parallel and generates a number of 4D points in a normalized coordinate system *(+/-1, +/-1)*. The fourth dimension is a homogeneous coordinate (generally 1).

3. Graphics primitives (points, lines, and triangles) are generated from the data points returned by the vertex shader (**primitive assembly** and **rasterization**).

4. The fragment shader processes all primitive pixels in parallel and returns each pixel's color as RGBA components.

In this recipe's example, there is only one GPU variable: the `a_position` attribute. An **attribute** is a variable that takes one value per data point. **Uniforms** are global variables (shared by all data points), whereas **varyings** are used to pass values from the vertex shader to the fragment shader (with automatic linear interpolation for a pixel between two or three vertices).

In `vispy.gloo`, a `Program` is created with the vertex and fragment shaders. Then, the variables declared in the shaders can be set with the `program['varname'] = value` syntax. When `varname` is an attribute variable, the value can just be a NumPy 2D array. In this array, every line contains the components of every data point.

Similarly, we can declare uniforms and textures in our program.

Finally, the `program.draw()` function renders the data using the specified primitive type. Here, the `line_strip` primitive type tells the GPU to run through all vertices (as returned by the vertex buffer) and to draw a line segment from one point to the next. If there are *n* points, there will be *n-1* line segments.

Other primitive types include points and triangles, with several ways of generating lines or triangles from a list of vertices.

In addition, an index buffer can be provided. An index buffer contains indices pointing to the vertex buffers. Using an index buffer would allow us to reuse any vertex multiple times during the primitive assembly stage. For example, when rendering a cube with a `triangles` primitive type (one triangle is generated for every triplet of points), we can use a vertex buffer with eight data points and an index buffer with thirty-six indices (three points per triangle, two triangles per face, and six faces).

There's more...

The example shown here is extremely simple. The approach provided by OpenGL and Vispy is nevertheless particularly powerful. It gives us full control on the rendering pipeline, and it allows us to leverage the computational power of GPUs in a nearly optimal way.

High performance is achieved by minimizing the number of data transfers to the GPU. When displaying static data (for example, a scatter plot), it is possible to send the data to the GPU at initialization time only. Yet, rendering dynamic data is reasonably fast; the order of magnitude of data transfers is roughly 1 GBps.

Additionally, it is critical to use as few OpenGL draw calls as possible. Every draw incurs a significant overhead. High performance is achieved by rendering all similar primitive types at once (**batch rendering**). GPUs are particularly efficient with batch rendering, even when the properties of the points are different (for example, points with various sizes and colors).

Finally, geometric or pixel transformations can be executed on the GPU with very high performance using the shaders. The massive architecture of GPUs, consisting of hundreds or thousands of computing units, is fully leveraged when transformations are implemented in the shaders.

General-purpose computations can be done in the shaders in the context of visualization. There is one major drawback compared to proper GPGPU frameworks like CUDA or OpenCL: in the vertex shader, a given thread has access to one data point only. Similarly, in the fragment shader, a thread has only access to one pixel. Yet, certain types of simulations or visualization effects require interactions between vertices or pixels. There are ways to mitigate this issue, but they lead to a drop in performance.

However, it is possible to interoperate OpenGL with CUDA/OpenCL. Buffers can be shared between OpenGL and the GPGPU framework. Complex CUDA/OpenCL computations can be implemented on vertex buffers or textures in real-time, leading to highly efficient rendering of numerical simulations.

Vispy for scientific visualization

As we have seen in this recipe, Vispy requires the user to know OpenGL and GLSL. However, higher-level graphical interfaces are currently being developed. These interfaces will bring to scientists the power of GPUs for high-performance interactive visualization.

Visuals will provide reusable, reactive graphical components like shapes, polygons, 3D meshes, graphs, and others. These visuals will be fully customizable and can be used without knowledge of OpenGL. A **shader composition system** will allow advanced users to reuse snippets of GLSL code in a modular way.

Visuals will be organized within a **scene graph** implementing GPU-based **transformations**.

Scientific plotting interfaces will be implemented. Vispy can also serve as a high-performance backend for existing plotting libraries such as matplotlib.

Vispy will also support full integration in the IPython notebook using WebGL.

Eventually, Vispy will be able to implement many kinds of scientific visualizations:

  ▶ Scatter plots can be rendered efficiently with **point sprites**, using one vertex per data point. Panning and zooming can be implemented in the vertex shader, enabling fast interactive visualization of millions of points.

  ▶ Static or dynamic (real-time) digital signals can be displayed with polylines. High-quality rendering of curves can be achieved using an OpenGL implementation of **Anti-Grain Geometry**, a high-quality 2D rendering library.

  ▶ Graphs can be displayed by combining points and line segments.

  ▶ 3D meshes can be displayed with triangles and index buffers. Geometric transformations and realistic lighting can be implemented in the vertex and fragment shaders.

  ▶ Real-time streams of images can be displayed efficiently with textures.

  ▶ Axes, grids, ticks, text, and labels can be rendered efficiently in the fragment shader.

Many examples can be found in Vispy's gallery.

Here are a few references:

  ▶ Vispy's gallery available at `http://vispy.org/gallery.html`

  ▶ A modern OpenGL tutorial, by Nicolas P. Rougier, available at `http://www.loria.fr/~rougier/teaching/opengl/`

- ▶ *Hardware-accelerated interactive data visualization for neuroscience in Python,* an article available at `http://journal.frontiersin.org/Journal/10.3389/fninf.2013.00036/full`

- ▶ The Vispy users mailing list available at `http://groups.google.com/forum/#!forum/vispy`

- ▶ The Vispy-dev mailing list available at `http://groups.google.com/forum/#!forum/vispy-dev`

- ▶ The Anti-Grain Geometry library on Wikipedia, available at `http://en.wikipedia.org/wiki/Anti-Grain_Geometry`

7
Statistical Data Analysis

In this chapter, we will cover the following topics:

- Exploring a dataset with pandas and matplotlib
- Getting started with statistical hypothesis testing – a simple z-test
- Getting started with Bayesian methods
- Estimating the correlation between two variables with a contingency table and a chi-squared test
- Fitting a probability distribution to data with the maximum likelihood method
- Estimating a probability distribution nonparametrically with a kernel density estimation
- Fitting a Bayesian model by sampling from a posterior distribution with a Markov chain Monte Carlo method
- Analyzing data with the R programming language in the IPython notebook

Introduction

In the previous chapters, we reviewed technical aspects of high-performance interactive computing in Python. We now begin the second part of this book by illustrating a variety of scientific questions that can be tackled with Python.

In this chapter, we introduce statistical methods for data analysis. In addition to covering statistical packages such as pandas, statsmodels, and PyMC, we will explain the basics of the underlying mathematical principles. Therefore, this chapter will be most profitable if you have basic experience with probability theory and calculus.

The next chapter, *Chapter 8, Machine Learning*, is closely related; the underlying mathematics is very similar, but the goals are slightly different. In this chapter, we show how to gain insight into real-world data and how to make informed decisions in the presence of uncertainty. In the next chapter, the goal is to *learn from data*, that is, to generalize and to predict outcomes from partial observations.

In this introduction, we will give a broad, high-level overview of the methods we will see in this chapter.

What is statistical data analysis?

The goal of statistical data analysis is to understand a complex, real-world phenomenon from partial and uncertain observations. The uncertainty in the data results in uncertainty in the knowledge we get about the phenomenon. A major goal of the theory is to *quantify* this uncertainty.

It is important to make the distinction between the mathematical theory underlying statistical data analysis, and the decisions made after conducting an analysis. The former is perfectly rigorous; perhaps surprisingly, mathematicians were able to build an exact mathematical framework to deal with uncertainty. Nevertheless, there is a subjective part in the way statistical analysis yields actual human decisions. Understanding the risk and the uncertainty behind statistical results is critical in the decision-making process.

In this chapter, we will see the basic notions, principles, and theories behind statistical data analysis, covering in particular how to make decisions with a quantified risk. Of course, we will always show how to implement these methods with Python.

A bit of vocabulary

There are many terms that need introduction before we get started with the recipes. These notions allow us to classify statistical techniques within multiple dimensions.

Exploration, inference, decision, and prediction

Exploratory methods allow us to get a preliminary look at a dataset through basic statistical aggregates and interactive visualization. We covered these basic methods in the first chapter of this book and in the book *Learning IPython for Interactive Computing and Data Visualization, Packt Publishing*. The first recipe of this chapter, *Exploring a dataset with pandas and matplotlib*, shows another example.

Statistical inference consists of getting information about an unknown process through partial and uncertain observations. In particular, **estimation** entails obtaining approximate quantities for the mathematical variables describing this process. Three recipes in this chapter deal with statistical inference:

> ▸ The *Fitting a probability distribution to data with the maximum likelihood method* recipe

> ▸ The *Estimating a probability distribution nonparametrically with a kernel density estimation* recipe

> ▸ The *Fitting a Bayesian model by sampling from a posterior distribution with a Markov chain Monte Carlo method* recipe

Decision theory allows us to make decisions about an unknown process from random observations, with a controlled risk. The following two recipes show how to make statistical decisions:

> ▸ The *Getting started with statistical hypothesis testing: a simple z-test* recipe

> ▸ The *Estimating the correlation between two variables with a contingency table and a chi-squared test* recipe

Prediction consists of learning from data, that is, predicting the outcomes of a random process based on a limited number of observations. This is the topic of the next chapter, *Chapter 8*, *Machine Learning*.

Univariate and multivariate methods

In most cases, you can consider two dimensions in your data:

> ▸ **Observations** (or **samples**, for machine learning people)

> ▸ **Variables** (or **features**)

Typically, observations are independent realizations of the same random process. Each observation is made of one or several variables. Most of the time, variables are either numbers, or elements belonging to a finite set (that is, taking a finite number of values). The first step in an analysis is to understand what your observations and variables are.

Your problem is **univariate** if you have one variable. It is **bivariate** if you have two variables and **multivariate** if you have at least two variables. Univariate methods are typically simpler. That being said, univariate methods may be used on multivariate data, using one dimension at a time. Although interactions between variables cannot be explored in that case, it is often an interesting first approach.

Frequentist and Bayesian methods

There are at least two different ways of considering uncertainty, resulting in two different classes of methods for inference, decision, and other statistical questions. These are called **frequentist and Bayesian methods**. Some people prefer frequentist methods, while others prefer Bayesian methods.

Frequentists interpret a probability as a **statistical average** across many independent realizations (law of large numbers). Bayesians interpret it as a **degree of belief** (no need for many realizations). The Bayesian interpretation is very useful when only a single trial is considered. In addition, Bayesian theory takes into account our **prior knowledge** about a random process. This prior probability distribution is updated into a posterior distribution as we get more and more data.

Both frequentist and Bayesian methods have their advantages and disadvantages. For instance, one could say that frequentist methods might be easier to apply than Bayesian methods, but more difficult to interpret. For classic misuses of frequentist methods, see `www.refsmmat.com/statistics/`.

In any case, if you are a beginner in statistical data analysis, you probably want to learn the basics of both approaches before choosing sides. This chapter introduces you to both types of methods.

The following recipes are exclusively Bayesian:

  ▶ The *Getting started with Bayesian methods* recipe
  ▶ The *Fitting a Bayesian model by sampling from a posterior distribution with a Markov chain Monte Carlo method* recipe

Jake Vanderplas has written several blog posts about frequentism and Bayesianism, with examples in Python. The first post of the series is available at `http://jakevdp.github.io/blog/2014/03/11/frequentism-and-bayesianism-a-practical-intro/`.

Parametric and nonparametric inference methods

In many cases, you base your analysis on a **probabilistic model**. This model describes how your data is generated. A probabilistic model has no reality; it is only a mathematical object that guides you in your analysis. A good model can be helpful, whereas a bad model may misguide you.

With a **parametric method**, you assume that your model belongs to a known family of probability distributions. The model has one or multiple numerical *parameters* that you can *estimate*.

With a **nonparametric model**, you do not make such an assumption in your model. This gives you more flexibility. However, these methods are typically more complicated to implement and to interpret.

The following recipes are parametric and nonparametric, respectively:

- ▸ The *Fitting a probability distribution to data with the maximum likelihood method* recipe
- ▸ The *Estimating a probability distribution nonparametrically with a kernel density estimation* recipe

This chapter only gives you an idea of the wide range of possibilities that Python offers for statistical data analysis. You can find many books and online courses that cover statistical methods in much greater detail, such as:

- ▸ Statistics on WikiBooks at `http://en.wikibooks.org/wiki/Statistics`
- ▸ Free statistical textbooks available at `http://stats.stackexchange.com/questions/170/free-statistical-textbooks`

Exploring a dataset with pandas and matplotlib

In this first recipe, we will show how to conduct a preliminary analysis of a dataset with pandas. This is typically the first step after getting access to the data. pandas lets us load the data very easily, explore the variables, and make basic plots with matplotlib.

We will take a look at a dataset containing all ATP matches played by four tennis players until 2012. Here, we will focus on Roger Federer.

Getting ready

Download the *Tennis* dataset from the book's GitHub repository at `https://github.com/ipython-books/cookbook-data`, and extract it to the current directory.

How to do it...

1. We import NumPy, pandas, and matplotlib:

```
In [1]: import numpy as np
        import pandas as pd
        import matplotlib.pyplot as plt
        %matplotlib inline
```

2. The dataset is a CSV file, that is, a text file with comma-separated values. pandas lets us load this file with a single function:

```
In [2]: player = 'Roger Federer'
        filename = "data/{name}.csv".format(
                    name=player.replace(' ', '-'))
        df = pd.read_csv(filename)
```

We can have a first look at this dataset by just displaying it in the IPython notebook:

```
In [3]: df
Out[3]: Int64Index: 1179 entries, 0 to 1178
        Data columns (total 70 columns):
        year                        1179  non-null values
        tournament                  1179  non-null values
        . . .
        player2 total points total  1027  non-null values
        dtypes: float64(49), int64(2), object(19)
```

3. There are many columns. Each row corresponds to a match played by Roger Federer. Let's add a Boolean variable indicating whether he has won the match or not. The `tail()` method displays the last rows of the column:

```
In [4]: df['win'] = df['winner'] == player
        df['win'].tail()
Out[4]: 1174      False
        1175      True
        1176      True
        1177      True
        1178      False
        Name: win, dtype: bool
```

4. df['win'] is a Series object. It is very similar to a NumPy array, except that each value has an index (here, the match index). This object has a few standard statistical functions. For example, let's look at the proportion of matches won:

```
In [5]: print(("{player} has won {vic:.0f}% "
               "of his ATP matches.").format(
               player=player, vic=100*df['win'].mean()))
Roger Federer has won 82% of his ATP matches.
```

5. Now, we are going to look at the evolution of some variables across time. The df['start date'] field contains the start date of the tournament as a string. We can convert the type to a date type using the pd.to_datetime() function:

```
In [6]: date = pd.to_datetime(df['start date'])
```

6. We are now looking at the proportion of double faults in each match (taking into account that there are logically more double faults in longer matches!). This number is an indicator of the player's state of mind, his level of self-confidence, his willingness to take risks while serving, and other parameters.

```
In [7]: df['dblfaults'] = (df['player1 double faults'] /
                            df['player1 total points total'])
```

7. We can use the `head()` and `tail()` methods to take a look at the beginning and the end of the column, and `describe()` to get summary statistics. In particular, let's note that some rows have NaN values (that is, the number of double faults is not available for all matches).

```
In [8]: df['dblfaults'].tail()
Out[8]: 1174     0.018116
        1175     0.000000
        1176     0.000000
        1177     0.011561
        1178          NaN
        Name: dblfaults, dtype: float64
In [9]: df['dblfaults'].describe()
Out[9]: count    1027.000000
        mean        0.012129
        std         0.010797
        min         0.000000
        25%         0.004444
        50%         0.010000
        75%         0.018108
        max         0.060606
        dtype: float64
```

8. A very powerful feature in pandas is `groupby()`. This function allows us to group together rows that have the same value in a particular column. Then, we can aggregate this group by value to compute statistics in each group. For instance, here is how we can get the proportion of wins as a function of the tournament's surface:

```
In [10]: df.groupby('surface')['win'].mean()
Out[10]: surface
         Indoor: Carpet    0.736842
         Indoor: Clay      0.833333
         Indoor: Hard      0.836283
         Outdoor: Clay     0.779116
         Outdoor: Grass    0.871429
         Outdoor: Hard     0.842324
         Name: win, dtype: float64
```

9. Now, we are going to display the proportion of double faults as a function of the tournament date, as well as the yearly average. To do this, we also use `groupby()`:

```
In [11]: gb = df.groupby('year')
```

10. `gb` is a `GroupBy` instance. It is similar to a `DataFrame` object, but there are multiple rows per group (all matches played in each year). We can aggregate these rows using the `mean()` operation. We use the matplotlib `plot_date()` function because the x-axis contains dates:

```
In [12]: plt.plot_date(date, df['dblfaults'],
                        alpha=.25, lw=0)
         plt.plot_date(gb['start date'].max(),
                       gb['dblfaults'].mean(), '-', lw=3)
         plt.xlabel('Year')
         plt.ylabel('Proportion of double faults per
                    match.')
```

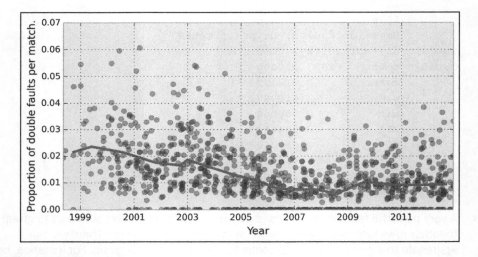

There's more...

pandas is an excellent tool for data wrangling and exploratory analysis. pandas accepts all sorts of formats (text-based, and binary files) and it lets us manipulate tables in many ways. In particular, the `groupby()` function is extremely powerful. This library is covered in much greater detail in a book by Wes McKinney, *Python for Data Analysis*.

What we covered here is only the first step in a data-analysis process. We need more advanced statistical methods to obtain reliable information about the underlying phenomena, make decisions and predictions, and so on. This is the topic of the following recipes.

In addition, more complex datasets demand more sophisticated analysis methods. For example, digital recordings, images, sounds, and videos require specific signal processing treatments before we can apply statistical techniques. These questions will be covered in subsequent chapters.

Getting started with statistical hypothesis testing – a simple z-test

Statistical hypothesis testing allows us to make decisions in the presence of incomplete data. By definition, these decisions are uncertain. Statisticians have developed rigorous methods to evaluate this risk. Nevertheless, some subjectivity is always involved in the decision-making process. The theory is just a tool that helps us make decisions in an uncertain world.

Here, we introduce the most basic ideas behind statistical hypothesis testing. We will follow an extremely simple example: coin tossing. More precisely, we will show how to perform a **z-test**, and we will briefly explain the mathematical ideas underlying it. This kind of method (also called the *frequentist method*), although widely used in science, is subject to many criticisms. We will show later a more modern approach based on Bayesian theory. It is very helpful to understand both approaches, because many studies and publications still follow frequentist methods.

Getting ready

You need to have a basic knowledge of probability theory for this recipe (random variables, distributions, expectancy, variance, central limit theorem, and so on).

How to do it...

Many frequentist methods for hypothesis testing roughly involve the following steps:

1. Writing down the hypotheses, notably the **null hypothesis**, which is the *opposite* of the hypothesis we want to prove (with a certain degree of confidence).
2. Computing a **test statistic**, a mathematical formula depending on the test type, the model, the hypotheses, and the data.
3. Using the computed value to accept the hypothesis, reject it, or fail to conclude.

Here, we flip a coin n times and we observe h heads. We want to know whether the coin is fair (null hypothesis). This example is extremely simple yet quite useful for pedagogical purposes. Besides, it is the basis of many more complex methods.

We denote the Bernoulli distribution by *B(q)* with the unknown parameter *q*. You can refer to `http://en.wikipedia.org/wiki/Bernoulli_distribution` for more information.

A Bernoulli variable is:

  ▸ 0 (tail) with probability *1-q*

  ▸ 1 (head) with probability *q*

Here are the steps required to conduct a simple statistical *z*-test:

1. Let's suppose that after *n=100* flips, we get *h=61* heads. We choose a significance level of 0.05: is the coin fair or not? Our null hypothesis is: *the coin is fair (q = 1/2)*:

```
In [1]: import numpy as np
        import scipy.stats as st
        import scipy.special as sp
In [2]: n = 100   # number of coin flips
        h = 61    # number of heads
        q = .5    # null-hypothesis of fair coin
```

2. Let's compute the **z-score**, which is defined by the following formula (`xbar` is the estimated average of the distribution). We will explain this formula in the next section, *How it works...*.

```
In [3]: xbar = float(h)/n
        z = (xbar - q) * np.sqrt(n / (q*(1-q))); z
Out[3]: 2.1999999999999997
```

3. Now, from the z-score, we can compute the p-value as follows:

```
In [4]: pval = 2 * (1 - st.norm.cdf(z)); pval
Out[4]: 0.02780689502699718
```

4. This p-value is less than 0.05, so we reject the null hypothesis and conclude that *the coin is probably not fair*.

How it works...

The coin tossing experiment is modeled as a sequence of *n* independent random variables $x_i \in \{0,1\}$ following the Bernoulli distribution *B(q)*. Each x_i represents one coin flip. After our experiment, we get actual values (samples) for these variables. A different notation is sometimes used to distinguish between the random variables (probabilistic objects) and the actual values (samples).

The following formula gives the **sample mean** (proportion of heads here):

$$\bar{x} = \frac{1}{n}\sum_i x_i$$

Knowing the expectancy $\mu = q$ and variance $\sigma^2 = q(1-q)$ of the distribution $B(q)$, we compute:

$$E[\overline{x}] = \mu = q$$

$$\mathrm{var}(\overline{x}) = \frac{\sigma^2}{n} = \frac{q(1-q)}{n}$$

The z-test is the normalized version of $\overline{x}$ (we remove its mean, and divide by the standard deviation, thus we get a variable with mean 0 and standard deviation 1):

$$z = \frac{\overline{x} - E[\overline{x}]}{\mathrm{std}(\overline{x})} = (\overline{x} - q)\sqrt{\frac{n}{q(1-q)}}$$

Under the null hypothesis, what is the probability of obtaining a z-test higher than some quantity z_0? This probability is called the (two-sided) **p-value**. According to the central limit theorem, the z-test approximately follows a standard Gaussian distribution $N(0,1)$ for large n, so we get:

$$p = P\left[|z| > z_0\right] = 2P[z > z_0] \simeq 2\left(1 - \Phi(z_0)\right)$$

The following diagram illustrates the z-score and the p-value:

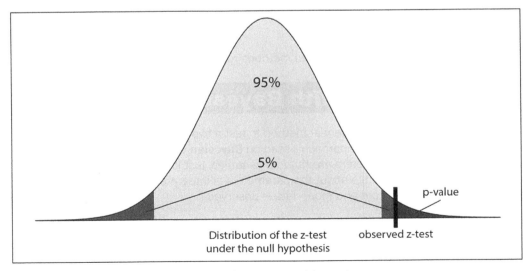

Illustration of the z-score and the p-value

In this formula, Φ is the **cumulative distribution function** of a standard normal distribution. In SciPy, we can get it with `scipy.stats.norm.cdf`. So, given the z-test computed from the data, we compute the p-value: the probability of observing a z-test more extreme than the observed test, under the null hypothesis.

If the p-value is less than five percent (a frequently-chosen significance level, for arbitrary and historical reasons), we conclude that either:

 ▶ The null hypothesis is false, thus we conclude that the coin is unfair.

 ▶ The null hypothesis is true, and it's just bad luck if we obtained these values. We cannot make a conclusion.

We cannot disambiguate between these two options in this framework, but typically the first option is chosen. We hit the limits of frequentist statistics, although there are ways to mitigate this problem (for example, by conducting several independent studies and looking at all of their conclusions).

There's more...

Many statistical tests following this pattern exist. Reviewing all those tests is largely beyond the scope of this book, but you can take a look at the reference at `http://en.wikipedia.org/wiki/Statistical_hypothesis_testing`.

As a p-value is not easy to interpret, it can lead to wrong conclusions, even in peer-reviewed scientific publications. For an in-depth treatment of the subject, see `www.refsmmat.com/statistics/`.

See also

 ▶ The *Getting started with Bayesian methods* recipe

Getting started with Bayesian methods

In the last recipe, we used a frequentist method to test a hypothesis on incomplete data. Here, we will see an alternative approach based on **Bayesian theory**. The main idea is to consider that *unknown parameters are random variables*, just like the variables describing the experiment. Prior knowledge about the parameters is integrated into the model. This knowledge is updated as more and more data is observed.

Frequentists and Bayesians interpret probabilities differently. Frequentists interpret a probability as a limit of frequencies when the number of samples tends to infinity. Bayesians interpret it as a belief; this belief is updated as more and more data is observed.

Here, we revisit the previous coin flipping example with a Bayesian approach. This example is sufficiently simple to permit an analytical treatment. In general, as we will see later in this chapter, analytical results cannot be obtained and numerical methods become essential.

Getting ready

This is a math-heavy recipe. Knowledge of basic probability theory (random variables, distributions, Bayes formula) and calculus (derivatives, integrals) is recommended. We use the same notations as in the previous recipe.

How to do it...

Let q be the probability of obtaining a head. Whereas q was just a fixed number in the previous recipe, we consider here that it is a **random variable**. Initially, this variable follows a distribution called the **prior probability distribution**. It represents our knowledge about q before we start flipping the coin. We will update this distribution after each trial (posterior distribution).

1. First, we assume that q is a *uniform* random variable in the interval [0, 1]. That's our prior distribution: for all q, $P(q)=1$.

2. Then, we flip our coin n times. We note x_i the outcome of the ith flip (0 for tail and 1 for head).

3. What is the probability distribution of q knowing the observations x_i? **Bayes' theorem** allows us to compute the **posterior distribution** analytically (see the next section for the mathematical details):

$$P\left(q \mid \{x_i\}\right) = \frac{P\left(\{x_i\} \mid q\right) P(q)}{\int_0^1 P\left(\{x_i\} \mid q\right) P(q) \, dq} = (n+1) \binom{n}{h} q^h (1-q)^{n-h}$$

4. We define the posterior distribution according to the previous mathematical formula. We remark that this expression is *(n+1)* times the **probability mass function** (**PMF**) of the binomial distribution, which is directly available in `scipy.stats`. (For more information on Binomial distribution, refer to `http://en.wikipedia.org/wiki/Binomial_distribution`.)

```
In [1]: import numpy as np
        import scipy.stats as st
        import matplotlib.pyplot as plt
        %matplotlib inline
In [2]: posterior = lambda n, h, q: ((n+1) *
                                st.binom(n, q).pmf(h))
```

5. Let's plot this distribution for an observation of *h=61* heads and *n=100* total flips:

```
In [3]: n = 100
        h = 61
        q = np.linspace(0., 1., 1000)
        d = posterior(n, h, q)
In [4]: plt.plot(q, d, '-k')
        plt.ylim(0, d.max()+1)
```

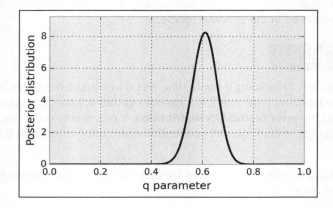

This curve represents our belief about the parameter *q* after we have observed 61 heads.

How it works...

In this section, we explain Bayes' theorem, and we give the mathematical details underlying this example.

Bayes' theorem

There is a very general idea in data science that consists of explaining data with a mathematical model. This is formalized with a one-way process, *model → data*.

Once this process is formalized, the task of the data scientist is to exploit the data to recover information about the model. In other words, we want to *invert* the original process and get *data → model*.

In a probabilistic setting, the direct process is represented as a **conditional probability distribution** *P(data | model)*. This is the probability of observing the data when the model is entirely specified.

Similarly, the inverse process is *P(model | data)*. It gives us information about the model (what we're looking for), knowing the observations (what we have).

Bayes' theorem is at the core of a general framework for inverting a probabilistic process of *model → data*. It can be stated as follows:

$$P(\text{model} \mid \text{data}) = \frac{P(\text{data} \mid \text{model}) \, P(\text{model})}{P(\text{data})}$$

This equation gives us information about our model, knowing the observed data. Bayes' equation is widely used in signal processing, statistics, machine learning, inverse problems, and in many other scientific applications.

In Bayes' equation, *P(model)* reflects our prior knowledge about the model. Also, *P(data)* is the distribution of the data. It is generally expressed as an integral of *P(data|model)P(model)*.

In conclusion, Bayes' equation gives us a general roadmap for data inference:

1. Specify a mathematical model for the direct process *model → data* (the *P(data|model)* term).
2. Specify a prior probability distribution for the model (*P(model) term*).
3. Perform analytical or numerical calculations to solve this equation.

Computation of the posterior distribution

In this recipe's example, we found the posterior distribution with the following equation (deriving directly from Bayes' theorem):

$$P(q \mid \{x_i\}) = \frac{P(\{x_i\} \mid q) P(q)}{\int_0^1 P(\{x_i\} \mid q) P(q) \, dq}$$

Knowing that the x_i are independent, we get (*h* being the number of heads):

$$P(\{x_i\} \mid q) = \prod_{i=1}^{n} P(x_i \mid q) = q^h (1-q)^{n-h}$$

In addition, we can compute analytically the following integral (using an integration by parts and an induction):

$$\int_0^1 P(\{x_i\} \mid q) \, P(q) \, dq = \int_0^1 q^h (1-q)^{n-h} \, dq = \frac{1}{(n+1) \binom{n}{h}}$$

Finally, we get:

$$P\big(q \,|\, \{x_i\}\big) = \frac{P\big(\{x_i\} \,|\, q\big) P(q)}{\int_0^1 P\big(\{x_i\} \,|\, q\big) P(q)\, dq} = (n+1)\binom{n}{h} q^h (1-q)^{n-h}$$

Maximum a posteriori estimation

We can get a point estimate from the posterior distribution. For example, the **maximum a posteriori** (**MAP**) estimation consists of considering the *maximum* of the posterior distribution as an estimate for q. We can find this maximum analytically or numerically. For more information on MAP, refer to `http://en.wikipedia.org/wiki/Maximum_a_posteriori_estimation`.

Here, we can get this estimate analytically by deriving the posterior distribution with respect to q. We get (assuming *1 ≤ h ≤ n-1*):

$$\frac{dP\big(q \,|\, \{x_i\}\big)}{dq} = (n+1)\frac{n!}{(n-h)!h!}\Big(hq^{h-1}(1-q)^{n-h} - (n-h)q^h(1-q)^{n-h-1}\Big)$$

This expression is equal to zero when $q = h/n$. This is the MAP estimate of the parameter q. This value happens to be the proportion of heads obtained in the experiment.

There's more...

In this recipe, we showed a few basic notions in Bayesian theory. We illustrated them with a simple example. The fact that we were able to derive the posterior distribution analytically is not very common in real-world applications. This example is nevertheless informative because it explains the core mathematical ideas behind the complex numerical methods we will see later.

Credible interval

The posterior distribution indicates the plausible values for q given the observations. We could use it to derive a **credible interval**, likely to contain the actual value. Credible intervals are the Bayesian analog to confidence intervals in frequentist statistics. For more information on credible intervals, refer to `http://en.wikipedia.org/wiki/Credible_interval`.

Conjugate distributions

In this recipe, the prior and posterior distributions are **conjugate**, meaning that they belong to the same family (the beta distribution). For this reason, we were able to compute the posterior distribution analytically. You will find more details about conjugate distributions at `http://en.wikipedia.org/wiki/Conjugate_prior`.

Non-informative (objective) prior distributions

We chose a uniform distribution as prior distribution for the unknown parameter q. It is a simple choice and it leads to tractable computations. It reflects the intuitive fact that we do not favor any particular value a priori. However, there are rigorous ways of choosing completely uninformative priors (see http://en.wikipedia.org/wiki/Prior_ probability#Uninformative_priors). An example is the Jeffreys prior, based on the idea that the prior distribution should not depend on the parameterization of the parameters. For more information on Jeffreys prior, refer to http://en.wikipedia.org/wiki/ Jeffreys_prior. In our example, the Jeffreys prior is:

$$P(q) = \frac{1}{\sqrt{q(1-q)}}$$

See also

 ▸ The *Fitting a Bayesian model by sampling from a posterior distribution with a Markov chain Monte Carlo method* recipe

Estimating the correlation between two variables with a contingency table and a chi-squared test

Whereas univariate methods deal with single-variable observations, multivariate methods consider observations with several features. Multivariate datasets allow the study of *relations* between variables, more particularly their correlation or lack thereof (that is, independence).

In this recipe, we will take a look at the same tennis dataset as in the first recipe of this chapter. Following a frequentist approach, we will estimate the correlation between the number of aces and the proportion of points won by a tennis player.

Getting ready

Download the *Tennis* dataset on the book's GitHub repository at https://github.com/ ipython-books/cookbook-data, and extract it in the current directory.

How to do it...

1. Let's import NumPy, pandas, SciPy.stats, and matplotlib:

```
In [1]: import numpy as np
        import pandas as pd
```

```
import scipy.stats as st
import matplotlib.pyplot as plt
%matplotlib inline
```

2. We load the dataset corresponding to Roger Federer:

```
In [2]: player = 'Roger Federer'
        filename = "data/{name}.csv".format(
                 name=player.replace(' ', '-'))
        df = pd.read_csv(filename)
```

3. Each row corresponds to a match, and the 70 columns contain many player characteristics during that match:

```
In [3]: print("Number of columns: " + str(len(df.columns)))
        df[df.columns[:4]].tail()
Number of columns: 70
            year                 tournament   start date
     1174   2012   Australian Open, Australia   16.01.2012
     1175   2012                 Doha, Qatar   02.01.2012
     1176   2012                 Doha, Qatar   02.01.2012
     1177   2012                 Doha, Qatar   02.01.2012
     1178   2012                 Doha, Qatar   02.01.2012
```

4. Here, we only look at the proportion of points won, and the (relative) number of aces:

```
In [4]: npoints = df['player1 total points total']
        points = df['player1 total points won'] / npoints
        aces = df['player1 aces'] / npoints
In [5]: plt.plot(points, aces, '.')
        plt.xlabel('% of points won')
        plt.ylabel('% of aces')
        plt.xlim(0., 1.)
        plt.ylim(0.)
```

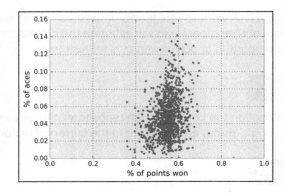

If the two variables were independent, we would not see any trend in the cloud of points. On this plot, it is a bit hard to tell. Let's use pandas to compute a coefficient correlation.

5. We create a new `DataFrame` object with only these fields (note that this step is not compulsory). We also remove the rows where one field is missing (using `dropna()`):

```
In [6]: df_bis = pd.DataFrame({'points': points,
                               'aces': aces}).dropna()
        df_bis.tail()
Out[6]:         aces       points
        1173  0.024390   0.585366
        1174  0.039855   0.471014
        1175  0.046512   0.639535
        1176  0.020202   0.606061
        1177  0.069364   0.531792
```

6. Let's compute the Pearson's correlation coefficient between the relative number of aces in the match, and the number of points won:

```
In [7]: df_bis.corr()
Out[7]:           aces       points
        aces    1.000000   0.255457
        points  0.255457   1.000000
```

A correlation of ~0.26 seems to indicate a positive correlation between our two variables. In other words, the more aces in a match, the more points the player wins (which is not very surprising!).

7. Now, to determine if there is a *statistically significant* correlation between the variables, we use a **chi-squared test** of the independence of variables in a **contingency table**.

8. First, we binarize our variables. Here, the value corresponding to the number of aces is `True` if the player is serving more aces than usual in a match, and `False` otherwise:

```
In [8]: df_bis['result'] = df_bis['points'] > \
                           df_bis['points'].median()
        df_bis['manyaces'] = df_bis['aces'] > \
                             df_bis['aces'].median()
```

9. Then, we create a contingency table, with the frequencies of all four possibilities (True and True, True and False, and so on):

```
In [9]: pd.crosstab(df_bis['result'], df_bis['manyaces'])
Out[9]: manyaces  False   True
        result
        False      300     214
        True       214     299
```

10. Finally, we compute the chi-squared test statistic and the associated p-value. The null hypothesis is the independence between the variables. SciPy implements this test in `scipy.stats.chi2_contingency`, which returns several objects. We're interested in the second result, which is the p-value:

```
In [10]: st.chi2_contingency(_)
Out[10]: (27.809858855369555,
          1.3384233799633629e-07,
          1L,
          array([[ 257.25024343,  256.74975657],
                 [ 256.74975657,  256.25024343]]))
```

The p-value is much lower than 0.05, so we reject the null hypothesis and conclude that there is a statistically significant correlation between the proportion of aces and the proportion of points won in a match (for Roger Federer!).

> As always, correlation does not imply causation. Here, it is likely that external factors influence both variables. See http://en.wikipedia.org/wiki/Correlation_does_not_imply_causation for more details.

How it works...

We give here a few details about the statistical concepts used in this recipe.

Pearson's correlation coefficient

Pearson's correlation coefficient measures the linear correlation between two random variables, *X* and *Y*. It is a normalized version of the covariance:

$$\rho \frac{\text{cov}(X, Y)}{\sqrt{\text{var}(X)\text{var}(Y)}} = \frac{E\big((X - E(X))(Y - E(Y))\big)}{\sqrt{\text{var}(X)\text{var}(Y)}}$$

It can be estimated by substituting, in this formula, the expectancy with the sample mean, and the variance with the sample variance. More details about its inference can be found at http://en.wikipedia.org/wiki/Pearson_product-moment_correlation_coefficient.

Contingency table and chi-squared test

The contingency table contains the frequencies O_{ij} of all combinations of outcomes, when there are multiple random variables that can take a finite number of values. Under the null hypothesis of independence, we can compute the *expected* frequencies E_{ij}, based on the marginal sums (sums in each row). The chi-squared statistic, by definition, is:

$$\chi = \sum_{i,j} \frac{\left(O_{ij} - E_{ij}\right)^2}{E_{ij}}$$

When there are sufficiently many observations, this variable approximately follows a chi-squared distribution (the distribution of the sum of normal variables squared). Once we get the p-value, as explained in the *Getting started with statistical hypothesis testing – a simple z-test* recipe, we can reject or accept the null hypothesis of independence. Then, we can conclude (or not) that there exists a significant correlation between the variables.

There's more...

There are many other sorts of chi-squared tests, that is, tests where the test statistic follows a chi-squared distribution. These tests are widely used for testing the goodness-of-fit of a distribution, or testing the independence of variables. More information can be found in the following pages:

- Chi2 test in SciPy documentation available at `http://docs.scipy.org/doc/scipy/reference/generated/scipy.stats.chi2_contingency.html`
- Contingency table introduced at `http://en.wikipedia.org/wiki/Contingency_table`
- Chi-squared test introduced at `http://en.wikipedia.org/wiki/Pearson's_chi-squared_test`

See also

- The *Getting started with statistical hypothesis testing – a simple z-test* recipe

Fitting a probability distribution to data with the maximum likelihood method

A good way to explain a dataset is to apply a probabilistic model to it. Finding an adequate model can be a job in its own. Once a model is chosen, it is necessary to compare it to the data. This is what statistical estimation is about. In this recipe, we apply the **maximum likelihood method** on a dataset of survival times after heart transplant (1967-1974 study).

Getting ready

As usual in this chapter, a background in probability theory and real analysis is recommended. In addition, you need the statsmodels package to retrieve the test dataset. For more information on statsmodels, refer to `http://statsmodels.sourceforge.net`. On Anaconda, you can install statsmodel with the `conda install statsmodels` command.

How to do it...

1. statsmodels is a Python package for conducting statistical data analyses. It also contains real-world datasets that we can use when experimenting with new methods. Here, we load the *heart* dataset:

    ```
    In [1]: import numpy as np
            import scipy.stats as st
            import statsmodels.datasets as ds
            import matplotlib.pyplot as plt
            %matplotlib inline
    In [2]: data = ds.heart.load_pandas().data
    ```

2. Let's take a look at this `DataFrame`:

    ```
    In [3]: data.tail()
    Out[3]:      survival   censors    age
            64         14         1   40.3
            65        167         0   26.7
            66        110         0   23.7
            67         13         0   28.9
            68          1         0   35.2
    ```

    This dataset contains censored and uncensored data: a censor of 0 means that the patient was alive at the end of the study, and thus we don't know the exact survival time. We only know that the patient survived *at least* the indicated number of days. For simplicity here, we only keep uncensored data (we thereby introduce a bias toward patients that did not survive very long after their transplant):

    ```
    In [4]: data = data[data.censors==1]
            survival = data.survival
    ```

3. Let's take a look at the data graphically, by plotting the raw survival data and the histogram:

    ```
    In [5]: plt.subplot(121)
            plt.plot(sorted(survival)[::-1], 'o')
            plt.xlabel('Patient')
            plt.ylabel('Survival time (days)')
            plt.subplot(122)
            plt.hist(survival, bins=15)
    ```

```
plt.xlabel('Survival time (days)')
plt.ylabel('Number of patients')
```

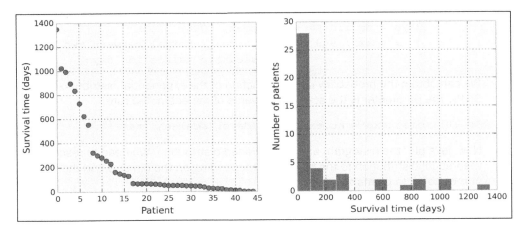

4. We observe that the histogram is decreasing very rapidly. Fortunately, the survival rates today are much higher (~70 percent after 5 years). Let's try to fit an exponential distribution (more information on the exponential distribution is available at `http://en.wikipedia.org/wiki/Exponential_distribution`) to the data. According to this model, S (number of days of survival) is an exponential random variable with the parameter λ, and the observations s_i are sampled from this distribution. Let the sample mean be:

$$\overline{s} = \frac{1}{n}\sum s_i$$

The likelihood function of an exponential distribution is as follows, by definition (see proof in the next section):

$$\mathcal{L}\left(\lambda,\{s_i\}\right) = P\left(\{s_i\} \mid \lambda\right) = \lambda^n \exp\left(-\lambda n\overline{s}\right)$$

The **maximum likelihood estimate** for the rate parameter is, by definition, the value λ that maximizes the likelihood function. In other words, it is the parameter that maximizes the probability of observing the data, assuming that the observations are sampled from an exponential distribution.

Here, it can be shown that the likelihood function has a maximum value when $\lambda = 1/\overline{s}$, which is the maximum likelihood estimate for the rate parameter. Let's compute this parameter numerically:

```
In [6]: smean = survival.mean()
        rate = 1./smean
```

5. To compare the fitted exponential distribution to the data, we first need to generate linearly spaced values for the x-axis (days):

```
In [7]: smax = survival.max()
        days = np.linspace(0., smax, 1000)
        dt = smax / 999.  # bin size: interval between two
                          # consecutive values in `days`
```

We can obtain the probability density function of the exponential distribution with SciPy. The parameter is the scale, the inverse of the estimated rate.

```
In [8]: dist_exp = st.expon.pdf(days, scale=1./rate)
```

6. Now, let's plot the histogram and the obtained distribution. We need to rescale the theoretical distribution to the histogram (depending on the bin size and the total number of data points):

```
In [9]: nbins = 30
        plt.hist(survival, nbins)
        plt.plot(days, dist_exp*len(survival)*smax/nbins,
                 '-r', lw=3)
```

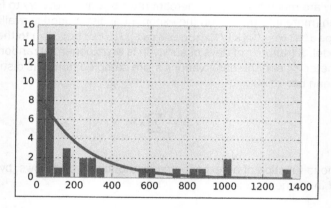

The fit is far from perfect. We were able to find an analytical formula for the maximum likelihood estimate here. In more complex situations, that is not always possible. Thus we may need to resort to numerical methods. SciPy actually integrates numerical maximum likelihood routines for a large number of distributions. Here, we use this other method to estimate the parameter of the exponential distribution.

```
In [10]: dist = st.expon
         args = dist.fit(survival); args
Out[10]: (0.99999999994836486, 222.28880590143666)
```

7. We can use these parameters to perform a **Kolmogorov-Smirnov test**, which assesses the goodness of fit of the distribution with respect to the data. This test is based on a distance between the **empirical distribution function** of the data and the **cumulative distribution function** (**CDF**) of the reference distribution.

```
In [11]: st.kstest(survival, dist.cdf, args)
Out[11]: (0.36199685486406347, 8.6470960143358866e-06)
```

The second output value is the p-value. Here, it is very low: the null hypothesis (stating that the observed data stems from an exponential distribution with a maximum likelihood rate parameter) can be rejected with high confidence. Let's try another distribution, the **Birnbaum-Sanders distribution**, which is typically used to model failure times. (More information on the Birnbaum-Sanders distribution is available at http://en.wikipedia.org/wiki/Birnbaum-Saunders_distribution.)

```
In [12]: dist = st.fatiguelife
         args = dist.fit(survival)
         st.kstest(survival, dist.cdf, args)
Out[12]: (0.18773446101946889, 0.073211497000863268)
```

This time, the p-value is 0.07, so that we would not reject the null hypothesis with a five percent confidence level. When plotting the resulting distribution, we observe a better fit than with the exponential distribution:

```
In [13]: dist_fl = dist.pdf(days, *args)
         nbins = 30
         plt.hist(survival, nbins)
         plt.plot(days, dist_exp*len(survival)*smax/nbins,
                  '-r', lw=3, label='exp')
         plt.plot(days, dist_fl*len(survival)*smax/nbins,
                  '-g', lw=3, label='BS')
         plt.xlabel("Survival time (days)")
         plt.ylabel("Number of patients")
         plt.legend()
```

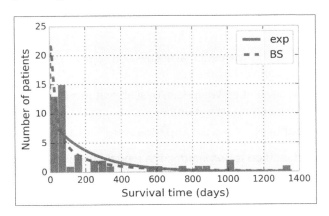

How it works...

Here, we give the calculations leading to the maximum likelihood estimation of the rate parameter for an exponential distribution:

$$\mathcal{L}(\lambda, \{s_i\}) = P(\{s_i\} \mid \lambda)$$

$$= \prod_{i=1}^{n} P(s_i \mid \lambda) \qquad \text{(by independence of the } s_i\text{)}$$

$$= \prod_{i=1}^{n} \lambda \exp(-\lambda s_i)$$

$$= \lambda^n \exp\left(-\lambda \sum_{i=1}^{n} s_i\right)$$

$$= \lambda^n \exp(-\lambda n \overline{s})$$

Here, $\overline{s}$ is the sample mean. In more complex situations, we would require numerical optimization methods in which the principle is to maximize the likelihood function using a standard numerical optimization algorithm (see *Chapter 9, Numerical Optimization*).

To find the maximum of this function, let's compute its derivative function with respect to λ:

$$\frac{d\mathcal{L}(\lambda, \{s_i\})}{d\lambda} = \lambda^{n-1} \exp(-\lambda n \overline{s})(n - n\lambda \overline{s})$$

The root of this derivative is therefore $\lambda = 1 / \overline{s}$

There's more...

Here are a few references:

- Maximum likelihood on Wikipedia, available at http://en.wikipedia.org/wiki/Maximum_likelihood
- Kolmogorov-Smirnov test on Wikipedia, available at http://en.wikipedia.org/wiki/Kolmogorov-Smirnov_test
- Goodness of fit at http://en.wikipedia.org/wiki/Goodness_of_fit

The maximum likelihood method is *parametric*: the model belongs to a prespecified parametric family of distributions. In the next recipe, we will see a nonparametric kernel-based method.

See also

▶ The *Estimating a probability distribution nonparametrically with a kernel density estimation* recipe

Estimating a probability distribution nonparametrically with a kernel density estimation

In the previous recipe, we applied a **parametric estimation method**. We had a statistical model (the exponential distribution) describing our data, and we estimated a single parameter (the rate of the distribution). **Nonparametric estimation** deals with statistical models that do not belong to a known family of distributions. The parameter space is then *infinite-dimensional* instead of finite-dimensional (that is, we estimate *functions* rather than *numbers*).

Here, we use a **kernel density estimation** (**KDE**) to estimate the density of probability of a spatial distribution. We look at the geographical locations of tropical cyclones from 1848 to 2013, based on data provided by the NOAA, the US' National Oceanic and Atmospheric Administration.

Getting ready

Download the *Storms* dataset from the book's GitHub repository at `https://github.com/ipython-books/cookbook-data`, and extract it in the current directory. The data was obtained from `www.ncdc.noaa.gov/ibtracs/index.php?name=wmo-data`.

You also need matplotlib's toolkit **basemap**, available at `http://matplotlib.org/basemap/`. With Anaconda, you can install it with conda install basemap. Windows users can also find an installer at `www.lfd.uci.edu/~gohlke/pythonlibs/`.

How to do it...

1. Let's import the usual packages. The kernel density estimation with a Gaussian kernel is implemented in SciPy.stats:

```
In [1]: import numpy as np
        import pandas as pd
        import scipy.stats as st
        import matplotlib.pyplot as plt
        from mpl_toolkits.basemap import Basemap
        %matplotlib inline
```

2. Let's open the data with pandas:

```
In [2]: df = pd.read_csv(
            "data/Allstorms.ibtracs_wmo.v03r05.csv")
```

3. The dataset contains information about most storms since 1848. A single storm may appear multiple times across several consecutive days.

```
In [3]: df[df.columns[[0,1,3,8,9]]].head()
Out[3]:      Serial_Num Season Basin  Latitude  Longitude
          0  1848011S09080   1848    SI      -8.6       79.8
          1  1848011S09080   1848    SI      -9.0       78.9
          2  1848011S09080   1848    SI     -10.4       73.2
          3  1848011S09080   1848    SI     -12.8       69.9
          4  1848011S09080   1848    SI     -13.9       68.9
```

4. We use pandas' `groupby()` function to obtain the average location of every storm:

```
In [4]: dfs = df.groupby('Serial_Num')
        pos = dfs[['Latitude', 'Longitude']].mean()
        y, x = pos.values.T
        pos.head()
Out[4]:                   Latitude   Longitude
        Serial_Num
        1848011S09080  -15.918182   71.854545
        1848011S15057  -24.116667   52.016667
        1848061S12075  -20.528571   65.342857
        1851080S15063  -17.325000   55.400000
        1851080S21060  -23.633333   60.200000
```

5. We display the storms on a map with basemap. This toolkit allows us to easily project the geographical coordinates on the map.

```
In [5]: m = Basemap(projection='mill', llcrnrlat=-65,
                    urcrnrlat=85, llcrnrlon=-180,
                    urcrnrlon=180)
        x0, y0 = m(-180, -65)
        x1, y1 = m(180, 85)
        m.drawcoastlines()
        m.fillcontinents(color='#dbc8b2')
        xm, ym = m(x, y)
        m.plot(xm, ym, '.r', alpha=.1)
```

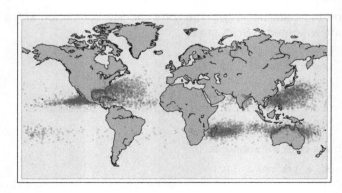

6. To perform the kernel density estimation, we stack the x and y coordinates of the storms into a (2, N) array:

```
In [6]: h = np.vstack((xm, ym))
In [7]: kde = st.gaussian_kde(h)
```

7. The `gaussian_kde()` routine returned a Python function. To see the results on a map, we need to evaluate this function on a 2D grid spanning the entire map. We create this grid with `meshgrid()`, and we pass the x and y values to the `kde` function. `kde` accepts a (2, N) array as input, requiring us to tweak the shape of the array:

```
In [8]: k = 50
        tx, ty = np.meshgrid(np.linspace(x0, x1, 2*k),
                             np.linspace(y0, y1, k))
        v = kde(np.vstack((tx.ravel(),
                           ty.ravel()))).reshape((k, 2*k))
```

8. Finally, we display the estimated density with `imshow()`:

```
In [9]: m.drawcoastlines()
        m.fillcontinents(color='#dbc8b2')
        xm, ym = m(x, y)
        m.imshow(v, origin='lower', extent=[x0,x1,y0,y1],
                 cmap=plt.get_cmap('Reds'))
```

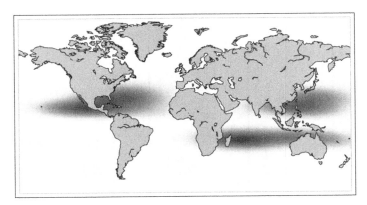

How it works...

The **kernel density estimator** of a set of *n* points {x} is given as:

$$\hat{f}_h(x) = \frac{1}{nh}\sum_{i=1}^{n} K\left(\frac{x-x_i}{h}\right)$$

Here, *h>0* is a scaling parameter (the **bandwidth**) and *K(u)* is the **kernel**, a symmetric function that integrates to 1. This estimator is to be compared with a classical histogram, where the kernel would be a *top-hat* function (a rectangle function taking its values in *{0,1}*), but the blocks would be located on a regular grid instead of the data points. For more information on kernel density estimator, refer to `http://en.wikipedia.org/wiki/Kernel_density_estimation`.

Multiple kernels can be chosen. Here, we chose a **Gaussian kernel**, so that the KDE is the superposition of Gaussian functions centered on all the data points. It is an estimation of the density.

The choice of the bandwidth is not trivial; there is a tradeoff between a too low value (small bias, high variance: overfitting) and a too high value (high bias, small variance: underfitting). We will return to this important concept of **bias-variance tradeoff** in the next chapter. For more information on the bias-variance tradeoff, refer to `http://en.wikipedia.org/wiki/Bias-variance_dilemma`.

The following figure illustrates the KDE. The dataset contains four points in *[0,1]* (black lines). The estimated density is a smooth curve, represented here with multiple bandwidth values.

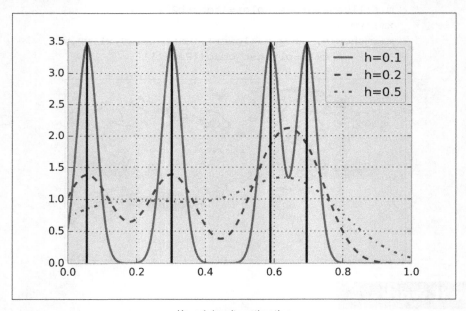

Kernel density estimation

 There are other KDE implementations in statsmodels and scikit-learn. You can find more information at `http://jakevdp.github.io/blog/2013/12/01/kernel-density-estimation/`.

See also

▸ The *Fitting a probability distribution to data with the maximum likelihood method* recipe

Fitting a Bayesian model by sampling from a posterior distribution with a Markov chain Monte Carlo method

In this recipe, we illustrate a very common and useful method for characterizing a posterior distribution in a Bayesian model. Imagine that you have some data and you want to obtain information about the underlying random phenomenon. In a frequentist approach, you could try to fit a probability distribution within a given family of distributions, using a parametric method such as the maximum likelihood method. The optimization procedure would yield parameters that maximize the probability of observing the data if given the null hypothesis.

In a Bayesian approach, you consider the parameters themselves as random variables. Their prior distributions reflect your initial knowledge about these parameters. After the observations, your knowledge is updated, and this is reflected in the posterior distributions of the parameters.

A typical goal for Bayesian inference is to characterize the posterior distributions. Bayes' theorem gives an analytical way to do this, but it is often impractical in real-world problems due to the complexity of the models and the number of dimensions. A **Markov chain Monte Carlo** method, such as the **Metropolis-Hastings algorithm**, gives a numerical method to approximate a posterior distribution.

Here, we introduce the **PyMC** package, which gives an effective and natural interface for fitting a probabilistic model to data in a Bayesian framework. We will look at the annual frequency of storms in the northern Atlantic Ocean since the 1850s using data from NOAA, the US' National Oceanic and Atmospheric Administration.

This recipe is largely inspired by a tutorial on PyMC's website (see the link in the *There's more...* section).

Getting ready

You can find the instructions to install PyMC on the package's website. In this recipe, we will use PyMC2. The new version (PyMC3) is still in development at the time of writing, and it is likely to be significantly different. For more information on PyMC, refer to `http://pymc-devs.github.io/pymc/`. With Anaconda, you can try `conda install -c https://conda.binstar.org/pymc pymc`. Windows users can also find an installer at `www.lfd.uci.edu/~gohlke/pythonlibs/`.

You also need to download the *Storms* dataset from the book's GitHub repository at `https://github.com/ipython-books/cookbook-data` and extract it in the current directory.

How to do it...

1. Let's import the standard packages and PyMC:

```
In [1]: import numpy as np
        import pandas as pd
        import pymc
        import matplotlib.pyplot as plt
        %matplotlib inline
```

2. Let's import the data with pandas:

```
In [2]: df = pd.read_csv(
            "data/Allstorms.ibtracs_wmo.v03r05.csv",
            delim_whitespace=False)
```

3. With pandas, it only takes a single line of code to get the annual number of storms in the North Atlantic Ocean. We first select the storms in that basin (`NA`), then we group the rows by year (`Season`), and then we take the number of unique storms (`Serial_Num`), as each storm can span several days (the `nunique()` method):

```
In [3]: cnt = df[df['Basin'] == ' NA'].groupby('Season') \
                        ['Serial_Num'].nunique()
        years = cnt.index
        y0, y1 = years[0], years[-1]
        arr = cnt.values
        plt.plot(years, arr, '-ok')
        plt.xlim(y0, y1)
        plt.xlabel("Year")
        plt.ylabel("Number of storms")
```

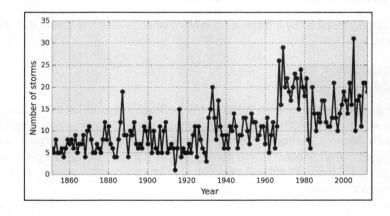

4. Now, we define our probabilistic model. We assume that storms arise following a time-dependent Poisson process with a deterministic rate. We assume that this rate is a piecewise-constant function that takes a first value `early_mean` before a switch point `switchpoint`, and a second value `late_mean` after that point. These three unknown parameters are treated as random variables (we will describe them more in the *How it works...* section).

A Poisson process (`http://en.wikipedia.org/wiki/Poisson_process`) is a particular **point process**, that is, a stochastic process describing the random occurrence of instantaneous events. The Poisson process is fully random: the events occur independently at a given rate. See also *Chapter 13, Stochastic Dynamical Systems*.

```
In [4]: switchpoint = pymc.DiscreteUniform('switchpoint',
                                            lower=0,
                                            upper=len(arr))
        early_mean = pymc.Exponential('early_mean', beta=1)
        late_mean = pymc.Exponential('late_mean', beta=1)
```

5. We define the piecewise-constant rate as a Python function:

```
In [5]: @pymc.deterministic(plot=False)
        def rate(s=switchpoint, e=early_mean, l=late_mean):
            out = np.empty(len(arr))
            out[:s] = e
            out[s:] = l
            return out
```

6. Finally, the observed variable is the annual number of storms. It follows a Poisson variable with a random mean (the rate of the underlying Poisson process). This fact is a known mathematical property of Poisson processes.

```
In [6]: storms = pymc.Poisson('storms', mu=rate, value=arr,
                              observed=True)
```

7. Now, we use the MCMC method to sample from the posterior distribution, given the observed data. The `sample()` method launches the fitting iterative procedure:

```
In [7]: model = pymc.Model([switchpoint, early_mean,
                            late_mean,
                            rate, storms])
In [8]: mcmc = pymc.MCMC(model)
        mcmc.sample(iter=10000, burn=1000, thin=10)
         [----       17%              ] 1774 of 10000 complete
         [----------100%-----------] 10000 of 10000 complete
```

8. Let's plot the sampled Markov chains. Their stationary distribution corresponds to the posterior distribution we want to characterize.

```
In [9]: plt.subplot(311)
        plt.plot(mcmc.trace('switchpoint')[:])
        plt.ylabel("Switch point")
        plt.subplot(312)
        plt.plot(mcmc.trace('early_mean')[:])
        plt.ylabel("Early mean")
        plt.subplot(313)
        plt.plot(mcmc.trace('late_mean')[:])
        plt.xlabel("Iteration")
        plt.ylabel("Late mean")
```

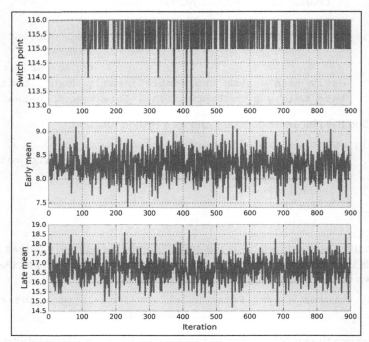

9. We also plot the distribution of the samples, which correspond to the posterior distributions of our parameters, after the data points have been taken into account:

```
In [10]: plt.subplot(131)
         plt.hist(mcmc.trace('switchpoint')[:] + y0, 15)
         plt.xlabel("Switch point")
         plt.ylabel("Distribution")
         plt.subplot(132)
         plt.hist(mcmc.trace('early_mean')[:], 15)
         plt.xlabel("Early mean")
```

```
plt.subplot(133)
plt.hist(mcmc.trace('late_mean')[:], 15)
plt.xlabel("Late mean")
```

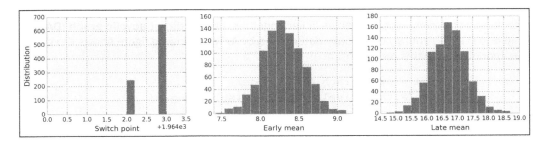

10. Taking the sample mean of these distributions, we get posterior estimates for the three unknown parameters, including the year where the frequency of storms suddenly increased:

```
In [11]: yp = y0 + mcmc.trace('switchpoint')[:].mean()
         em = mcmc.trace('early_mean')[:].mean()
         lm = mcmc.trace('late_mean')[:].mean()
         print((yp, em, lm))
(1966.681111111111, 8.2843072252292682, 16.728831395584947)
```

11. Now, we can plot the estimated rate on top of the observations:

```
In [12]: plt.plot(years, arr, '-ok')
         plt.axvline(yp, color='k', ls='--')
         plt.plot([y0, yp], [em, em], '-b', lw=3)
         plt.plot([yp, y1], [lm, lm], '-r', lw=3)
         plt.xlim(y0, y1)
         plt.xlabel("Year")
         plt.ylabel("Number of storms")
```

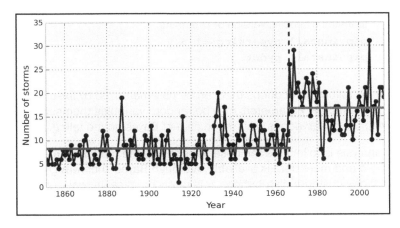

How it works...

The general idea is to define a Bayesian probabilistic model and to fit it to the data. This model may be the starting point of an estimation or decision task. The model is essentially described by stochastic or deterministic variables linked together within a **direct acyclic graph** (**DAG**). *A* is linked to *B* if *B* is entirely or partially determined by *A*. The following figure shows the graph of the model used in this recipe:

```
In [13]: graph = pymc.graph.graph(model)
         from IPython.display import display_png
         display_png(graph.create_png(), raw=True)
```

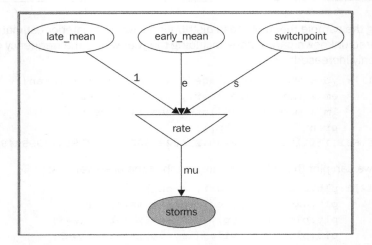

 As you can see, PyMC can create graph representations of the models. You need to install GraphViz (refer to www.graphviz.org), pydot, and pyparsing. Because of an unfortunate bug, you might need to install a specific version of pyparsing:

```
pip install pyparsing==1.5.7
pip install pydot
```

Stochastic variables follow distributions that can be parameterized by fixed numbers or other variables in the model. Parameters may be random variables themselves, reflecting knowledge prior to the observations. This is the core of Bayesian modeling.

The goal of the analysis is to include the observations into the model in order to update our knowledge as more and more data is available. Although Bayes' theorem gives us an exact way to compute those posterior distributions, it is rarely practical in real-world problems. This is notably due to the complexity of the models. Alternatively, numerical methods have been developed in order to tackle this problem.

The **Markov chain Monte Carlo** (**MCMC**) method used here allows us to sample from a complex distribution by simulating a Markov chain that has the desired distribution as its equilibrium distribution. The **Metropolis-Hastings algorithm** is a particular application of this method to our current example.

This algorithm is implemented in the MCMC class in PyMC. The `burn` parameter determines how many initial iterations are thrown away. This is necessary because it takes a number of iterations for the Markov chain to converge to its equilibrium distribution. The `thin` parameter corresponds to the number of steps to skip in the evaluation of the distribution so as to minimize the autocorrelation of the samples. You will find more information at `http://pymc-devs.github.io/pymc/modelfitting.html`.

There's more...

Here are a few references:

► A great PyMC tutorial that we largely took inspiration from is available at `http://pymc-devs.github.io/pymc/tutorial.html`

► A must-read free e-book on the subject, by Cameron Davidson-Pilon, entirely written in the IPython notebook, available at `http://camdavidsonpilon.github.io/Probabilistic-Programming-and-Bayesian-Methods-for-Hackers/`

► The Markov chain Monte Carlo method introduced at `http://en.wikipedia.org/wiki/Markov_chain_Monte_Carlo`

► The Metropolis-Hastings algorithm introduced at `http://en.wikipedia.org/wiki/Metropolis-Hastings_algorithm`

See also

► The *Getting started with Bayesian methods* recipe

Analyzing data with the R programming language in the IPython notebook

R (`www.r-project.org`) is a free domain-specific programming language for statistics. Its syntax is well-adapted to statistical modeling and data analysis. By contrast, Python's syntax is typically more convenient for general-purpose programming. Luckily, IPython allows you to have the best of both worlds. For example, you can insert R code snippets anywhere in a normal IPython notebook. You can continue using Python and pandas for data loading and wrangling, and switch to R to design and fit statistical models. Using R instead of Python for these tasks is more than a matter of programming syntax; R comes with an impressive statistical toolbox that is still unmatched by Python.

In this recipe, we will show how to use R from IPython, and we illustrate the most basic capabilities of R with a simple data analysis example.

Getting ready

You need the statsmodels package for this recipe. You can find installation instructions in the previous recipe, *Fitting a probability distribution to data with the maximum likelihood method*.

You also need R. There are three steps to use R from IPython. First, install R and rpy2 (R to Python interface). Of course, you only need to do this step once. Then, to use R in an IPython session, you need to load the IPython R extension.

1. Download R for your operating system from `http://cran.r-project.org/mirrors.html` and install it. On Ubuntu, you can do `sudo apt-get install r-base-dev`.

2. Download rpy2 from `http://rpy.sourceforge.net/rpy2.html` and install it. With Anaconda on Linux, you can try `conda install -c https://conda.binstar.org/r rpy2`. Alternatively, you can do `pip install rpy2`.

3. Then, to execute R code in an IPython notebook, execute `%load_ext rmagic` first.

> rpy2 does not appear to work well on Windows. We recommend using Linux or Mac OS X.

How to do it...

Here, we will use the following workflow: first, we load data from Python. Then, we use R to design and fit a model, and to make some plots in the IPython notebook. We could also load data from R, or design and fit a statistical model with Python's statsmodels package, and so on. In particular, the analysis we do here could be done entirely in Python, without resorting to the R language. This recipe merely shows the basics of R and illustrates how R and Python can play together within an IPython session.

1. Let's load the *longley* dataset with the statsmodels package. This dataset contains a few economic indicators in the US from 1947 to 1962. We also load the IPython R extension:

```
In [1]: import statsmodels.datasets as sd
In [2]: data = sd.longley.load_pandas()
In [3]: %load_ext rmagic
```

2. We define x and y as the exogeneous (independent) and endogenous (dependent) variables, respectively. The endogenous variable quantifies the total employment in the country.

```
In [4]: data.endog_name, data.exog_name
Out[4]: ('TOTEMP', ['GNPDEFL', 'GNP', 'UNEMP',
                     'ARMED', 'POP', 'YEAR'])
In [5]: y, x = data.endog, data.exog
```

3. For convenience, we add the endogenous variable to the x DataFrame:

```
In [6]: x['TOTEMP'] = y
In [7]: x
Out[7]:     GNPDEFL      GNP   UNEMP       POP   YEAR   TOTEMP
       0        83.0   234289    2356    107608   1947    60323
       1        88.5   259426    2325    108632   1948    61122
       2        88.2   258054    3682    109773   1949    60171
       ...
       13      114.2   502601    3931    125368   1960    69564
       14      115.7   518173    4806    127852   1961    69331
       15      116.9   554894    4007    130081   1962    70551
```

4. We will make a simple plot in R. First, we need to pass Python variables to R. We can use the `%R -i var1,var2` magic. Then, we can call R's `plot()` command:

```
In [8]: gnp = x['GNP']
        totemp = x['TOTEMP']
In [9]: %R -i totemp,gnp plot(gnp, totemp)
```

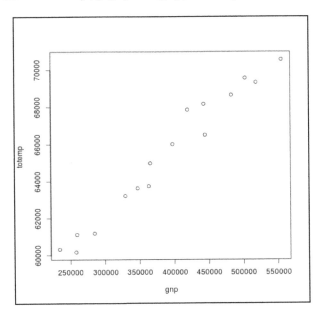

5. Now that the data has been passed to R, we can fit a linear model to the data. The `lm()` function lets us perform a linear regression. Here, we want to express `totemp` (total employment) as a function of the country's GNP:

```
In [10]: %%R
         # Least-squares regression
         fit <- lm(totemp ~ gnp);
         # Display the coefficients of the fit.
         print(fit$coefficients)
         plot(gnp, totemp)  # Plot the data points.
         abline(fit)  # And plot the linear regression.
  (Intercept)          gnp
5.184359e+04 3.475229e-02
```

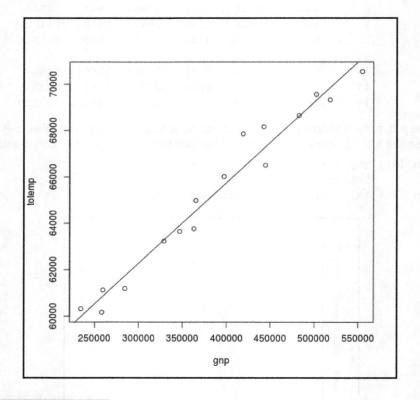

How it works...

The `-i` and `-o` options of the `%R` magic allow us to pass variables back and forth between IPython and R. The variable names need to be separated by commas. You can find more information about the `%R` magic in the documentation available at `http://rpy.sourceforge.net/`.

In R, the tilde (~) expresses the dependence of a dependent variable upon one or several independent variables. The `lm()` function allows us to fit a simple linear regression model to the data. Here, `totemp` is expressed as a function of `gnp`:

$$\text{totemp} = a \times \text{gnp} + b$$

Here, *b* (intercept) and *a* are the coefficients of the linear regression model. These two values are returned by `fit$coefficients` in R, where `fit` is the fitted model.

Our data points do not satisfy this relation exactly, of course. The coefficients are chosen so as to minimize the error between this linear prediction and the actual values. This is typically done by minimizing the following least squares error:

$$r(a,b) = \sum_{i=1}^{n} \left(\text{totemp}_i - \left(a \times \text{gnp}_i + b \right) \right)^2$$

The data points are *(gnp$_i$, totemp$_i$)* here. The coefficients *a* and *b* that are returned by `lm()` make this sum minimal: they fit the data best.

There's more...

Regression is an important statistical concept that we will see in greater detail in the next chapter. Here are a few references:

- ► Regression analysis on Wikipedia, available at `http://en.wikipedia.org/wiki/Regression_analysis`
- ► Least squares method on Wikipedia, available at `en.wikipedia.org/wiki/Linear_least_squares_(mathematics)`

R is an excellent platform for advanced statistics. Python has a few statistical packages such as pandas and statsmodels that implement many common features, but the number of statistical toolboxes in R remains unmatched by Python at this time. Yet, Python has a much wider range of possibilities outside of statistics and is an excellent general-purpose language that comes with an impressive number of various packages.

Thanks to the multilanguage capabilities of IPython, you don't necessarily have to choose between those languages. You can keep using Python and switch to R when you need highly specific statistical features that are still missing in Python.

Here are a few references about R:

- ► Introduction to R available at `http://cran.r-project.org/doc/manuals/R-intro.html`
- ► R tutorial available at `www.cyclismo.org/tutorial/R/`

- ▶ CRAN, or Comprehensive R Archive Network, containing many packages for R, available at `http://cran.r-project.org`

- ▶ IPython and R tutorial available at `http://nbviewer.ipython.org/github/ipython/ipython/blob/master/examples/Builtin%20Extensions/R%20Magics.ipynb`

See also

- ▶ The *Exploring a dataset with pandas and matplotlib* recipe

8

Machine Learning

In this chapter, we will cover the following topics:

- ▸ Getting started with scikit-learn
- ▸ Predicting who will survive on the Titanic with logistic regression
- ▸ Learning to recognize handwritten digits with a K-nearest neighbors classifier
- ▸ Learning from text – Naive Bayes for Natural Language Processing
- ▸ Using support vector machines for classification tasks
- ▸ Using a random forest to select important features for regression
- ▸ Reducing the dimensionality of a dataset with a Principal Component Analysis
- ▸ Detecting hidden structures in a dataset with clustering

Introduction

In the previous chapter, we were interested in getting insight into data, understanding complex phenomena through partial observations, and making informed decisions in the presence of uncertainty. Here, we are still interested in analyzing and processing data using statistical tools. However, the goal is not necessarily to *understand* the data, but to *learn* from it.

Learning from data is close to what we do as humans. From our experience, we intuitively learn general facts and relations about the world, even if we don't fully understand their complexity. The increasing computational power of computers makes them able to learn from data too. That's the heart of **machine learning**, a modern and fascinating branch of artificial intelligence, computer science, statistics, and applied mathematics. For more information on machine learning, refer to http://en.wikipedia.org/wiki/Machine_learning.

This chapter is a hands-on introduction to some of the most basic methods in machine learning. These methods are routinely used by data scientists. We will use these methods with **scikit-learn**, a popular and user-friendly Python package for machine learning.

A bit of vocabulary

In this introduction, we will explain the fundamental definitions and concepts of machine learning.

Learning from data

In machine learning, most data can be represented as a table of numerical values. Every row is called an **observation**, a **sample**, or a **data point**. Every column is called a **feature** or a **variable**.

Let's call N the number of rows (or the number of points) and D the number of columns (or number of features). The number D is also called the **dimensionality** of the data. The reason is that we can view this table as a set E of **vectors** in a space with D dimensions (or **vector space**). Here, a vector **x** contains D numbers $(x_1, ..., x_D)$, also called **components**. This mathematical point of view is very useful and we will use it throughout this chapter.

We generally make the distinction between supervised learning and unsupervised learning:

- **Supervised learning** is when we have a **label** y associated with a data point x. The goal is to *learn* the mapping from x to y from our data. The data gives us this mapping for a finite set of points, but what we want is to *generalize* this mapping to the full set E.

- **Unsupervised learning** is when we don't have any labels. What we want to do is discover some form of hidden structure in the data.

Supervised learning

Mathematically, supervised learning consists of finding a function f that maps the set of points E to a set of labels F, knowing a finite set of associations (x, y), which is given by our data. This is what *generalization* is about: after observing the pairs (x, y), given a new x, we are able to find the corresponding y by applying the function f to x. For more information on supervised learning, refer to `http://en.wikipedia.org/wiki/Supervised_learning`.

It is a common practice to split the set of data points into two subsets: the **training set** and the **test set**. We learn the function f on the training set and test it on the test set. This is essential when assessing the predictive power of a model. By training and testing a model on the same set, our model might not be able to generalize well. This is the fundamental concept of **overfitting**, which we will detail later in this chapter.

We generally make the distinction between classification and regression, two particular instances of supervised learning.

Classification is when our labels *y* can only take a finite set of values (categories). Examples include:

▶ **Handwritten digit recognition**: *x* is an image with a handwritten digit; *y* is a digit between 0 and 9

▶ **Spam filtering**: *x* is an e-mail and *y* is 1 or 0, depending on whether that e-mail is spam or not

Regression is when our labels *y* can take any real (continuous) value. Examples include:

▶ Predicting stock market data

▶ Predicting sales

▶ Detecting the age of a person from a picture

A classification task yields a division of our space *E* in different regions (also called **partition**), each region being associated to one particular value of the label *y*. A regression task yields a mathematical model that associates a real number to any point *x* in the space *E*. This difference is illustrated in the following figure:

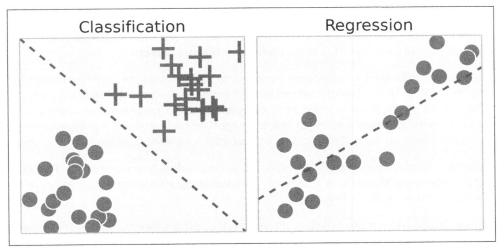

Difference between classification and regression

Classification and regression can be combined. For example, in the **probit model**, although the dependent variable is binary (classification), the *probability* that this variable belongs to one category can also be modeled (regression). We will see an example in the recipe about logistic regression. For more information on the probit model, refer to http://en.wikipedia.org/wiki/Probit_model.

Unsupervised learning

Broadly speaking, unsupervised learning helps us discover systemic structures in our data. This is harder to grasp than supervised learning, in that there is generally no precise question and answer. For more information on unsupervised learning, refer to `http://en.wikipedia.org/wiki/Unsupervised_learning`.

Here are a few important terms related to unsupervised learning:

- **Clustering**: Grouping similar points together within **clusters**
- **Density estimation**: Estimating a probability density function that can explain the distribution of the data points
- **Dimension reduction**: Getting a simple representation of high-dimensional data points by projecting them onto a lower-dimensional space (notably for **data visualization**)
- **Manifold learning**: Finding a low-dimensional manifold containing the data points (also known as **nonlinear dimension reduction**)

Feature selection and feature extraction

In a supervised learning context, when our data contains many features, it is sometimes necessary to choose a subset of them. The features we want to keep are those that are most relevant to our question. This is the problem of **feature selection**.

Additionally, we might want to extract new features by applying complex transformations on our original dataset. This is **feature extraction**. For example, in computer vision, training a classifier directly on the pixels is not the most efficient method in general. We might want to extract the relevant points of interest or make appropriate mathematical transformations. These steps depend on our dataset and on the questions we want to answer.

For example, it is often necessary to preprocess the data before learning models. **Feature scaling** (or **data normalization**) is a common **preprocessing** step where features are linearly rescaled to fit in the range *[-1,1]* or *[0,1]*.

Feature extraction and feature selection involve a balanced combination of domain expertise, intuition, and mathematical methods. These early steps are crucial, and they might be even more important than the learning steps themselves. The reason is that the few dimensions that are relevant to our problem are generally hidden in the high dimensionality of our dataset. We need to uncover the low-dimensional structure of interest to improve the efficiency of the learning models.

We will see a few feature selection and feature extraction methods in this chapter. Methods that are specific to signals, images, or sounds will be covered in *Chapter 10, Signal Processing,* and *Chapter 11, Image and Audio Processing*.

Here are a few further references:

- ▸ Feature selection in scikit-learn, documented at `http://scikit-learn.org/stable/modules/feature_selection.html`
- ▸ Feature selection on Wikipedia at `http://en.wikipedia.org/wiki/Feature_selection`

Overfitting, underfitting, and the bias-variance tradeoff

A central notion in machine learning is the trade-off between **overfitting** and **underfitting**. A model may be able to represent our data accurately. However, if it is *too* accurate, it might not generalize well to unobserved data. For example, in facial recognition, a too-accurate model would be unable to identify someone who styled their hair differently that day. The reason is that our model might learn irrelevant features in the training data. On the contrary, an insufficiently trained model would not generalize well either. For example, it would be unable to correctly recognize twins. For more information on overfitting, refer to `http://en.wikipedia.org/wiki/Overfitting`.

A popular solution to reduce overfitting consists of adding *structure* to the model, for example, with **regularization**. This method favors simpler models during training (Occam's razor). You will find more information at `http://en.wikipedia.org/wiki/Regularization_%28mathematics%29`.

The **bias-variance dilemma** is closely related to the issue of overfitting and underfitting. The **bias** of a model quantifies how precise it is across training sets. The **variance** quantifies how sensitive the model is to small changes in the training set. A **robust** model is not overly sensitive to small changes. The dilemma involves minimizing both bias and variance; we want a precise and robust model. Simpler models tend to be less accurate but more robust. Complex models tend to be more accurate but less robust. For more information on the bias-variance dilemma, refer to `http://en.wikipedia.org/wiki/Bias-variance_dilemma`.

The importance of this trade-off cannot be overstated. This question pervades the entire discipline of machine learning. We will see concrete examples in this chapter.

Model selection

As we will see in this chapter, there are many supervised and unsupervised algorithms. For example, well-known classifiers that we will cover in this chapter include logistic regression, nearest-neighbors, Naive Bayes, and support vector machines. There are many other algorithms that we can't cover here.

No model performs uniformly better than the others. One model may perform well on one dataset and badly on another. This is the question of **model selection**.

We will see systematic methods to assess the quality of a model on a particular dataset (notably cross-validation). In practice, machine learning is not an "exact science" in that it frequently involves trial and error. We need to try different models and empirically choose the one that performs best.

That being said, understanding the details of the learning models allows us to gain intuition about which model is best adapted to our current problem.

Here are a few references on this question:

▸ Model selection on Wikipedia, available at `http://en.wikipedia.org/wiki/Model_selection`

▸ Model evaluation in scikit-learn's documentation, available at `http://scikit-learn.org/stable/modules/model_evaluation.html`

▸ Blog post on how to choose a classifier, available at `http://blog.echen.me/2011/04/27/choosing-a-machine-learning-classifier/`

Machine learning references

Here are a few excellent, math-heavy textbooks on machine learning:

▸ *Pattern Recognition and Machine Learning, Christopher M. Bishop, (2006), Springer*

▸ *Machine Learning – A Probabilistic Perspective, Kevin P. Murphy, (2012), MIT Press*

▸ *The Elements of Statistical Learning, Trevor Hastie, Robert Tibshirani, Jerome Friedman, (2009), Springer*

Here are a few books more oriented toward programmers without a strong mathematical background:

▸ *Machine Learning for Hackers, Drew Conway, John Myles White, (2012), O'Reilly Media*

▸ *Machine Learning in Action, Peter Harrington, (2012), Manning Publications Co.*

You will find many other references online.

Important classes of machine learning methods that we couldn't cover in this chapter include neural networks and deep learning. Deep learning is the subject of very active research in machine learning. Many state-of-the-art results are currently achieved by using deep learning methods. For more information on deep learning, refer to `http://en.wikipedia.org/wiki/Deep_learning`.

Getting started with scikit-learn

In this recipe, we introduce the basics of the machine learning **scikit-learn** package (http://scikit-learn.org). This package is the main tool we will use throughout this chapter. Its clean API makes it really easy to define, train, and test models. Plus, scikit-learn is specifically designed for speed and (relatively) big data.

We will show here a very basic example of linear regression in the context of curve fitting. This toy example will allow us to illustrate key concepts such as linear models, overfitting, underfitting, regularization, and cross-validation.

Getting ready

You can find all instructions to install scikit-learn in the main documentation. For more information, refer to http://scikit-learn.org/stable/install.html. With anaconda, you can type conda install scikit-learn in a terminal.

How to do it...

We will generate a one-dimensional dataset with a simple model (including some noise), and we will try to fit a function to this data. With this function, we can predict values on new data points. This is a **curve fitting regression** problem.

1. First, let's make all the necessary imports:

```
In [1]: import numpy as np
        import scipy.stats as st
        import sklearn.linear_model as lm
        import matplotlib.pyplot as plt
        %matplotlib inline
```

2. We now define a deterministic nonlinear function underlying our generative model:

```
In [2]: f = lambda x: np.exp(3 * x)
```

3. We generate the values along the curve on *[0,2]*:

```
In [3]: x_tr = np.linspace(0., 2, 200)
        y_tr = f(x_tr)
```

4. Now, let's generate data points within *[0,1]*. We use the function *f* and we add some Gaussian noise:

```
In [4]: x = np.array([0, .1, .2, .5, .8, .9, 1])
        y = f(x) + np.random.randn(len(x))
```

5. Let's plot our data points on *[0,1]*:

```
In [5]: plt.plot(x_tr[:100], y_tr[:100], '--k')
        plt.plot(x, y, 'ok', ms=10)
```

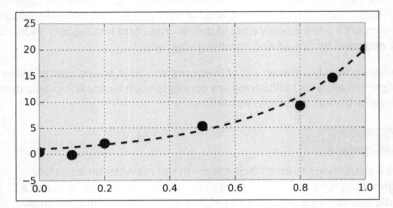

In the image, the dotted curve represents the generative model.

6. Now, we use scikit-learn to fit a linear model to the data. There are three steps. First, we create the model (an instance of the `LinearRegression` class). Then, we fit the model to our data. Finally, we predict values from our trained model.

```
In [6]: # We create the model.
        lr = lm.LinearRegression()
        # We train the model on our training dataset.
        lr.fit(x[:, np.newaxis], y)
        # Now, we predict points with our trained model.
        y_lr = lr.predict(x_tr[:, np.newaxis])
```

> We need to convert x and x_tr to column vectors, as it is a general convention in scikit-learn that observations are rows, while features are columns. Here, we have seven observations with one feature.

7. We now plot the result of the trained linear model. We obtain a regression line in green here:

```
In [7]: plt.plot(x_tr, y_tr, '--k')
        plt.plot(x_tr, y_lr, 'g')
        plt.plot(x, y, 'ok', ms=10)
        plt.xlim(0, 1)
```

```
plt.ylim(y.min()-1, y.max()+1)
plt.title("Linear regression")
```

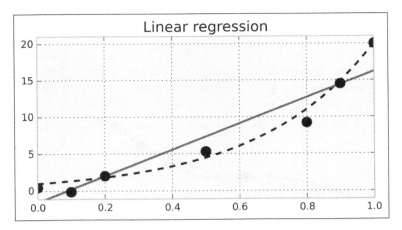

8. The linear fit is not well-adapted here, as the data points are generated according to a nonlinear model (an exponential curve). Therefore, we are now going to fit a nonlinear model. More precisely, we will fit a polynomial function to our data points. We can still use linear regression for this, by precomputing the exponents of our data points. This is done by generating a **Vandermonde matrix**, using the np.vander function. We will explain this trick in *How it works...*. In the following code, we perform and plot the fit:

```
In [8]: lrp = lm.LinearRegression()
        plt.plot(x_tr, y_tr, '--k')
        for deg in [2, 5]:
            lrp.fit(np.vander(x, deg + 1), y)
            y_lrp = lrp.predict(np.vander(x_tr, deg + 1))
            plt.plot(x_tr, y_lrp,
                     label='degree ' + str(deg))
            plt.legend(loc=2)
            plt.xlim(0, 1.4)
            plt.ylim(-10, 40)
            # Print the model's coefficients.
            print(' '.join(['%.2f' % c for c in
                            lrp.coef_]))
        plt.plot(x, y, 'ok', ms=10)
```

```
        plt.title("Linear regression")
25.00 -8.57 0.00
-132.71 296.80 -211.76 72.80 -8.68 0.00
```

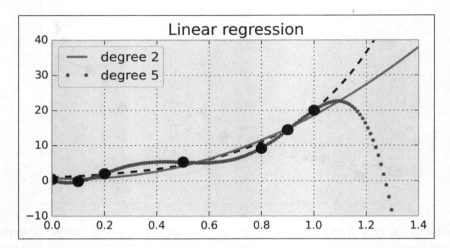

We have fitted two polynomial models of degree 2 and 5. The degree 2 polynomial appears to fit the data points less precisely than the degree 5 polynomial. However, it seems more robust; the degree 5 polynomial seems really bad at predicting values outside the data points (look for example at the $x \geq 1$ portion). This is what we call overfitting; by using a too-complex model, we obtain a better fit on the trained dataset, but a less robust model outside this set.

 Note the large coefficients of the degree 5 polynomial; this is generally a sign of overfitting.

9. We will now use a different learning model called **ridge regression**. It works like linear regression except that it prevents the polynomial's coefficients from becoming too big. This is what happened in the previous example. By adding a **regularization term** in the **loss function**, ridge regression imposes some structure on the underlying model. We will see more details in the next section.

   The ridge regression model has a meta-parameter, which represents the weight of the regularization term. We could try different values with trial and error using the Ridge class. However, scikit-learn provides another model called RidgeCV, which includes a parameter search with **cross-validation**. In practice, this means that we don't have to tweak this parameter by hand—scikit-learn does it for us. As the models of scikit-learn always follow the fit-predict API, all we have to do is replace lm.LinearRegression() with lm.RidgeCV() in the previous code. We will give more details in the next section.

```
In [9]: ridge = lm.RidgeCV()
        plt.plot(x_tr, y_tr, '--k')

        for deg in [2, 5]:
            ridge.fit(np.vander(x, deg + 1), y);
            y_ridge = ridge.predict(np.vander(x_tr, deg+1))
            plt.plot(x_tr, y_ridge,
                     label='degree ' + str(deg))
            plt.legend(loc=2)
            plt.xlim(0, 1.5)
            plt.ylim(-5, 80)
            # Print the model's coefficients.
            print(' '.join(['%.2f' % c
                            for c in ridge.coef_]))

        plt.plot(x, y, 'ok', ms=10)
        plt.title("Ridge regression")
11.36 4.61 0.00
2.84 3.54 4.09 4.14 2.67 0.00
```

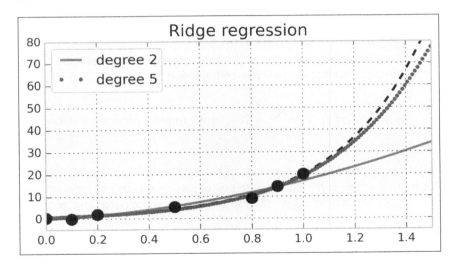

This time, the degree 5 polynomial seems more precise than the simpler degree 2 polynomial (which now causes **underfitting**). Ridge regression mitigates the overfitting issue here. Observe how the degree 5 polynomial's coefficients are much smaller than in the previous example.

How it works...

In this section, we explain all the aspects covered in this recipe.

The scikit-learn API

scikit-learn implements a clean and coherent API for supervised and unsupervised learning. Our data points should be stored in a *(N,D)* matrix *X*, where *N* is the number of observations and *D* is the number of features. In other words, each row is an observation. The first step in a machine learning task is to define what the matrix *X* is exactly.

In a supervised learning setup, we also have a *target*, an *N*-long vector *y* with a scalar value for each observation. This value is either continuous or discrete, depending on whether we have a regression or classification problem, respectively.

In scikit-learn, models are implemented in classes that have the `fit()` and `predict()` methods. The `fit()` method accepts the data matrix *X* as input, and *y* as well for supervised learning models. This method *trains* the model on the given data.

The `predict()` method also takes data points as input (as a *(M,D)* matrix). It returns the labels or transformed points as predicted by the trained model.

Ordinary least squares regression

Ordinary least squares regression is one of the simplest regression methods. It consists of approaching the output values y_i with a linear combination of X_{ij}:

$$\forall i \in \{1,...,N\}, \ \hat{y}_i = \sum_{j=1}^{D} w_j X_{ij}, \text{ or, in matrix form} : \hat{y} = XW$$

Here, $w = (w_1, ..., w_D)$ is the (unknown) **parameter vector**. Also, $\hat{y}$ represents the model's output. We want this vector to match the data points *y* as closely as possible. Of course, the exact equality $\hat{y} = y$ cannot hold in general (there is always some noise and uncertainty—models are always idealizations of reality). Therefore, we want to *minimize* the difference between these two vectors. The ordinary least squares regression method consists of minimizing the following **loss function**:

$$\min_{W} \| y - Xw \|_2^2 = \min_{W} \left(\sum_{i=1}^{N} (y_i - \hat{y}_i)^2 \right)$$

This sum of the components squared is called the **L² norm**. It is convenient because it leads to *differentiable* loss functions so that gradients can be computed and common optimization procedures can be performed.

Polynomial interpolation with linear regression

Ordinary least squares regression fits a linear model to the data. The model is linear both in the data points X_i and in the parameters w_j. In our example, we obtain a poor fit because the data points were generated according to a nonlinear generative model (an exponential function).

However, we can still use the linear regression method with a model that is linear in w_j but nonlinear in x_i. To do this, we need to increase the number of dimensions in our dataset by using a basis of polynomial functions. In other words, we consider the following data points:

$$x_i, x_i^2, ..., x_i^D$$

Here, D is the maximum degree. The input matrix X is therefore the **Vandermonde matrix** associated to the original data points x_i. For more information on the Vandermonde matrix, refer to http://en.wikipedia.org/wiki/Vandermonde_matrix.

Here, it is easy to see that training a linear model on these new data points is equivalent to training a polynomial model on the original data points.

Ridge regression

Polynomial interpolation with linear regression can lead to overfitting if the degree of the polynomials is too large. By capturing the random fluctuations (noise) instead of the general trend of the data, the model loses some of its predictive power. This corresponds to a divergence of the polynomial's coefficients w_j.

A solution to this problem is to prevent these coefficients from growing unboundedly. With **ridge regression** (also known as **Tikhonov regularization**), this is done by adding a *regularization* term to the loss function. For more details on Tikhonov regularization, refer to http://en.wikipedia.org/wiki/Tikhonov_regularization.

$$\min_{w} \| y - Xw \|_2^2 + \alpha \| w \|_2^2$$

By minimizing this loss function, we not only minimize the error between the model and the data (first term, related to the bias), but also the size of the model's coefficients (second term, related to the variance). The bias-variance trade-off is quantified by the hyperparameter α, which specifies the relative weight between the two terms in the loss function.

Here, ridge regression led to a polynomial with smaller coefficients, and thus a better fit.

Cross-validation and grid search

A drawback of the ridge regression model compared to the ordinary least squares model is the presence of an extra hyperparameter α. The quality of the prediction depends on the choice of this parameter. One possibility would be to fine-tune this parameter manually, but this procedure can be tedious and can also lead to overfitting problems.

To solve this problem, we can use a **grid search**; we loop over many possible values for α, and we evaluate the performance of the model for each possible value. Then, we choose the parameter that yields the best performance.

How can we assess the performance of a model with a given α value? A common solution is to use **cross-validation**. This procedure consists of splitting the dataset into a training set and a test set. We fit the model on the train set, and we test its predictive performance on the *test set*. By testing the model on a different dataset than the one used for training, we reduce overfitting.

There are many ways to split the initial dataset into two parts like this. One possibility is to remove *one* sample to form the train set and to put this one sample into the test set. This is called **Leave-One-Out** cross-validation. With *N* samples, we obtain *N* sets of train and test sets. The cross-validated performance is the average performance on all these set decompositions.

As we will see later, scikit-learn implements several easy-to-use functions to do cross-validation and grid search. In this recipe, there exists a special estimator called `RidgeCV` that implements a cross-validation and grid search procedure that is specific to the ridge regression model. Using this class ensures that the best hyperparameter α is found automatically for us.

There's more...

Here are a few references about least squares:

- Ordinary least squares on Wikipedia, available at `http://en.wikipedia.org/wiki/Ordinary_least_squares`
- Linear least squares on Wikipedia, available at `http://en.wikipedia.org/wiki/Linear_least_squares_(mathematics)`

Here are a few references about cross-validation and grid search:

- Cross-validation in scikit-learn's documentation, available at `http://scikit-learn.org/stable/modules/cross_validation.html`
- Grid search in scikit-learn's documentation, available at `http://scikit-learn.org/stable/modules/grid_search.html`
- Cross-validation on Wikipedia, available at `http://en.wikipedia.org/wiki/Cross-validation_%28statistics%29`

Here are a few references about scikit-learn:

- scikit-learn basic tutorial available at `http://scikit-learn.org/stable/tutorial/basic/tutorial.html`
- scikit-learn tutorial given at the SciPy 2013 conference, available at `https://github.com/jakevdp/sklearn_scipy2013`

▶ The *Using support vector machines for classification tasks* recipe

Predicting who will survive on the Titanic with logistic regression

In this recipe, we will introduce **logistic regression**, a basic classifier. We will also show how to perform a **grid search** with **cross-validation**.

We will apply these techniques on a **Kaggle** dataset where the goal is to predict survival on the Titanic based on real data.

> Kaggle (`www.kaggle.com/competitions`) hosts machine learning competitions where anyone can download a dataset, train a model, and test the predictions on the website. The author of the best model might even win a prize! It is a fun way to get started with machine learning.

Getting ready

Download the *Titanic* dataset from the book's GitHub repository at `https://github.com/ipython-books/cookbook-data`.

The dataset has been obtained from `www.kaggle.com/c/titanic-gettingStarted`.

How to do it...

1. We import the standard packages:

```
In [1]: import numpy as np
        import pandas as pd
        import sklearn
        import sklearn.linear_model as lm
        import sklearn.cross_validation as cv
        import sklearn.grid_search as gs
        import matplotlib.pyplot as plt
        %matplotlib inline
```

2. We load the training and test datasets with pandas:

```
In [2]: train = pd.read_csv('data/titanic_train.csv')
        test = pd.read_csv('data/titanic_test.csv')
In [3]: train[train.columns[[2,4,5,1]]].head()
Out[3]:
```

```
     Pclass     Sex   Age   Survived
0         3    male    22          0
1         1  female    38          1
2         3  female    26          1
3         1  female    35          1
4         3    male    35          0
```

3. Let's keep only a few fields for this example, and also convert the `sex` field to a binary variable so that it can be handled correctly by NumPy and scikit-learn. Finally, we remove the rows that contain `NaN` values:

```
In [4]: data = train[['Sex', 'Age', 'Pclass', 'Survived']].copy()
        data['Sex'] = data['Sex'] == 'female'
        data = data.dropna()
```

4. Now, we convert this `DataFrame` object to a NumPy array so that we can pass it to scikit-learn:

```
In [5]: data_np = data.astype(np.int32).values
        X = data_np[:,:-1]
        y = data_np[:,-1]
```

5. Let's have a look at the survival of male and female passengers as a function of their age:

```
In [6]: # We define a few boolean vectors.
        female = X[:,0] == 1
        survived = y == 1
        # This vector contains the age of the passengers.
        age = X[:,1]
        # We compute a few histograms.
        bins_ = np.arange(0, 81, 5)
        S = {'male': np.histogram(age[survived & ~female],
                                  bins=bins_)[0],
             'female': np.histogram(age[survived & female],
                                    bins=bins_)[0]}
        D = {'male': np.histogram(age[~survived & ~female],
                                  bins=bins_)[0],
             'female': np.histogram(age[~survived &
                                        female],
                                    bins=bins_)[0]}
In [7]: # We now plot the data.
        bins = bins_[:-1]
        for i, sex, color in zip((0, 1),
                                 ('male', 'female'),
                                 ('#3345d0', '#cc3dc0')):
            plt.subplot(121 + i)
            plt.bar(bins, S[sex], bottom=D[sex],
                    color=color,
```

```
            width=5, label='survived')
      plt.bar(bins, D[sex], color='k', width=5,
            label='died')
      plt.xlim(0, 80)
      plt.grid(None)
      plt.title(sex + " survival")
      plt.xlabel("Age (years)")
      plt.legend()
```

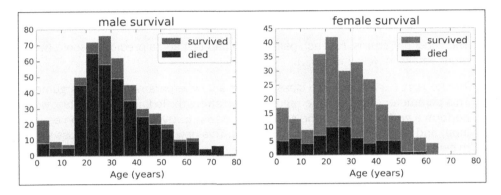

6. Let's try to train a `LogisticRegression` classifier in order to predict the survival of people based on their gender, age, and class. We first need to create a train and a test dataset:

```
In [8]: # We split X and y into train and test datasets.
        (X_train, X_test, y_train,
        y_test) = cv.train_test_split(X, y, test_size=.05)
In [9]: # We instanciate the classifier.
        logreg = lm.LogisticRegression()
```

7. We train the model and we get the predicted values on the test set:

```
In [10]: logreg.fit(X_train, y_train)
        y_predicted = logreg.predict(X_test)
```

The following figure shows the actual and predicted results:

```
In [11]: plt.imshow(np.vstack((y_test, y_predicted)),
                interpolation='none', cmap='bone')
        plt.xticks([]); plt.yticks([])
        plt.title(("Actual and predicted survival "
                "outcomes on the test set"))
```

In this screenshot, the first line shows the survival of several people from the test set (white for survival, black otherwise). The second line shows the values predicted by the model.

8. To get an estimation of the model's performance, we compute the cross-validation score with the `cross_val_score()` function. This function uses a three-fold stratified cross-validation procedure by default, but this can be changed with the `cv` keyword argument:

```
In [12]: cv.cross_val_score(logreg, X, y)
Out[12]: array([ 0.78661088,  0.78991597,  0.78059072])
```

This function returns, for each pair of train and test set, a prediction score (we give more details in *How it works...*).

9. The `LogisticRegression` class accepts a C hyperparameter as an argument. This parameter quantifies the regularization strength. To find a good value, we can perform a grid search with the generic `GridSearchCV` class. It takes an estimator as input and a dictionary of parameter values. This new estimator uses cross-validation to select the best parameter:

```
In [13]: grid = gs.GridSearchCV(logreg,
                         {'C': np.logspace(-5, 5, 50)})
         grid.fit(X_train, y_train)
         grid.best_params_
Out[13]: {'C':  5.35}
```

10. Here is the performance of the best estimator:

```
In [14]: cv.cross_val_score(grid.best_estimator_, X, y)
Out[14]: array([ 0.78661088,  0.79831933,  0.78481013])
```

Performance is slightly better after the C hyperparameter has been chosen with a grid search.

How it works...

Logistic regression is *not* a regression model, it is a classification model. Yet, it is closely related to linear regression. This model predicts the probability that a binary variable is 1, by applying a **sigmoid function** (more precisely, a logistic function) to a linear combination of the variables. The equation of the sigmoid is:

$$\forall i \in \{1,...,N\}, \hat{y}_i = f(x_i w) \text{ where } f(x) = \frac{1}{1+\exp(-x)}$$

The following figure shows a logistic function:

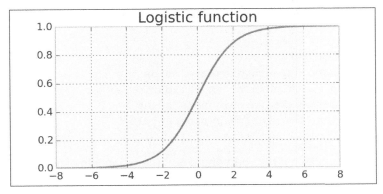

A logistic function

If a binary variable has to be obtained, we can round the value to the closest integer.

The parameter *w* is obtained with an optimization procedure during the learning step.

There's more...

Here are a few references:

- Logistic regression on Wikipedia, available at http://en.wikipedia.org/wiki/Logistic_regression
- Logistic regression in scikit-learn's documentation, available at http://scikit-learn.org/stable/modules/linear_model.html#logistic-regression

See also

- The *Getting started with scikit-learn* recipe
- The *Learning to recognize handwritten digits with a K-nearest neighbors classifier* recipe
- The *Using support vector machines for classification tasks* recipe

Learning to recognize handwritten digits with a K-nearest neighbors classifier

In this recipe, we will see how to recognize handwritten digits with a **K-nearest neighbors** (**K-NN**) classifier. This classifier is a simple but powerful model, well-adapted to complex, highly nonlinear datasets such as images. We will explain how it works later in this recipe.

How to do it...

1. We import the modules:

```
In [1]: import numpy as np
        import sklearn
        import sklearn.datasets as ds
        import sklearn.cross_validation as cv
        import sklearn.neighbors as nb
        import matplotlib.pyplot as plt
        %matplotlib inline
```

2. Let's load the *digits* dataset, part of the `datasets` module of scikit-learn. This dataset contains handwritten digits that have been manually labeled:

```
In [2]: digits = ds.load_digits()
        X = digits.data
        y = digits.target
        print((X.min(), X.max()))
        print(X.shape)
0.0 16.0
(1797L, 64L)
```

In the matrix X, each row contains *8 * 8=64* pixels (in grayscale, values between 0 and 16). The row-major ordering is used.

3. Let's display some of the images along with their labels:

```
In [3]: nrows, ncols = 2, 5
        plt.gray()
        for i in range(ncols * nrows):
            ax = plt.subplot(nrows, ncols, i + 1)
            ax.matshow(digits.images[i,...])
            plt.xticks([]); plt.yticks([])
            plt.title(digits.target[i])
```

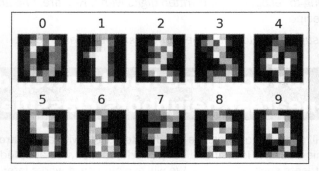

4. Now, let's fit a K-nearest neighbors classifier on the data:

```
In [4]: (X_train, X_test, y_train,
         y_test) = cv.train_test_split(X, y, test_size=.25)
In [5]: knc = nb.KNeighborsClassifier()
In [6]: knc.fit(X_train, y_train);
```

5. Let's evaluate the score of the trained classifier on the test dataset:

```
In [7]: knc.score(X_test, y_test)
Out[7]: 0.98888888888888893
```

6. Now, let's see if our classifier can recognize a *handwritten* digit!

```
In [8]: # Let's draw a 1.
        one = np.zeros((8, 8))
        one[1:-1, 4] = 16   # The image values are
                            # in [0,16].
        one[2, 3] = 16
In [9]: plt.imshow(one, interpolation='none')
        plt.grid(False)
        plt.xticks(); plt.yticks()
        plt.title("One")
```

Can our model recognize this number? Let's see:

```
In [10]: knc.predict(one.ravel())
Out[10]: array([1])
```

Good job!

How it works...

This example illustrates how to deal with images in scikit-learn. An image is a 2D *(N, M)* matrix, which has *NM* features. This matrix needs to be flattened when composing the data matrix; each row is a full image.

The idea of K-nearest neighbors is as follows: given a new point in the feature space, find the K closest points from the training set and assign the label of the majority of those points.

The distance is generally the Euclidean distance, but other distances can be used too.

The following image shows the space partition obtained with a 15-nearest-neighbors classifier on a toy dataset (with three labels):

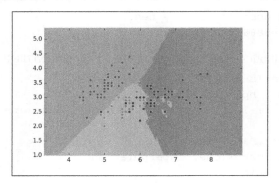

K-nearest neighbors space partition

The number K is a hyperparameter of the model. If it is too small, the model will not generalize well (high variance). In particular, it will be highly sensitive to outliers. By contrast, the precision of the model will worsen if K is too large. At the extreme, if K is equal to the total number of points, the model will always predict the exact same value disregarding the input (high bias). There are heuristics to choose this hyperparameter (see the next section).

It should be noted that no model is learned by a K-nearest neighbor algorithm; the classifier just stores all data points and compares any new target points with them. This is an example of **instance-based learning**. It is in contrast to other classifiers such as the logistic regression model, which explicitly learns a simple mathematical model on the training data.

The K-nearest neighbors method works well on complex classification problems that have irregular decision boundaries. However, it might be computationally intensive with large training datasets because a large number of distances have to be computed for testing. Dedicated tree-based data structures such as **K-D trees** or **ball trees** can be used to accelerate the search of nearest neighbors.

The K-nearest neighbors method can be used for classification, like here, and also for regression problems. The model assigns the average of the target value of the nearest neighbors. In both cases, different weighting strategies can be used.

There's more...

Here are a few references:

- ▶ The K-NN algorithm in scikit-learn's documentation, available at `http://scikit-learn.org/stable/modules/neighbors.html`
- ▶ The K-NN algorithm on Wikipedia, available at `http://en.wikipedia.org/wiki/K-nearest_neighbors_algorithm`
- ▶ Blog post about how to choose the K hyperparameter, available at `http://datasciencelab.wordpress.com/2013/12/27/finding-the-k-in-k-means-clustering/`
- ▶ Instance-based learning on Wikipedia, available at `http://en.wikipedia.org/wiki/Instance-based_learning`

See also

- ▶ The *Predicting who will survive on the Titanic with logistic regression* recipe
- ▶ The *Using support vector machines for classification tasks* recipe

Learning from text – Naive Bayes for Natural Language Processing

In this recipe, we show how to handle text data with scikit-learn. Working with text requires careful preprocessing and feature extraction. It is also quite common to deal with highly sparse matrices.

We will learn to recognize whether a comment posted during a public discussion is considered insulting to one of the participants. We will use a labeled dataset from Impermium, released during a Kaggle competition.

Getting ready

Download the *Troll* dataset from the book's GitHub repository at `https://github.com/ipython-books/cookbook-data`.

This dataset was obtained from Kaggle, at `www.kaggle.com/c/detecting-insults-in-social-commentary`.

How to do it...

1. Let's import our libraries:

```
In [1]: import numpy as np
        import pandas as pd
        import sklearn
        import sklearn.cross_validation as cv
        import sklearn.grid_search as gs
        import sklearn.feature_extraction.text as text
        import sklearn.naive_bayes as nb
        import matplotlib.pyplot as plt
        %matplotlib inline
```

2. Let's open the CSV file with pandas:

```
In [2]: df = pd.read_csv("data/troll.csv")
```

3. Each row is a comment. We will consider two columns: whether the comment is insulting (1) or not (0) and the unicode-encoded contents of the comment:

```
In [3]: df[['Insult', 'Comment']].tail()
        Insult                                                  Comment
   3942      1    "you are both morons and that is..."
   3943      0    "Many toolbars include spell check...
   3944      0    "@LambeauOrWrigley\xa0\xa0@K.Moss\xa0\n...
   3945      0    "How about Felix? He is sure turning into...
   3946      0    "You're all upset, defending this hipster...
```

4. Now, we are going to define the feature matrix X and the labels y:

```
In [4]: y = df['Insult']
```

Obtaining the feature matrix from the text is not trivial. scikit-learn can only work with numerical matrices. So how do we convert text into a matrix of numbers? A classical solution is to first extract a **vocabulary**, a list of words used throughout the corpus. Then, we count, for each sample, the frequency of each word. We end up with a **sparse matrix**, a huge matrix containing mostly zeros. Here, we do this in two lines. We will give more details in *How it works...*.

 The general rule here is that whenever one of our features is categorical (that is, the presence of a word, a color belonging to a fixed set of *n* colors, and so on), we should *vectorize* it by considering one binary feature per item in the class. For example, instead of a feature `color` being `red`, `green`, or `blue`, we should consider three *binary* features `color_red`, `color_green`, and `color_blue`. We give further references in the *There's more...* section.

```
In [5]: tf = text.TfidfVectorizer()
        X = tf.fit_transform(df['Comment'])
        print(X.shape)
(3947, 16469)
```

5. There are 3947 comments and 16469 different words. Let's estimate the sparsity of this feature matrix:

```
In [6]: print(("Each sample has ~{0:.2f}% non-zero"
               "features.").format(
           100 * X.nnz / float(X.shape[0] * X.shape[1])))
Each sample has ~0.15% non-zero features.
```

6. Now, we are going to train a classifier as usual. We first split the data into a train and test set:

```
In [7]: (X_train, X_test, y_train,
         y_test) = cv.train_test_split(X, y,
                                       test_size=.2)
```

7. We use a **Bernoulli Naive Bayes classifier** with a grid search on the α parameter:

```
In [8]: bnb = gs.GridSearchCV(nb.BernoulliNB(),
                              param_grid={
                              'alpha': np.logspace(-2., 2., 50)})
        bnb.fit(X_train, y_train)
```

8. Let's check the performance of this classifier on the test dataset:

```
In [9]: bnb.score(X_test, y_test)
Out[9]: 0.76455696202531642
```

9. Let's take a look at the words corresponding to the largest coefficients (the words we find frequently in insulting comments):

```
In [10]: # We first get the words corresponding
         # to each feature.
         names = np.asarray(tf.get_feature_names())
         # Next, we display the 50 words with the largest
         # coefficients.
         print(','.join(names[np.argsort(
             bnb.best_estimator_.coef_[0,:])[::-1][:50]]))
you,are,your,to,the,and,of,that,is,it,in,like,on,have,for,not,re,j
ust,an,with,so,all,***,***be,get,***,***up,this,what,xa0,don,***,*
**go,no,do,can,but,***,***or,as,if,***,***who,know,about,because,h
ere,***,***me,was
```

10. Finally, let's test our estimator on a few test sentences:

```
In [11]: print(bnb.predict(tf.transform([
            "I totally agree with you.",
            "You are so stupid.",
            "I love you."
            ])))
[0 1 1]
```

That's not bad, but we can probably do better.

How it works...

scikit-learn implements several utility functions to obtain a sparse feature matrix from text data. A **vectorizer** such as `CountVectorizer()` extracts a vocabulary from a corpus (`fit`) and constructs a sparse representation of the corpus based on this vocabulary (`transform`). Each sample is represented by the vocabulary's word frequencies. The trained instance also contains attributes and methods to map feature indices to the corresponding words (`get_feature_names()`) and conversely (`vocabulary_`).

N-grams can also be extracted. These are pairs or tuples of words occurring successively (the `ngram_range` keyword).

The frequency of the words can be weighted in different ways. Here, we have used **tf-idf**, or **term frequency-inverse document frequency**. This quantity reflects how important a word is to a corpus. Frequent words in comments have a high weight except if they appear in most comments (which means that they are common terms, for example, "the" and "and" would be filtered out using this technique).

Naive Bayes algorithms are Bayesian methods based on the naive assumption of independence between the features. This strong assumption drastically simplifies the computations and leads to very fast yet decent classifiers.

There's more...

Here are a few references:

- Text feature extraction in scikit-learn's documentation, available at `http://scikit-learn.org/stable/modules/feature_extraction.html#text-feature-extraction`

- Term frequency-inverse document-frequency on Wikipedia, available at `http://en.wikipedia.org/wiki/tf-idf`

- Vectorizer in scikit-learn's documentation, available at `http://scikit-learn.org/stable/modules/generated/sklearn.feature_extraction.DictVectorizer.html`

- Naive Bayes classifier on Wikipedia, at `http://en.wikipedia.org/wiki/Naive_Bayes_classifier`
- Naive Bayes in scikit-learn's documentation, available at `http://scikit-learn.org/stable/modules/naive_bayes.html`
- Impermium Kaggle challenge, at `http://blog.kaggle.com/2012/09/26/impermium-andreas-blog/`
- Document classification example in scikit-learn's documentation, at `http://scikit-learn.org/stable/auto_examples/document_classification_20newsgroups.html`

 Besides scikit-learn, which has good support for text processing, we should also mention NLTK (available at `www.nltk.org`), a Natural Language Toolkit in Python.

See also

- The *Predicting who will survive on the Titanic with logistic regression* recipe
- The *Learning to recognize handwritten digits with a K-nearest neighbors classifier* recipe
- The *Using support vector machines for classification tasks* recipe

Using support vector machines for classification tasks

In this recipe, we introduce **support vector machines**, or **SVMs**. These powerful models can be used for classification and regression. Here, we illustrate how to use linear and nonlinear SVMs on a simple classification task.

How to do it...

1. Let's import the packages:

```
In [1]: import numpy as np
        import pandas as pd
        import sklearn
        import sklearn.datasets as ds
        import sklearn.cross_validation as cv
        import sklearn.grid_search as gs
        import sklearn.svm as svm
        import matplotlib.pyplot as plt
        %matplotlib inline
```

2. We generate 2D points and assign a binary label according to a linear operation on the coordinates:

```
In [2]: X = np.random.randn(200, 2)
        y = X[:, 0] + X[:, 1] > 1
```

3. We now fit a linear **Support Vector Classifier** (**SVC**). This classifier tries to separate the two groups of points with a linear boundary (a line here, but more generally a hyperplane):

```
In [3]: # We train the classifier.
        est = svm.LinearSVC()
        est.fit(X, y)
```

4. We define a function that displays the boundaries and decision function of a trained classifier:

```
In [4]: # We generate a grid in the square [-3,3 ]^2.
        xx, yy = np.meshgrid(np.linspace(-3, 3, 500),
                             np.linspace(-3, 3, 500))
        # This function takes a SVM estimator as input.
        def plot_decision_function(est):
            # We evaluate the decision function on the
            # grid.
            Z = est.decision_function(np.c_[xx.ravel(),
                                            yy.ravel()])
            Z = Z.reshape(xx.shape)
            cmap = plt.cm.Blues
            # We display the decision function on the grid.
            plt.imshow(Z,
                       extent=(xx.min(), xx.max(),
                               yy.min(), yy.max()),
                       aspect='auto', origin='lower',
                       cmap=cmap)
            # We display the boundaries.
            plt.contour(xx, yy, Z, levels=[0],
                        linewidths=2,
                        colors='k')
            # We display the points with their true labels.
            plt.scatter(X[:, 0], X[:, 1], s=30, c=.5+.5*y,
                        lw=1, cmap=cmap, vmin=0, vmax=1)
            plt.axhline(0, color='k', ls='--')
            plt.axvline(0, color='k', ls='--')
            plt.xticks(())
            plt.yticks(())
            plt.axis([-3, 3, -3, 3])
```

5. Let's take a look at the classification results with the linear SVC:

```
In [5]: plot_decision_function(est)
        plt.title("Linearly separable, linear SVC")
```

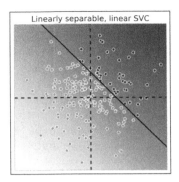

The linear SVC tried to separate the points with a line and it did a pretty good job here.

6. We now modify the labels with an XOR function. A point's label is 1 if the coordinates have different signs. This classification is not linearly separable. Therefore, a linear SVC fails completely:

```
In [6]: y = np.logical_xor(X[:, 0]>0, X[:, 1]>0)
        # We train the classifier.
        est = gs.GridSearchCV(svm.LinearSVC(),
                       {'C': np.logspace(-3., 3., 10)})
        est.fit(X, y)
        print("Score: {0:.1f}".format(
                   v.cross_val_score(est, X, y).mean()))
        # Plot the decision function.
        plot_decision_function(est)
        plt.title("XOR, linear SVC")
Score: 0.6
```

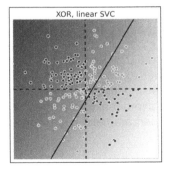

7. Fortunately, it is possible to use nonlinear SVCs by using nonlinear **kernels**. Kernels specify a nonlinear transformation of the points into a higher dimensional space. Transformed points in this space are assumed to be more linearly separable. By default, the SVC classifier in scikit-learn uses the **Radial Basis Function** (**RBF**) kernel:

```
In [7]: y = np.logical_xor(X[:, 0]>0, X[:, 1]>0)
        est = gs.GridSearchCV(svm.SVC(),
                     {'C': np.logspace(-3., 3., 10),
                      'gamma': np.logspace(-3., 3., 10)})
        est.fit(X, y)
        print("Score: {0:.3f}".format(
             cv.cross_val_score(est, X, y).mean()))
        plot_decision_function(est.best_estimator_)
        plt.title("XOR, non-linear SVC")
Score: 0.975
```

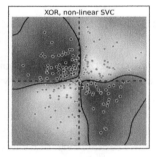

This time, the nonlinear SVC successfully managed to classify these nonlinearly separable points.

How it works...

A two-class linear SVC tries to find a hyperplane (defined as a linear equation) that best separates the two sets of points (grouped according to their labels). There is also the constraint that this separating hyperplane needs to be as far as possible from the points. This method works best when such a hyperplane exists. Otherwise, this method can fail completely, as we saw in the XOR example. XOR is known as being a nonlinearly separable operation.

The SVM classes in scikit-learn have a *C* hyperparameter. This hyperparameter trades off misclassification of training examples against simplicity of the decision surface. A low *C* value makes the decision surface smooth, while a high *C* value aims at classifying all training examples correctly. This is another example where a hyperparameter quantifies the bias-variance trade-off. This hyperparameter can be chosen with cross-validation and grid search.

The linear SVC can also be extended to multiclass problems. The multiclass SVC is directly implemented in scikit-learn.

The nonlinear SVC works by considering a nonlinear transformation $\varphi(x)$ from the original space into a higher dimensional space. This nonlinear transformation can increase the linear separability of the classes. In practice, all dot products are replaced by the $k(x,x') = \varphi(x) \cdot \varphi(x')$ kernel.

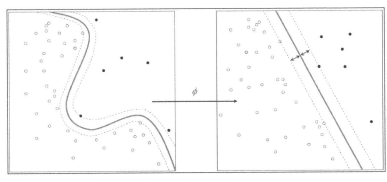

Nonlinear SVC

There are several widely-used nonlinear kernels. By default, SVC uses Gaussian radial basis functions:

$$k(\mathrm{x},\mathrm{x}') = \exp\left(-\gamma \| \mathrm{x} - \mathrm{x}' \|^2\right)$$

Here, γ is a hyperparameter of the model that can be chosen with grid search and cross-validation.

The φ function does not need to be computed explicitly. This is the **kernel trick**; it suffices to know the kernel $k(x, x')$. The existence of a function φ corresponding to a given kernel $k(x, x')$ is guaranteed by a mathematical theorem in functional analysis.

There's more...

Here are a few references about support vector machines:

- Exclusive OR on Wikipedia, available at `http://en.wikipedia.org/wiki/Exclusive_or`

- Support vector machines on Wikipedia, available at `http://en.wikipedia.org/wiki/Support_vector_machine`

- SVMs in scikit-learn's documentation, available at `http://scikit-learn.org/stable/modules/svm.html`

> ▸ Kernel trick on Wikipedia, available at `http://en.wikipedia.org/wiki/Kernel_method`

> ▸ Notes about the kernel trick available at `www.eric-kim.net/eric-kim-net/posts/1/kernel_trick.html`

> ▸ An example with a nonlinear SVM available at `http://scikit-learn.org/0.11/auto_examples/svm/plot_svm_nonlinear.html` (this example inspired this recipe)

See also

> ▸ The *Predicting who will survive on the Titanic with logistic regression* recipe

> ▸ The *Learning to recognize handwritten digits with a K-nearest neighbors classifier* recipe

Using a random forest to select important features for regression

Decision trees are frequently used to represent workflows or algorithms. They also form a method for nonparametric supervised learning. A tree mapping observations to target values is learned on a training set and gives the outcomes of new observations.

Random forests are ensembles of decision trees. Multiple decision trees are trained and aggregated to form a model that is more performant than any of the individual trees. This general idea is the purpose of **ensemble learning**.

There are many types of ensemble methods. Random forests are an instance of **bootstrap aggregating**, also called **bagging**, where models are trained on randomly drawn subsets of the training set.

Random forests yield information about the importance of each feature for the classification or regression task. In this recipe, we will find the most influential features of Boston house prices using a classic dataset that contains a range of diverse indicators about the houses' neighborhood.

How to do it...

1. We import the packages:

```
In [1]: import numpy as np
        import sklearn as sk
        import sklearn.datasets as skd
        import sklearn.ensemble as ske
        import matplotlib.pyplot as plt
```

```
%matplotlib inline
```

2. We load the Boston dataset:

```
In [2]: data = skd.load_boston()
```

The details of this dataset can be found in `data['DESCR']`. Here is the description of some features:

- *CRIM*: Per capita crime rate by town
- *NOX*: Nitric oxide concentration (parts per 10 million)
- *RM*: Average number of rooms per dwelling
- *AGE*: Proportion of owner-occupied units built prior to 1940
- *DIS*: Weighted distances to five Boston employment centers
- *PTRATIO*: Pupil-teacher ratio by town
- *LSTAT*: Percentage of lower status of the population
- *MEDV*: Median value of owner-occupied homes in $1000s

The target value is *MEDV*.

3. We create a `RandomForestRegressor` model:

```
In [3]: reg = ske.RandomForestRegressor()
```

4. We get the samples and the target values from this dataset:

```
In [4]: X = data['data']
        y = data['target']
```

5. Let's fit the model:

```
In [5]: reg.fit(X, y)
```

6. The importance of our features can be found in `reg.feature_importances_`. We sort them by decreasing order of importance:

```
In [6]: fet_ind = np.argsort(reg.feature_importances_) \
                                                    [::-1]
        fet_imp = reg.feature_importances_[fet_ind]
```

7. Finally, we plot a histogram of the features' importance:

```
In [7]: ax = plt.subplot(111)
        plt.bar(np.arange(len(fet_imp)),
                fet_imp, width=1, lw=2)
        plt.grid(False)
        ax.set_xticks(np.arange(len(fet_imp))+.5)
```

```
ax.set_xticklabels(data['feature_names'][fet_ind])
plt.xlim(0, len(fet_imp))
```

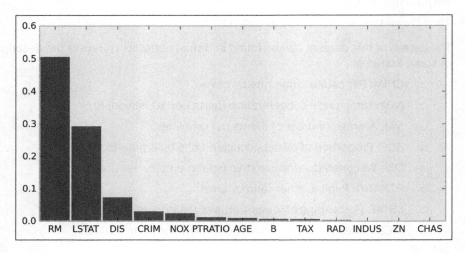

We find that *LSTAT* (proportion of lower status of the population) and *RM* (number of rooms per dwelling) are the most important features determining the price of a house. As an illustration, here is a scatter plot of the price as a function of *LSTAT*:

```
In [8]: plt.scatter(X[:,-1], y)
        plt.xlabel('LSTAT indicator')
        plt.ylabel('Value of houses (k$)')
```

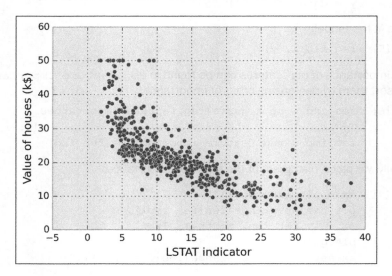

How it works...

Several algorithms can be used to train a decision tree. scikit-learn uses the **CART**, or **Classification and Regression Trees**, algorithm. This algorithm constructs binary trees using the feature and threshold that yield the largest information gain at each node. Terminal nodes give the outcomes of input values.

Decision trees are simple to understand. They can also be visualized with **pydot**, a Python package for drawing graphs and trees. This is useful when we want to understand what a tree has learned exactly (**white box model**); the conditions that apply on the observations at each node can be expressed easily with Boolean logic.

However, decision trees may suffer from overfitting, notably when they are too deep, and they might be unstable. Additionally, global convergence toward an optimal model is not guaranteed, particularly when greedy algorithms are used for training. These problems can be mitigated by using ensembles of decision trees, notably random forests.

In a random forest, multiple decision trees are trained on bootstrap samples of the training dataset (randomly sampled with replacement). Predictions are made with the averages of individual trees' predictions (bootstrap aggregating or bagging). Additionally, random subsets of the features are chosen at each node (**random subspace method**). These methods lead to an overall better model than the individual trees.

There's more...

Here are a few references:

- ► Ensemble learning in scikit-learn's documentation, available at `http://scikit-learn.org/stable/modules/ensemble.html`
- ► API reference of `RandomForestRegressor` available at `http://scikit-learn.org/stable/modules/generated/sklearn.ensemble.RandomForestRegressor.html`
- ► Random forests on Wikipedia, available at `http://en.wikipedia.org/wiki/Random_forest`
- ► Decision tree learning on Wikipedia, available at `http://en.wikipedia.org/wiki/Decision_tree_learning`
- ► Bootstrap aggregating on Wikipedia, available at `http://en.wikipedia.org/wiki/Bootstrap_aggregating`
- ► Random subspace method on Wikipedia, available at `http://en.wikipedia.org/wiki/Random_subspace_method`
- ► Ensemble learning on Wikipedia, available at `http://en.wikipedia.org/wiki/Ensemble_learning`

See also

▶ The *Using support vector machines for classification tasks* recipe

Reducing the dimensionality of a dataset with a principal component analysis

In the previous recipes, we presented *supervised learning* methods; our data points came with discrete or continuous labels, and the algorithms were able to learn the mapping from the points to the labels.

Starting with this recipe, we will present **unsupervised learning** methods. These methods might be helpful prior to running a supervised learning algorithm. They can give a first insight into the data.

Let's assume that our data consists of points x_i without any labels. The goal is to discover some form of hidden structure in this set of points. Frequently, data points have intrinsic low dimensionality: a small number of features suffice to accurately describe the data. However, these features might be hidden among many other features not relevant to the problem. Dimension reduction can help us find these structures. This knowledge can considerably improve the performance of subsequent supervised learning algorithms.

Another useful application of unsupervised learning is **data visualization**; high-dimensional datasets are hard to visualize in 2D or 3D. Projecting the data points on a subspace or submanifold yields more interesting visualizations.

In this recipe, we will illustrate a basic unsupervised linear method, **principal component analysis** (**PCA**). This algorithm lets us project data points linearly on a low-dimensional subspace. Along the **principal components**, which are vectors forming a basis of this low-dimensional subspace, the variance of the data points is maximum.

We will use the classic *Iris flower* dataset as an example. This dataset contains the width and length of the petal and sepal of 150 iris flowers. These flowers belong to one of three categories: *Iris setosa*, *Iris virginica*, and *Iris versicolor*. We have access to the category in this dataset (labeled data). However, because we are interested in illustrating an unsupervised learning method, we will only use the data matrix *without* the labels.

How to do it...

1. We import NumPy, matplotlib, and scikit-learn:

```
In [1]: import numpy as np
        import sklearn
        import sklearn.decomposition as dec
        import sklearn.datasets as ds
```

5. We now display the same dataset, but in a new coordinate system (or equivalently, a linearly transformed version of the initial dataset):

```
In [5]: plt.scatter(X_bis[:,0], X_bis[:,1], c=y,
                 s=30, cmap=plt.cm.rainbow)
```

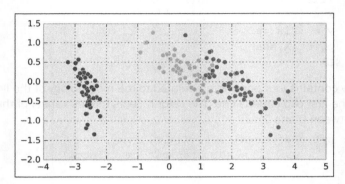

Points belonging to the same classes are now grouped together, even though the PCA estimator did *not* use the labels. The PCA was able to find a projection maximizing the variance, which corresponds here to a projection where the classes are well separated.

6. The scikit.decomposition module contains several variants of the classic PCA estimator: ProbabilisticPCA, SparsePCA, RandomizedPCA, KernelPCA, and others. As an example, let's take a look at KernelPCA, a nonlinear version of PCA:

```
In [6]: X_ter = dec.KernelPCA(kernel='rbf'). \
                              fit_transform(X)
        plt.scatter(X_ter[:,0], X_ter[:,1], c=y, s=30,
                 cmap=plt.cm.rainbow)
```

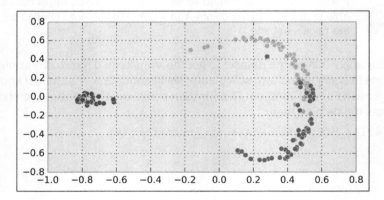

How it works...

Let's look at the mathematical ideas behind PCA. This method is based on a matrix decomposition called **Singular Value Decomposition (SVD)**:

$$X = U \sum V^{T}$$

Here, *X* is the *(N,D)* data matrix, *U* and *V* are orthogonal matrices, and $\sum$ is a *(N,D)* diagonal matrix.

PCA transforms *X* into *X'* defined by:

$$X' = XV = U \sum$$

The diagonal elements of $\sum$ are the **singular values** of X. By convention, they are generally sorted in descending order. The columns of *U* are orthonormal vectors called the **left singular vectors** of *X*. Therefore, the columns of *X'* are the left singular vectors multiplied by the singular values.

In the end, PCA converts the initial set of observations, which are made of possibly correlated variables, into vectors of linearly uncorrelated variables called **principal components**.

The first new feature (or first component) is a transformation of all original features such that the dispersion (variance) of the data points is the highest in that direction. In the subsequent principal components, the variance is decreasing. In other words, PCA gives us an alternative representation of our data where the new features are sorted according to how much they account for the variability of the points.

There's more...

Here are a few further references:

- ► Iris flower dataset on Wikipedia, available at `http://en.wikipedia.org/wiki/Iris_flower_data_set`
- ► PCA on Wikipedia, available at `http://en.wikipedia.org/wiki/Principal_component_analysis`
- ► SVD decomposition on Wikipedia, available at `http://en.wikipedia.org/wiki/Singular_value_decomposition`
- ► Iris dataset example available at `http://scikit-learn.org/stable/auto_examples/datasets/plot_iris_dataset.html`
- ► Decompositions in scikit-learn's documentation, available at `http://scikit-learn.org/stable/modules/decomposition.html`

▶ Unsupervised learning tutorial with scikit-learn available at `http://scikit-learn.org/dev/tutorial/statistical_inference/unsupervised_learning.html`

See also

▶ The *Detecting hidden structures in a dataset with clustering* recipe

Detecting hidden structures in a dataset with clustering

A large part of unsupervised learning is devoted to the **clustering** problem. The goal is to group similar points together in a totally unsupervised way. Clustering is a hard problem, as the very definition of **clusters** (or **groups**) is not necessarily well posed. In most datasets, stating that two points should belong to the same cluster may be context-dependent or even subjective.

There are many clustering algorithms. We will see a few of them in this recipe, applied to a toy example.

How to do it...

1. Let's import the libraries:

```
In [1]: from itertools import permutations
        import numpy as np
        import sklearn
        import sklearn.decomposition as dec
        import sklearn.cluster as clu
        import sklearn.datasets as ds
        import sklearn.grid_search as gs
        import matplotlib.pyplot as plt
        %matplotlib inline
```

2. Let's generate a random dataset with three clusters:

```
In [2]: X, y = ds.make_blobs(n_samples=200, n_features=2,
                             centers=3)
```

3. We need a couple of functions to relabel and display the results of the clustering algorithms:

```
In [3]: def relabel(cl):
            """Relabel a clustering with three clusters
            to match the original classes."""
            if np.max(cl) != 2:
```

```
            return cl
        perms = np.array(list(permutations((0, 1, 2))))
        i = np.argmin([np.sum(np.abs(perm[cl] - y))
                         for perm in perms])
        p = perms[i]
        return p[cl]
In [4]: def display_clustering(labels, title):
        """Plot the data points with the cluster
        colors."""
        # We relabel the classes when there are 3
        # clusters.
        labels = relabel(labels)
        # Display the points with the true labels on
        # the left, and with the clustering labels on
        # the right.
        for i, (c, title) in enumerate(zip(
                [y, labels], ["True labels", title])):
            plt.subplot(121 + i)
            plt.scatter(X[:,0], X[:,1], c=c, s=30,
                         linewidths=0,
                         cmap=plt.cm.rainbow)
            plt.xticks([]); plt.yticks([])
            plt.title(title)
```

4. Now, we cluster the dataset with the **K-means** algorithm, a classic and simple clustering algorithm:

```
In [5]: km = clu.KMeans()
        km.fit(X)
        display_clustering(km.labels_, "KMeans")
```

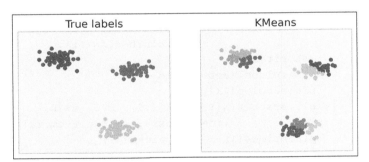

 If you're reading the printed version of this book, you might not be able to distinguish the colors. You will find the colored images on the book's website.

5. This algorithm needs to know the number of clusters at initialization time. In general, however, we do not necessarily know the number of clusters in the dataset. Here, let's try with n_clusters=3 (that's cheating, because we happen to know that there are 3 clusters!):

```
In [6]: km = clu.KMeans(n_clusters=3)
        km.fit(X)
        display_clustering(km.labels_, "KMeans(3)")
```

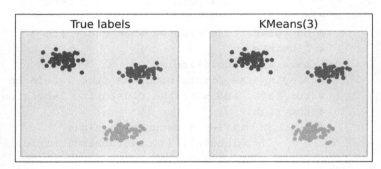

6. Let's try a few other clustering algorithms implemented in scikit-learn. The simplicity of the API makes it really easy to try different methods; it is just a matter of changing the name of the class:

```
In [7]: plt.subplot(231)
        plt.scatter(X[:,0], X[:,1], c=y, s=30,
                    linewidths=0, cmap=plt.cm.rainbow)
        plt.xticks([]); plt.yticks([])
        plt.title("True labels")
        for i, est in enumerate([clu.SpectralClustering(3),
                                  clu.AgglomerativeClustering(3),
                                  clu.MeanShift(),
                                  clu.AffinityPropagation(),
                                  clu.DBSCAN()]):
            est.fit(X)
            c = relabel(est.labels_)
            plt.subplot(232 + i)
            plt.scatter(X[:,0], X[:,1], c=c, s=30,
                        linewidths=0, cmap=plt.cm.rainbow)
            plt.xticks([]); plt.yticks([])
            plt.title(est.__class__.__name__)
```

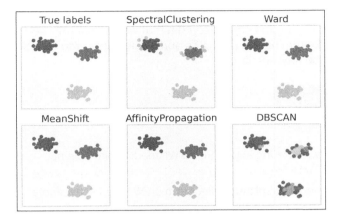

The first two algorithms required the number of clusters as input. The next two did not, but they were able to find the right number: 3. The last one failed at finding the correct number of clusters (this is *overclustering*—too many clusters have been found).

How it works...

The K-means clustering algorithm consists of partitioning the data points x_j into K clusters S_i so as to minimize the within-cluster sum of squares:

$$\arg \min_{S} \sum_{i=1}^{K} \sum_{x_j \in S_i} \| x_j - \mu_i \|_2^2$$

Here, μ_i is the center of the cluster i (average of all points in S_i).

Although it is very hard to solve this problem exactly, approximation algorithms exist. A popular one is **Lloyd's algorithm**. It consists of starting from an initial set of K means μ_i and alternating between two steps:

- ▶ In the *assignment* step, the points are assigned to the cluster associated to the closest mean
- ▶ In the *update* step, the means are recomputed from the last assignments

The algorithm converges to a solution that is not guaranteed to be optimal.

The **expectation-maximization algorithm** can be seen as a probabilistic version of the K-means algorithm. It is implemented in the `mixture` module of scikit-learn.

The other clustering algorithms used in this recipe are explained in the scikit-learn documentation. There is no clustering algorithm that works uniformly better than all the others, and every algorithm has its strengths and weaknesses. You will find more details in the references in the next section.

There's more...

Here are a few references:

- ▶ The K-means clustering algorithm on Wikipedia, available at `http://en.wikipedia.org/wiki/K-means_clustering`
- ▶ The expectation-maximization algorithm on Wikipedia, available at `http://en.wikipedia.org/wiki/Expectation-maximization_algorithm`
- ▶ Clustering in scikit-learn's documentation, available at `http://scikit-learn.org/stable/modules/clustering.html`

See also

- ▶ The *Reducing the dimensionality of a dataset with principal component analysis* recipe

9
Numerical Optimization

In this chapter, we will cover the following topics:

- ▶ Finding the root of a mathematical function
- ▶ Minimizing a mathematical function
- ▶ Fitting a function to data with nonlinear least squares
- ▶ Finding the equilibrium state of a physical system by minimizing its potential energy

Introduction

Mathematical optimization is a wide area of applied mathematics. It consists of finding the best solution to a given problem. Many real-world problems can be expressed in an optimization framework. What is the shortest path on the road from point A to point B? What is the best strategy to solve a puzzle? What is the most energy-efficient shape of a car (automotive aerodynamics)? Mathematical optimization is relevant in many domains including engineering, economics, finance, operations research, image processing, data analysis, and others.

Mathematically, an optimization problem generally consists of finding the maximum or minimum value of a function. We sometimes use the terms **continuous optimization** or **discrete optimization**, according to whether the function variable is real-valued or discrete.

In this chapter, we will focus on numerical methods for solving continuous optimization problems. Many optimization algorithms are implemented in the `scipy.optimize` module. We will come across other instances of optimization problems in several other chapters of this book. For example, we will see discrete optimization problems in *Chapter 14, Graphs, Geometry, and Geographic Information Systems*. In this introduction, we will give a few important definitions and key concepts related to mathematical optimization.

The objective function

We will study methods to find a root or an **extremum** of a real-valued function *f* called the **objective function**. An extremum is either a maximum or a minimum of a function. This mathematical function is generally implemented in a Python function. It can accept one or several variables, it can be continuous or not, and so on. The more assumptions we have about the function, the easier it can be optimized.

> A maximum of *f* is a minimum of *-f*, so any minimization algorithm can be used to maximize a function by considering the *opposite* of that function. Therefore, from now on, when we talk about *minimization*, we will really mean *minimization or maximization*.

Convex functions are generally easier to optimize than non-convex functions, as they satisfy certain useful properties. For example, any local minimum is necessarily a global minimum. The field of **convex optimization** deals with algorithms that are specifically adapted to the optimization of convex functions on convex domains. Convex optimization is an advanced topic, and we can't cover much of it here.

Differentiable functions have gradients, and these gradients can be particularly useful in optimization algorithms. Similarly, **continuous functions** are typically easier to optimize than non-continuous functions.

Also, functions with a single variable are easier to optimize than functions with multiple variables.

The choice of the most adequate optimization algorithm depends on the properties satisfied by the objective function.

Local and global minima

A **minimum** of a function *f* is a point x_0 such that $f(x) \geq f(x_0)$, for a particular set of points *x* in *E*. When this inequality is satisfied on the whole set *E*, we refer to x_0 as a **global minimum**. When it is only satisfied locally (around the point x_0), we say that x_0 is a **local minimum**. A **maximum** is defined similarly.

If *f* is differentiable, an extremum x_0 satisfies:

$$f'(x_0) = 0$$

Therefore, finding the extrema of an objective function is closely related to finding the roots of the derivative. However, a point x_0 satisfying this property is not necessarily an extremum.

It is more difficult to find global minima than to find local minima. In general, when an algorithm finds a local minimum, there is no guarantee that it is also a global minimum. Frequently, an algorithm seeking a global minimum stays *stuck* in a local minimum. This problem needs to be accounted for, specifically in global minimization algorithms. However, things are simpler with convex functions since these do not have strictly local minima. Moreover, there are many cases where finding a local minimum is good enough (for example, when looking for a good solution to a problem rather than the absolute best solution). Finally, let's note that a global minimum or maximum does not necessarily exist (the function can go to infinity). In that case, it may be necessary to constrain the space search; this is the subject of **constrained optimization**.

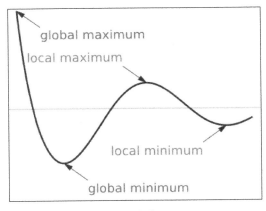

Local and global extrema

Constrained and unconstrained optimization

▶ **Unconstrained optimization**: Finding the minimum of a function *f* on the full set *E* where *f* is defined

▶ **Constrained optimization**: Finding the minimum of a function *f* on a subset *E'* of *E*; this set is generally described by equalities and inequalities:

$$x \in E' \Leftrightarrow \forall i, j, \quad g_i(x) = c_i, \quad h_j(x) \le d_j$$

Here, the g_i and h_j are arbitrary functions defining the constraints.

For example, optimizing the aerodynamic shape of a car requires constraints on parameters such as the volume and mass of the car, the cost of the production process, and others.

Constrained optimization is generally harder than unconstrained optimization.

Deterministic and stochastic algorithms

Some global optimization algorithms are **deterministic**, others are **stochastic**. Typically, deterministic methods are adapted to well-behaved functions, whereas stochastic methods may be useful with highly irregular and noisy functions.

The reason is that deterministic algorithms may be stuck in local minima, particularly if there are many non-global local minima. By spending some time exploring the space *E*, stochastic algorithms may have a chance of finding a global minimum.

References

- ▶ The SciPy lecture notes are an excellent reference on mathematical optimization with SciPy and are available at `http://scipy-lectures.github.io/advanced/mathematical_optimization/index.html`

- ▶ Reference manual of `scipy.optimize` available at `http://docs.scipy.org/doc/scipy/reference/optimize.html`

- ▶ Overview of mathematical optimization on Wikipedia, available at `http://en.wikipedia.org/wiki/Mathematical_optimization`

- ▶ Extrema, minima, and maxima on Wikipedia, available at `http://en.wikipedia.org/wiki/Maxima_and_minima`

- ▶ Convex optimization on Wikipedia, available at `http://en.wikipedia.org/wiki/Convex_optimization`

- ▶ Advanced optimization methods for image processing by Gabriel Peyré, available at `http://github.com/gpeyre/numerical-tours`

Finding the root of a mathematical function

In this short recipe, we will see how to use SciPy to find the root of a simple mathematical function of a single real variable.

How to do it...

1. Let's import NumPy, SciPy, `scipy.optimize`, and matplotlib:

```
In [1]: import numpy as np
        import scipy as sp
```

```
import scipy.optimize as opt
import matplotlib.pyplot as plt
%matplotlib inline
```

2. We define the mathematical function *f(x)=cos(x)-x* in Python. We will try to find a root of this function numerically. Here, a root corresponds to a fixed point of the cosine function:

```
In [2]: f = lambda x: np.cos(x) - x
```

3. Let's plot this function on the interval *[-5, 5]* (using 1000 samples):

```
In [3]: x = np.linspace(-5, 5, 1000)
        y = f(x)
        plt.plot(x, y)
        plt.axhline(0, color='k')
        plt.xlim(-5,5)
```

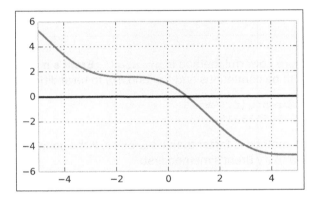

4. We see that this function has a unique root on this interval (this is because the function's sign changes on this interval). The scipy.optimize module contains a few root-finding functions that are adapted here. For example, the bisect() function implements the **bisection method** (also called the **dichotomy method**). It takes as input the function and the interval to find the root in:

```
In [4]: opt.bisect(f, -5, 5)
Out[4]: 0.7390851332155535
```

Let's visualize the root on the plot:

```
In [5]: plt.plot(x, y)
        plt.axhline(0, color='k')
        plt.scatter([_], [0], c='r', s=100)
        plt.xlim(-5,5)
```

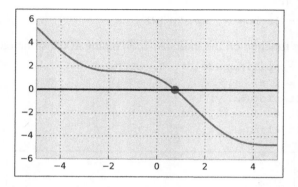

5. A faster and more powerful method is `brentq()` (**Brent's method**). This algorithm also requires *f* to be continuous and *f(a)* and *f(b)* to have different signs:

```
In [6]: opt.brentq(f, -5, 5)
Out[6]: 0.7390851332151607
```

The `brentq()` method is faster than `bisect()`. If the conditions are satisfied, it is a good idea to try Brent's method first:

```
In [7]: %timeit opt.bisect(f, -5, 5)
        %timeit opt.brentq(f, -5, 5)
1000 loops, best of 3: 331 µs per loop
10000 loops, best of 3: 71 µs per loop
```

How it works...

The bisection method consists of iteratively cutting an interval in half and selecting a subinterval that necessarily contains a root. This method is based on the fact that, if *f* is a continuous function of a single real variable, *f(a)>0*, and *f(b)<0*, then *f* has a root in *(a,b)* (**intermediate value theorem**).

Brent's method is a popular hybrid algorithm combining root bracketing, interval bisection, and inverse quadratic interpolation. It is a default method that works in many cases.

Let's also mention **Newton's method**. The idea is to approximate *f(x)* by its tangent (found with *f'(x)*) and find the intersection with the *y=0* line. If *f* is regular enough, the intersection point will be closer to the actual root of *f*. By iterating this operation, the algorithm generally converges to the sought solution.

There's more...

Here are a few references:

- Documentation of `scipy.optimize` available at `http://docs.scipy.org/doc/scipy/reference/optimize.html#root-finding`
- A course on root finding with SciPy available at `http://quant-econ.net/scipy.html#roots-and-fixed-points`
- The Bisection method on Wikipedia, available at `http://en.wikipedia.org/wiki/Bisection_method`
- The intermediate value theorem on Wikipedia, available at `http://en.wikipedia.org/wiki/Intermediate_value_theorem`
- Brent's method on Wikipedia, available at `http://en.wikipedia.org/wiki/Brent%27s_method`
- Newton's method on Wikipedia, available at `http://en.wikipedia.org/wiki/Newton%27s_method`

See also

- The *Minimizing a mathematical function* recipe

Minimizing a mathematical function

Mathematical optimization deals mainly with the problem of finding a minimum or a maximum of a mathematical function. Frequently, a real-world numerical problem can be expressed as a function minimization problem. Such examples can be found in statistical inference, machine learning, graph theory, and other areas.

Although there are many function minimization algorithms, a generic and universal method does not exist. Therefore, it is important to understand the differences between existing classes of algorithms, their specificities, and their respective use cases. We should also have a good understanding of our problem and our objective function; is it continuous, differentiable, convex, multidimensional, regular, or noisy? Is our problem constrained or unconstrained? Are we seeking local or global minima?

In this recipe, we will demonstrate a few usage examples of the function minimization algorithms implemented in SciPy.

How to do it...

1. We import the libraries:

```
In [1]: import numpy as np
        import scipy as sp
        import scipy.optimize as opt
        import matplotlib.pyplot as plt
        %matplotlib inline
```

2. First, let's define a simple mathematical function (the opposite of the **cardinal sine**). This function has many local minima but a single global minimum (http://en.wikipedia.org/wiki/Sinc_function):

```
In [2]: f = lambda x: 1-np.sin(x)/x
```

3. Let's plot this function on the interval *[-20, 20]* (with 1000 samples):

```
In [3]: x = np.linspace(-20., 20., 1000)
        y = f(x)
In [4]: plt.plot(x, y)
```

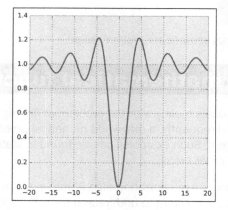

4. The scipy.optimize module comes with many function minimization routines. The minimize() function offers a unified interface to many algorithms. The **Broyden–Fletcher–Goldfarb–Shanno** (**BFGS**) algorithm (the default algorithm in minimize()) gives good results in general. The minimize() function requires an initial point as argument. For scalar univariate functions, we can also use minimize_scalar():

```
In [5]: x0 = 3
        xmin = opt.minimize(f, x0).x
```

Starting from x_0=3, the algorithm was able to find the actual global minimum, as shown in the following figure:

```
In [6]: plt.plot(x, y)
        plt.scatter(x0, f(x0), marker='o', s=300)
        plt.scatter(xmin, f(xmin), marker='v', s=300)
        plt.xlim(-20, 20)
```

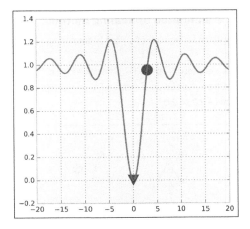

5. Now, if we start from an initial point that is further away from the actual global minimum, the algorithm converges towards a *local* minimum only:

```
In [7]: x0 = 10
        xmin = opt.minimize(f, x0).x
In [8]: plt.plot(x, y)
        plt.scatter(x0, f(x0), marker='o', s=300)
        plt.scatter(xmin, f(xmin), marker='v', s=300)
        plt.xlim(-20, 20)
```

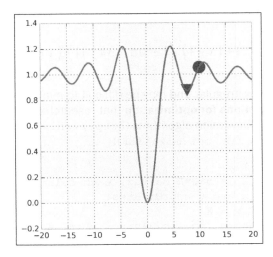

6. Like most function minimization algorithms, the BFGS algorithm is efficient at finding *local* minima, but not necessarily *global* minima, especially on complicated or noisy objective functions. A general strategy to overcome this problem is to combine such algorithms with an exploratory grid search on the initial points. Another option is to use a different class of algorithms based on heuristics and stochastic methods. A popular example is the **simulated annealing method**:

```
In [9]: xmin = opt.minimize(f, x0, method='Anneal').x
In [10]: plt.plot(x, y)
         plt.scatter(x0, f(x0), marker='o', s=300)
         plt.scatter(xmin, f(xmin), marker='v', s=300)
         plt.xlim(-20, 20)
```

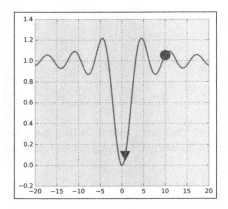

This time, the algorithm was able to find the global minimum.

7. Now, let's define a new function, in two dimensions this time, called the **Lévi function**:

$$f(x, y) = \sin^2(3\pi x) + (x-1)^2\left(1+\sin^2(3\pi y)\right) + (y-1)^2\left(1+\sin^2(2\pi y)\right)$$

This function is very irregular and may be difficult to minimize in general. It is one of the many **test functions for optimization** that researchers have developed to study and benchmark optimization algorithms (http://en.wikipedia.org/wiki/Test_functions_for_optimization):

```
In [11]: def g(X):
             # X is a 2*N matrix, each column contains
             # x and y coordinates.
             x, y = X
             return (np.sin(3*np.pi*x)**2 +
                     (x-1)**2 * (1+np.sin(3*np.pi*y)**2) +
                     (y-1)**2 * (1+np.sin(2*np.pi*y)**2))
```

8. Let's display this function with `imshow()`, on the square *[-10,10]*^{2}:

```
In [12]: n = 200
         k = 10
         X, Y = np.mgrid[-k:k:n*1j,-k:k:n*1j]
In [13]: Z = g(np.vstack((X.ravel(),
                          Y.ravel())))).reshape(n,n)
In [14]: # We use a logarithmic scale for the color here.
         plt.imshow(np.log(Z), cmap=plt.cm.hot_r)
         plt.xticks([]); plt.yticks([])
```

9. The BFGS algorithm also works in multiple dimensions:

```
In [15]: x0, y0 = opt.minimize(g, (8, 3)).x
In [16]: plt.imshow(np.log(Z), cmap=plt.cm.hot_r,
                    extent=(-k, k, -k, k), origin=0)
         plt.scatter([x0], [y0], c=['r'], s=100)
         plt.xticks([]); plt.yticks([])
```

How it works...

Many function minimization algorithms are based on the fundamental idea of **gradient descent**. If a function *f* is differentiable, then at every point, the opposite of its gradient points to the direction of the greatest decrease rate of the function. By following this direction, we can expect to find a local minimum.

This operation is generally done iteratively, by following the direction of the gradient with a small step. The way this step is computed depends on the optimization method.

Newton's method can also be used in this context of function minimization. The idea is to find a root of *f'* with Newton's method, thereby making use of the *second* derivative *f''*. In other words, we approximate *f* with a *quadratic* function instead of a *linear* function. In multiple dimensions, this is done by computing the **Hessian** (second derivatives) of *f*. By performing this operation iteratively, we can expect the algorithm to converge towards a local minimum.

When the computation of the Hessian is too costly, we can compute an *approximation* of the Hessian. Such methods are called **Quasi-Newton methods**. The BFGS algorithm belongs to this class of algorithms.

These algorithms make use of the objective function's gradient. If we can compute an analytical expression of the gradient, we should provide it to the minimization routine. Otherwise, the algorithm will compute an approximation of the gradient that may not be reliable.

The **simulated annealing** algorithm is a generic probabilistic metaheuristic for the global optimization problem. It is based on an analogy with thermodynamic systems: by increasing and decreasing the temperature, the configuration may converge to a state of low energy.

There are many stochastic global optimization methods based on metaheuristics. They are generally less well-theoretically grounded than the deterministic optimization algorithms previously described, and convergence is not always guaranteed. However, they may be useful in situations where the objective function is very irregular and noisy, with many local minima. The **Covariance Matrix Adaptation Evolution Strategy** (**CMA-ES**) algorithm is a metaheuristic that performs well in many situations. It is currently not implemented in SciPy, but there's a Python implementation in one of the references given later.

SciPy's `minimize()` function accepts a `method` keyword argument to specify the minimization algorithm to use. This function returns an object containing the results of the optimization. The `x` attribute is the point reaching the minimum.

There's more...

Here are a few further references:

- The `scipy.optimize` reference documentation available at `http://docs.scipy.org/doc/scipy/reference/optimize.html`
- An excellent lecture on mathematical optimization with SciPy available at `http://scipy-lectures.github.io/advanced/mathematical_optimization/`
- Definition of the gradient on Wikipedia, available at `http://en.wikipedia.org/wiki/Gradient`

- ► Newton's method on Wikipedia, available at `http://en.wikipedia.org/wiki/Newton%27s_method_in_optimization`

- ► Quasi-Newton methods on Wikipedia, available at `http://en.wikipedia.org/wiki/Quasi-Newton_method`

- ► Metaheuristics for function minimization on Wikipedia, available at `http://en.wikipedia.org/wiki/Metaheuristic`

- ► Simulated annealing on Wikipedia, available at `http://en.wikipedia.org/wiki/Simulated_annealing`

- ► The CMA-ES algorithm described at `http://en.wikipedia.org/wiki/CMA-ES`

- ► A Python implementation of CMA-ES available at `http://www.lri.fr/~hansen/cmaes_inmatlab.html#python`

See also

- ► The *Finding the root of a mathematical function* recipe

Fitting a function to data with nonlinear least squares

In this recipe, we will show an application of numerical optimization to **nonlinear least squares curve fitting**. The goal is to fit a function, depending on several parameters, to data points. In contrast to the linear least squares method, this function does not have to be linear in those parameters.

We will illustrate this method on artificial data.

How to do it...

1. Let's import the usual libraries:

```
In [1]: import numpy as np
        import scipy.optimize as opt
        import matplotlib.pyplot as plt
        %matplotlib inline
```

2. We define a logistic function with four parameters:

$$f_{a,b,c,d}(x) = \frac{a}{1 + \exp(-c(x-d))} + b$$

```
In [2]: def f(x, a, b, c, d):
            return a/(1 + np.exp(-c * (x-d))) + b
```

3. Let's define four random parameters:

```
In [3]: a, c = np.random.exponential(size=2)
        b, d = np.random.randn(2)
```

4. Now, we generate random data points by using the sigmoid function and adding a bit of noise:

```
In [4]: n = 100
        x = np.linspace(-10., 10., n)
        y_model = f(x, a, b, c, d)
        y = y_model + a * .2 * np.random.randn(n)
```

5. Here is a plot of the data points, with the particular sigmoid used for their generation (in dashed black):

```
In [5]: plt.plot(x, y_model, '--k')
        plt.plot(x, y, 'o')
```

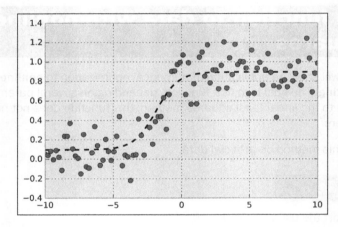

6. We now assume that we only have access to the data points and not the underlying generative function. These points could have been obtained during an experiment. By looking at the data, the points appear to approximately follow a sigmoid, so we may want to try to fit such a curve to the points. That's what **curve fitting** is about. SciPy's curve_fit() function allows us to fit a curve defined by an arbitrary Python function to the data:

```
In [6]: (a_, b_, c_, d_), _ = opt.curve_fit(f, x, y,
                                             (a, b, c, d))
```

7. Now, let's take a look at the fitted sigmoid curve:

```
In [7]: y_fit = f(x, a_, b_, c_, d_)
In [8]: plt.plot(x, y_model, '--k')
        plt.plot(x, y, 'o')
        plt.plot(x, y_fit, '-')
```

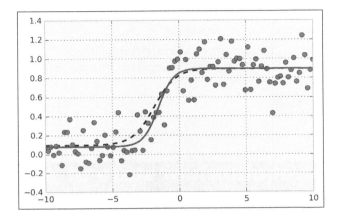

The fitted sigmoid appears to be reasonably close to the original sigmoid used for data generation.

How it works...

In SciPy, nonlinear least squares curve fitting works by minimizing the following cost function:

$$S(\beta) = \sum_{i=1}^{n} \left(y_i - f_\beta(x_i) \right)^2$$

Here, β is the vector of parameters (in our example, $\beta = (a,b,c,d)$).

Nonlinear least squares is really similar to linear least squares for linear regression. Whereas the function *f* is *linear* in the parameters with the linear least squares method, it is *not linear* here. Therefore, the minimization of $S(\beta)$ cannot be done analytically by solving the derivative of S with respect to β. SciPy implements an iterative method called the **Levenberg-Marquardt algorithm** (an extension of the Gauss–Newton algorithm).

There's more...

Here are further references:

- ► Reference documentation of `curvefit` available at `http://docs.scipy.org/doc/scipy/reference/generated/scipy.optimize.curve_fit.html`
- ► Nonlinear least squares on Wikipedia, available at `http://en.wikipedia.org/wiki/Non-linear_least_squares`
- ► Levenberg-Marquardt algorithm on Wikipedia, available at `http://en.wikipedia.org/wiki/Levenberg%E2%80%93Marquardt_algorithm`

See also

- ► The *Minimizing a mathematical function* recipe

Finding the equilibrium state of a physical system by minimizing its potential energy

In this recipe, we will give an application example of the function minimization algorithms described earlier. We will try to numerically find the equilibrium state of a physical system by minimizing its potential energy.

More specifically, we'll consider a structure made of masses and springs, attached to a vertical wall and subject to gravity. Starting from an initial position, we'll search for the equilibrium configuration where the gravity and elastic forces compensate.

How to do it...

1. Let's import NumPy, SciPy, and matplotlib:

   ```
   In [1]: import numpy as np
           import scipy.optimize as opt
           import matplotlib.pyplot as plt
           %matplotlib inline
   ```

2. We define a few constants in the International System of Units:

   ```
   In [2]: g = 9.81  # gravity of Earth
           m = .1  # mass, in kg
           n = 20  # number of masses
           e = .1  # initial distance between the masses
           l = e  # relaxed length of the springs
           k = 10000  # spring stiffness
   ```

3. We define the initial positions of the masses. They are arranged on a two-dimensional grid with two lines and *n/2* columns:

```
In [3]: P0 = np.zeros((n, 2))
        P0[:,0] = np.repeat(e*np.arange(n//2), 2)
        P0[:,1] = np.tile((0,-e), n//2)
```

4. Now, let's define the connectivity matrix between the masses. Coefficient *(i,j)* is 1 if masses *i* and *j* are connected by a spring, 0 otherwise:

```
In [4]: A = np.eye(n, n, 1) + np.eye(n, n, 2)
```

5. We also specify the spring stiffness of each spring. It is *l*, except for *diagonal* springs where it is $l\sqrt{2}$:

```
In [5]: L = l * (np.eye(n, n, 1) + np.eye(n, n, 2))
        for i in range(n//2-1):
            L[2*i+1,2*i+2] *= np.sqrt(2)
```

6. We get the indices of the spring connections:

```
In [6]: I, J = np.nonzero(A)
```

7. This `dist` function computes the distance matrix (distance between any pair of masses):

```
In [7]: dist = lambda P: np.sqrt(
                (P[:,0]-P[:,0][:, np.newaxis])**2 +
                (P[:,1]-P[:,1][:, np.newaxis])**2)
```

8. We define a function that displays the system. The springs are colored according to their tension:

```
In [8]: def show_bar(P):
            # Wall.
            plt.axvline(0, color='k', lw=3)
            # Distance matrix.
            D = dist(P)
            # We plot the springs.
            for i, j in zip(I, J):
                # The color depends on the spring tension,
                # which is proportional to the spring
                # elongation.
                c = D[i,j] - L[i,j]
                plt.plot(P[[i,j],0], P[[i,j],1],
                        lw=2, color=plt.cm.copper(c*150))
            # We plot the masses.
            plt.plot(P[[I,J],0], P[[I,J],1], 'ok',)
            # We configure the axes.
            plt.axis('equal')
```

```
        plt.xlim(P[:,0].min()-e/2, P[:,0].max()+e/2)
        plt.ylim(P[:,1].min()-e/2, P[:,1].max()+e/2)
        plt.xticks([]); plt.yticks([])
```

9. Here is the system in its initial configuration:

```
In [9]: show_bar(P0)
        plt.title("Initial configuration")
```

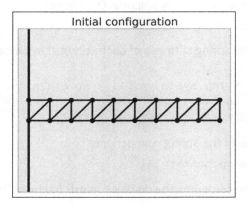

10. To find the equilibrium state, we need to minimize the total potential energy of the system. The following function computes the energy of the system given the positions of the masses. This function is explained in the *How it works...* section:

```
In [10]: def energy(P):
             # The argument P is a vector (flattened
             # matrix). We convert it to a matrix here.
             P = P.reshape((-1, 2))
             # We compute the distance matrix.
             D = dist(P)
             # The potential energy is the sum of the
             # gravitational and elastic potential
             # energies.
             return (g * m * P[:,1].sum() +
                     .5 * (k * A * (D - L)**2).sum())
```

11. Let's compute the potential energy of the initial configuration:

```
In [11]: energy(P0.ravel())
Out[11]: -0.98099
```

12. Now, let's minimize the potential energy with a function minimization method. We need a **constrained optimization algorithm**, because we make the assumption that the first two masses are fixed to the wall. Therefore, their positions cannot change. The **L-BFGS-B** algorithm, a variant of the BFGS algorithm, accepts bound constraints. Here, we force the first two points to stay at their initial positions, whereas there are no constraints on the other points. The `minimize()` function accepts a `bounds` list containing, for each dimension, a pair of `[min, max]` values:

```
In [12]: bounds = np.c_[P0[:2,:].ravel(),
                        P0[:2,:].ravel()].tolist() + \
                        [[None, None]] * (2*(n-2))
In [13]: P1 = opt.minimize(energy, P0.ravel(),
                        method='L-BFGS-B',
                        bounds=bounds).x \
                        .reshape((-1, 2))
```

13. Let's display the stable configuration:

```
In [14]: show_bar(P1)
         plt.title("Equilibrium configuration")
```

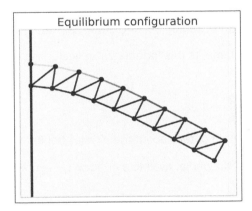

This configuration looks realistic. The tension appears to be maximal on the top springs near the wall.

How it works...

This example is conceptually simple. The state of the system is only described by the positions of the masses. If we can write a Python function that returns the total energy of the system, finding the equilibrium is just a matter of minimizing this function. This is the **principle of minimum total potential energy**, due to the second law of thermodynamics.

Here, we give an expression of the total energy of the system. Since we are only interested in the *equilibrium*, we omit any kinetic aspect and we only consider potential energy due to gravity (**gravitational force**) and spring forces (**elastic potential energy**).

Letting U be the total potential energy of the system, U can be expressed as the sum of the gravitational potential energies of the masses and the elastic potential energies of the springs. Therefore:

$$U = \sum_{i=1}^{n} mgy_i + \frac{1}{2} \sum_{i,j=1}^{n} ka_{ij} \left(\left\| \mathbf{p}_i - \mathbf{p}_j \right\| - l_{ij} \right)^2$$

Here:

> ▶ m is the mass
> ▶ g is the gravity of Earth
> ▶ k is the stiffness of the springs
> ▶ $p_i = (x, y)$ is the position of mass i
> ▶ a_{ij} is 1 if masses i and j are attached by a spring, 0 otherwise
> ▶ l_{ij} is the relaxed length of spring (i,j), or 0 if masses i and j are not attached

The energy() function implements this formula using vectorized computations on NumPy arrays.

There's more...

The following references contain details about the physics behind this formula:

> ▶ Potential energy on Wikipedia, available at http://en.wikipedia.org/wiki/Potential_energy
> ▶ Elastic potential energy on Wikipedia, available at http://en.wikipedia.org/wiki/Elastic_potential_energy
> ▶ Hooke's law, which is the linear approximation of the springs' response, described at http://en.wikipedia.org/wiki/Hooke%27s_law
> ▶ Principle of minimum energy on Wikipedia, available at http://en.wikipedia.org/wiki/Minimum_total_potential_energy_principle

Here is a reference about the optimization algorithm:

 ▶ L-BFGS-B algorithm on Wikipedia, available at `http://en.wikipedia.org/wiki/Limited-memory_BFGS#L-BFGS-B`

See also

 ▶ The *Minimizing a mathematical function* recipe

10
Signal Processing

In this chapter, we will cover the following topics:

- ► Analyzing the frequency components of a signal with a Fast Fourier Transform
- ► Applying a linear filter to a digital signal
- ► Computing the autocorrelation of a time series

Introduction

Signals are mathematical functions that describe the variation of a quantity across time or space. Time-dependent signals are often called **time series**. Examples of time series include share prices, which are typically presented as successive points in time spaced at uniform time intervals. In physics or biology, experimental devices record the evolution of variables such as electromagnetic waves or biological processes.

In signal processing, a general objective consists of extracting meaningful and relevant information from raw, noisy measurements. Signal processing topics include signal acquisition, transformation, compression, filtering, and feature extraction, among others. When dealing with a complex dataset, it can be beneficial to clean it before applying more advanced mathematical analysis methods (such as machine learning, for instance).

In this concise chapter, we will illustrate and explain the main foundations of signal processing. In the next chapter, *Chapter 11, Image and Audio Processing*, we will see particular signal processing methods adapted to images and sounds.

First, we will give some important definitions in this introduction.

Analog and digital signals

Signals can be time-dependent or space-dependent. In this chapter, we will focus on time-dependent signals.

Let $x(t)$ be a time-varying signal. We say that:

- This signal is **analog** if t is a continuous variable and $x(t)$ is a real number
- This signal is **digital** if t is a discrete variable (**discrete-time signal**) and $x(t)$ can only take a finite number of values (**quantified signal**)

The following figure shows the difference between an analog signal (the continuous curve) and a digital signal (dots):

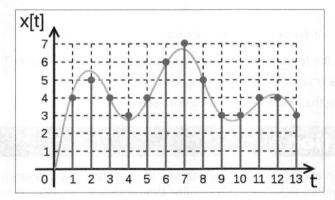

Difference between the analog and digital (quantified) signals

Analog signals are found in mathematics and in most physical systems such as electric circuits. Yet, computers being discrete machines, they can only understand digital signals. This is why computational science especially deals with digital signals.

A digital signal recorded by an experimental device is typically characterized by two important quantities:

- **The sampling rate**: The number of values (or samples) recorded every second (in Hertz)
- **The resolution**: The precision of the quantization, usually in bits per sample (also known as **bit depth**)

Digital signals with high sampling rates and bit depths are more accurate, but they require more memory and processing power. These two parameters are limited by the experimental devices that record the signals.

The Nyquist–Shannon sampling theorem

Let's consider a continuous (analog) time-varying signal x(t). We record this physical signal with an experimental device, and we obtain a digital signal with a sampling rate of f_s. As the original analog signal has an infinite precision, whereas the recorded signal has a finite precision, we expect to lose information in the analog-to-digital process.

The **Nyquist–Shannon sampling** theorem states that under certain conditions on the analog signal and the sampling rate, it is possible not to lose any information in the process. In other words, under these conditions, we can recover the original continuous signal from the sampled digital signal. For more details, refer to http://en.wikipedia.org/wiki/Nyquist%E2%80%93Shannon_sampling_theorem.

Let's define these conditions. The **Fourier transform** $\hat{x}(f)$ of x(t) is defined by:

$$\hat{x}(f) = \int_{-\infty}^{+\infty} x(t) e^{-2i\pi ft} dt$$

Here, the Fourier transform is a representation of a time-dependent signal in the frequency domain. The **Nyquist criterion** states that:

$$\exists B < f_s/2, \quad \forall |f| > B, \quad \hat{x}(f) = 0.$$

In other words, the signal must be **bandlimited**, meaning that it must not contain any frequency higher than a certain cutoff frequency B. Additionally, the sampling rate f_s needs to be at least twice as large as this frequency B. Here are a couple of definitions:

▶ The **Nyquist rate** is *2B*. For a given bandlimited analog signal, it is the minimal sampling rate required to sample the signal without loss.

▶ The **Nyquist frequency** is $f_s/2$. For a given sampling rate, it is the maximal frequency that the signal can contain in order to be sampled without loss.

Under these conditions, we can theoretically reconstruct the original analog signal from the sampled digital signal.

Compressed sensing

Compressed sensing is a modern and important approach to signal processing. It acknowledges that many real-world signals are intrinsically low dimensional. For example, speech signals have a very specific structure depending on the general physical constraints of the human vocal tract.

Even if a speech signal has many frequencies in the Fourier domain, it may be well approximated by a **sparse decomposition** on an adequate basis (dictionary). By definition, a decomposition is sparse if most of the coefficients are zero. If the dictionary is chosen well, every signal is a combination of a small number of the basis signals.

This dictionary contains elementary signals that are specific to the signals considered in a given problem. This is different from the Fourier transform that decomposes a signal on a *universal* basis of sine functions. In other words, with sparse representations, the Nyquist condition can be circumvented. We can precisely reconstruct a continuous signal from a sparse representation containing fewer samples than what the Nyquist condition requires.

Sparse decompositions can be found with sophisticated algorithms. In particular, these problems may be turned into convex optimization problems that can be tackled with specific numerical optimization methods.

Compressed sensing has many applications in signal compression, image processing, computer vision, biomedical imaging, and many other scientific and engineering areas.

Here are further references about compressed sensing:

- `http://en.wikipedia.org/wiki/Compressed_sensing`
- `http://en.wikipedia.org/wiki/Sparse_approximation`

References

Here are a few references:

- *Understanding Digital Signal Processing*, Richard G. Lyons, *Pearson Education, (2010)*.
- For good coverage of compressed sensing, refer to the book *A Wavelet Tour of Signal Processing: The Sparse Way, Mallat Stéphane, Academic Press, (2008)*.
- The book *Python for Signal Processing* by Jose Unpingco contains many more details than what we can cover in this chapter. The code is available as IPython notebooks on GitHub (`http://python-for-signal-processing.blogspot.com`).
- Digital Signal Processing on WikiBooks available at `http://en.wikibooks.org/wiki/Digital_Signal_Processing`.

Analyzing the frequency components of a signal with a Fast Fourier Transform

In this recipe, we will show how to use a **Fast Fourier Transform** (**FFT**) to compute the spectral density of a signal. The spectrum represents the energy associated to frequencies (encoding periodic fluctuations in a signal). It is obtained with a Fourier transform, which is a frequency representation of a time-dependent signal. A signal can be transformed back and forth from one representation to the other without information loss.

In this recipe, we will illustrate several aspects of the Fourier Transform. We will apply this tool to weather data spanning 20 years in France obtained from the US National Climatic Data Center.

Getting ready

Download the *Weather* dataset from the book's GitHub repository at `http://github.com/ipython-books/cookbook-data`, and extract it in the current directory.

The data has been obtained from `www.ncdc.noaa.gov/cdo-web/datasets#GHCND`.

How to do it...

1. Let's import the packages, including `scipy.fftpack`, which includes many FFT-related routines:

    ```
    In [1]: import datetime
            import numpy as np
            import scipy as sp
            import scipy.fftpack
            import pandas as pd
            import matplotlib.pyplot as plt
            %matplotlib inline
    ```

2. We import the data from the CSV file. The number `-9999` is used for N/A values. pandas can easily handle this. In addition, we tell pandas to parse dates contained in the `DATE` column:

    ```
    In [2]: df0 = pd.read_csv('data/weather.csv',
                              na_values=(-9999),
                              parse_dates=['DATE'])
    In [3]: df = df0[df0['DATE']>='19940101']
    In [4]: df.head()
    Out[4]:     STATION              DATE         PRCP  TMAX  TMIN
            365 FR013055001 1994-01-01 00:00:00      0   104    72
            366 FR013055001 1994-01-02 00:00:00      4   128    49
    ```

3. Each row contains the precipitation and extreme temperatures recorded each day by one weather station in France. For every date in the calendar, we want to get a single average temperature for the whole country. The `groupby()` method provided by pandas lets us do this easily. We also remove any N/A value with `dropna()`:

```
In [5]: df_avg = df.dropna().groupby('DATE').mean()
In [6]: df_avg.head()
Out[6]:
    DATE          PRCP         TMAX         TMIN
1994-01-01   178.666667   127.388889   70.333333
1994-01-02   122.000000   152.421053   81.736842
```

4. Now, we get the list of dates and the list of corresponding temperatures. The unit is in tenths of a degree, and we get the average value between the minimal and maximal temperature, which explains why we divide by 20.

```
In [7]: date = df_avg.index.to_datetime()
        temp = (df_avg['TMAX'] + df_avg['TMIN']) / 20.
        N = len(temp)
```

5. Let's take a look at the evolution of the temperature:

```
In [8]: plt.plot_date(date, temp, '-', lw=.5)
        plt.ylim(-10, 40)
        plt.xlabel('Date')
        plt.ylabel('Mean temperature')
```

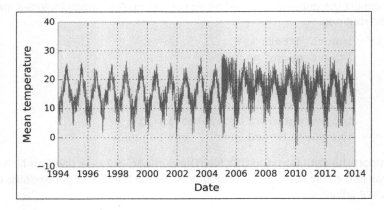

6. We now compute the Fourier transform and the spectral density of the signal. The first step is to compute the FFT of the signal using the `fft()` function:

```
In [9]: temp_fft = sp.fftpack.fft(temp)
```

7. Once the FFT has been obtained, we need to take the square of its absolute value in order to get the **power spectral density (PSD)**:

```
In [10]: temp_psd = np.abs(temp_fft) ** 2
```

8. The next step is to get the frequencies corresponding to the values of the PSD. The `fftfreq()` utility function does just that. It takes the length of the PSD vector as input as well as the frequency unit. Here, we choose an annual unit: a frequency of 1 corresponds to 1 year (365 days). We provide *1/365* because the original unit is in days.

```
In [11]: fftfreq = sp.fftpack.fftfreq(len(temp_psd),
                                      1./365)
```

9. The `fftfreq()` function returns positive and negative frequencies. We are only interested in positive frequencies here, as we have a real signal (this will be explained in the *How it works...* section of this recipe).

```
In [12]: i = fftfreq>0
```

10. We now plot the power spectral density of our signal, as a function of the frequency (in unit of *1/year*). We choose a logarithmic scale for the *y* axis (**decibels**).

```
In [13]: plt.plot(fftfreq[i], 10*np.log10(temp_psd[i]))
         plt.xlim(0, 5)
         plt.xlabel('Frequency (1/year)')
         plt.ylabel('PSD (dB)')
```

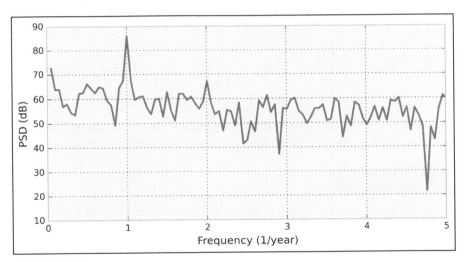

Because the fundamental frequency of the signal is the yearly variation of the temperature, we observe a peak for *f=1*.

11. Now, we cut out frequencies higher than the fundamental frequency:

```
In [14]: temp_fft_bis = temp_fft.copy()
         temp_fft_bis[np.abs(fftfreq) > 1.1] = 0
```

12. Next, we perform an **inverse FFT** to convert the modified Fourier transform back to the temporal domain. This way, we recover a signal that mainly contains the fundamental frequency, as shown in the following figure:

```
In [15]: temp_slow = np.real(sp.fftpack.ifft(temp_fft_bis))
In [16]: plt.plot_date(date, temp, '-', lw=.5)
         plt.plot_date(date, temp_slow, '-')
         plt.xlim(datetime.date(1994, 1, 1),
                  datetime.date(2000, 1, 1))
         plt.ylim(-10, 40)
         plt.xlabel('Date')
         plt.ylabel('Mean temperature')
```

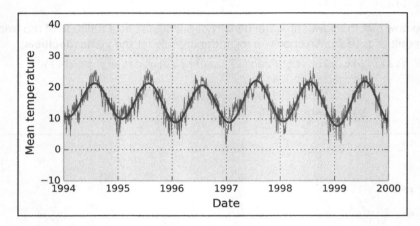

We get a smoothed version of the signal, because the fast variations have been lost when we have removed the high frequencies in the Fourier transform.

How it works...

Broadly speaking, the Fourier transform is an alternative representation of a signal as a superposition of periodic components. It is an important mathematical result that any well-behaved function can be represented under this form. Whereas a time-varying signal is most naturally considered as a function of time, the Fourier transform represents it as a function of the frequency. A magnitude and a phase, which are both encoded in a single complex number, are associated to each frequency.

The Discrete Fourier Transform

Let's consider a digital signal x represented by a vector $(x_0, ..., x_{(N-1)})$. We assume that this signal is regularly sampled. The **Discrete Fourier Transform** (**DFT**) of x is $X = (X_0, ..., X_{(N-1)})$ defined as:

$$\forall k \in \{0,...,N-1\}, \quad X_k = \sum_{n=0}^{N-1} x_n e^{-2i\pi kn/N}.$$

The DFT can be computed efficiently with the Fast Fourier Transform (FFT), an algorithm that exploits symmetries and redundancies in this definition to considerably speed up the computation. The complexity of the FFT is $O(N \log N)$ instead of $O(N^2)$ for the naive DFT. The FFT is one of the most important algorithms of the digital universe.

Here is an intuitive explanation of what the DFT describes. Instead of representing our signal on a real line, let's represent it on a circle. We can play the whole signal by making 1, 2, or any number k of laps on the circle. Therefore, when k is fixed, we represent each value x_n of the signal with an angle $2\pi kn/N$ and a distance from the original equal to x_n.

If the signal shows a certain periodicity of k laps, it means that many correlated values will superimpose at that exact frequency so that the coefficient X_k will be large. In other words, the modulus $|X_k|$ of the k-th coefficient represents the *energy* of the signal associated to this frequency.

In the following figure, the signal is a sine wave at the frequency *f=3 Hz*. The points of this signal are in blue, positioned at an angle $2\pi kn/N$. Their algebraic sum in the complex plane is in red. These vectors represent the different coefficients of the signal's DFT.

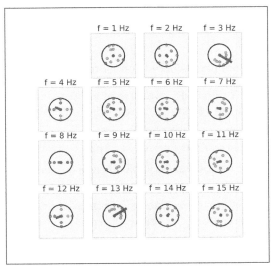

An illustration of the DFT

The next figure represents the previous signal's **power spectral density (PSD)**:

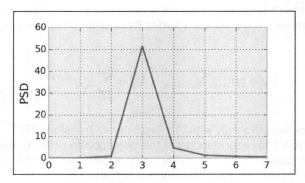

The PSD of the signal in the previous example

Inverse Fourier Transform

By considering all possible frequencies, we have an exact representation of our digital signal in the frequency domain. We can recover the initial signal with an **Inverse Fast Fourier Transform** that computes an **Inverse Discrete Fourier Transform**. The formula is very similar to the DFT:

$$\forall k \in \{0,...,N-1\}, \quad x_k = \frac{1}{N}\sum_{n=0}^{N-1} X_n e^{2i\pi kn/N}.$$

The DFT is useful when periodic patterns are to be found. However, generally speaking, the Fourier transform cannot detect *transient* changes at specific frequencies. More local spectral methods are required, such as the **wavelet transform**.

There's more...

The following links contain more details about Fourier transforms:

- Introduction to the FFT with SciPy, available at `http://scipy-lectures.github.io/intro/scipy.html#fast-fourier-transforms-scipy-fftpack`
- Reference documentation for the fftpack in SciPy, available at `http://docs.scipy.org/doc/scipy/reference/fftpack.html`
- Fourier Transform on Wikipedia, available at `http://en.wikipedia.org/wiki/Fourier_transform`
- Discrete Fourier Transform on Wikipedia, available at `http://en.wikipedia.org/wiki/Discrete_Fourier_transform`
- Fast Fourier Transform on Wikipedia, available at `http://en.wikipedia.org/wiki/Fast_Fourier_transform`
- Decibel on Wikipedia, available at `https://en.wikipedia.org/wiki/Decibel`

See also

▶ The *Applying a linear filter to a digital signal* recipe

▶ The *Computing the autocorrelation of a time series* recipe

Applying a linear filter to a digital signal

Linear filters play a fundamental role in signal processing. With a linear filter, one can extract meaningful information from a digital signal.

In this recipe, we will show two examples using stock market data (the NASDAQ stock exchange). First, we will smooth out a very noisy signal with a low-pass filter to extract its slow variations. We will also apply a high-pass filter on the original time series to extract the fast variations. These are just two common examples among a wide variety of applications of linear filters.

Getting ready

Download the *Nasdaq* dataset from the book's GitHub repository at `https://github.com/ipython-books/cookbook-data` and extract it in the current directory.

The data has been obtained from `http://finance.yahoo.com/q/hp?s=^IXIC&a=00&b=1&c=1990&d=00&e=1&f=2014&g=d`.

How to do it...

1. Let's import the packages:

    ```
    In [1]: import numpy as np
            import scipy as sp
            import scipy.signal as sg
            import pandas as pd
            import matplotlib.pyplot as plt
            %matplotlib inline
    ```

2. We load the NASDAQ data with pandas:

    ```
    In [2]: nasdaq_df = pd.read_csv('data/nasdaq.csv')
    In [3]: nasdaq_df.head()
    Out[3]:    Date      Open     High     Low      Close
    0  2013-12-31  4161.51  4177.73  4160.77  4176.59
    1  2013-12-30  4153.58  4158.73  4142.18  4154.20
    ```

3. Let's extract two columns: the date and the daily closing value:

```
In [4]: date = pd.to_datetime(nasdaq_df['Date'])
        nasdaq = nasdaq_df['Close']
```

4. Let's take a look at the raw signal:

```
In [5]: plt.plot_date(date, nasdaq, '-')
```

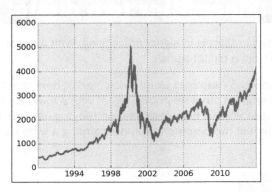

5. Now, we will follow the first approach to get the slow variations of the signal. We will convolve the signal with a triangular window, which corresponds to a **FIR filter**. We will explain the idea behind this method in the *How it works...* section of this recipe. For now, let's just say that we replace each value with a weighted mean of the signal around this value:

```
In [6]: # We get a triangular window with 60 samples.
        h = sg.get_window('triang', 60)
        # We convolve the signal with this window.
        fil = sg.convolve(nasdaq, h/h.sum())
In [7]: # We plot the original signal...
        plt.plot_date(date, nasdaq, '-', lw=1)
        # ... and the filtered signal.
        plt.plot_date(date, fil[:len(nasdaq)-1], '-')
```

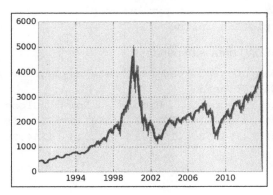

6. Now, let's use another method. We create an IIR Butterworth low-pass filter to extract the slow variations of the signal. The `filtfilt()` method allows us to apply a filter forward and backward in order to avoid phase delays:

```
In [8]: plt.plot_date(date, nasdaq, '-', lw=1)
        # We create a 4-th order Butterworth low-pass
        # filter.
        b, a = sg.butter(4, 2./365)
        # We apply this filter to the signal.
        plt.plot_date(date, sg.filtfilt(b, a, nasdaq),
                      '-')
```

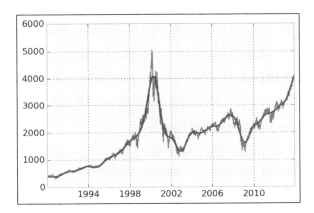

7. Finally, we use the same method to create a high-pass filter and extract the *fast* variations of the signal:

```
In [9]: plt.plot_date(date, nasdaq, '-', lw=1)
        b, a = sg.butter(4, 2*5./365, btype='high')
        plt.plot_date(date, sg.filtfilt(b, a, nasdaq),
                      '-', lw=.5)
```

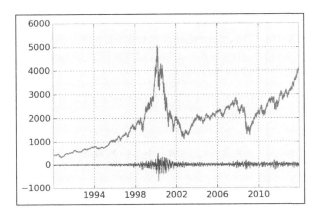

The fast variations around 2000 correspond to the dot-com bubble burst, reflecting the high-market volatility and the fast fluctuations of the stock market indices at that time. For more details, refer to `http://en.wikipedia.org/wiki/Dot-com_bubble`.

How it works...

In this section, we explain the very basics of linear filters in the context of digital signals.

A **digital signal** is a discrete sequence (x_n) indexed by $n \geq 0$. Although we often assume infinite sequences, in practice, a signal is represented by a *vector* of the finite size N.

In the continuous case, we would rather manipulate time-dependent functions $f(t)$. Loosely stated, we can go from continuous signals to discrete signals by discretizing time and transforming integrals into sums.

What are linear filters?

A **linear filter** F transforms an input signal $x = (x_n)$ to an output signal $y = (y_n)$. This transformation is *linear*—the transformation of the sum of two signals is the sum of the transformed signals: $F(x+y) = F(x)+F(y)$.

In addition to this, multiplying the input signal by a constant λ yields the same output as multiplying the original output signal by the same constant: $F(\lambda x) = \lambda F(x)$.

A **Linear Time-Invariant** (**LTI**) filter has an additional property: if the signal (x_n) is transformed to (y_n), then the *shifted* signal $(x_{(n-k)})$ is transformed to $(y_{(n-k)})$, for any fixed k. In other words, the system is time-invariant because the output does not depend on the particular time the input is applied.

[From now on, we will only consider LTI filters.]

Linear filters and convolutions

A very important result in the LTI system theory is that LTI filters can be described by a single signal: the impulse response h. This is the output of the filter in response to an impulse signal. For digital filters, the impulse signal is *(1, 0, 0, 0, ...)*.

It can be shown that $x = (x_n)$ is transformed to $y = (y_n)$ defined by the **convolution** of the impulse response h with the signal x:

$$y = h * x, \quad or \quad y_n = \sum_{k=0}^{n} h_k x_{n-k}$$

The convolution is a fundamental mathematical operation in signal processing. Intuitively, and considering a convolution function peaking around zero, the convolution is equivalent to taking a local average of the signal (*x* here), weighted by a given window (*h* here).

It is implied, by our notations, that we restrict ourselves to **causal** filters (h_n = 0 for *n* < 0). This property means that the output of the signal only depends on the present and the past of the input, not the future. This is a natural property in many situations.

The FIR and IIR filters

The **support** of a signal *(h_n)* is the set of *n* such that $h_n \neq 0$. LTI filters can be classified into two categories:

▸ A **Finite Impulse Response** (FIR) filter has an impulse response with finite support

▸ A **Infinite Impulse Response** (IIR) filter has an impulse response with infinite support

A FIR filter can be described by a finite impulse response of size *N* (a vector). It works by convolving a signal with its impulse response. Let's define $b_n = h_n$ for $n \leq N$. Then, y_n is a linear combination of the last *N+1* values of the input signal:

$$y_n = \sum_{k=0}^{N} b_k x_{n-k}$$

On the other hand, an IIR filter is described by an infinite impulse response that cannot be represented exactly under this form. For this reason, we often use an alternative representation:

$$y_n = \frac{1}{a_0}\left(\sum_{k=0}^{N} b_k x_{n-k} - \sum_{l=1}^{M} a_l y_{n-l}\right)$$

This **difference equation** expresses y_n as a linear combination of the last *N+1* values of the *input* signal (the **feedforward** term, like for a FIR filter) *and* a linear combination of the last *M* values of the *output* signal (**feedback** term). The feedback term makes the IIR filter more complex than a FIR filter in that the output depends not only on the input but also on the previous values of the output (dynamics).

Filters in the frequency domain

We only described filters in the temporal domain. Alternate representations in other domains exist such as Laplace transforms, Z-transforms, and Fourier transforms.

In particular, the *Fourier transform* has a very convenient property: it transforms convolutions into multiplications in the frequency domain. In other words, in the frequency domain, an LTI filter multiplies the Fourier transform of the input signal by the Fourier transform of the impulse response.

The low-, high-, and band-pass filters

Filters can be characterized by their effects on the amplitude of the input signal's frequencies. They are as follows:

> ▶ A **low-pass filter** attenuates the components of the signal at frequencies *higher* than a **cutoff frequency**
>
> ▶ A **high-pass filter** attenuates the components of the signal at frequencies *lower* than a **cutoff frequency**
>
> ▶ A **band-pass filter** passes the components of the signal at frequencies within a certain range and attenuates those outside

In this recipe, we first convolved the input signal with a triangular window (with finite support). It can be shown that this operation corresponds to a low-pass FIR filter. It is a particular case of the **moving average** method, which computes a local weighted average of every value in order to smooth out the signal.

Then, we applied two instances of the **Butterworth filter**, a particular kind of IIR filter that can act as a low-pass, high-pass, or band-pass filter. In this recipe, we first used it as a low-pass filter to smooth out the signal, before using it as a high-pass filter to extract fast variations of the signal.

There's more...

Here are some general references about digital signal processing and linear filters:

> ▶ Digital signal processing on Wikipedia, available at `http://en.wikipedia.org/wiki/Digital_signal_processing`
>
> ▶ Linear filters on Wikipedia, available at `http://en.wikipedia.org/wiki/Linear_filter`
>
> ▶ LTI filters on Wikipedia, available at `http://en.wikipedia.org/wiki/LTI_system_theory`

Here are some references about impulse responses, convolutions, and FIR/IIR filters:

> ▶ Impulse responses described at `http://en.wikipedia.org/wiki/Impulse_response`
>
> ▶ Convolution described at `http://en.wikipedia.org/wiki/Convolution`

- ▶ FIR filters described at `http://en.wikipedia.org/wiki/Finite_impulse_response`
- ▶ IIR filters described at `http://en.wikipedia.org/wiki/Infinite_impulse_response`
- ▶ Low-pass filters described at `http://en.wikipedia.org/wiki/Low-pass_filter`
- ▶ High-pass filters described at `http://en.wikipedia.org/wiki/High-pass_filter`
- ▶ Band-pass filters described at `http://en.wikipedia.org/wiki/Band-pass_filter`

See also

- ▶ The *Analyzing the frequency components of a signal with a Fast Fourier Transform* recipe

Computing the autocorrelation of a time series

The autocorrelation of a time series can inform us about repeating patterns or serial correlation. The latter refers to the correlation between the signal at a given time and at a later time. The analysis of the autocorrelation can thereby inform us about the timescale of the fluctuations. Here, we use this tool to analyze the evolution of baby names in the US, based on the data provided by the United States Social Security Administration.

Getting ready

Download the *Babies* dataset from the book's GitHub repository at `https://github.com/ipython-books/cookbook-data`, and extract it in the current directory.

The data has been obtained from `www.data.gov` (`http://catalog.data.gov/dataset/baby-names-from-social-security-card-applications-national-level-data-6315b`).

How to do it...

1. We import the following packages:

```
In [1]: import os
        import numpy as np
        import pandas as pd
        import matplotlib.pyplot as plt
        %matplotlib inline
```

2. We read the data with pandas. The dataset contains one CSV file per year. Each file contains all baby names given that year with the respective frequencies. We load the data in a dictionary, containing one `DataFrame` per year:

```
In [2]: files = [file for file in os.listdir('data/')
                 if file.startswith('yob')]
In [3]: years = np.array(sorted([int(file[3:7])
                                 for file in files]))
In [4]: data = {year:
                pd.read_csv(
                  'data/yob{y:d}.txt'.format(y=year),
                  index_col=0, header=None,
                  names=['First name', 'Gender', 'Number'])
                        for year in years}
In [5]: data[2012].head()
Out[5]:      Gender  Number
First name
Sophia         F     22158
Emma           F     20791
Isabella       F     18931
Olivia         F     17147
Ava            F     15418
```

3. We write functions to retrieve the frequencies of baby names as a function of the name, gender, and birth year:

```
In [6]: def get_value(name, gender, year):
            """Return the number of babies born a given
            year, with a given gender and a given name."""
            try:
                return data[year] \
                       [data[year]['Gender'] == gender] \
                       ['Number'][name]
            except KeyError:
                return 0
In [7]: def get_evolution(name, gender):
```

```
"""Return the evolution of a baby name over the
years."""
return np.array([get_value(name, gender, year)
                 for year in years])
```

4. Let's define a function that computes the autocorrelation of a signal. This function is essentially based on NumPy's `correlate()` function.

```
In [8]: def autocorr(x):
            result = np.correlate(x, x, mode='full')
            return result[result.size/2:]
```

5. Now, we create a function that displays the evolution of a baby name as well as its (normalized) autocorrelation:

```
In [9]: def autocorr_name(name, gender):
            x = get_evolution(name, gender)
            z = autocorr(x)
            # Evolution of the name.
            plt.subplot(121)
            plt.plot(years, x, '-o', label=name)
            plt.title("Baby names")
            # Autocorrelation.
            plt.subplot(122)
            plt.plot(z / float(z.max()), '-', label=name)
            plt.legend()
            plt.title("Autocorrelation")
```

6. Let's take a look at two female names:

```
In [10]: autocorr_name('Olivia', 'F')
         autocorr_name('Maria', 'F')
```

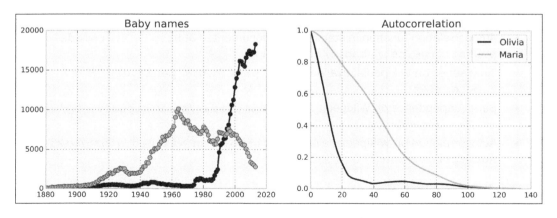

The autocorrelation of Olivia is decaying much faster than Maria's. This is mainly because of the steep increase of the name Olivia at the end of the twentieth century. By contrast, the name Maria is varying more slowly globally, and its autocorrelation is decaying somewhat slower.

How it works...

A **time series** is a sequence indexed by time. Important applications include stock markets, product sales, weather forecasting, biological signals, and many others. Time series analysis is an important part of statistical data analysis, signal processing, and machine learning.

There are various definitions of the autocorrelation. Here, we define the autocorrelation of a time series (x_n) as:

$$R(k) = \frac{1}{N} \sum_n x_n x_{n+k}$$

In the previous plot, we normalized the autocorrelation by its maximum so as to compare the autocorrelation of two signals. The autocorrelation quantifies the average similarity between the signal and a shifted version of the same signal, as a function of the delay between the two. In other words, the autocorrelation can give us information about repeating patterns as well as the timescale of the signal's fluctuations. The faster the autocorrelation decays to zero, the faster the signal varies.

There's more...

Here are a few references:

- ▶ NumPy's correlation function documentation, available at `http://docs.scipy.org/doc/numpy/reference/generated/numpy.correlate.html`
- ▶ Autocorrelation function in statsmodels, documented at `http://statsmodels.sourceforge.net/stable/tsa.html`
- ▶ Time series on Wikipedia, available at `http://en.wikipedia.org/wiki/Time_series`
- ▶ Serial dependence on Wikipedia, available at `http://en.wikipedia.org/wiki/Serial_dependence`
- ▶ Autocorrelation on Wikipedia, available at `http://en.wikipedia.org/wiki/Autocorrelation`

See also

- ▶ The *Analyzing the frequency components of a signal with a Fast Fourier Transform* recipe

11
Image and Audio Processing

In this chapter, we will cover the following topics:

- ▶ Manipulating the exposure of an image
- ▶ Applying filters on an image
- ▶ Segmenting an image
- ▶ Finding points of interest in an image
- ▶ Detecting faces in an image with OpenCV
- ▶ Applying digital filters to speech sounds
- ▶ Creating a sound synthesizer in the notebook

Introduction

In the previous chapter, we covered signal processing techniques for one-dimensional, time-dependent signals. In this chapter, we will see signal processing techniques for images and sounds.

Generic signal processing techniques can be applied to images and sounds, but many image or audio processing tasks require specialized algorithms. For example, we will see algorithms for segmenting images, detecting points of interest in an image, or detecting faces. We will also hear the effect of linear filters on speech sounds.

scikit-image is one of the main image processing packages in Python. We will use it in most of the image processing recipes in this chapter. For more on scikit-image, refer to `http://scikit-image.org`.

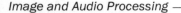

We will also use **OpenCV** (http://opencv.org), a C++ computer vision library that has a Python wrapper. It implements algorithms for specialized image and video processing tasks, but it can be a bit difficult to use. An interesting (and simpler) alternative is **SimpleCV** (http://simplecv.org).

In this introduction, we will discuss the particularities of images and sounds from a signal processing point of view.

Images

A **grayscale** image is a bidimensional signal represented by a function, *f*, that maps each pixel to an **intensity**. The intensity can be a real value between 0 (dark) and 1 (light). In a colored image, this function maps each pixel to a triplet of intensities, generally, the **red**, **green**, and **blue** (**RGB**) components.

On a computer, images are digitally sampled. The intensities are no longer real values, but integers or floating point numbers. On one hand, the mathematical formulation of continuous functions allows us to apply analytical tools such as derivatives and integrals. On the other hand, we need to take into account the digital nature of the images we deal with.

Sounds

From a signal processing perspective, a sound is a time-dependent signal that has sufficient power in the hearing frequency range (about 20 Hz to 20 kHz). Then, according to the Nyquist-Shannon theorem (introduced in *Chapter 10*, *Signal Processing*), the sampling rate of a digital sound signal needs to be at least 40 kHz. A sampling rate of 44100 Hz is frequently chosen.

References

Here are a few references:

▶ Image processing on Wikipedia, available at http://en.wikipedia.org/wiki/Image_processing

▶ Advanced image processing algorithms, by Gabriel Peyré, available at https://github.com/gpeyre/numerical-tours

▶ Audio signal processing on Wikipedia, available at http://en.wikipedia.org/wiki/Audio_signal_processing

▶ Particularities of the 44100 Hz sampling rate explained at http://en.wikipedia.org/wiki/44,100_Hz

Manipulating the exposure of an image

The **exposure** of an image tells us whether the image is too dark, too light, or balanced. It can be measured with a histogram of the intensity values of all pixels. Improving the exposure of an image is a basic image-editing operation. As we will see in this recipe, that can be done easily with scikit-image.

Getting ready

You need scikit-image for this recipe. You will find the installation instructions at `http://scikit-image.org/download.html`. With Anaconda, you can just type `conda install scikit-image` in a terminal.

You also need to download the *Beach* dataset from the book's GitHub repository at `https://github.com/ipython-books/cookbook-data`.

How to do it...

1. Let's import the packages:

```
In [1]: import numpy as np
        import matplotlib.pyplot as plt
        import skimage.exposure as skie
        %matplotlib inline
```

2. We open an image with matplotlib. We only take a single RGB component to have a grayscale image (there are better ways to convert a colored image to a grayscale image):

```
In [2]: img = plt.imread('data/pic1.jpg')[...,0]
```

3. We create a function that displays the image along with its **histogram** of the intensity values (that is, the exposure):

```
In [3]: def show(img):
            # Display the image.
            plt.subplot(121)
            plt.imshow(img, cmap=plt.cm.gray)
            plt.axis('off')
            # Display the histogram.
            plt.subplot(122)
            plt.hist(img.ravel(), lw=0, bins=256)
            plt.xlim(0, img.max())
            plt.yticks([])
            plt.show()
```

4. Let's display the image along with its histogram:

```
In [4]: show(img)
```

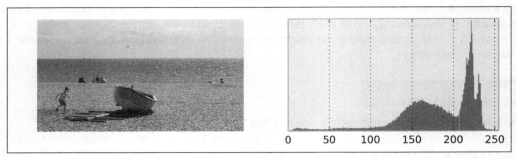

An image and its histogram

The histogram is unbalanced and the image appears overexposed (many pixels are too bright).

5. Now, we rescale the intensity of the image using scikit-image's `rescale_intensity` function. The `in_range` and `out_range` parameters define a linear mapping from the original image to the modified image. The pixels that are outside `in_range` are clipped to the extremal values of `out_range`. Here, the darkest pixels (intensity less than 100) become completely black (0), whereas the brightest pixels (>240) become completely white (255):

```
In [5]: show(skie.rescale_intensity(img,
            in_range=(100, 240), out_range=(0, 255)))
```

A crude exposure manipulation technique

Many intensity values seem to be missing in the histogram, which reflects the poor quality of this basic exposure correction technique.

6. We now use a more advanced exposure correction technique called **Contrast Limited Adaptive Histogram Equalization** (**CLAHE**):

```
In [6]: show(skie.equalize_adapthist(img))
```

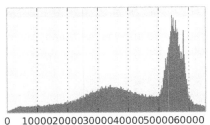

Result of the Contrast Limited Adaptive Histogram Equalization method for exposure correction

The histogram seems more balanced, and the image now appears more contrasted.

How it works...

An image's histogram represents the distribution of the pixels' intensity values. It is a central tool in image editing, image processing, and computer vision.

The `rescale_intensity()` function stretches or shrinks the intensity levels of the image. One use case is to ensure that the whole range of values allowed by the data type is used by the image.

The `equalize_adapthist()` function works by splitting the image into rectangular sections and computing the histogram for each section. Then, the intensity values of the pixels are redistributed to improve the contrast and enhance the details.

There's more...

Here are some references:

- Image histogram on Wikipedia, available at `http://en.wikipedia.org/wiki/Image_histogram`
- Histogram equalization on Wikipedia, available at `http://en.wikipedia.org/wiki/Histogram_equalization`
- Adaptive histogram equalization on Wikipedia, available at `http://en.wikipedia.org/wiki/Adaptive_histogram_equalization`
- Contrast on Wikipedia, available at `http://en.wikipedia.org/wiki/Contrast_(vision)`

See also

- The *Applying filters on an image* recipe

Applying filters on an image

In this recipe, we apply filters on an image for various purposes: blurring, denoising, and edge detection.

How it works...

1. Let's import the packages:

```
In [1]: import numpy as np
        import matplotlib.pyplot as plt
        import skimage
        import skimage.filter as skif
        import skimage.data as skid
        %matplotlib inline
```

2. We create a function that displays a grayscale image:

```
In [2]: def show(img):
            plt.imshow(img, cmap=plt.cm.gray)
            plt.axis('off')
            plt.show()
```

3. Now, we load the Lena image (bundled in scikit-image). We select a single RGB component to get a grayscale image:

```
In [3]: img = skimage.img_as_float(skid.lena())[...,0]
In [4]: show(img)
```

4. Let's apply a blurring **Gaussian filter** to the image:

```
In [5]: show(skif.gaussian_filter(img, 5.))
```

5. We now apply a **Sobel filter** that enhances the edges in the image:

```
In [6]: sobimg = skif.sobel(img)
        show(sobimg)
```

6. We can threshold the filtered image to get a *sketch effect*. We obtain a binary image that only contains the edges. We use a notebook widget to find an adequate thresholding value; by adding the @interact decorator, we display a slider on top of the image. This widget lets us control the threshold dynamically.

```
In [7]: from IPython.html import widgets
        @widgets.interact(x=(0.01, .4, .005))
        def edge(x):
            show(sobimg<x)
```

7. Finally, we add some noise to the image to illustrate the effect of a denoising filter:

```
In [8]: img = skimage.img_as_float(skid.lena())
        # We take a portion of the image to show the
        # details.
        img = img[200:-100, 200:-150]
        # We add Gaussian noise.
        img = np.clip(img + 0.3*np.random.rand(*img.shape),
                      0, 1)
In [9]: show(img)
```

8. The `denoise_tv_bregman()` function implements total-variation denoising using the Split Bregman method:

```
In [10]: show(skimage.restoration.denoise_tv_bregman(img,
                                                      5.))
```

How it works...

Many filters used in image processing are linear filters. These filters are very similar to those seen in *Chapter 10*, *Signal Processing*; the only difference is that they work in two dimensions. Applying a linear filter to an image amounts to performing a discrete **convolution** of the image with a particular function. The Gaussian filter applies a convolution with a Gaussian function to blur the image.

The Sobel filter computes an approximation of the gradient of the image. Therefore, it can detect fast-varying spatial changes in the image, which generally correspond to edges.

Image denoising refers to the process of removing noise from an image. **Total variation denoising** works by finding a *regular* image close to the original (noisy) image. Regularity is quantified by the **total variation** of the image:

$$V\left(x\right) = \sum_{i,j} \sqrt{\left|x_{i+1,j} - x_{i,j}\right|^2 + \left|x_{i,j+1} - x_{i,j}\right|^2}$$

The **Split Bregman method** is a variant based on the L^1 norm. It is an instance of **compressed sensing**, which aims to find regular and sparse approximations of real-world noisy measurements.

There's more...

Here are a few references:

- API reference of the skimage.filter module available at `http://scikit-image.org/docs/dev/api/skimage.filter.html`
- Noise reduction on Wikipedia, available at `http://en.wikipedia.org/wiki/Noise_reduction`
- Gaussian filter on Wikipedia, available at `http://en.wikipedia.org/wiki/Gaussian_filter`
- Sobel filter on Wikipedia, available at `http://en.wikipedia.org/wiki/Sobel_operator`
- Image denoising on Wikipedia, available at `http://en.wikipedia.org/wiki/Noise_reduction`
- Total variation denoising on Wikipedia, available at `http://en.wikipedia.org/wiki/Total_variation_denoising`
- The Split Bregman algorithm explained at `www.ece.rice.edu/~tag7/Tom_Goldstein/Split_Bregman.html`

See also

- The *Manipulating the exposure of an image* recipe

Segmenting an image

Image segmentation consists of partitioning an image into different regions that share certain characteristics. This is a fundamental task in computer vision, facial recognition, and medical imaging. For example, an image segmentation algorithm can automatically detect the contours of an organ in a medical image.

scikit-image provides several segmentation methods. In this recipe, we will demonstrate how to segment an image containing different objects.

How to do it...

1. Let's import the packages:

```
In [1]: import numpy as np
        import matplotlib.pyplot as plt
        from skimage.data import coins
        from skimage.filter import threshold_otsu
        from skimage.segmentation import clear_border
        from skimage.morphology import closing, square
        from skimage.measure import regionprops, label
        from skimage.color import lab2rgb
        %matplotlib inline
```

2. We create a function that displays a grayscale image:

```
In [2]: def show(img, cmap=None):
            cmap = cmap or plt.cm.gray
            plt.imshow(img, cmap=cmap)
            plt.axis('off')
            plt.show()
```

3. We get a test image bundled in scikit-image, showing various coins on a plain background:

```
In [3]: img = coins()
In [4]: show(img)
```

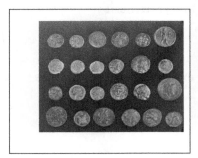

4. The first step to segment the image is finding an intensity threshold separating the (bright) coins from the (dark) background. **Otsu's method** defines a simple algorithm to automatically find such a threshold.

```
In [5]: threshold_otsu(img)
Out[5]: 107
In [6]: show(img>107)
```

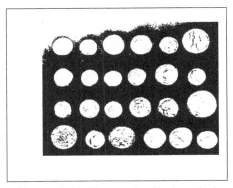

The thresholded image using Otsu's method

5. There appears to be a problem in the top-left corner of the image, with part of the background being too bright. Let's use a notebook widget to find a better threshold:

```
In [7]: from IPython.html import widgets
        @widgets.interact(t=(10, 240))
        def threshold(t):
            show(img>t)
```

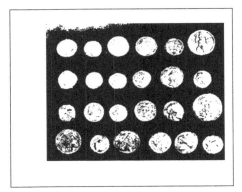

The thresholded image using a manually selected threshold

6. The threshold 120 looks better. The next step consists of cleaning the binary image by smoothing the coins and removing the border. scikit-image contains a few functions for these purposes.

```
In [8]: img_bin = clear_border(closing(img>120, square(5)))
        show(img_bin)
```

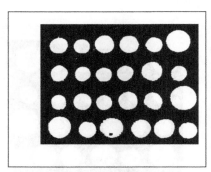

The thresholded image with cleared borders

7. Next, we perform the segmentation task itself with the `label()` function. This function detects the connected components in the image and attributes a unique label to every component. Here, we color code the labels in the binary image:

```
In [9]: labels = label(img_bin)
        show(labels, cmap=plt.cm.rainbow)
```

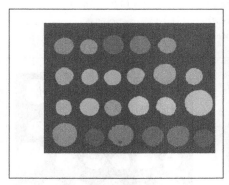

The segmented image

8. Small artifacts in the image result in spurious labels that do not correspond to coins. Therefore, we only keep components with more than 100 pixels. The `regionprops()` function allows us to retrieve specific properties of the components (here, the area and the bounding box):

```
In [10]: regions = regionprops(labels,
                               ['Area', 'BoundingBox'])
```

```
boxes = np.array([label['BoundingBox']
                  for label in regions
                  if label['Area'] > 100])
print("There are {0:d} coins.".format(len(boxes)))
There are 24 coins.
```

9. Finally, we show the label number on top of each component in the original image:

```
In [11]: plt.imshow(img, cmap=plt.cm.gray)
         plt.axis('off')
         xs = boxes[:,[1,3]].mean(axis=1)
         ys = boxes[:,[0,2]].mean(axis=1)
         for i, box in enumerate(boxes):
             plt.text(xs[i]-5, ys[i]+5, str(i))
```

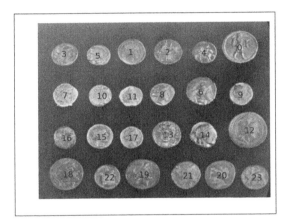

How it works...

To clean up the coins in the thresholded image, we used **mathematical morphology** techniques. These methods, based on set theory, geometry, and topology, allow us to manipulate shapes.

For example, let's explain **dilation** and **erosion**. First, if *A* is a set of pixels in an image, and *b* is a 2D vector, we denote A_b the set *A* translated by *b* as:

$$A_b = \{a + b \mid a \in A\}$$

Let *B* be a set of vectors with integer components. We call *B* the **structuring element** (here, we used a square). This set represents the neighborhood of a pixel. The dilation of *A* by *B* is:

$$A \oplus B = \bigcup_{b \in B} A_b$$

The erosion of *A* by *B* is:

$$A \ominus B = \{ z \in E \mid B_z \subseteq A \}$$

A dilation extends a set by adding pixels close to its boundaries. An erosion removes the pixels of the set that are too close to the boundaries. The **closing** of a set is a dilation followed by an erosion. This operation can remove small dark spots and connect small bright cracks. In this recipe, we used a square structuring element.

There's more...

Here are a few references:

- ▸ SciPy lecture notes on image processing available at `http://scipy-lectures.github.io/packages/scikit-image/`
- ▸ Image segmentation on Wikipedia, available at `http://en.wikipedia.org/wiki/Image_segmentation`
- ▸ Otsu's method to find a threshold explained at `http://en.wikipedia.org/wiki/Otsu's_method`
- ▸ Segmentation tutorial with scikit-image (which inspired this recipe) available at `http://scikit-image.org/docs/dev/user_guide/tutorial_segmentation.html`
- ▸ Mathematical morphology on Wikipedia, available at `http://en.wikipedia.org/wiki/Mathematical_morphology`
- ▸ API reference of the `skimage.morphology` module available at `http://scikit-image.org/docs/dev/api/skimage.morphology.html`

See also

- ▸ The *Computing connected components in an image* recipe in *Chapter 14, Graphs, Geometry, and Geographic Information Systems*

Finding points of interest in an image

In an image, **points of interest** are positions where there might be edges, corners, or interesting objects. For example, in a landscape picture, points of interest can be located near a house or a person. Detecting points of interest is useful in image recognition, computer vision, or medical imaging.

In this recipe, we will find points of interest in an image with scikit-image. This will allow us to crop an image around the subject of the picture, even when this subject is not in the center of the image.

Getting ready

Download the *Child* dataset from the book's GitHub repository at https://github.com/ipython-books/cookbook-data, and extract it into the current directory.

How to do it...

1. Let's import the packages:

    ```
    In [1]: import numpy as np
            import matplotlib.pyplot as plt
            import skimage
            import skimage.feature as sf
            %matplotlib inline
    ```

2. We create a function to display a colored or grayscale image:

    ```
    In [2]: def show(img, cmap=None):
                cmap = cmap or plt.cm.gray
                plt.imshow(img, cmap=cmap)
                plt.axis('off')
    ```

3. We load an image:

    ```
    In [3]: img = plt.imread('data/pic2.jpg')
    In [4]: show(img)
    ```

4. Let's find salient points in the image with the Harris corner method. The first step consists of computing the **Harris corner measure response image** with the `corner_harris()` function (we will explain this measure in *How it works...*). This function requires a grayscale image, thus we select the first RGB component:

```
In [5]: corners = sf.corner_harris(img[:,:,0])
In [6]: show(corners)
```

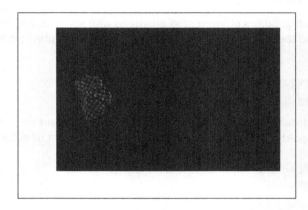

We see that the patterns in the child's coat are well detected by this algorithm.

5. The next step is to detect corners from this measure image, using the `corner_peaks()` function:

```
In [7]: peaks = sf.corner_peaks(corners)
In [8]: show(img)
        plt.plot(peaks[:,1], peaks[:,0], 'or', ms=4)
```

6. Finally, we create a box around the corner points to define our region of interest:

```
In [9]: ymin, xmin = peaks.min(axis=0)
        ymax, xmax = peaks.max(axis=0)
        w, h = xmax-xmin, ymax-ymin
In [10]: k = .25
         xmin -= k*w
         xmax += k*w
         ymin -= k*h
         ymax += k*h
In [11]: show(img[ymin:ymax,xmin:xmax])
```

How it works...

Let's explain the method used in this recipe. The first step consists of computing the **structure tensor** (or **Harris matrix**) of the image:

$$A = \begin{bmatrix} \langle I_x^2 \rangle & \langle I_x I_y \rangle \\ \langle I_x I_y \rangle & \langle I_y^2 \rangle \end{bmatrix}$$

Here, $I(x,y)$ is the image, I_x and I_y are the partial derivatives, and the brackets denote the local spatial average around neighboring values.

This tensor associates a *(2,2)* positive symmetric matrix at each point. This matrix is used to calculate a sort of autocorrelation of the image at each point.

Let λ and μ be the two eigenvalues of this matrix (the matrix is diagonalizable because it is real and symmetric). Roughly, a corner is characterized by a large variation of the autocorrelation in all directions, or in large positive eigenvalues λ and μ. The corner measure image is defined as:

$$M = \det(A) - k \times \text{trace}(A)^2 = \lambda\mu - k(\lambda + \mu)^2$$

Here, *k* is a tunable parameter. *M* is large when there is a corner. Finally, `corner_peaks()` finds corner points by looking at local maxima in the corner measure image.

There's more...

Here are a few references:

- A corner detection example with scikit-image available at `http://scikit-image.org/docs/dev/auto_examples/plot_corner.html`
- An image processing tutorial with scikit-image available at `http://blog.yhathq.com/posts/image-processing-with-scikit-image.html`
- Corner detection on Wikipedia, available at `http://en.wikipedia.org/wiki/Corner_detection`
- Structure tensor on Wikipedia, available at `http://en.wikipedia.org/wiki/Structure_tensor`
- Interest point detection on Wikipedia, available at `http://en.wikipedia.org/wiki/Interest_point_detection`
- API reference of the `skimage.feature` module available at `http://scikit-image.org/docs/dev/api/skimage.feature.html`

Detecting faces in an image with OpenCV

OpenCV (**Open Computer Vision**) is an open source C++ library for computer vision. It features algorithms for image segmentation, object recognition, augmented reality, face detection, and other computer vision tasks.

In this recipe, we will use OpenCV in Python to detect faces in a picture.

Getting ready

You need OpenCV and the Python wrapper. You can find installation instructions on OpenCV's website, `http://docs.opencv.org/trunk/doc/py_tutorials/py_tutorials.html`.

On Windows, you can install Chris Gohlke's package, available at `www.lfd.uci.edu/~gohlke/pythonlibs/#opencv`.

You also need to download the *Family* dataset from the book's GitHub repository at `https://github.com/ipython-books/cookbook-data`.

> OpenCV is not compatible with Python 3 at the time of this writing. Therefore, this recipe requires Python 2.

How to do it...

1. First, we import the packages:

    ```
    In [1]: import numpy as np
            import cv2
            import matplotlib.pyplot as plt
            %matplotlib inline
    ```

2. We open the JPG image with OpenCV:

    ```
    In [2]: img = cv2.imread('data/pic3.jpg')
    ```

3. Then, we convert it to a grayscale image using OpenCV's `cvtColor()` function. For face detection, it is sufficient and faster to use grayscale images.

    ```
    In [3]: gray = cv2.cvtColor(img, cv2.COLOR_BGR2GRAY)
    ```

4. To detect faces, we will use the **Viola–Jones object detection framework**. A cascade of Haar-like classifiers has been trained on many images to detect faces (more details are given in the next section). The result of the training is stored in an XML file (part of the *Family* dataset available on the book's GitHub repository). We load this cascade from this XML file with OpenCV's `CascadeClassifier` class:

    ```
    In [4]: face_cascade = cv2.CascadeClassifier(
                'data/haarcascade_frontalface_default.xml')
    ```

5. Finally, the `detectMultiScale()` method of the classifier detects the objects on a grayscale image and returns a list of rectangles around these objects:

```
In [5]: for x,y,w,h in \
                face_cascade.detectMultiScale(gray, 1.3):
            cv2.rectangle(gray, (x,y), (x+w,y+h),
                          (255,0,0), 2)
        plt.imshow(gray, cmap=plt.cm.gray)
        plt.axis('off')
```

We see that, although all detected objects are indeed faces, one face out of four is not detected. This is probably due to the fact that this face is not perfectly facing the camera, whereas the faces in the training set were. This shows that the efficacy of this method is limited by the quality and generality of the training set.

How it works...

The Viola–Jones object detection framework works by training a cascade of boosted classifiers with Haar-like features. First, we consider a set of features:

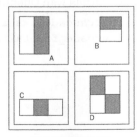

Haar-like features

A feature is positioned at a particular location and size in the image. It covers a small window in the image (for example, 24 x 24 pixels). The sum of all pixels in the black area is subtracted to the sum of the pixels in the white area. This operation can be done efficiently with integral images.

Then, the set of all classifiers is trained with a boosting technique; only the best features are kept for the next stage during training. The training set contains positive and negative images (with and without faces). Although the classifiers yield poor performance *individually*, the cascade of boosted classifiers is both efficient and fast. This method is therefore well-adapted to real-time processing.

The XML file has been obtained in OpenCV's package. There are multiple files corresponding to different training sets. You can also train your own cascade with your own training set.

There's more...

Here are a few references:

- A cascade tutorial with OpenCV (C++) available at `http://docs.opencv.org/doc/tutorials/objdetect/cascade_classifier/cascade_classifier.html`
- Documentation to train a cascade, available at `http://docs.opencv.org/doc/user_guide/ug_traincascade.html`
- Haar cascades library, available at `https://github.com/Itseez/opencv/tree/master/data/haarcascades`
- OpenCV's cascade classification API reference available at `http://docs.opencv.org/modules/objdetect/doc/cascade_classification.html`
- The Viola–Jones object detection framework on Wikipedia, available at `http://en.wikipedia.org/wiki/Viola%E2%80%93Jones_object_detection_framework`
- Boosting or how to create one strong classifier from many weak classifiers, explained at `http://en.wikipedia.org/wiki/Boosting_(machine_learning)`

Applying digital filters to speech sounds

In this recipe, we will show how to play sounds in the notebook. We will also illustrate the effect of simple digital filters on speech sounds.

Getting ready

You need the **pydub** package. You can install it with `pip install pydub` or download it from `https://github.com/jiaaro/pydub/`.

This package requires the open source multimedia library FFmpeg for the decompression of MP3 files, available at `www.ffmpeg.org`.

The code given here works with Python 3. You will find the Python 2 version in the book's GitHub repository.

How to do it...

1. Let's import the packages:

```
In [1]: import urllib
        from io import BytesIO
        import numpy as np
        import scipy.signal as sg
        import pydub
        import matplotlib.pyplot as plt
        from IPython.display import Audio, display
        %matplotlib inline
```

2. We create a Python function to generate a sound from an English sentence. This function uses Google's **Text-To-Speech** (**TTS**) API. We retrieve the sound in the MP3 format, and convert it to the Wave format with pydub. Finally, we retrieve the raw sound data by removing the wave header with NumPy:

```
In [2]: def speak(sentence):
            url = ("http://translate.google.com/"
                   "translate_tts?tl=en&q=") +
                       urllib.parse.quote_plus(sentence)
            req = urllib.request.Request(url,
                        headers={'User-Agent': ''})
            mp3 = urllib.request.urlopen(req).read()
            # We convert the mp3 bytes to wav.
            audio = pydub.AudioSegment.from_mp3(
                                        BytesIO(mp3))
            wave = audio.export('_', format='wav')
            wave.seek(0)
            wave = wave.read()
            # We get the raw data by removing the 24
            # first bytes of the header.
            x = np.frombuffer(wave, np.int16)[24:] / 2.**15
```

3. We create a function that plays a sound (represented by a NumPy vector) in the notebook, using IPython's `Audio` class:

```
In [3]: def play(x, fr, autoplay=False):
            display(Audio(x, rate=fr, autoplay=autoplay))
```

4. Let's play the sound "Hello world." We also display the waveform with matplotlib:

```
In [4]: x, fr = speak("Hello world")
        play(x, fr)
        t = np.linspace(0., len(x)/fr, len(x))
        plt.plot(t, x, lw=1)
```

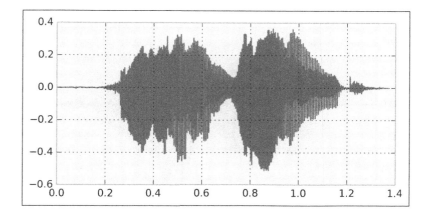

5. Now, we will hear the effect of a Butterworth low-pass filter applied to this sound (500 Hz cutoff frequency):

```
In [5]: b, a = sg.butter(4, 500./(fr/2.), 'low')
        x_fil = sg.filtfilt(b, a, x)
In [6]: play(x_fil, fr)
        plt.plot(t, x, lw=1)
        plt.plot(t, x_fil, lw=1)
```

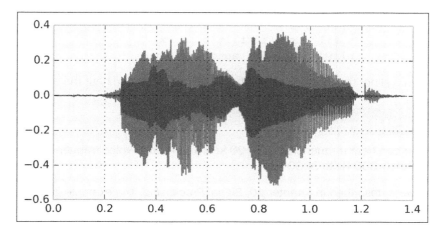

We hear a muffled voice.

6. Now, with a high-pass filter (1000 Hz cutoff frequency):

```
In [7]: b, a = sg.butter(4, 1000./(fr/2.), 'high')
        x_fil = sg.filtfilt(b, a, x)
In [8]: play(x_fil, fr)
        plt.plot(t, x, lw=1)
        plt.plot(t, x_fil, lw=1)
```

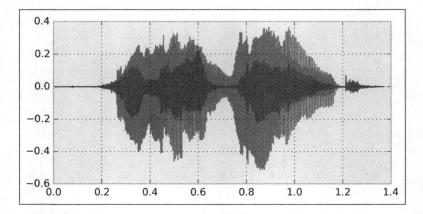

It sounds like a phone call.

7. Finally, we can create a simple widget to quickly test the effect of a high-pass filter with an arbitrary cutoff frequency:

```
In [9]: from IPython.html import widgets
        @widgets.interact(t=(100., 5000., 100.))
        def highpass(t):
            b, a = sg.butter(4, t/(fr/2.), 'high')
            x_fil = sg.filtfilt(b, a, x)
            play(x_fil, fr, autoplay=True)
```

We get a slider that lets us change the cutoff frequency and hear the effect in real-time.

How it works...

The human ear can hear frequencies up to 20 kHz. The human voice frequency band ranges from approximately 300 Hz to 3000 Hz.

Digital filters were described in *Chapter 10, Signal Processing*. The example given here allows us to hear the effect of low- and high-pass filters on sounds.

There's more...

Here are a few references:

- ▶ Audio signal processing on Wikipedia, available at `http://en.wikipedia.org/wiki/Audio_signal_processing`
- ▶ Audio filters on Wikipedia, available at `http://en.wikipedia.org/wiki/Audio_filter`
- ▶ Voice frequency on Wikipedia, available at `http://en.wikipedia.org/wiki/Voice_frequency`
- ▶ **PyAudio**, an audio Python package that uses the PortAudio library, available at `http://people.csail.mit.edu/hubert/pyaudio/`

See also

- ▶ The *Creating a sound synthesizer in the notebook* recipe

Creating a sound synthesizer in the notebook

In this recipe, we will create a small electronic piano in the notebook. We will synthesize sinusoidal sounds with NumPy instead of using recorded tones.

How to do it...

1. We import the modules:

```
In [1]: import numpy as np
        import matplotlib.pyplot as plt
        from IPython.display import (Audio, display,
                                     clear_output)
        from IPython.html import widgets
        from functools import partial
        %matplotlib inline
```

2. We define the sampling rate and the duration of the notes:

```
In [2]: rate = 16000.
        duration = 0.5
        t = np.linspace(0., duration, rate * duration)
```

3. We create a function that generates and plays the sound of a note (sine function) at a given frequency, using NumPy and IPython's `Audio` class:

```
In [3]: def synth(f):
            x = np.sin(f * 2. * np.pi * t)
            display(Audio(x, rate=rate, autoplay=True))
```

4. Here is the fundamental 440 Hz note:

```
In [4]: synth(440)
```

5. Now, we generate the note frequencies of our piano. The chromatic scale is obtained by a geometric progression with the common ratio $2^{1/12}$:

```
In [5]: notes = zip(('C,C#,D,D#,E,F,F#,G,G#,'
                      'A,A#,B,C').split(','),
                      440. * 2 ** (np.arange(3, 17) / 12.))
```

6. Finally, we create the piano with the notebook widgets. Each note is a button, and all buttons are contained in a horizontal box container. Clicking on one note plays a sound at the corresponding frequency. The piano layout is the same as the one used in the *Using interactive widgets – a piano in the notebook* recipe of *Chapter 3, Mastering the Notebook*.

```
In [6]: container = widgets.ContainerWidget()
        buttons = []
        for note, f in notes:
            button = widgets.ButtonWidget(description=note)
            def on_button_clicked(f, b):
                clear_output()
                synth(f)
            button.on_click(partial(on_button_clicked, f))
            button.set_css({...})
            buttons.append(button)
        container.children = buttons
        display(container)
        container.remove_class('vbox')
        container.add_class('hbox')
```

 The IPython API used here to design the layout is based on IPython 2.x; it will be slightly different in IPython 3.0.

How it works...

A **pure tone** is a tone with a sinusoidal waveform. It is the simplest way of representing a musical note. A note generated by a musical instrument is typically much more complex. Although the sound contains many frequencies, we generally perceive a musical tone (**fundamental frequency**).

By generating another periodic function instead of a sinusoidal waveform, we would hear the same tone, but a different **timbre**. Electronic music synthesizers are based on this idea.

There's more...

Here are a few references:

▶ Synthesizer on Wikipedia, available at `http://en.wikipedia.org/wiki/Synthesizer`

▶ Equal temperament on Wikipedia, available at `http://en.wikipedia.org/wiki/Equal_temperament`

▶ Chromatic scale on Wikipedia, available at `http://en.wikipedia.org/wiki/Chromatic_scale`

▶ Pure tone on Wikipedia, available at `http://en.wikipedia.org/wiki/Pure_tone`

▶ Timbre on Wikipedia, available at `http://en.wikipedia.org/wiki/Timbre`

See also

▶ The *Applying digital filters to speech sounds* recipe

▶ The *Using interactive widgets – a piano in the notebook* recipe in *Chapter 3, Mastering the Notebook*

12

Deterministic Dynamical Systems

In this chapter, we will cover the following topics:

- ▶ Plotting the bifurcation diagram of a chaotic dynamical system
- ▶ Simulating an elementary cellular automaton
- ▶ Simulating an ordinary differential equation with SciPy
- ▶ Simulating a partial differential equation – reaction-diffusion systems and Turing patterns

Introduction

The previous chapters dealt with classical approaches in data science: statistics, machine learning, and signal processing. In this chapter and the next chapter, we will cover a different type of approach. Instead of analyzing data directly, we will simulate mathematical models that represent how our data was generated. A representative model gives us an explanation of the real-world processes underlying our data.

Specifically, we will cover a few examples of dynamical systems. These mathematical equations describe the evolution of quantities over time and space. They can represent a wide variety of real-world phenomena in physics, chemistry, biology, economics, social sciences, computer science, engineering, and other disciplines.

In this chapter, we will consider deterministic dynamical systems. This term is used in contrast to stochastic systems, which incorporate randomness in their rules. We will cover stochastic systems in the next chapter.

Types of dynamical systems

The types of deterministic dynamical systems we will consider here are:

- **Discrete-time dynamical systems** (iterated functions)
- **Cellular automata**
- **Ordinary Differential Equations** (**ODEs**)
- **Partial Differential Equations** (**PDEs**)

In these models, the quantities of interest depend on one or several **independent variables**. Often, these variables include time and/or space. The independent variables can be discrete or continuous, resulting in different types of models and different analysis and simulation techniques.

A **discrete-time dynamical system** is described by the iterative application of a function on an initial point: $f(x)$, $f(f(x))$, $f(f(f(x)))$, and so on. This type of system can lead to complex and **chaotic** behaviors.

A **cellular automaton** is represented by a discrete grid of cells that can be in a finite number of states. Rules describe how the state of a cell evolves according to the states of the neighboring cells. These simple models can lead to highly sophisticated behaviors.

An **ODE** describes the dependence of a continuous function on its derivative with respect to the independent variable. In differential equations, the unknown variable is a *function* instead of a *number*. ODEs notably arise when the rate of change of a quantity depends on the current value of this quantity. For example, in classical mechanics, the laws of motion (including movement of planets and satellites) can be described by ODEs.

PDEs are similar to ODEs, but they involve several independent variables (for example, time and space). These equations contain **partial derivatives** of the function with respect to the different independent variables. For example, PDEs describe the propagation of waves (acoustic, electromagnetic, or mechanical waves) and fluids (**fluid dynamics**). They are also important in quantum mechanics.

Differential equations

ODEs and PDEs can be one-dimensional or multidimensional, depending on the dimensionality of the target space. Systems of multiple differential equations can be seen as multidimensional equations.

The **order** of an ODE or a PDE refers to the maximal derivative order in the equation. For example, a first-order equation only involves simple derivatives, a second-order equation also involves second-order derivatives (the derivatives of the derivatives), and so on.

Ordinary or partial differential equations come with additional rules: **initial and boundary conditions**. These formulas describe the behavior of the sought functions on the spatial and temporal domain boundaries. For example, in classical mechanics, boundary conditions include the initial position and initial speed of a physical body subject to forces.

Dynamical systems are often classified between **linear** and **nonlinear** systems, depending on whether the rules are linear or not (with respect to the unknown function). Nonlinear equations are typically much harder to study mathematically and numerically than linear equations. They can lead to extremely complex behaviors.

For example, the **Navier–Stokes equations**, a set of nonlinear PDEs that describe the motion of fluid substances, can lead to **turbulence**, a highly chaotic behavior seen in many fluid flows. Despite their high importance in meteorology, medicine, and engineering, fundamental properties of the Navier-Stokes equations remain unknown at this time. For example, the existence and smoothness problem in three dimensions is one of the seven Clay Mathematics Institute's Millennium Prize Problems. One million dollars is offered to anyone who comes up with a solution.

References

Here are a few references:

- Overview of dynamical systems on Wikipedia, available at `http://en.wikipedia.org/wiki/Dynamical_system`

- Mathematical definition of dynamical systems available at `http://en.wikipedia.org/wiki/Dynamical_system_%28definition%29`

- List of dynamical systems topics available at `http://en.wikipedia.org/wiki/List_of_dynamical_systems_and_differential_equations_topics`

- Navier-Stokes equations on Wikipedia, available at `http://en.wikipedia.org/wiki/Navier%E2%80%93Stokes_equations`

- A course on Computational Fluid Dynamics by Prof. Lorena Barba, written in the IPython notebook, available at `https://github.com/barbagroup/CFDPython`

Plotting the bifurcation diagram of a chaotic dynamical system

A **chaotic** dynamical system is highly sensitive to initial conditions; small perturbations at any given time yield completely different trajectories. The trajectories of a chaotic system tend to have complex and unpredictable behaviors.

Many real-world phenomena are chaotic, particularly those that involve nonlinear interactions among many agents (complex systems). Famous examples can be found in meteorology, economics, biology, and other disciplines.

In this recipe, we will simulate a famous chaotic system: the **logistic map**. This is an archetypal example of how chaos can arise from a very simple nonlinear equation. The logistic map models the evolution of a population, taking into account both reproduction and density-dependent mortality (starvation).

We will draw the system's **bifurcation diagram**, which shows the possible long-term behaviors (equilibria, fixed points, periodic orbits, and chaotic trajectories) as a function of the system's parameter. We will also compute an approximation of the system's **Lyapunov exponent**, characterizing the model's sensitivity to initial conditions.

How to do it...

1. Let's import NumPy and matplotlib:

```
In [1]: import numpy as np
        import matplotlib.pyplot as plt
        %matplotlib inline
```

2. We define the logistic function by:

$$f_r(x) = rx(1-x)$$

Our discrete dynamical system is defined by the recursive application of the logistic function:

$$x_{n+1}^{(r)} = f_r\left(x_n^{(r)}\right) = rx_n^{(r)}\left(1 - x_n^{(r)}\right)$$

3. Here is the implementation of this function in Python:

```
In [2]: def logistic(r, x):
            return r*x*(1-x)
```

4. We simulate this system for 10000 values of *r* linearly spaced between 2.5 and 4, and vectorize the simulation with NumPy by considering a vector of independent systems (one dynamical system per parameter value):

```
In [3]: n = 10000
        r = np.linspace(2.5, 4.0, n)
```

5. Let's simulate 1000 iterations of the logistic map and keep the last 100 iterations to display the bifurcation diagram:

```
In [4]: iterations = 1000
        last = 100
```

6. We initialize our system with the same initial condition x_0 = 0.00001:

```
In [5]: x = 1e-5 * np.ones(n)
```

7. We also compute an approximation of the Lyapunov exponent for every value of *r*. The Lyapunov exponent is defined by:

$$\lambda(r) = \lim_{n \to \infty} \frac{1}{n} \sum_{i=0}^{n-1} \log \left| \frac{df_r}{dx}\left(x_i^{(r)}\right) \right|$$

8. We first initialize the `lyapunov` vector:

```
In [6]: lyapunov = np.zeros(n)
```

9. Now, we simulate the system and plot the bifurcation diagram. The simulation only involves the iterative evaluation of the `logistic()` function on our vector x. Then, to display the bifurcation diagram, we draw one pixel per point $x_n^{(r)}$ during the last 100 iterations:

```
In [7]: plt.subplot(211)
        for i in range(iterations):
            x = logistic(r, x)
            # We compute the partial sum of the
            # Lyapunov exponent.
            lyapunov += np.log(abs(r-2*r*x))
            # We display the bifurcation diagram.
            if i >= (iterations - last):
                plt.plot(r, x, ',k', alpha=.02)
        plt.xlim(2.5, 4)
        plt.title("Bifurcation diagram")

        # We display the Lyapunov exponent.
        plt.subplot(212)
        plt.plot(r[lyapunov<0],
                 lyapunov[lyapunov<0] / iterations,
                 ',k', alpha=0.1)
        plt.plot(r[lyapunov>=0],
```

```
                                lyapunov[lyapunov>=0] / iterations,
                                ',r', alpha=0.25)
                plt.xlim(2.5, 4)
                plt.ylim(-2, 1)
                plt.title("Lyapunov exponent")
```

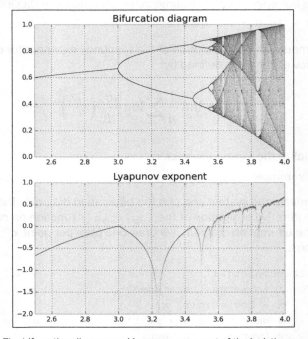

The bifurcation diagram and Lyapunov exponent of the logistic map

The bifurcation diagram brings out the existence of a fixed point for *r<3*, then two and four equilibria, and a chaotic behavior when r belongs to certain areas of the parameter space.

We observe an important property of the Lyapunov exponent: it is positive when the system is chaotic (in red here).

There's more...

Here are some references:

▶ Chaos theory on Wikipedia, available at http://en.wikipedia.org/wiki/Chaos_theory

▶ Complex systems on Wikipedia, available at http://en.wikipedia.org/wiki/Complex_system

- The logistic map on Wikipedia, available at `https://en.wikipedia.org/wiki/Logistic_map`

- Iterated functions (discrete dynamical systems) on Wikipedia, available at `http://en.wikipedia.org/wiki/Iterated_function`

- Bifurcation diagrams on Wikipedia, available at `http://en.wikipedia.org/wiki/Bifurcation_diagram`

- Lyapunov exponent on Wikipedia, available at `http://en.wikipedia.org/wiki/Lyapunov_exponent`

See also

- The *Simulating an ordinary differential equation with SciPy* recipe

Simulating an elementary cellular automaton

Cellular automata are discrete dynamical systems evolving on a grid of cells. These cells can be in a finite number of states (for example, on/off). The evolution of a cellular automaton is governed by a set of rules, describing how the state of a cell changes according to the state of its neighbors.

Although extremely simple, these models can initiate highly complex and chaotic behaviors. Cellular automata can model real-world phenomena such as car traffic, chemical reactions, propagation of fire in a forest, epidemic propagations, and much more. Cellular automata are also found in nature. For example, the patterns of some seashells are generated by natural cellular automata.

An **elementary cellular automaton** is a binary, one-dimensional automaton, where the rules concern the immediate left and right neighbors of every cell.

In this recipe, we will simulate elementary cellular automata with NumPy using their Wolfram code.

How to do it...

1. We import NumPy and matplotlib:

```
In [1]: import numpy as np
        import matplotlib.pyplot as plt
        %matplotlib inline
```

2. We will use the following vector to obtain numbers written in binary representation:

```
In [2]: u = np.array([[4], [2], [1]])
```

3. Let's write a function that performs an iteration on the grid, updating all cells at once according to the given rule in binary representation (we will give all explanations in the *How it works...* section). The first step consists of stacking circularly-shifted versions of the grid to get the LCR (left, center, right) triplets of each cell (y). Then, we convert these triplets into 3-bit numbers (z). Finally, we compute the next state of every cell using the specified rule:

```
In [3]: def step(x, rule_binary):
            """Compute a single stet of an elementary
            cellular automaton."""
            # The columns contain the L, C, R values
            # of all cells.
            y = np.vstack((np.roll(x, 1), x,
                            np.roll(x, -1))).astype(np.int8)
            # We get the LCR pattern numbers
            # between 0 and 7.
            z = np.sum(y * u, axis=0).astype(np.int8)
            # We get the patterns given by the rule.
            return rule_binary[7-z]
```

4. We now write a function that simulates any elementary cellular automaton. First, we compute the binary representation of the rule (**Wolfram Code**). Then, we initialize the first row of the grid with random values. Finally, we apply the function `step()` iteratively on the grid:

```
In [4]: def generate(rule, size=80, steps=80):
            """Simulate an elementary cellular automaton
            given its rule (number between 0 and 255)."""
            # Compute the binary representation of the
            # rule.
            rule_binary = np.array(
                [int(x) for x in np.binary_repr(rule, 8)],
                dtype=np.int8)
            x = np.zeros((steps, size), dtype=np.int8)
            # Random initial state.
            x[0,:] = np.random.rand(size) < .5
            # Apply the step function iteratively.
            for i in range(steps-1):
                x[i+1,:] = step(x[i,:], rule_binary)
            return x
```

5. Now, we simulate and display nine different automata:

```
In [5]: rules = [  3,  18,  30,
                  90, 106, 110,
                 158, 154, 184]
        for i, rule in enumerate(rules):
```

```
x = generate(rule)
plt.subplot(331+i)
plt.imshow(x, interpolation='none',
           cmap=plt.cm.binary)
plt.xticks([]); plt.yticks([])
plt.title(str(rule))
```

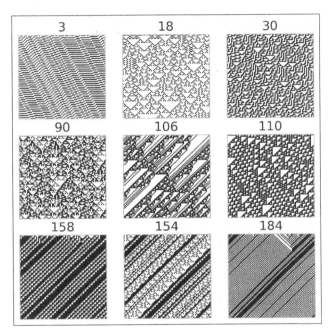

How it works...

Let's consider an elementary cellular automaton in one dimension. Every cell C has two neighbors (L and R), and it can be either off (0) or on (1). Therefore, the future state of a cell depends on the current state of L, C, and R. This triplet can be encoded as a number between 0 and 7 (three digits in binary representation).

A particular elementary cellular automaton is entirely determined by the outcome of each of these eight configurations. Therefore, there are 256 different elementary cellular automata (2^8). Each of these automata is identified by a number between 0 and 255.

We consider all eight LCR states in order: 111, 110, 101, ..., 001, 000. Each of the eight digits in the binary representation of the automaton's number corresponds to a LCR state (using the same order). For example, in the **Rule 110 automaton** (`01101110` in binary representation), the state 111 yields a new state of 0 for the center cell, 110 yields 1, 101 yields 1, and so on. It has been shown that this particular automaton is **Turing complete** (or **universal**); it can theoretically simulate any computer program.

There's more...

Other types of cellular automata include **Conway's Game of Life**, in two dimensions. This famous system yields various dynamic patterns. It is also Turing complete.

Here are a few references:

▸ Cellular automata on Wikipedia, available at `http://en.wikipedia.org/wiki/Cellular_automaton`

▸ Elementary cellular automata on Wikipedia, available at `http://en.wikipedia.org/wiki/Elementary_cellular_automaton`

▸ Rule 110, described at `http://en.wikipedia.org/wiki/Rule_110`

▸ The Wolfram code, explained at `http://en.wikipedia.org/wiki/Wolfram_code`, assigns a 1D elementary cellular automaton to any number between 0 and 255

▸ Conway's Game of Life on Wikipedia, available at `http://en.wikipedia.org/wiki/Conway's_Game_of_Life`

Simulating an ordinary differential equation with SciPy

Ordinary Differential Equations (**ODEs**) describe the evolution of a system subject to internal and external dynamics. Specifically, an ODE links a quantity depending on a single independent variable (time, for example) to its derivatives. In addition, the system can be under the influence of external factors. A first-order ODE can typically be written as:

$$y'(t) = f(t, y(t))$$

More generally, an *n*-th order ODE involves successive derivatives of *y* until the order *n*. The ODE is said to be linear or nonlinear depending on whether *f* is linear in *y* or not.

ODEs naturally appear when the rate of change of a quantity depends on its value. Therefore, ODEs are found in many scientific disciplines such as mechanics (evolution of a body subject to dynamic forces), chemistry (concentration of reacting products), biology (spread of an epidemic), ecology (growth of a population), economics, and finance, among others.

Whereas simple ODEs can be solved analytically, many ODEs require a numerical treatment. In this recipe, we will simulate a simple linear second-order autonomous ODE, describing the evolution of a particle in the air subject to gravity and viscous resistance. Although this equation could be solved analytically, here we will use SciPy to simulate it numerically.

How to do it...

1. Let's import NumPy, SciPy (the `integrate` package), and matplotlib:

```
In [1]: import numpy as np
        import scipy.integrate as spi
        import matplotlib.pyplot as plt
        %matplotlib inline
```

2. We define a few parameters appearing in our model:

```
In [2]: m = 1.    # particle's mass
        k = 1.    # drag coefficient
        g = 9.81  # gravity acceleration
```

3. We have two variables: *x* and *y* (two dimensions). We note *u=(x,y)*. The ODE that we are going to simulate is:

$$\ddot{\mathbf{u}} = -\frac{k}{m}\dot{\mathbf{u}} + \mathbf{g}$$

Here, *g* is the gravity acceleration vector.

 Time derivatives are denoted with *dots* above variables (one dot means *first derivative* and two dots means *second derivative*).

In order to simulate this second-order ODE with SciPy, we can convert it to a first-order ODE (another option would be to solve *u'* first before integrating the solution). To do this, we consider two 2D variables: *u* and *u'*. We note *v = (u, u')*. We can express *v'* as a function of *v*. Now, we create the initial vector v_0 at time *t=0*: it has four components.

```
In [3]: # The initial position is (0, 0).
        v0 = np.zeros(4)
        # The initial speed vector is oriented
        # to the top right.
        v0[2] = 4.
        v0[3] = 10.
```

4. Let's create a Python function *f* that takes the current vector $v(t_0)$ and a time t_0 as arguments (with optional parameters) and that returns the derivative $v'(t_0)$:

```
In [4]: def f(v, t0, k):
            # v has four components: v=[u, u'].
            u, udot = v[:2], v[2:]
```

```
# We compute the second derivative u'' of u.
udotdot = -k/m * udot
udotdot[1] -= g
# We return v'=[u', u''].
return np.r_[udot, udotdot]
```

5. Now, we simulate the system for different values of *k*. We use the SciPy `odeint()` function, defined in the `scipy.integrate` package.

```
In [5]:  # We want to evaluate the system on 30 linearly
         # spaced times between t=0 and t=3.
         t = np.linspace(0., 3., 30)
         # We simulate the system for different values of k.
         for k in np.linspace(0., 1., 5):
             # We simulate the system and evaluate $v$ on
             # the given times.
             v = spi.odeint(f, v0, t, args=(k,))
             # We plot the particle's trajectory.
             plt.plot(v[:,0], v[:,1], 'o-',
                      mew=1, ms=8, mec='w',
                      label='k={0:.1f}'.format(k))
         plt.legend()
         plt.xlim(0, 12)
         plt.ylim(0, 6)
```

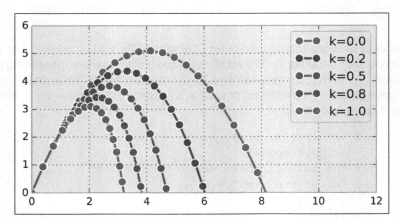

In the preceding figure, the most outward trajectory (blue) corresponds to drag-free motion (without air resistance). It is a parabola. In the other trajectories, we can observe the increasing effect of air resistance, parameterized with `k`.

How it works...

Let's explain how we obtained the differential equation from our model. Let $u = (x,y)$ encode the 2D position of our particle with mass m. This particle is subject to two forces: gravity $g = (0, -9.81)$ (in m/s) and air drag $F = -ku'$. This last term depends on the particle's speed and is only valid at low speed. With higher speeds, we need to use more complex nonlinear expressions.

Now, we use **Newton's second law of motion** in classical mechanics. This law states that in an inertial reference frame, the mass multiplied by the acceleration of the particle is equal to the sum of all forces applied to that particle. Here, we obtain:

$$m\,\ddot{\mathbf{u}} = \mathbf{F} + \mathbf{g}$$

We immediately obtain our second-order ODE:

$$\ddot{\mathbf{u}} = -\frac{k}{m}\dot{\mathbf{u}} + \mathbf{g}$$

We transform it into a single-order system of ODEs with $v=(u, u')$:

$$\dot{\mathbf{v}} = \left(\dot{\mathbf{u}}, \ddot{\mathbf{u}}\right) = \left(\dot{\mathbf{u}}, -\frac{k}{m}\dot{\mathbf{u}} + \mathbf{g}\right)$$

The last term can be expressed as a function of v only.

The SciPy `odeint()` function is a black-box solver; we simply specify the function that describes the system, and SciPy solves it automatically.

This function leverages the FORTRAN library **ODEPACK**, which contains well-tested code that has been used for decades by many scientists and engineers.

An example of a simple numerical solver is the **Euler method**. To numerically solve the autonomous ODE $y'=f(y)$, the method consists of discretizing time with a time step dt and replacing y' with a first-order approximation:

$$y'(t) \simeq \frac{y(t+dt) - y(t)}{dt}$$

Then, starting from an initial condition $y_0 = y(t_0)$, the method evaluates y successively with the following recurrence relation:

$$y_{n+1} = y_n + dt \cdot f(y_n) \quad \text{with} \quad t = n \cdot dt, \quad y_n = y(n \cdot dt)$$

There's more...

Here are a few references:

- ▶ The documentation of the `integrate` package in SciPy available at `http://docs.scipy.org/doc/scipy/reference/integrate.html`

- ▶ ODEs on Wikipedia, available at `http://en.wikipedia.org/wiki/Ordinary_differential_equation`

- ▶ Newton's laws of motion on Wikipedia, available at `http://en.wikipedia.org/wiki/Newton's_laws_of_motion`

- ▶ Air resistance on Wikipedia, available at `http://en.wikipedia.org/wiki/Drag_%28physics%29`

- ▶ Some numerical methods for ODEs described at `http://en.wikipedia.org/wiki/Numerical_methods_for_ordinary_differential_equations`

- ▶ The Euler method on Wikipedia, available at `http://en.wikipedia.org/wiki/Euler_method`

- ▶ Documentation of the ODEPACK package in FORTRAN available at `www.netlib.org/odepack/opks-sum`

See also

- ▶ The *Plotting the bifurcation diagram of a chaotic dynamical system* recipe

Simulating a partial differential equation – reaction-diffusion systems and Turing patterns

Partial Differential Equations (**PDEs**) describe the evolution of dynamical systems involving both time and space. Examples in physics include sound, heat, electromagnetism, fluid flow, and elasticity, among others. Examples in biology include tumor growth, population dynamics, and epidemic propagations.

PDEs are hard to solve analytically. Therefore, PDEs are often studied via numerical simulations.

In this recipe, we will illustrate how to simulate a **reaction-diffusion system** described by a PDE called the **FitzHugh–Nagumo equation**. A reaction-diffusion system models the evolution of one or several variables subject to two processes: reaction (transformation of the variables into each other) and diffusion (spreading across a spatial region). Some chemical reactions can be described by this type of model, but there are other applications in physics, biology, ecology, and other disciplines.

Here, we simulate a system that has been proposed by Alan Turing as a model of animal coat pattern formation. Two chemical substances influencing skin pigmentation interact according to a reaction-diffusion model. This system is responsible for the formation of patterns that are reminiscent of the pelage of zebras, jaguars, and giraffes.

We will simulate this system with the finite difference method. This method consists of discretizing time and space and replacing the derivatives with their discrete equivalents.

How to do it...

1. Let's import the packages:

```
In [1]: import numpy as np
        import matplotlib.pyplot as plt
        %matplotlib inline
```

2. We will simulate the following system of partial differential equations on the domain $E=[-1,1]^2$:

$$\frac{\partial u}{\partial t} = a\Delta u + u - u^3 - v + k$$

$$\tau\frac{\partial u}{\partial t} = b\Delta v + u - v$$

The variable u represents the concentration of a substance favoring skin pigmentation, whereas v represents another substance that reacts with the first and impedes pigmentation.

At initialization time, we assume that u and v contain independent random numbers on every grid point. We also take **Neumann boundary conditions**: we require the spatial derivatives of the variables with respect to the normal vectors to be null on the domain's boundaries.

3. Let's define the four parameters of the model:

```
In [2]: a = 2.8e-4
        b = 5e-3
        tau = .1
        k = -.005
```

4. We discretize time and space. The following condition ensures that the discretization scheme we use here is stable:

$$dt \leq \frac{dx^2}{2}$$

```
In [3]: size = 80   # size of the 2D grid
        dx = 2./size   # space step
In [4]: T = 10.0   # total time
        dt = .9 * dx**2/2   # time step
        n = int(T/dt)
```

5. We initialize the variables *u* and *v*. The matrices U and V contain the values of these variables on the vertices of the 2D grid. These variables are initialized with a uniform noise between 0 and 1:

```
In [5]: U = np.random.rand(size, size)
        V = np.random.rand(size, size)
```

6. Now, we define a function that computes the discrete Laplace operator of a 2D variable on the grid, using a five-point stencil finite difference method. This operator is defined by:

$$\Delta u(x, y) \simeq \frac{u(x+h, y)+u(x-h, y)+u(x, y+h)+u(x, y-h)-4u(x, y)}{dx^2}$$

We can compute the values of this operator on the grid using vectorized matrix operations. Because of side effects on the edges of the matrix, we need to remove the borders of the grid in the computation:

```
In [6]: def laplacian(Z):
            Ztop = Z[0:-2,1:-1]
            Zleft = Z[1:-1,0:-2]
            Zbottom = Z[2:,1:-1]
            Zright = Z[1:-1,2:]
            Zcenter = Z[1:-1,1:-1]
            return (Ztop + Zleft + Zbottom + Zright \
                    - 4 * Zcenter) / dx**2
```

7. Now, we simulate the system of equations using the finite difference method. At each time step, we compute the right-hand sides of the two equations on the grid using discrete spatial derivatives (Laplacians). Then, we update the variables using a discrete time derivative:

```
In [7]: for i in range(n):
            # We compute the Laplacian of u and v.
            deltaU = laplacian(U)
            deltaV = laplacian(V)
            # We take the values of u and v
            # inside the grid.
            Uc = U[1:-1,1:-1]
```

```
Vc = V[1:-1,1:-1]
# We update the variables.
U[1:-1,1:-1], V[1:-1,1:-1] = (
    Uc + dt * (a*deltaU + Uc - Uc**3 - Vc + k),
    Vc + dt * (b*deltaV + Uc - Vc) / tau)
# Neumann conditions: derivatives at the edges
# are null.
for Z in (U, V):
    Z[0,:] = Z[1,:]
    Z[-1,:] = Z[-2,:]
    Z[:,0] = Z[:,1]
    Z[:,-1] = Z[:,-2]
```

8. Finally, we display the variable u after a time T of simulation:

```
In [8]: plt.imshow(U, cmap=plt.cm.copper, extent=[-1,1,-1,1])
```

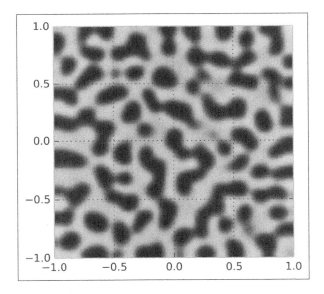

Whereas the variables were completely random at initialization time, we observe the formation of patterns after a sufficiently long simulation time.

How it works...

Let's explain how the finite difference method allowed us to implement the update step. We start from the following system of equations:

$$\frac{\partial u}{\partial t}(t;x,y) = a\Delta u(t;x,y) + u(t;x,y) - u(t;x,y)^3 - v(t;x,y) + k$$

$$\tau \frac{\partial v}{\partial t}(t;x,y) = b\Delta v(t;x,y) + u(t;x,y) - v(t;x,y)$$

We first use the following scheme for the discrete Laplace operator:

$$\Delta u(x,y) \simeq \frac{u(x+h,y) + u(x-h,y) + u(x,y+h) + u(x,y-h) - 4u(x,y)}{dx^2}$$

We also use this scheme for the time derivative of *u* and *v*:

$$\frac{\partial u}{\partial t}(t;x,y) \simeq \frac{u(t+dt;x,y) - u(t;x,y)}{dt}$$

We end up with the following iterative update step:

$$u(t+dt;x,y) = u(t;x,y) + dt\left(a\Delta u(t;x,y) + u(t;x,y) - u(t;x,y)^3 - v(t;x,y) + k\right)$$

$$v(t+dt;x,y) = v(t;x,y) + \frac{dt}{\tau}\left(b\Delta v(t;x,y) + u(t;x,y) - v(t;x,y)\right)$$

Here, our Neumann boundary conditions state that the spatial derivatives with respect to the normal vectors are null on the boundaries of the domain *E*:

$$\forall w \in \{u,v\}, \forall t \geq 0, \forall x,y \in \partial E$$

$$\frac{\partial w}{\partial x}(t;-1,y) = \frac{\partial w}{\partial x}(t;1,y) = \frac{\partial w}{\partial y}(t;x,-1) = \frac{\partial w}{\partial y}(t;x,1) = 0$$

We implement these boundary conditions by duplicating values in matrices U and V on the edges (see the preceding code).

In order to ensure that our numerical scheme converges to a numerical solution that is close to the actual (unknown) mathematical solution, the stability of the scheme needs to be ascertained. One can show that a sufficient condition for the stability is:

$$dt \le \frac{dx^2}{2}$$

There's more...

Here are further references on partial differential equations, reaction-diffusion systems, and numerical simulations of those systems:

- ► Partial differential equations on Wikipedia, available at `http://en.wikipedia.org/wiki/Partial_differential_equation`
- ► Reaction-diffusion systems on Wikipedia, available at `http://en.wikipedia.org/wiki/Reaction%E2%80%93diffusion_system`
- ► FitzHugh-Nagumo system on Wikipedia, available at `http://en.wikipedia.org/wiki/FitzHugh%E2%80%93Nagumo_equation`
- ► Neumann boundary conditions on Wikipedia, available at `http://en.wikipedia.org/wiki/Neumann_boundary_condition`
- ► Von Neumann stability analysis on Wikipedia, available at `http://en.wikipedia.org/wiki/Von_Neumann_stability_analysis`
- ► A course on Computational Fluid Dynamics by Prof. Lorena Barba, written in the IPython notebook, available at `https://github.com/barbagroup/CFDPython`

See also

- ► The *Simulating an elementary cellular automaton* recipe
- ► The *Simulating an ordinary differential equation with SciPy* recipe

13
Stochastic Dynamical Systems

In this chapter, we will cover the following topics:

- ▶ Simulating a discrete-time Markov chain
- ▶ Simulating a Poisson process
- ▶ Simulating a Brownian motion
- ▶ Simulating a stochastic differential equation

Introduction

Stochastic dynamical systems are dynamical systems subjected to the effect of noise. The randomness brought by the noise takes into account the variability observed in real-world phenomena. For example, the evolution of a share price typically exhibits long-term behaviors along with faster, smaller-amplitude oscillations, reflecting day-to-day or hour-to-hour variations.

Applications of stochastic systems to data science include methods for statistical inference (such as Markov chain Monte Carlo) and stochastic modeling for time series or geospatial data.

Stochastic discrete-time systems include discrete-time **Markov chains**. The **Markov property** means that the state of a system at time $n+1$ only depends on its state at time n. **Stochastic cellular automata**, which are stochastic extensions of cellular automata, are particular Markov chains.

As far as continuous-time systems are concerned, Ordinary Differential Equations with noise yield **Stochastic Differential Equations (SDEs)**. Partial Differential Equations with noise yield **Stochastic Partial Differential Equations (SPDEs)**.

Point processes are another type of stochastic process. These processes model the random occurrence of instantaneous events over time (arrival of customers in a queue or action potentials in the nervous system) or space (locations of trees in a forest, cities in a territory, or stars in the sky).

Mathematically, the theory of stochastic dynamical systems is based on probability theory and measure theory. The study of continuous-time stochastic systems builds upon stochastic calculus, an extension of infinitesimal calculus (including derivatives and integrals) to stochastic processes.

In this chapter, we will see how to simulate different kinds of stochastic systems with Python.

References

Here are a few references on the subject:

▶ An overview of stochastic dynamical systems, available at `www.scholarpedia.org/article/Stochastic_dynamical_systems`

▶ The Markov property on Wikipedia, available at `https://en.wikipedia.org/wiki/Markov_property`

Simulating a discrete-time Markov chain

Discrete-time Markov chains are stochastic processes that undergo transitions from one state to another in a state space. Transitions occur at every time step. Markov chains are characterized by their lack of memory in that the probability to undergo a transition from the current state to the next depends only on the current state, not the previous ones. These models are widely used in scientific and engineering applications.

Continuous-time Markov processes also exist and we will cover particular instances later in this chapter.

Markov chains are relatively easy to study mathematically and to simulate numerically. In this recipe, we will simulate a simple Markov chain modeling the evolution of a population.

How to do it...

1. Let's import NumPy and matplotlib:

```
In [1]: import numpy as np
        import matplotlib.pyplot as plt
        %matplotlib inline
```

2. We consider a population that cannot comprise more than *N=100* individuals, and define the birth and death rates:

```
In [2]: N = 100   # maximum population size
        a = 0.5/N  # birth rate
        b = 0.5/N  # death rate
```

3. We simulate a Markov chain on the finite space *{0, 1, ..., N}*. Each state represents a population size. The x vector will contain the population size at each time step. We set the initial state to $x_0=25$ (that is, there are 25 individuals in the population at initialization time):

```
In [3]: nsteps = 1000
        x = np.zeros(nsteps)
        x[0] = 25
```

4. Now we simulate our chain. At each time step *t*, there is a new birth with probability ax_t, and independently, there is a new death with probability bx_t. These probabilities are proportional to the size of the population at that time. If the population size reaches *0* or *N*, the evolution stops:

```
In [4]: for t in range(nsteps - 1):
            if 0 < x[t] < N-1:
                # Is there a birth?
                birth = np.random.rand() <= a*x[t]
                # Is there a death?
                death = np.random.rand() <= b*x[t]
                # We update the population size.
                x[t+1] = x[t] + 1*birth - 1*death
            # The evolution stops if we reach 0 or N.
            else:
                x[t+1] = x[t]
```

5. Let's look at the evolution of the population size:

```
In [5]: plt.plot(x)
```

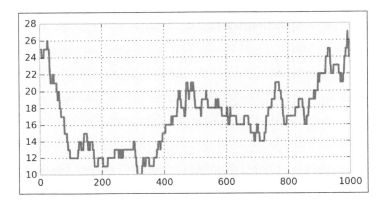

We see that, at every time step, the population size can stay stable, increase, or decrease by 1.

6. Now, we will simulate many independent trials of this Markov chain. We could run the previous simulation with a loop, but it would be very slow (two nested `for` loops). Instead, we *vectorize* the simulation by considering all independent trials at once. There is a single loop over time. At every time step, we update all trials simultaneously with vectorized operations on vectors. The x vector now contains the population size of all trials, at a particular time. At initialization time, the population sizes are set to random numbers between 0 and N:

```
In [6]: ntrials = 100
        x = np.random.randint(size=ntrials,
                              low=0, high=N)
```

7. We define a function that performs the simulation. At every time step, we find the trials that undergo births and deaths by generating random vectors, and we update the population sizes with vector operations:

```
In [7]: def simulate(x, nsteps):
            """Run the simulation."""
            for _ in range(nsteps - 1):
                # Which trials to update?
                upd = (0 < x) & (x < N-1)
                # In which trials do births occur?
                birth = 1*(np.random.rand(ntrials) <= a*x)
                # In which trials do deaths occur?
                death = 1*(np.random.rand(ntrials) <= b*x)
                # We update the population size for all
                # trials.
                x[upd] += birth[upd] - death[upd]
```

8. Now, let's look at the histograms of the population size at different times. These histograms represent the probability distribution of the Markov chain, estimated with independent trials (the Monte Carlo method):

```
In [8]: bins = np.linspace(0, N, 25)
In [9]: nsteps_list = [10, 1000, 10000]
        for i, nsteps in enumerate(nsteps_list):
            plt.subplot(1, len(nsteps_list), i + 1)
            simulate(x, nsteps)
            plt.hist(x, bins=bins)
            plt.xlabel("Population size")
            if i == 0:
                plt.ylabel("Histogram")
            plt.title("{0:d} time steps".format(nsteps))
```

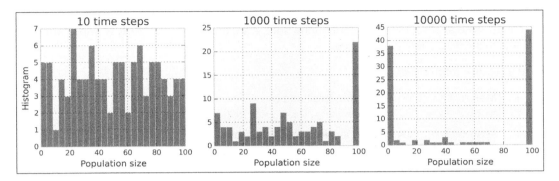

Whereas, initially, the population sizes look uniformly distributed between *0* and *N*, they appear to converge to *0* or *N* after a sufficiently long time. This is because the states *0* and *N* are **absorbing**; once reached, the chain cannot leave these states. Furthermore, these states can be reached from any other state.

How it works...

Mathematically, a discrete-time Markov chain on a space *E* is a sequence of random variables $X_1, X_2 \ldots$ that satisfy the Markov property:

$$\forall n \geq 1, \quad P(X_{n+1} \mid X_1, X_2, \ldots, X_n) = P(X_{n+1} \mid X_n)$$

A (stationary) Markov chain is characterized by the probability of transitions $P(X_j \mid X_i)$. These values form a matrix called the **transition matrix**. This matrix is the adjacency matrix of a directed graph called the **state diagram**. Every node is a state, and the node *i* is connected to the node *j* if the chain has a non-zero probability of transition between these nodes.

There's more...

Simulating a single Markov chain in Python is not particularly efficient because we need a `for` loop. However, simulating many independent chains following the same process can be made efficient with vectorization and parallelization (all tasks are independent, thus the problem is **embarrassingly parallel**). This is useful when we are interested in statistical properties of the chain (example of the Monte Carlo method).

There is a vast literature on Markov chains. Many theoretical results can be established with linear algebra and probability theory. You can find references and textbooks on Wikipedia.

Many generalizations of discrete-time Markov chains exist. Markov chains can be defined on infinite state spaces, or with a continuous time. Also, the Markov property is important in a broad class of stochastic processes.

Here are a few references:

▶ Markov chains on Wikipedia, available at
`https://en.wikipedia.org/wiki/Markov_chain`

▶ Absorbing Markov chains on Wikipedia, available at
`https://en.wikipedia.org/wiki/Absorbing_Markov_chain`

▶ Monte-Carlo methods on Wikipedia, available at
`https://en.wikipedia.org/wiki/Monte_Carlo_method`

See also

▶ The *Simulating a Brownian motion* recipe

Simulating a Poisson process

A **Poisson process** is a particular type of **point process**, a stochastic model that represents random occurrences of instantaneous events. Roughly speaking, the Poisson process is the least structured, or the most random, point process.

The Poisson process is a particular continuous-time Markov process.

Point processes, and notably Poisson processes, can model random instantaneous events such as the arrival of clients in a queue or on a server, telephone calls, radioactive disintegrations, action potentials of nerve cells, and many other phenomena.

In this recipe, we will show different methods to simulate a homogeneous stationary Poisson process.

How to do it...

1. Let's import NumPy and matplotlib:

```
In [1]: import numpy as np
        import matplotlib.pyplot as plt
        %matplotlib inline
```

2. Let's specify the `rate` value, that is, the average number of events per second:

    ```
    In [2]: rate = 20.  # average number of events per second
    ```

3. First, we will simulate the process using small time bins of 1 millisecond:

    ```
    In [3]: dt = .001  # time step
            n = int(1./dt)  # number of time steps
    ```

4. On every time bin, the probability that an event occurs is about *rate * dt* if *dt* is small enough. Besides, as the Poisson process has no memory, the occurrence of an event is independent from one bin to another. Therefore, we can sample Bernoulli random variables (either 1 or 0, respectively representing an experiment's success or failure) in a vectorized way in order to simulate our process:

    ```
    In [4]: x = np.zeros(n)
            x[np.random.rand(n) <= rate*dt] = 1
    ```

    The x vector contains zeros and ones on all time bins, 1 corresponding to the occurrence of an event:

    ```
    In [5]: x[:5]
    Out[5]: array([ 0.,  1.,  0.,  0.,  0. ])
    ```

5. Let's display the simulated process. We draw a vertical line for each event:

    ```
    In [6]: plt.vlines(np.nonzero(x)[0], 0, 1)
            plt.xticks([]); plt.yticks([])
    ```

6. Another way of representing that same object is by considering the associated **counting process** *N(t)*,which is the number of events that have occurred until time *t*. Here, we can display this process using the `cumsum()` function:

```
In [7]: plt.plot(np.linspace(0., 1., n), np.cumsum(x))
        plt.xlabel("Time")
        plt.ylabel("Counting process")
```

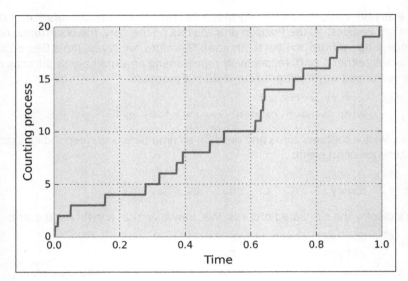

7. The other (and more efficient) way of simulating the homogeneous Poisson process is to use the property that the time intervals between two successive events follow an exponential distribution. Furthermore, these intervals are independent. Thus, we can sample them in a vectorized way. Finally, we get our process by cumulatively summing all of these intervals:

```
In [8]: y = np.cumsum(np.random.exponential(
                      1./rate, size=int(rate)))
```

The `y` vector contains another realization of our Poisson process, but the data structure is different. Every component of the vector is an event time:

```
In [9]: y[:5]
Out[9]: array([ 0.006,   0.111,   0.244,   0.367,   0.365])
```

8. Finally, let's display the simulated process:

```
In [10]: plt.vlines(y, 0, 1)
         plt.xticks([]); plt.yticks([])
```

How it works...

For a Poisson process with rate λ, the number of events in a time window of length τ follows a Poisson distribution:

$$\forall k \geq 0, \quad P\big[N(t+\tau) - N(t) = k\big] = e^{-\lambda\tau}\frac{(\lambda\tau)^k}{k!}$$

When $\tau = dt$ is small, we can show that, at first order, this probability is about $\lambda\tau$.

Also, the **holding times** (delays between two consecutive events) are independent and follow an exponential distribution. The Poisson process satisfies other useful properties, such as the independent and stationary increments. This property justifies the first simulation method used in this recipe.

There's more...

In this recipe, we only considered homogeneous time-dependent Poisson processes. Other types of Poisson processes include inhomogeneous (or non-homogeneous) processes that are characterized by a time-varying rate, and multidimensional spatial Poisson processes.

Here are further references:

▸ The Poisson process on Wikipedia, available at
  `http://en.wikipedia.org/wiki/Poisson_process`

▸ Point processes on Wikipedia, available at
  `http://en.wikipedia.org/wiki/Point_process`

▸ Continuous-time processes on Wikipedia, available at
  `http://en.wikipedia.org/wiki/Continuous-time_process`

▸ Renewal theory on Wikipedia, available at
  `http://en.wikipedia.org/wiki/Renewal_theory`

▸ Spatial Poisson processes on Wikipedia, available at
  `http://en.wikipedia.org/wiki/ Spatial_Poisson_process`

See also

▶ The *Simulating a discrete-time Markov chain* recipe

Simulating a Brownian motion

The **Brownian motion** (or **Wiener process**) is a fundamental object in mathematics, physics, and many other scientific and engineering disciplines. This model describes the movement of a particle suspended in a fluid resulting from random collisions with the quick molecules in the fluid (diffusion). More generally, the Brownian motion models a continuous-time **random walk**, where a particle evolves in space by making independent random steps in all directions.

Mathematically, the Brownian motion is a particular Markov continuous stochastic process. The Brownian motion is at the core of mathematical domains such as stochastic calculus and the theory of stochastic processes, but it is also central in applied fields such as quantitative finance, ecology, and neuroscience.

In this recipe, we will show how to simulate and plot a Brownian motion in two dimensions.

How to do it...

1. Let's import NumPy and matplotlib:

```
In [1]: import numpy as np
        import matplotlib.pyplot as plt
        %matplotlib inline
```

2. We simulate Brownian motions with 5000 time steps:

```
In [2]: n = 5000
```

3. We simulate two independent one-dimensional Brownian processes to form a single two-dimensional Brownian process. The (discrete) Brownian motion makes independent Gaussian jumps at each time step. Therefore, we merely have to compute the cumulative sum of independent normal random variables (one for each time step):

```
In [3]: x = np.cumsum(np.random.randn(n))
        y = np.cumsum(np.random.randn(n))
```

4. Now, to display the Brownian motion, we could just use `plot(x, y)`. However, the result would be monochromatic and a bit boring. We would like to use a gradient of color to illustrate the progression of the motion in time (the hue is a function of time). matplotlib forces us to use a small hack based on `scatter()`. This function allows us to assign a different color to each point at the expense of dropping out line segments between points. To work around this issue, we linearly interpolate the process to give the illusion of a continuous line:

```
In [4]: k = 10  # We add 10 intermediary points between two
                 # successive points.
        # We interpolate x and y.
        x2 = np.interp(np.arange(n*k), np.arange(n)*k, x)
        y2 = np.interp(np.arange(n*k), np.arange(n)*k, y)
In [5]: # Now, we draw our points with a gradient of
        # colors.
        plt.scatter(x2, y2, c=range(n*k), linewidths=0,
                    marker='o', s=3, cmap=plt.cm.jet)
        plt.axis('equal')
        plt.xticks([]); plt.yticks([])
```

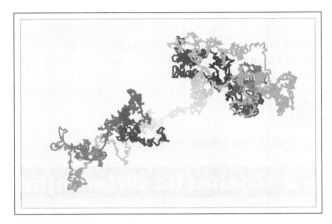

How it works...

The Brownian motion *W(t)* has several important properties. First, it gives rise (almost surely) to continuous trajectories. Second, its increments $W(t+\tau)-W(t)$ are independent on non-overlapping intervals. Third, these increments are Gaussian random variables. More precisely:

$$\forall t, \tau > 0, \quad W(t+\tau) - W(t) \sim N(0, \tau)$$

In particular, the density of *W(t)* is a normal distribution with variance *t*.

Additionally, the Brownian motion, and stochastic processes in general, have deep connections with partial differential equations. Here, the density of *W(t)* is a solution of the **heat equation**, a particular diffusion equation. More generally, the **Fokker-Planck equation** is a partial differential equation satisfied by the density of solutions of a stochastic differential equation.

There's more...

The Brownian motion is a limit of a random walk with an infinitesimal step size. We used this property here to simulate the process.

Here are a few references:

- ▶ The Brownian motion (physical phenomenon) described at http://en.wikipedia.org/wiki/Brownian_motion
- ▶ The Wiener process (mathematical object) explained at http://en.wikipedia.org/wiki/Wiener_process
- ▶ The Brownian motion is a particular type of the Lévy process; refer to http://en.wikipedia.org/wiki/L%C3%A9vy_process
- ▶ The Fokker-Planck equation links stochastic processes to partial differential equations; refer to http://en.wikipedia.org/wiki/Fokker%E2%80%93Planck_equation

See also

- ▶ The *Simulating a stochastic differential equation* recipe

Simulating a stochastic differential equation

Stochastic differential equations (**SDEs**) model dynamical systems that are subject to noise. They are widely used in physics, biology, finance, and other disciplines.

In this recipe, we simulate an **Ornstein-Uhlenbeck process**, which is a solution of the **Langevin equation**. This model describes the stochastic evolution of a particle in a fluid under the influence of friction. The particle's movement is due to collisions with the molecules of the fluid (diffusion). The difference with the Brownian motion is the presence of friction.

The Ornstein-Uhlenbeck process is stationary, Gaussian, and Markov, which makes it a good candidate to represent stationary random noise.

We will simulate this process with a numerical method called the **Euler-Maruyama method**. It is a simple generalization to SDEs of the Euler method for ODEs.

How to do it...

1. Let's import NumPy and matplotlib:

```
In [1]: import numpy as np
        import matplotlib.pyplot as plt
        %matplotlib inline
```

2. We define a few parameters for our model:

```
In [2]: sigma = 1.  # Standard deviation.
        mu = 10.0  # Mean.
        tau = 0.05  # Time constant.
```

3. Let's define a few simulation parameters:

```
In [3]: dt = 0.001  # Time step.
        T = 1.0  # Total time.
        n = int(T/dt)  # Number of time steps.
        t = np.linspace(0., T, n)  # Vector of times.
```

4. We also define renormalized variables (to avoid recomputing these constants at every time step):

```
In [4]: sigma_bis = sigma * np.sqrt(2. / tau)
        sqrtdt = np.sqrt(dt)
```

5. We create a vector that will contain all successive values of our process during the simulation:

```
In [5]: x = np.zeros(n)
```

6. Now, let's simulate the process with the Euler-Maruyama method. It is really like the standard Euler method for ODEs, but with an extra stochastic term (which is just a scaled normal random variable). We will give the equation of the process along with the details of this method in the *How it works...* section:

```
In [6]: for i in range(n-1):
            x[i+1] = x[i] + dt*(-(x[i]-mu)/tau) + \
                 sigma_bis * sqrtdt * np.random.randn()
```

7. Let's display the evolution of the process:

```
In [7]: plt.plot(t, x)
```

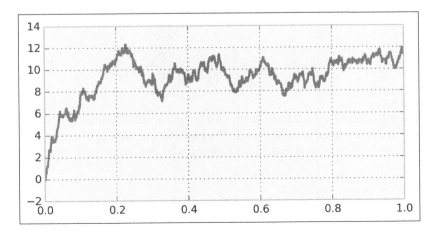

8. Now, we are going to take a look at the time evolution of the distribution of the process. To do this, we will simulate many independent realizations of the same process in a vectorized way. We define a vector x that will contain all realizations of the process at a given time (that is, we do not keep all realizations at all times in memory). This vector will be overwritten at every time step. We will show the estimated distribution (histograms) at several points in time:

```
In [8]: ntrials = 10000
        X = np.zeros(ntrials)
In [9]: # We create bins for the histograms.
        bins = np.linspace(-2., 14., 50);
        for i in range(n):
            # We update the process independently for all
            # trials.
            X += dt*(-(X-mu)/tau) + \
                sigma_bis*sqrtdt*np.random.randn(ntrials)
            # We display the histogram for a few points in
            # time.
            if i in (5, 50, 900):
                hist, _ = np.histogram(X, bins=bins)
                plt.plot((bins[1:]+bins[:-1])/2,  hist,
                        label="t={0:.2f}".format(i*dt))
        plt.legend()
```

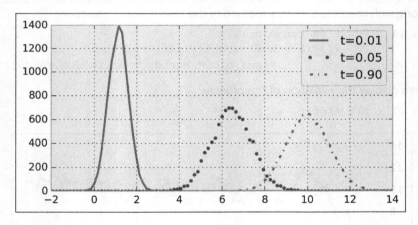

The distribution of the process tends to a Gaussian distribution with mean $\mu = 10$ and standard deviation $\sigma = 1$. The process would be stationary if the initial distribution was also a Gaussian with the adequate parameters.

How it works...

The Langevin equation that we use in this recipe is the following stochastic differential equation:

$$dx = -\frac{(x-\mu)}{\tau}dt + \sigma\sqrt{\frac{2}{\tau}}dW$$

Here, *x(t)* is our stochastic process, *dx* is the infinitesimal increment, μ is the mean, σ is the standard deviation, and τ is the time constant. Also, *W* is a Brownian motion (or the Wiener process) that underlies our SDE.

The first term on the right-hand side is the deterministic term (in *dt*), while the second term is the stochastic term. Without that last term, the equation would be a regular deterministic ODE.

The infinitesimal step of a Brownian motion is a Gaussian random variable. Specifically, the derivative (in a certain sense) of a Brownian motion is a **white noise**, a sequence of independent Gaussian random variables.

The Euler-Maruyama method involves discretizing time and adding infinitesimal steps to the process at every time step. This method involves a deterministic term (like in the standard Euler method for ODEs) and a stochastic term (random Gaussian variable). Specifically, for an equation:

$$dx = a(t,x)dt + b(t,x)dW$$

The numerical scheme is (with *t=n * dt*):

$$x_{n+1} = x_n + dx = x_n + a(t,x_n)dt + b(t,x_n)\sqrt{dt}\xi, \quad \xi \sim N(0,1)$$

Here, ξ is a random Gaussian variable with variance *1* (independent at each time step). The normalization factor $\sqrt{dt}$ comes from the fact that the infinitesimal step for a Brownian motion has the standard deviation $\sqrt{dt}$.

There's more...

The mathematics of SDEs comprises the theory of stochastic calculus, Itō calculus, martingales, and other topics. Although these theories are quite involved, simulating stochastic processes numerically can be relatively straightforward, as we have seen in this recipe.

The error of the Euler-Maruyama method is of order $\sqrt{dt}$. The Milstein method is a more precise numerical scheme, of order dt.

Here are a few references on these topics:

▶ Stochastic differential equations on Wikipedia, available at
`http://en.wikipedia.org/wiki/Stochastic_differential_equation`

▶ White noise, described at `http://en.wikipedia.org/wiki/White_noise`

▶ The Langevin equation on Wikipedia, available at
`http://en.wikipedia.org/wiki/Langevin_equation`

▶ The Ornstein-Uhlenbeck process described at `http://en.wikipedia.org/wiki/`
`Ornstein%E2%80%93Uhlenbeck_process`

▶ Diffusion processes described at `http://en.wikipedia.org/wiki/`
`Diffusion_process`

▶ Itō calculus, described at `http://en.wikipedia.org/wiki/It%C5%8D_`
`calculus`

▶ The Euler-Maruyama method, explained at `http://en.wikipedia.org/wiki/`
`Euler%E2%80%93Maruyama_method`

▶ The Milstein method on Wikipedia, available at `http://en.wikipedia.org/`
`wiki/Milstein_method`

See also

▶ The *Simulating a Brownian motion* recipe

14
Graphs, Geometry, and Geographic Information Systems

In this chapter, we will cover the following topics:

- ► Manipulating and visualizing graphs with NetworkX
- ► Analyzing a social network with NetworkX
- ► Resolving dependencies in a Directed Acyclic Graph with a topological sort
- ► Computing connected components in an image
- ► Computing the Voronoi diagram of a set of points
- ► Manipulating geospatial data with Shapely and basemap
- ► Creating a route planner for a road network

Introduction

In this chapter, we will cover Python's capabilities in graph theory, geometry, and geography.

Graphs are mathematical objects describing relations between items. They are ubiquitous in science and engineering, as they can represent many kinds of real-world relations: friends in a social network, atoms in a molecule, website links, cells in a neural network, neighboring pixels in an image, and so on. Graphs are also classical data structures in computer science. Finally, many domain-specific problems may be re-expressed as graph problems, and then solved with well-known algorithms.

We will also see a few recipes related to **geometry** and **Geographic Information Systems** (**GIS**), which refers to the processing and analysis of any kind of spatial, geographical, or topographical data.

In this introduction, we will give a brief overview of these topics.

Graphs

Mathematically, a **graph** $G = (V, E)$ is defined by a set V of **vertices** or **nodes**, and a set E of **edges** (two-element subsets of V). Two nodes v and v' are said to be **connected** if (v, v') is an edge (element of E).

- ▸ If the edges are *unordered* (meaning that $(v,v') = (v',v)$), the graph is said to be **undirected**
- ▸ If the edges are *ordered* (meaning that $(v,v') \neq (v',v)$), the graph is said to be **directed**

An edge in an undirected graph is represented by a line segment between the two nodes. In a directed graph, it is represented by an arrow.

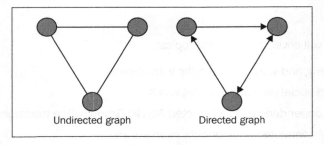

Undirected graph   Directed graph

Undirected and directed graphs

A graph can be represented by different data structures, notably an **adjacency list** (for each vertex, a list of adjacent vertices) or an **adjacency matrix** (matrix of connections between vertices).

Problems in graph theory

Here are a few examples of classical graph problems:

- ▸ **Graph traversal**: How to walk through a graph, discussed at
  http://en.wikipedia.org/wiki/Graph_traversal
- ▸ **Graph coloring**: How to color nodes in a graph such that no two adjacent vertices share the same color, discussed at http://en.wikipedia.org/wiki/Graph_coloring

- ▶ **Connected components**: How to find connected components in a graph, explained at `http://en.wikipedia.org/wiki/Connected_component_%28graph_theory%29`

- ▶ **Shortest paths**: What is the shortest path from one node to another in a given graph?, discussed at `http://en.wikipedia.org/wiki/Shortest_path_problem`

- ▶ **Hamiltonian paths**: Does a graph include a Hamiltonian path, visiting every vertex exactly once?, explained at `http://en.wikipedia.org/wiki/Hamiltonian_path`

- ▶ **Eulerian paths**: Does a graph include an Eulerian path, visiting every _edge_ exactly once?, discussed at `http://en.wikipedia.org/wiki/Eulerian_path`

- ▶ **Traveling Salesman Problem**: What is the shortest route visiting every node exactly once (Hamiltonian path)?, explained at `http://en.wikipedia.org/wiki/Traveling_salesman_problem`

Random graphs

Random graphs are particular kinds of graphs defined with probabilistic rules. They are useful for understanding the structure of large real-world graphs such as social graphs.

In particular, **small-world networks** have sparse connections, but most nodes can be reached from every other node in a small number of steps. This property is due to the existence of a small number of **hubs** that have a high number of connections.

Graphs in Python

Although graphs can be manipulated with native Python structures, it is more convenient to use a dedicated library implementing specific data structures and manipulation routines. In this chapter, we will use **NetworkX**, a pure Python library. Alternative Python libraries include **python-graph** and **graph-tool** (largely written in C++).

NetworkX implements a flexible data structure for graphs, and it contains many algorithms. NetworkX also lets us draw graphs easily with matplotlib.

Geometry in Python

Shapely is a Python library used to manipulate 2D geometrical shapes such as points, lines, and polygons. It is most notably useful in Geographic Information Systems.

It is not straightforward to combine Shapely with matplotlib. Fortunately, the **descartes** package makes this task much easier.

Geographical Information Systems in Python

There are several Python modules used to manipulate geographical data and plotting maps.

In this chapter, we will use matplotlib's basemap, Shapely, descartes, and Fiona to handle GIS files.

The ESRI **shapefile** is a popular geospatial vector data format. It can be read by basemap, NetworkX, and Fiona.

We will also use the **OpenStreetMap** service, a free, open source, collaborative service providing maps of the world.

Other GIS/mapping systems in Python that we couldn't cover in this chapter include **GeoPandas**, **Kartograph**, **Vincent**, and **cartopy**.

References

Here are a few references about graphs:

- Graph theory on Wikipedia, available at `http://en.wikipedia.org/wiki/Graph_theory`
- Data structures for graphs, described at `http://en.wikipedia.org/wiki/Graph_(abstract_data_type)`
- Random graphs on Wikipedia, available at `http://en.wikipedia.org/wiki/Random_graph`
- Small-world graphs on Wikipedia, available at `http://en.wikipedia.org/wiki/Small-world_network`
- NetworkX package, available at `http://networkx.github.io`
- The python-graph package, available at `https://code.google.com/p/python-graph/`
- The graph-tool package, available at `http://graph-tool.skewed.de`

Here are a few references about geometry and maps in Python:

- Basemap at `http://matplotlib.org/basemap/`
- Shapely at `http://toblerity.org/shapely/project.html`
- Fiona at `http://toblerity.org/fiona/`
- descartes at `https://pypi.python.org/pypi/descartes`
- Shapefile at `http://en.wikipedia.org/wiki/Shapefile`
- OpenStreetMap at `www.openstreetmap.org`

- ▶ Folium at `https://github.com/wrobstory/folium`
- ▶ GeoPandas at `http://geopandas.org`
- ▶ Kartograph at `http://kartograph.org`
- ▶ Cartopy at `http://scitools.org.uk/cartopy/`
- ▶ Vincent at `https://github.com/wrobstory/vincent`

Manipulating and visualizing graphs with NetworkX

In this recipe, we will show how to create, manipulate, and visualize graphs with NetworkX.

Getting ready

You can find the installation instructions for NetworkX in the official documentation at `http://networkx.github.io/documentation/latest/install.html`.

With Anaconda, you can type `conda install networkx` in a terminal. Alternatively, you can type `pip install networkx`. On Windows, you can also use Chris Gohlke's installer, available at `www.lfd.uci.edu/~gohlke/pythonlibs/#networkx`.

How to do it...

1. Let's import NumPy, NetworkX, and matplotlib:

```
In [1]: import numpy as np
        import networkx as nx
        import matplotlib.pyplot as plt
        %matplotlib inline
```

2. There are many different ways of creating a graph. Here, we create a list of edges (pairs of node indices):

```
In [2]: n = 10  # Number of nodes in the graph.
        # Each node is connected to the two next nodes,
        # in a circular fashion.
        adj = [(i, (i+1)%n) for i in range(n)]
        adj += [(i, (i+2)%n) for i in range(n)]
```

3. We instantiate a `Graph` object with our list of edges:

```
In [3]: g = nx.Graph(adj)
```

4. Let's check the list of nodes and edges of the graph, and its adjacency matrix:

```
In [4]: print(g.nodes())
[0, 1, 2, 3, 4, 5, 6, 7, 8, 9]
In [5]: print(g.edges())
[(0, 8), (0, 1), (0, 2), ..., (7, 9), (8, 9)]
In [6]: print(nx.adjacency_matrix(g))
[[ 0.  1.  1.  0.  0.  0.  0.  0.  1.  1.]
 [ 1.  0.  1.  1.  0.  0.  0.  0.  0.  1.]
 ...
 [ 1.  0.  0.  0.  0.  0.  1.  1.  0.  1.]
 [ 1.  1.  0.  0.  0.  0.  0.  1.  1.  0.]]
```

5. Let's display this graph. NetworkX comes with a variety of drawing functions. We can either specify the nodes' positions explicitly, or we can use an algorithm to automatically compute an interesting layout. Here, we use the `draw_circular()` function that simply positions nodes linearly on a circle:

```
In [7]: nx.draw_circular(g)
```

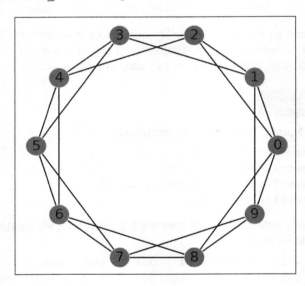

6. Graphs can be modified easily. Here, we add a new node connected to all existing nodes. We also specify a `color` attribute to this node. In NetworkX, every node and edge comes with a convenient Python dictionary containing arbitrary attributes.

```
In [8]: g.add_node(n, color='#fcff00')
        # We add an edge from every existing
        # node to the new node.
        for i in range(n):
            g.add_edge(i, n)
```

7. Now, let's draw the modified graph again. This time, we specify the nodes' positions and colors explicitly:

```
In [9]:  # We define custom node positions on a circle
         # except the last node which is at the center.
         t = np.linspace(0., 2*np.pi, n)
         pos = np.zeros((n+1, 2))
         pos[:n,0] = np.cos(t)
         pos[:n,1] = np.sin(t)
         # A node's color is specified by its 'color'
         # attribute, or a default color if this attribute
         # doesn't exist.
         color = [g.node[i].get('color', '#88b0f3')
                     for i in range(n+1)]
         # We now draw the graph with matplotlib.
         nx.draw_networkx(g, pos=pos, node_color=color)
         plt.axis('off')
```

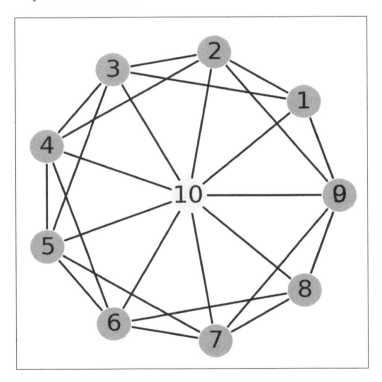

8. Let's also use an automatic layout algorithm:

```
In [10]: nx.draw_spectral(g, node_color=color)
         plt.axis('off')
```

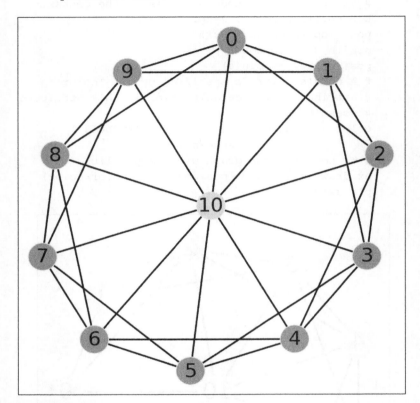

There's more...

In NetworkX, nodes are not necessarily integers. They can be numbers, strings, tuples, and instances of any hashable Python class.

In addition, every node and edge comes with optional attributes (which form a dictionary).

A few layout algorithms are implemented in NetworkX. The `draw_spectral()` function uses the eigenvectors of the graph's **Laplacian matrix**.

The `draw_spring()` function implements the **Fruchterman-Reingold force-directed** algorithm. Nodes are considered as masses subject to edge-dependent forces. A force-directed graph drawing algorithm minimizes the system's energy so as to find an equilibrium configuration. This results in an aesthetically appealing layout with as few crossing edges as possible.

Here are a few references:

- Graph drawing, described at `http://en.wikipedia.org/wiki/Graph_drawing`
- Laplacian matrix on Wikipedia, available at `http://en.wikipedia.org/wiki/Laplacian_matrix`
- Force-directed graph drawing, described at `http://en.wikipedia.org/wiki/Force-directed_graph_drawing`

See also

- The *Analyzing a social network with NetworkX* recipe

Analyzing a social network with NetworkX

In this recipe, we will show how to analyze social data in Python. Social data is generated by people's activity on social networks such as Facebook, Twitter, Google+, GitHub, and others.

In this recipe, we will analyze and visualize a Twitter user's social network with NetworkX.

Getting ready

First, you need to install the **Twitter** Python package. You can install it with `pip install twitter`. You'll find more information at `https://pypi.python.org/pypi/twitter`.

Then, you need to obtain authentication codes in order to access your Twitter data. The procedure is free. In addition to a Twitter account, you also need to create an *Application* on the Twitter Developers website at `https://dev.twitter.com/apps`. Then, you will be able to retrieve the **OAuth authentication codes** that are required for this recipe.

You need to create a `twitter.txt` text file in the current folder with the four private authentication keys. There must be one key per line, in the following order:

- API key
- API secret
- Access token
- Access token secret

Note that access to the Twitter API is limited. Most methods can only be called a few times within a given time window. Unless you study small networks or look at small portions of large networks, you will need to *throttle* your requests. In this recipe, we only consider a small portion of the network, so that the API limit should not be reached. Otherwise, you will have to wait a few minutes before the next time window starts. The API limits are available at `https://dev.twitter.com/docs/rate-limiting/1.1/limits`.

How to do it...

1. Let's import a few packages:

```
In [1]: import math
        import json
        import twitter
        import numpy as np
        import pandas as pd
        import networkx as nx
        import matplotlib.pyplot as plt
        %matplotlib inline
        from IPython.display import Image
```

2. We get the secret consumer and OAuth keys from our `twitter.txt` file:

```
In [2]: (CONSUMER_KEY,
         CONSUMER_SECRET,
         OAUTH_TOKEN,
         OAUTH_TOKEN_SECRET) = open(
                'twitter.txt', 'r').read().splitlines()
```

3. We now create an instance of the `Twitter` class that will give us access to the Twitter API:

```
In [3]: auth = twitter.oauth.OAuth(OAUTH_TOKEN,
                                   OAUTH_TOKEN_SECRET,
                                   CONSUMER_KEY,
                                   CONSUMER_SECRET)
        tw = twitter.Twitter(auth=auth)
```

4. We use the 1.1 version of the Twitter API in this recipe. The `twitter` library defines a direct mapping between the REST API and the attributes of the `Twitter` instance. Here, we execute the `account/verify_credentials` REST request to obtain the identifier of the authenticated user (me here, or you if you execute this notebook yourself!):

```
In [4]: me = tw.account.verify_credentials()
In [5]: myid = me['id']
```

5. Let's define a simple function that returns the identifiers of all followers of a given user (the authenticated user by default):

```
In [6]: def get_followers_ids(uid=None):
            # Retrieve the list of followers' ids of the
            # specified user.
            return tw.followers.ids(user_id=uid)['ids']
In [7]: # We get the list of my followers.
        my_followers_ids = get_followers_ids()
```

6. Now, we define a function that retrieves the full profile of Twitter users. As the `users/lookup` batch request is limited to 100 users per call, and only a small number of calls are allowed within a time window, we only look at a subset of all the followers:

```
In [8]: def get_users_info(users_ids, max=500):
            n = min(max, len(users_ids))
            # Get information about those users,
            # using batch requests.
            users = [tw.users.lookup(
                user_id=users_ids[100*i:100*(i+1)])
                    for i in range(int(math.ceil(n/100.)))]
            # We flatten this list of lists.
            users = [item for sublist in users
                    for item in sublist]
            return {user['id']: user for user in users}
In [9]: users_info = get_users_info(my_followers_ids)
In [10]: # Let's save this dictionary on the disk.
         with open('my_followers.json', 'w') as f:
             json.dump(users_info, f, indent=1)
```

7. We also start to define the graph with the followers, using an adjacency list (technically, a dictionary of lists). This is called the **ego graph**. This graph represents all *following* connections between our followers:

```
In [11]: adjacency = {myid: my_followers_ids}
```

8. Now, we are going to take a look at the part of the ego graph related to Python. Specifically, we will consider the followers of the 10 most followed users whose descriptions contain "Python":

```
In [12]: my_followers_python = \[user
            for user in users_info.values()
                if 'python' in user['description'].lower()]
In [13]: my_followers_python_best = \
            sorted(my_followers_python,
                key=lambda u: u['followers_count'])[::-1][:10]
```

The request for retrieving the followers of a given user is rate-limited. Let's check how many remaining calls we have:

```
In [14]: tw.application.rate_limit_status(
            resources='followers') \
            ['resources']['followers']['/followers/ids']
Out[14]: {u'limit': 15,
          u'remaining': 0,
          u'reset': 1388865551}
```

```
In [15]: for user in my_followers_python_best:
             # The call to get_followers_ids is
             # rate-limited.
             adjacency[user['id']] = list(set(
                 get_followers_ids(user['id'])). \
                 intersection(my_followers_ids))
```

9. Now that our graph is defined as an adjacency list in a dictionary, we will load it in NetworkX:

```
In [16]: g = nx.Graph(adjacency)
In [17]: # We only restrict the graph to the users
         # for which we were able to retrieve the profile.
         g = g.subgraph(users_info.keys())
In [18]: # We also save this graph on disk.
         with open('my_graph.json', 'w') as f:
             json.dump(nx.to_dict_of_lists(g), f, indent=1)
In [19]: # We remove isolated nodes for simplicity.
         g.remove_nodes_from([k
             for k, d in g.degree().items()
                 if d <= 1])
In [20]: # Since I am connected to all nodes,
         # by definition, we can remove me for simplicity.
         g.remove_nodes_from([myid])
```

10. Let's take a look at the graph's statistics:

```
In [21]: len(g.nodes()), len(g.edges())
Out[21]: (197, 1037)
```

11. We are now going to plot this graph. We will use different sizes and colors for the nodes, according to the number of followers and the number of tweets for each user. Most followed users will be bigger. Most active users will be redder.

```
In [22]: # Update the dictionary.
         deg = g.degree()
         for user in users_info.values():
             fc = user['followers_count']
             sc = user['statuses_count']
             # Is this user a Pythonista?
             user['python'] = 'python' in \
                                  user['description'].lower()
             # We compute the node size as a function of
             # the number of followers.
             user['node_size'] = math.sqrt(1 + 10 * fc)
             # The color is function of its activity
```

```
user['node_color'] = 10 * math.sqrt(1 + sc)
# We only display the name of the most
# followed users.
user['label'] = user['screen_name'] \
                    if fc > 2000 else ''
```

12. Finally, we use the `draw()` function to display the graph. We need to specify the nodes' sizes and colors as lists, and the labels as a dictionary:

```
In [23]: node_size = [users_info[uid]['node_size']
                      for uid in g.nodes()]
In [24]: node_color = [users_info[uid]['node_color']
                       for uid in g.nodes()]
In [25]: labels = {uid: users_info[uid]['label']
                   for uid in g.nodes()}
In [26]: nx.draw(g, cmap=plt.cm.OrRd, alpha=.8,
                 node_size=node_size,
                 node_color=node_color,
                 labels=labels, font_size=4, width=.1)
```

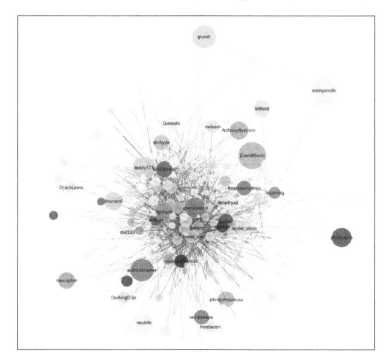

There's more...

A great reference on social data analysis with Python is Matthew A. Russel's book *Mining the Social Web, O'Reilly Media*. The code is available on GitHub as IPython notebooks at `https://github.com/ptwobrussell/Mining-the-Social-Web-2nd-Edition`. The following networks are covered: Twitter, Facebook, LinkedIn, Google+, GitHub, mailboxes, websites, and others.

See also

▶ The *Manipulating and visualizing graphs with NetworkX* recipe

Resolving dependencies in a directed acyclic graph with a topological sort

In this recipe, we will show an application of a well-known graph algorithm: **topological sorting**. Let's consider a directed graph describing dependencies between items. For example, in a package manager, before we can install a given package *P*, we may need to install *dependent* packages.

The set of dependencies forms a directed graph. With topological sorting, the package manager can resolve the dependencies and find the right installation order of the packages.

Topological sorting has many other applications. Here, we will illustrate this notion on real data from the Debian package manager. We will find the installation order of the required packages for IPython.

Getting ready

You need the `python-apt` package in order to build the package dependency graph. The package is available at `https://pypi.python.org/pypi/python-apt/`.

We also assume that this notebook is executed on a Debian system (such as Ubuntu). If you don't have such a system, you can download the *Debian* dataset directly from the book's GitHub repository at `https://github.com/ipython-books/cookbook-data`. Extract it in the current directory, and start directly from step 7 in this notebook.

How to do it...

1. We import the `apt` module and we build the list of packages:

```
In [1]: import json
        import apt
        cache = apt.Cache()
```

2. The `graph` dictionary will contain the adjacency list of a small portion of the dependency graph:

```
In [2]: graph = {}
```

3. We define a function that returns the list of dependencies of a package:

```
In [3]: def get_dependencies(package):
            if package not in cache:
                return []
            pack = cache[package]
            ver = pack.candidate or pack.versions[0]
            # We flatten the list of dependencies,
            # and we remove the duplicates.
            return sorted(set([item.name
                    for sublist in ver.dependencies
                    for item in sublist]))
```

4. We now define a *recursive* function that builds the dependency graph for a particular package. This function updates the `graph` variable:

```
In [4]: def get_dep_recursive(package):
            if package not in cache:
                return []
            if package not in graph:
                dep = get_dependencies(package)
                graph[package] = dep
            for dep in graph[package]:
                if dep not in graph:
                    graph[dep] = get_dep_recursive(dep)
            return graph[package]
```

5. Let's build the dependency graph for IPython:

```
In [5]: get_dep_recursive('ipython')
```

6. Finally, we save the adjacency list in JSON:

```
In [6]: with open('data/apt.json', 'w') as f:
            json.dump(graph, f, indent=1)
```

Start here if you don't have a Debian operating system (you first need to download the *Debian* dataset from the book's repository).

7. We import a few packages:

```
In [7]: import json
        import numpy as np
        import networkx as nx
        import matplotlib.pyplot as plt
        %matplotlib inline
```

8. Let's load the adjacency list from the JSON file:

```
In [8]: with open('data/apt.json', 'r') as f:
            graph = json.load(f)
```

9. Now, we create a directed graph (DiGraph in NetworkX) from our adjacency list. We reverse the graph to get a more natural ordering:

```
In [9]: g = nx.DiGraph(graph).reverse()
```

10. A topological sort only exists when the graph is a **directed acyclic graph** (**DAG**). This means that there is no cycle in the graph, that is, no circular dependency. Is our graph a DAG? Let's see:

```
In [10]: nx.is_directed_acyclic_graph(g)
Out[10]: False
```

11. What are the packages responsible for the cycles? We can find them with the simple_cycles() function:

```
In [11]: set([cycle[0] for cycle in nx.simple_cycles(g)])
Out[11]: {u'coreutils', u'libc6', u'multiarch-support',
          u'python-minimal', u'tzdata'}
```

12. Here, we can try to remove these packages. In an actual package manager, these cycles need to be carefully taken into account.

```
In [12]: g.remove_nodes_from(_)
In [13]: nx.is_directed_acyclic_graph(g)
Out[13]: True
```

13. The graph is now a DAG. Let's display it first:

```
In [14]: ug = g.to_undirected()
         deg = ug.degree()
In [15]: # The size of the nodes depends on the number
         # of dependencies.
         nx.draw(ug, font_size=6,
             node_size=[20*deg[k] for k in ug.nodes()])
```

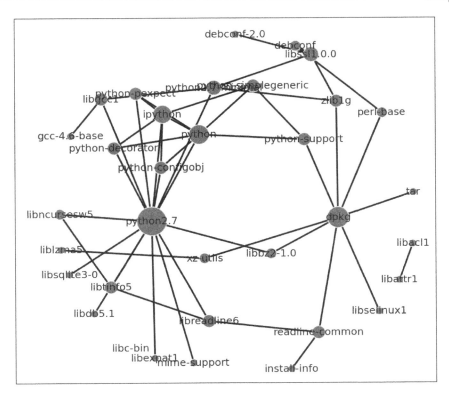

14. Finally, we can perform the topological sort, thereby obtaining a linear installation order satisfying all dependencies:

```
In [16]: nx.topological_sort(g)
Out[16]: [u'libexpat1',
          u'libdb5.1',
          u'debconf-2.0',
          ...
          u'python-pexpect',
          u'python-configobj',
          u'ipython']
```

There's more...

Directed acyclic graphs are found in many applications. They can represent causal relations, influence diagrams, dependencies, and other concepts. For example, the version history of a distributed revision control system such as Git is described with a DAG.

Topological sorting is useful in any scheduling task in general (project management and instruction scheduling).

Here are a few references:

- Topological sorting on Wikipedia, available at `http://en.wikipedia.org/wiki/Topological_sorting`
- Directed acyclic graphs, described at `http://en.wikipedia.org/wiki/Directed_acyclic_graph`

Computing connected components in an image

In this recipe, we will show an application of graph theory in image processing. We will compute **connected components** in an image. This method will allow us to label contiguous regions of an image, similar to the *bucket* fill tool of paint programs.

Finding connected components is also useful in many puzzle video games such as Minesweeper, bubble shooters, and others. In these games, contiguous sets of items with the same color need to be automatically detected.

How to do it...

1. Let's import the packages:

   ```
   In [1]: import itertools
           import numpy as np
           import networkx as nx
           import matplotlib.colors as col
           import matplotlib.pyplot as plt
           %matplotlib inline
   ```

2. We create a *10 x 10* image where each pixel can take one of three possible labels (or colors):

   ```
   In [2]: n = 10
   In [3]: img = np.random.randint(size=(n, n),
                                    low=0, high=3)
   ```

3. Now, we create the underlying 2D grid graph encoding the structure of the image. Each node is a pixel, and a node is connected to its nearest neighbors. NetworkX defines a `grid_2d_graph` function to generate this graph:

   ```
   In [4]: g = nx.grid_2d_graph(n, n)
   ```

```
In [5]: def show_image(img, **kwargs):
            plt.imshow(img,
                       origin='lower',
                       interpolation='none',
                       **kwargs)
            plt.axis('off')
In [6]: def show_graph(g, **kwargs):
            nx.draw(g,
               pos={(i, j): (j, i)
                     for (i, j) in g.nodes()},
               node_color=[img[i, j]
                            for (i, j) in g.nodes()],
               linewidths=1, edge_color='w',
               with_labels=False, node_size=30, **kwargs)
In [7]: cmap = plt.cm.Blues
```

5. Here is the original image superimposed with the underlying graph:

```
In [8]: show_image(img, cmap=cmap, vmin=-1)
        show_graph(g, cmap=cmap, vmin=-1)
```

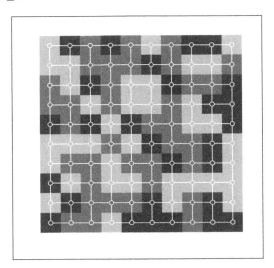

6. Now, we are going to find all contiguous dark blue regions containing more than three pixels. First, we consider the *subgraph* corresponding to all dark blue pixels:

```
In [9]: g2 = g.subgraph(zip(*np.nonzero(img==2)))
In [10]: show_image(img, cmap=cmap, vmin=-1)
         show_graph(g2, cmap=cmap, vmin=-1)
```

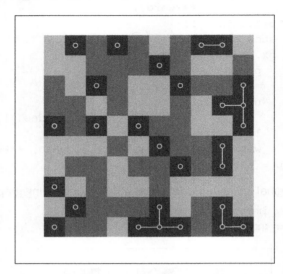

7. We see that the requested contiguous regions correspond to the *connected components* containing more than three nodes in the subgraph. We can use the `connected_components` function of NetworkX to find those components:

```
In [11]: components = [np.array(comp)
                for comp in nx.connected_components(g2)
                if len(comp)>=3]
         len(components)
Out[11]: 3
```

8. Finally, we assign a new color to each of these components, and we display the new image:

```
In [12]: # We copy the image, and assign a new label
         # to each found component.
         img_bis = img.copy()
         for i, comp in enumerate(components):
             img_bis[comp[:,0], comp[:,1]] = i + 3
In [13]: # We create a new discrete color map extending
         # the previous map with new colors.
         colors = [cmap(.5), cmap(.75), cmap(1.),
```

```
        '#f4f235', '#f4a535', '#f44b35']
    cmap2 = col.ListedColormap(colors, 'indexed')
In [14]: show_image(img_bis, cmap=cmap2)
```

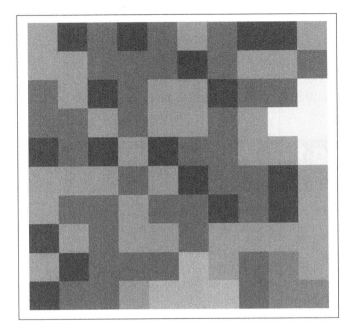

How it works...

The problem we solved is called **connected-component labeling**. It is also closely related to the **flood-fill algorithm**.

The idea to associate a grid graph to an image is quite common in image processing. Here, contiguous color regions correspond to **connected components** of subgraphs. A connected component can be defined as an equivalence class of the **reachability** relation. Two nodes are connected in the graph if there is a path from one node to the other. An equivalence class contains nodes that can be reached from one another.

Finally, the simple approach described here is only adapted to basic tasks on small images. More advanced algorithms are covered in *Chapter 11, Image and Audio Processing*.

There's more...

Here are a few references:

 ▶ Connected components on Wikipedia, available at `http://en.wikipedia.org/wiki/Connected_component_%28graph_theory%29`

 ▶ Connected-component labeling on Wikipedia, at `http://en.wikipedia.org/wiki/Connected-component_labeling`

 ▶ Flood-fill algorithm on Wikipedia, available at `http://en.wikipedia.org/wiki/Flood_fill`

Computing the Voronoi diagram of a set of points

The **Voronoi diagram** of a set of *seed* points divides space into several regions. Each region contains all points closer to one seed point than to any other seed point.

The Voronoi diagram is a fundamental structure in computational geometry. It is widely used in computer science, robotics, geography, and other disciplines. For example, the Voronoi diagram of a set of metro stations gives us the closest station from any point in the city.

In this recipe, we compute the Voronoi diagram of the set of metro stations in Paris using SciPy.

Getting ready

You need the Smopy module to display the OpenStreetMap map of Paris. You can install this package with `pip install smopy`.

You also need to download the *RATP* dataset from the book's GitHub repository at `https://github.com/ipython-books/cookbook-data` and extract it in the current directory. The data was obtained on RATP's open data website (Paris' public transport operator, `http://data.ratp.fr`).

How to do it...

1. Let's import NumPy, pandas, matplotlib, and SciPy:

```
In [1]: import numpy as np
        import pandas as pd
        import scipy.spatial as spatial
        import matplotlib.pyplot as plt
        import matplotlib.path as path
```

```
import matplotlib as mpl
import smopy
%matplotlib inline
```

2. Let's load the dataset with pandas:

```
In [2]: df = pd.read_csv('data/ratp.csv',
                         sep='#', header=None)
In [3]: df[df.columns[1:]].tail(2)
Out[3]:    1       2          3              4        5
11609   2.30   48.93       TIMBAUD   GENNEVILLIERS  tram
11610   2.23   48.91  VICTOR BASCH      COLOMBES    tram
```

3. The `DataFrame` object contains the coordinates, name, city, district, and type of station. Let's select all metro stations:

```
In [4]: metro = df[(df[5] == 'metro')]
In [5]: metro[metro.columns[1:]].tail(3)
Out[5]:
305   2.308   48.841  Volontaires   PARIS-15EME  metro
306   2.379   48.857     Voltaire   PARIS-11EME  metro
307   2.304   48.883       Wagram   PARIS-17EME  metro
```

4. We are going to extract the district number of Paris' stations. With pandas, we can use vectorized string operations using the `str` attribute of the corresponding column.

```
In [6]: # We only extract the district from stations
        # in Paris.
        paris = metro[4].str.startswith('PARIS').values
In [7]: # We create a vector of integers with the district
        # number of the corresponding station, or 0
        # if the station is not in Paris.
        districts = np.zeros(len(paris), dtype=np.int32)
        districts[paris] = metro[4][paris].\
                str.slice(6, 8).astype(np.int32)
        districts[~paris] = 0
        ndistricts = districts.max() + 1
```

5. We also extract the coordinates of all metro stations:

```
In [8]: lon = metro[1]
        lat = metro[2]
```

6. Now, let's retrieve Paris' map with OpenStreetMap. We specify the map's boundaries with the extreme latitude and longitude coordinates of all our metro stations. We use the lightweight Smopy module to generate the map:

```
In [9]: box = (lat[paris].min(), lon[paris].min(),
               lat[paris].max(), lon[paris].max())
        m = smopy.Map(box, z=12)
```

7. We now compute the Voronoi diagram of the stations using SciPy. A `Voronoi` object is created with the points coordinates. It contains several attributes we will use for display:

```
In [10]: vor = spatial.Voronoi(np.c_[lat, lon])
```

8. We create a generic function to display a Voronoi diagram. SciPy already implements such a function, but this function does not take infinite points into account. The implementation we will use has been obtained in Stack Overflow and is present at `http://stackoverflow.com/a/20678647/1595060`. This function is relatively long, and we won't copy it entirely here. The full version can be found in the book's GitHub repository.

```
In [11]: def voronoi_finite_polygons_2d(vor, radius=None):
             """Reconstruct infinite Voronoi regions in a
             2D diagram to finite regions."""
             ...
```

9. The `voronoi_finite_polygons_2d()` function returns a list of regions and a list of vertices. Every region is a list of vertex indices. The coordinates of all vertices are stored in `vertices`. From these structures, we can create a list of *cells*. Every cell represents a polygon as an array of vertex coordinates. We also use the `to_pixels()` method of the `smopy.Map` instance. This function converts latitude and longitude geographical coordinates to pixels in the image.

```
In [12]: regions, vertices = \
             voronoi_finite_polygons_2d(vor)
         cells = [m.to_pixels(vertices[region])
                  for region in regions]
```

10. Now, we compute the color of every polygon:

```
In [13]: cmap = plt.cm.Set3
         # We generate colors for districts using
         # a color map.
         colors_districts = cmap(
                 np.linspace(0., 1., ndistricts))[:,:3]
         # The color of every polygon, grey by default.
         colors = .25 * np.ones((len(districts), 3))
```

```
        # We give each polygon in Paris the color of
        # its district.
        colors[paris] = colors_districts[districts[paris]]
```

11. Finally, we display the map with the Voronoi diagram, using the `show_mpl()` method of the `Map` instance:

```
In [14]: ax = m.show_mpl()
         ax.add_collection(
             mpl.collections.PolyCollection(cells,
                 facecolors=colors, edgecolors='k',
                 alpha=0.35,))
```

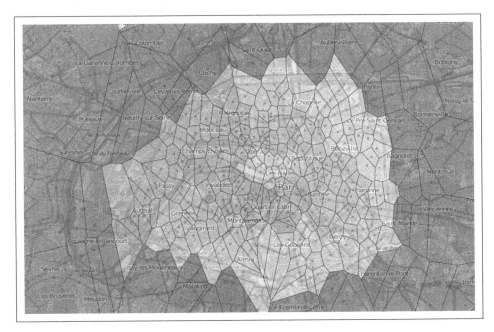

How it works...

Let's give the mathematical definition of the Voronoi diagram in a Euclidean space. If (x_i) is a set of points, the Voronoi diagram of this set of points is the collection of subsets V_i (called **cells** or **regions**) defined by:

$$V_i = \left\{ \mathbf{x} \in \mathbb{R}^d \mid \forall j \neq i, \quad \left\| \mathbf{x} - \mathbf{x}_i \right\| \leq \left\| \mathbf{x} - \mathbf{x}_j \right\| \right\}$$

The dual graph of the Voronoi diagram is the **Delaunay triangulation**. This geometrical object covers the convex hull of the set of points with triangles.

SciPy computes Voronoi diagrams with **Qhull**, a computational geometry library in C++.

There's more...

Here are further references:

▶ Voronoi diagram on Wikipedia, available at `http://en.wikipedia.org/wiki/Voronoi_diagram`

▶ Delaunay triangulation on Wikipedia, available at `http://en.wikipedia.org/wiki/Delaunay_triangulation`

▶ The documentation of `scipy.spatial.voronoi` available at `http://docs.scipy.org/doc/scipy-dev/reference/generated/scipy.spatial.Voronoi.html`

▶ The Qhull library available at `www.qhull.org`

See also

▶ The *Manipulating geospatial data with Shapely and basemap* recipe

Manipulating geospatial data with Shapely and basemap

In this recipe, we will show how to load and display geographical data in the Shapefile format. Specifically, we will use data from **Natural Earth** (`www.naturalearthdata.com`) to display the countries of Africa, color coded with their population and **Gross Domestic Product** (**GDP**).

Shapefile (`http://en.wikipedia.org/wiki/Shapefile`) is a popular geospatial vector data format for GIS software. It can be read by **Fiona**, a Python wrapper to **GDAL/OGR** (a C++ library supporting GIS file formats). We will also use **Shapely**, a Python package used to handle two-dimensional geometrical shapes, and **descartes**, used to render Shapely shapes in matplotlib. Finally, we will use **basemap** to plot maps.

Getting ready

You need the following packages:

▶ GDAL/OGR available at `www.gdal.org/ogr/`

▶ Fiona available at `http://toblerity.org/fiona/README.html`

▶ Shapely available at `http://toblerity.org/shapely/project.html`

▶ descartes available at `https://pypi.python.org/pypi/descartes`

▶ Basemap available at `http://matplotlib.org/basemap/`

With Anaconda, you can do:

```
conda install gdal
conda install fiona
conda install basemap
```

Shapely and descartes can be installed with:

```
pip install shapely
pip install descartes
```

On Windows, you can find binary installers for all of those packages except descartes on Chris Gohlke's webpage, `www.lfd.uci.edu/~gohlke/pythonlibs/`.

On other systems, you can find installation instructions on the projects' websites. GDAL/OGR is a C++ library that is required by Fiona. The other packages are regular Python packages.

Finally, you need to download the *Africa* dataset on the book's GitHub repository at `https://github.com/ipython-books/cookbook-data`. The data was obtained on Natural Earth's website, `www.naturalearthdata.com/downloads/10m-cultural-vectors/10m-admin-0-countries/`.

How to do it...

1. Let's import the packages:

```
In [1]: import numpy as np
        import matplotlib.pyplot as plt
        import matplotlib.collections as col
        from mpl_toolkits.basemap import Basemap
        import fiona
        import shapely.geometry as geom
        from descartes import PolygonPatch
        %matplotlib inline
```

2. We load the *Shapefile* dataset with Fiona. This dataset notably contains the borders of all countries in the world.

```
In [2]: # Natural Earth data
        countries = fiona.open(
                "data/ne_10m_admin_0_countries.shp")
```

3. We select the countries in Africa:

```
In [3]: africa = [c for c in countries
                  if c['properties']['CONTINENT'] == 'Africa']
```

4. Now, we create a basemap map showing the African continent:

```
In [4]: m = Basemap(llcrnrlon=-23.03,
                    llcrnrlat=-37.72,
                    urcrnrlon=55.20,
                    urcrnrlat=40.58)
```

5. Let's write a function converting the geographical coordinates of the countries' borders to map coordinates. This will allow us to display the borders in basemap:

```
In [5]: def _convert(poly, m):
            if isinstance(poly, list):
                return [_convert(_, m) for _ in poly]
            elif isinstance(poly, tuple):
                return m(*poly)
In [6]: for _ in africa:
            _['geometry']['coordinates'] = _convert(
                _['geometry']['coordinates'], m)
```

6. The next step is to create matplotlib `PatchCollection` objects from the *Shapefile* dataset loaded with Fiona. We use Shapely and descartes for this:

```
In [7]: def get_patch(shape, **kwargs):
            """Return a matplotlib PatchCollection from a
            geometry object loaded with fiona."""
            # Simple polygon.
            if isinstance(shape, geom.Polygon):
                return col.PatchCollection(
                    [PolygonPatch(shape, **kwargs)],
                    match_original=True)
            # Collection of polygons.
            elif isinstance(shape, geom.MultiPolygon):
                return col.PatchCollection(
                    [PolygonPatch(c, **kwargs)
                     for c in shape],
                    match_original=True)
In [8]: def get_patches(shapes, fc=None,
                        ec=None, **kwargs):
            """Return a list of matplotlib PatchCollection
            objects from a Shapefile dataset."""
            # fc and ec are the face and edge colors of the
            # countries. We ensure these are lists of
```

```
        # colors, with one element per country.
        if not isinstance(fc, list):
            fc = [fc] * len(shapes)
        if not isinstance(ec, list):
            ec = [ec] * len(shapes)
        # We convert each polygon to a matplotlib
        # PatchCollection object.
        return [get_patch(geom.shape(s['geometry']),
                        fc=fc_, ec=ec_, **kwargs)
                for s, fc_, ec_ in zip(shapes, fc, ec)]
```

7. We also define a function to get countries' colors depending on a specific field in the *Shapefile* dataset. Indeed, our dataset not only contains countries borders, but also a few administrative, economical, and geographical properties for each country. Here, we will choose the color according to the countries' population and GDP:

```
In [9]: def get_colors(field, cmap):
            """Return one color per country, depending on a
            specific field in the dataset."""
            values = [country['properties'][field]
                    for country in africa]
            values_max = max(values)
            return [cmap(v / values_max) for v in values]
```

8. Finally, we display the maps. We display the coastlines with basemap, and the countries with our *Shapefile* dataset:

```
In [10]: # Display the countries color-coded with
         # their population.
         ax = plt.subplot(121)
         m.drawcoastlines()
         patches = get_patches(africa,
                            fc=get_colors('POP_EST',
                                        plt.cm.Reds),
                            ec='k')
         for p in patches:
             ax.add_collection(p)
         plt.title("Population")
         # Display the countries color-coded with
         # their population.
         ax = plt.subplot(122)
         m.drawcoastlines()
         patches = get_patches(africa,
                            fc=get_colors('GDP_MD_EST',
```

```
                                               plt.cm.Blues),
                         ec='k')
        for p in patches:
            ax.add_collection(p)
        plt.title("GDP")
```

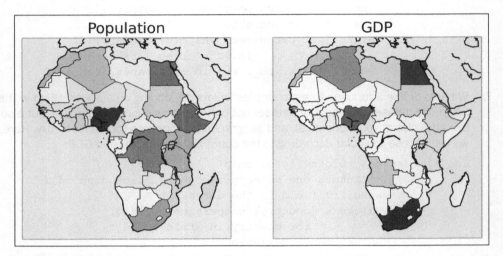

See also

▸ The *Creating a route planner for a road network* recipe

Creating a route planner for a road network

In this recipe, we build upon several techniques described in the previous recipes in order to create a simple GPS-like route planner in Python. We will retrieve California's road network data from the United States Census Bureau in order to find shortest paths in the road network graph. This allows us to display road itineraries between any two locations in California.

Getting ready

You need NetworkX and Smopy for this recipe. In order for NetworkX to read Shapefile datasets, you also need GDAL/OGR. You can find more information in the previous recipe.

You also need to download the *Road* dataset from the book's GitHub repository at https://github.com/ipython-books/cookbook-data, and extract it in the current directory.

> At the time of this writing, NetworkX's support of Shapefile doesn't seem to be compatible with Python 3.x. For this reason, this recipe has only been successfully tested with Python 2.x.

How to do it...

1. Let's import the packages:

```
In [1]: import networkx as nx
        import numpy as np
        import pandas as pd
        import json
        import smopy
        import matplotlib.pyplot as plt
        %matplotlib inline
```

2. We load the data (a Shapefile dataset) with NetworkX. This dataset contains detailed information about the primary roads in California. NetworkX's read_shp() function returns a graph, where each node is a geographical position, and each edge contains information about the road linking the two nodes. The data comes from the United States Census Bureau website at www.census.gov/geo/maps-data/data/tiger.html.

```
In [2]: g = nx.read_shp("data/tl_2013_06_prisecroads.shp")
```

3. This graph is not necessarily connected, but we need a connected graph in order to compute shortest paths. Here, we take the largest connected subgraph using the connected_component_subgraphs() function:

```
In [3]: sgs = list(nx.connected_component_subgraphs(
                     g.to_undirected()))
        largest = np.argmax([len(sg)
                                for sg in sgs])
        sg = sgs[largest]
        len(sg)
Out[3]: 464
```

4. We define two positions (with the latitude and longitude) and find the shortest path between these two positions:

```
In [4]: pos0 = (36.6026, -121.9026)
        pos1 = (34.0569, -118.2427)
```

5. Each edge in the graph contains information about the road, including a list of points along this road. We first create a function that returns this array of coordinates, for any edge in the graph:

```
In [5]: def get_path(n0, n1):
```

```
"""If n0 and n1 are connected nodes in the
graph, this function returns an array of point
coordinates along the road linking these
two nodes."""
return np.array(json.loads(
        sg[n0][n1]['Json'])['coordinates'])
```

6. We can notably use the road path to compute its length. We first need to define a function that computes the distance between any two points in geographical coordinates. This function has been found in Stack Overflow (http://stackoverflow.com/questions/8858838/need-help-calculating-geographical-distance):

```
In [6]: EARTH_R = 6372.8
        def geocalc(lat0, lon0, lat1, lon1):
            """Return the distance (in km) between two
            points in geographical coordinates."""
            lat0 = np.radians(lat0)
            lon0 = np.radians(lon0)
            lat1 = np.radians(lat1)
            lon1 = np.radians(lon1)
            dlon = lon0 - lon1
            y = np.sqrt(
                (np.cos(lat1)*np.sin(dlon))**2
                +(np.cos(lat0)*np.sin(lat1)
                  -np.sin(lat0)*np.cos(lat1)* \
                  np.cos(dlon))**2)
            x = np.sin(lat0)*np.sin(lat1) + \
                np.cos(lat0)*np.cos(lat1)*np.cos(dlon)
            c = np.arctan2(y, x)
            return EARTH_R * c
```

7. Now, we define a function computing a path's length:

```
In [7]: def get_path_length(path):
            return np.sum(geocalc(
                        path[1:,0], path[1:,1],
                        path[:-1,0], path[:-1,1]))
```

8. Now, we update our graph by computing the distance between any two connected nodes. We add this information in the distance attribute of the edges:

```
In [8]: # Compute the length of the road segments.
        for n0, n1 in sg.edges_iter():
            path = get_path(n0, n1)
            distance = get_path_length(path)
            sg.edge[n0][n1]['distance'] = distance
```

9. The last step before we can find the shortest path in the graph is to find the two nodes in the graph that are closest to the two requested positions:

```
In [9]: nodes = np.array(sg.nodes())
        # Get the closest nodes in the graph.
        pos0_i = np.argmin(np.sum(
                        (nodes[:,::-1] - pos0)**2,
                        axis=1))
        pos1_i = np.argmin(np.sum(
                        (nodes[:,::-1] - pos1)**2,
                        axis=1))
```

10. Now, we use NetworkX's `shortest_path()` function to compute the shortest path between our two positions. We specify that the weight of every edge is the length of the road between them:

```
In [10]: # Compute the shortest path.
         path = nx.shortest_path(sg,
                        source=tuple(nodes[pos0_i]),
                        target=tuple(nodes[pos1_i]),
                        weight='distance')
         len(path)
Out[10]: 19
```

11. The itinerary has been computed. The `path` variable contains the list of edges that form the shortest path between our two positions. Now, we can get information about the itinerary with pandas. The dataset has a few fields of interest, including the name and type (State, Interstate, and so on) of the roads:

```
In [11]: roads = pd.DataFrame([
                    sg.edge[path[i]][path[i + 1]]
                        for i in range(len(path)-1)],
                    columns=['FULLNAME', 'MTFCC',
                        'RTTYP', 'distance'])
         roads
Out[11]:   FULLNAME     MTFCC RTTYP    distance
0          State Rte 1  S1200    S     100.657768
1          State Rte 1  S1200    S      33.419581
...
16         Hollywood Fwy S1200   M      14.087627
17         Hollywood Fwy S1200   M       0.010107
```

Here is the total length of this itinerary:

```
In [12]: roads['distance'].sum()
Out[12]: 508.66421585288725
```

12. Finally, let's display the itinerary on the map. We first retrieve the map with Smopy:

```
In [13]: map = smopy.Map(pos0, pos1, z=7, margin=.1)
```

13. Our path contains connected nodes in the graph. Every edge between two nodes is characterized by a list of points (constituting a part of the road). Therefore, we need to define a function that concatenates the positions along every edge in the path. We have to concatenate the positions in the right order along our path. We choose the order based on the fact that the last point in an edge needs to be close to the first point in the next edge:

```
In [14]: def get_full_path(path):
             """Return the positions along a path."""
             p_list = []
             curp = None
             for i in range(len(path)-1):
                 p = get_path(path[i], path[i+1])
                 if curp is None:
                     curp = p
                 if np.sum((p[0]-curp)**2) > \
                                 np.sum((p[-1]-curp)**2):
                     p = p[::-1,:]
                 p_list.append(p)
                 curp = p[-1]
             return np.vstack(p_list)
```

14. We convert the path in pixels in order to display it on the Smopy map:

```
In [15]: linepath = get_full_path(path)
         x, y = map.to_pixels(linepath[:,1], linepath[:,0])
```

15. Finally, let's display the map, with our two positions and the computed itinerary between them:

```
In [16]: map.show_mpl()
         # Plot the itinerary.
         plt.plot(x, y, '-k', lw=1.5)
         # Mark our two positions.
         plt.plot(x[0], y[0], 'ob', ms=10)
         plt.plot(x[-1], y[-1], 'or', ms=10)
```

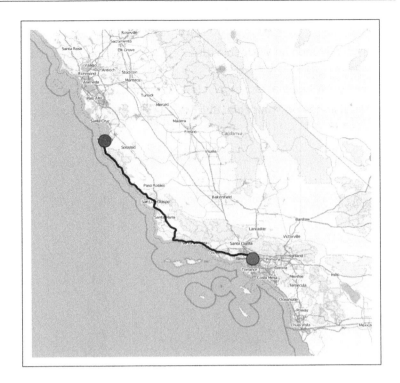

How it works...

We computed the shortest path with NetworkX's `shortest_path()` function. Here, this function used **Dijkstra's algorithm**. This algorithm has a wide variety of applications, for example in network routing protocols.

There are different ways to compute the geographical distance between two points. Here, we used a relatively precise formula: the **orthodromic distance** (also called **great-circle distance**), which assumes that the Earth is a perfect sphere. We could also have used a simpler formula since the distance between two successive points on a road is small.

There's more...

You can find more information about shortest path problems and Dijkstra's algorithm in the following references:

▶ Shortest paths on Wikipedia, available at http://en.wikipedia.org/wiki/Shortest_path_problem

▶ Dijkstra's algorithm, described at http://en.wikipedia.org/wiki/Dijkstra%27s_algorithm

Here are a few references about geographical distances:

- ▸ Geographical distance on Wikipedia, at `http://en.wikipedia.org/wiki/Geographical_distance`
- ▸ Great circles on Wikipedia, at `http://en.wikipedia.org/wiki/Great_circle`
- ▸ Great-circle distance on Wikipedia, at `http://en.wikipedia.org/wiki/Great-circle_distance`

15
Symbolic and Numerical Mathematics

In this chapter, we will cover the following topics:

- ▶ Diving into symbolic computing with SymPy
- ▶ Solving equations and inequalities
- ▶ Analyzing real-valued functions
- ▶ Computing exact probabilities and manipulating random variables
- ▶ A bit of number theory with SymPy
- ▶ Finding a Boolean propositional formula from a truth table
- ▶ Analyzing a nonlinear differential system – Lotka-Volterra (predator-prey) equations
- ▶ Getting started with Sage

Introduction

In this chapter, we will introduce **SymPy**, a Python library for symbolic mathematics. Whereas most of the book deals with numerical methods, we will see examples here where symbolic computations are more suitable.

SymPy is to symbolic computing what NumPy is to numerical computing. For example, SymPy can help us analyze a mathematical model before we run a simulation.

Although quite powerful, SymPy is a bit slow compared to other computer algebra systems. The main reason is that SymPy is written in pure Python. A faster and more powerful mathematics system is **Sage** (see also the *Getting started with Sage* recipe in this chapter). Sage is a heavy standalone program that has many big dependencies (including SymPy!), and it uses only Python 2 at the time of writing. It is essentially meant for interactive use. Sage includes an IPython-like notebook.

LaTeX

LaTeX is a document markup language widely used to write publication-quality mathematical equations. Equations written in LaTeX can be displayed in the browser with the **MathJax** JavaScript library. SymPy uses this system to display equations in the IPython notebook.

LaTeX equations can also be used in matplotlib. In this case, it is recommended to have a LaTeX installation on your local computer.

Here are a few references:

> ▸ LaTeX on Wikipedia, at `http://en.wikipedia.org/wiki/LaTeX`
> ▸ MathJax, available at `www.mathjax.org`
> ▸ LaTeX in matplotlib, described at `http://matplotlib.org/users/usetex.html`
> ▸ Documentation for displaying equations with SymPy, available at `http://docs.sympy.org/latest/tutorial/printing.html`
> ▸ To install LaTeX on your computer, refer to `http://latex-project.org/ftp.html`

Diving into symbolic computing with SymPy

In this recipe, we will give a brief introduction to symbolic computing with SymPy. We will see more advanced features of SymPy in the next recipes.

Getting ready

SymPy is a pure Python package with no other dependencies, and as such, it is very easy to install. With Anaconda, you can type `conda install sympy` in a terminal. On Windows, you can use Chris Gohlke's package (`www.lfd.uci.edu/~gohlke/pythonlibs/#sympy`). Finally, you can use the `pip install sympy` command.

How to do it...

SymPy can be used from a Python module, or interactively in IPython. In the notebook, all mathematical expressions are displayed with LaTeX, thanks to the MathJax JavaScript library.

Here is an introduction to SymPy:

1. First, we import SymPy and enable LaTeX printing in the IPython notebook:

```
In [1]: from sympy import *
        init_printing()
```

2. To deal with symbolic variables, we first need to declare them:

```
In [2]: var('x y')
Out[2]: (x, y)
```

3. The `var()` function creates symbols and injects them into the namespace. This function should only be used in the interactive mode. In a Python module, it is better to use the `symbols()` function that returns the symbols:

```
In [3]: x, y = symbols('x y')
```

4. We can create mathematical expressions with these symbols:

```
In [4]: expr1 = (x + 1)**2
        expr2 = x**2 + 2*x + 1
```

5. Are these expressions equal?

```
In [5]: expr1 == expr2
Out[5]: False
```

6. These expressions are mathematically equal, but not syntactically identical. To test whether they are mathematically equal, we can ask SymPy to simplify the difference algebraically:

```
In [6]: simplify(expr1-expr2)
Out[6]: 0
```

7. A very common operation with symbolic expressions is the substitution of a symbol by another symbol, expression, or a number, using the `subs()` method of a symbolic expression:

```
In [7]: expr1.subs(x, expr1)
```

$$Out[7]: \left((x+1)^2 + 1 \right)^2$$

```
In [8]: expr1.subs(x, pi)
```

$$Out[8]: (1 + \pi)^2$$

Substitution in a SymPy expression

8. A rational number cannot be written simply as `1/2` as this Python expression evaluates to 0. A possibility is to convert the number `1` into a SymPy integer object, for example by using the `S()` function:

    ```
    In [9]:  expr1.subs(x, S(1)/2)
    Out[9]:  9/4
    ```

9. Exactly represented numbers can be evaluated numerically with `evalf`:

    ```
    In [10]:  _.evalf()
    Out[10]:  2.25000000000000
    ```

10. We can easily create a Python function from a SymPy symbolic expression using the `lambdify()` function. The resulting function can notably be evaluated on NumPy arrays. This is quite convenient when we need to go from the symbolic world to the numerical world:

    ```
    In [11]:  f = lambdify(x, expr1)
    In [12]:  import numpy as np
              f(np.linspace(-2., 2., 5))
    Out[12]:  array([ 1.,   0.,   1.,   4.,   9.])
    ```

How it works...

A core idea in SymPy is to use the standard Python syntax to manipulate exact expressions. Although this is very convenient and natural, there are a few caveats. Symbols such as x, which represent mathematical variables, cannot be used in Python before being instantiated (otherwise, a `NameError` exception is thrown by the interpreter). This is in contrast to most other computer algebra systems. For this reason, SymPy offers ways to declare symbolic variables beforehand.

Another example is integer division; as `1/2` evaluates to `0` (in Python 2), SymPy has no way to know that the user intended to write a fraction instead. We need to convert the numerical integer 1 to the symbolic integer 1 before dividing it by 2.

Also, the Python equality refers to the equality between syntax trees rather than between mathematical expressions.

See also

▶ The *Solving equations and inequalities* recipe
▶ The *Getting started with Sage* recipe

Solving equations and inequalities

SymPy offers several ways to solve linear and nonlinear equations and systems of equations. Of course, these functions do not always succeed in finding closed-form exact solutions. In this case, we can fall back to numerical solvers and obtain approximate solutions.

Getting ready

We first need to import SymPy. We also initialize pretty printing in the notebook (see the first recipe of this chapter).

How to do it...

1. Let's define a few symbols:

    ```
    In [2]: var('x y z a')
    Out[2]: (x, y, z, a)
    ```

2. We use the `solve()` function to solve equations (the right-hand side is 0 by default):

    ```
    In [3]: solve(x**2 - a, x)
    Out[3]: [-sqrt(a), sqrt(a)]
    ```

3. We can also solve inequalities. Here, we need to use the `solve_univariate_inequality()` function to solve this univariate inequality in the real domain:

    ```
    In [4]: x = Symbol('x')
            solve_univariate_inequality(x**2 > 4, x)
    Out[4]: Or(x < -2, x > 2)
    ```

4. The `solve()` function also accepts systems of equations (here, a linear system):

    ```
    In [5]: solve([x + 2*y + 1, x - 3*y - 2], x, y)
    Out[5]: {x: 1/5, y: -3/5}
    ```

5. Nonlinear systems are also handled:

    ```
    In [6]: solve([x**2 + y**2 - 1, x**2 - y**2 - S(1)/2],
                  x, y)
    Out[6]: [(-sqrt(3)/2, -1/2), (-sqrt(3)/2, 1/2),
             (sqrt(3)/2, -1/2), (sqrt(3)/2, 1/2)]
    ```

6. Singular linear systems can also be solved (here, there is an infinite number of solutions because the two equations are collinear):

    ```
    In [7]: solve([x + 2*y + 1, -x - 2*y - 1], x, y)
    Out[7]: {x: -2*y - 1}
    ```

7. Now, let's solve a linear system using matrices containing symbolic variables:

```
In [8]: var('a b c d u v')
Out[8]: (a, b, c, d, u, v)
```

8. We create the **augmented matrix**, which is the horizontal concatenation of the system's matrix with the linear coefficients and the right-hand side vector. This matrix corresponds to the following system in *x,y*: *ax+by=u, cx+dy=v*:

```
In [9]: M = Matrix([[a, b, u], [c, d, v]]); M
Out[9]: Matrix([[a, b, u],
                 [c, d, v]])
In [10]: solve_linear_system(M, x, y)
Out[10]: {x: (-b*v + d*u)/(a*d - b*c),
          y: ( a*v - c*u)/(a*d - b*c)}
```

9. This system needs to be nonsingular in order to have a unique solution, which is equivalent to saying that the determinant of the system's matrix needs to be nonzero (otherwise the denominators in the preceding fractions are equal to zero):

```
In [11]: det(M[:2,:2])
Out[11]: a*d - b*c
```

There's more...

Matrix support in SymPy is quite rich; we can perform a large number of operations and decompositions (see the reference guide at http://docs.sympy.org/latest/modules/matrices/matrices.html).

Here are more references about linear algebra:

- Linear algebra on Wikipedia, at http://en.wikipedia.org/wiki/Linear_algebra#Further_reading
- Linear algebra on Wikibooks, at http://en.wikibooks.org/wiki/Linear_Algebra

Analyzing real-valued functions

SymPy contains a rich **calculus** toolbox to analyze real-valued functions: limits, power series, derivatives, integrals, Fourier transforms, and so on. In this recipe, we will show the very basics of these capabilities.

Getting ready

We first need to import SymPy. We also initialize pretty printing in the notebook (see the first recipe of this chapter).

How to do it...

1. Let's define a few symbols and a function (which is just an expression depending on x):

```
In [1]: var('x z')
Out[1]: (x, z)
In [2]: f = 1/(1+x**2)
```

2. Let's evaluate this function at 1:

```
In [3]: f.subs(x, 1)
Out[3]: 1/2
```

3. We can compute the derivative of this function:

```
In [4]: diff(f, x)
Out[4]: -2*x/(x**2 + 1)**2
```

4. What is f's limit to infinity? (Note the double o (oo) for the infinity symbol):

```
In [5]: limit(f, x, oo)
Out[5]: 0
```

5. Here's how to compute a Taylor series (here, around 0, of order 9). The **Big O** can be removed with the removeO() method.

```
In [6]: series(f, x0=0, n=9)
Out[6]: 1 - x**2 + x**4 - x**6 + x**8 + O(x**9)
```

6. We can compute definite integrals (here, over the entire real line):

```
In [7]: integrate(f, (x, -oo, oo))
Out[7]: pi
```

7. SymPy can also compute indefinite integrals:

```
In [8]: integrate(f, x)
Out[8]: atan(x)
```

8. Finally, let's compute f's Fourier transforms:

```
In [9]: fourier_transform(f, x, z)
Out[9]: pi*exp(-2*pi*z)
```

There's more...

SymPy includes a large number of other integral transforms besides the Fourier transform (http://docs.sympy.org/dev/modules/integrals/integrals.html). However, SymPy will not always be able to find closed-form solutions.

Here are a few general references about real analysis and calculus:

▸ Real analysis on Wikipedia, at `http://en.wikipedia.org/wiki/Real_analysis#Bibliography`

▸ Calculus on Wikibooks, at `http://en.wikibooks.org/wiki/Calculus`

Computing exact probabilities and manipulating random variables

SymPy includes a module named `stats` that lets us create and manipulate random variables. This is useful when we work with probabilistic or statistical models; we can compute symbolic expectancies, variances probabilities, and densities of random variables.

How to do it...

1. Let's import SymPy and the stats module:

```
In [1]: from sympy import *
        from sympy.stats import *
        init_printing()
```

2. Let's roll two dice, X and Y, with six faces each:

```
In [2]: X, Y = Die('X', 6), Die('Y', 6)
```

3. We can compute probabilities defined by equalities (with the `Eq` operator) or inequalities:

```
In [3]: P(Eq(X, 3))
Out[3]: 1/6
In [4]: P(X>3)
Out[4]: 1/2
```

4. Conditions can also involve multiple random variables:

```
In [5]: P(X>Y)
Out[5]: 5/12
```

5. We can compute conditional probabilities:

```
In [6]: P(X+Y>6, X<5)
Out[6]: 5/12
```

6. We can also work with arbitrary discrete or continuous random variables:

```
In [7]: Z = Normal('Z', 0, 1)   # Gaussian variable
In [8]: P(Z>pi)
Out[8]: -erf(sqrt(2)*pi/2)/2 + 1/2
```

7. We can compute expectancies and variances:

```
In [9]: E(Z**2), variance(Z**2)
Out[9]: (1, 2)
```

8. We can also compute densities:

```
In [10]: f = density(Z)
In [11]: var('x')
         f(x)
Out[11]: sqrt(2)*exp(-x**2/2)/(2*sqrt(pi))
```

9. We can plot these densities:

```
In [12]: %matplotlib inline
         plot(f(x), (x, -6, 6))
```

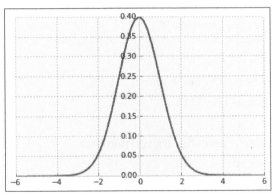

The Gaussian density

How it works...

SymPy's `stats` module contains many functions to define random variables with classical laws (binomial, exponential, and so on), discrete or continuous. It works by leveraging SymPy's powerful integration algorithms to compute exact probabilistic quantities as integrals of probability distributions. For example, $P(Z > \pi)$ is:

```
Eq(Integral(f(x), (x, pi, oo)),
   simplify(integrate(f(x), (x, pi, oo))))
```

$$\int_\pi^\infty \frac{\sqrt{2}e^{-\frac{x^2}{2}}}{2\sqrt{\pi}}\,dx = -\frac{1}{2}\,\mathrm{erf}\left(\frac{\sqrt{2}\pi}{2}\right) + \frac{1}{2}$$

Note that the equality condition is written using the `Eq` operator rather than the more standard `==` Python syntax. This is a general feature in SymPy; `==` means equality between Python variables, whereas `Eq` is the mathematical operation between symbolic expressions.

A bit of number theory with SymPy

SymPy contains many number-theory-related routines: obtaining prime numbers, integer decompositions, and much more. We will show a few examples here.

Getting ready

To display legends using LaTeX in matplotlib, you will need an installation of LaTeX on your computer (see this chapter's *Introduction*).

How to do it...

1. Let's import SymPy and the number theory package:

```
In [1]: from sympy import *
        init_printing()
In [2]: import sympy.ntheory as nt
```

2. We can test whether a number is prime:

```
In [3]: nt.isprime(2011)
Out[3]: True
```

3. We can find the next prime after a given number:

```
In [4]: nt.nextprime(2011)
Out[4]: 2017
```

4. What is the 1000th prime number?

```
In [5]: nt.prime(1000)
Out[5]: 7919
```

5. How many primes less than 2011 are there?

```
In [6]: nt.primepi(2011)
Out[6]: 305
```

6. We can plot $\pi(x)$, the **prime-counting function** (the number of prime numbers less than or equal to some number x). The famous **prime number theorem** states that this function is asymptotically equivalent to *x*/log(*x*). This expression approximately quantifies the distribution of prime numbers among all integers:

```
In [7]: import numpy as np
        import matplotlib.pyplot as plt
        %matplotlib inline
        x = np.arange(2, 10000)
        plt.plot(x, map(nt.primepi, x), '-k',
              label='$\pi(x)$')
```

```
plt.plot(x, x / np.log(x), '--k',
        label='$x/\log(x)$')
plt.legend(loc=2)
```

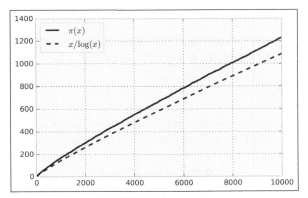

Distribution of prime numbers

7. Let's compute the integer factorization of a number:

```
In [8]: nt.factorint(1998)
Out[8]: {2: 1, 3: 3, 37: 1}
In [9]: 2 * 3**3 * 37
Out[9]: 1998
```

8. Finally, a small problem. A lazy mathematician is counting his marbles. When they are arranged in three rows, the last column contains one marble. When they form four rows, there are two marbles in the last column, and there are three with five rows. How many marbles are there? (Hint: The lazy mathematician has fewer than 100 marbles.)

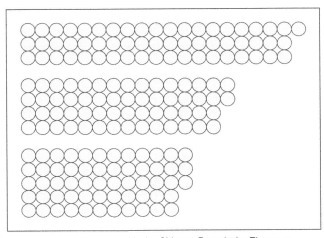

Counting marbles with the Chinese Remainder Theorem

The Chinese Remainder Theorem gives us the answer:

```
In [10]: from sympy.ntheory.modular import solve_congruence
In [11]: solve_congruence((1, 3), (2, 4), (3, 5))
Out[11]: (58, 60)
```

There are infinitely many solutions: 58 plus any multiple of 60. Since there are less than 100 marbles, 58 is the right answer.

How it works...

SymPy contains many number-theory-related functions. Here, we used the **Chinese Remainder Theorem** to find the solutions of the following system of arithmetic equations:

$$n \equiv a_1 \quad (\mathrm{mod}\ m_1)$$
$$\vdots$$
$$n \equiv a_k \quad (\mathrm{mod}\ m_k)$$

The Chinese Remainder Theorem

The triple bar is the symbol for modular congruence. Here, it means that m_i divides a_i-n. In other words, n and a_i are equal up to a multiple of m_i. Reasoning with congruences is very convenient when periodic scales are involved. For example, operations involving 12-hour clocks are done modulo 12. The numbers 11 and 23 are equivalent modulo 12 (they represent the same hour on the clock) because their difference is a multiple of 12.

In this recipe's example, three congruences have to be satisfied: the remainder of the number of marbles in the division with 3 is 1 (there's one extra marble in that arrangement), it is 2 in the division with 4, and 3 in the division with 5. With SymPy, we simply specify these values in the `solve_congruence()` function to get the solutions.

The theorem states that solutions exist as soon as the m_i are pairwise co-prime (any two distinct numbers among them are co-prime). All solutions are congruent modulo the product of the m_i. This fundamental theorem in number theory has several applications, notably in cryptography.

There's more...

Here are a few textbooks about number theory:

▶ Undergraduate level: *Elementary Number Theory, Gareth A. Jones, Josephine M. Jones, Springer, (1998)*

▸ Graduate level: *A Classical Introduction to Modern Number Theory, Kenneth Ireland, Michael Rosen, Springer, (1982)*

Here are a few references:

▸ Documentation on SymPy's number-theory module, available at `http://docs.sympy.org/dev/modules/ntheory.html`

▸ The Chinese Remainder Theorem on Wikipedia, at `http://en.wikipedia.org/wiki/Chinese_remainder_theorem`

▸ Applications of the Chinese Remainder Theorem, given at `http://mathoverflow.net/questions/10014/applications-of-the-chinese-remainder-theorem`

Finding a Boolean propositional formula from a truth table

The logic module in SymPy lets us manipulate complex Boolean expressions, also known as **propositional formulas**.

This recipe will show an example where this module can be useful. Let's suppose that, in a program, we need to write a complex `if` statement depending on three Boolean variables. We can think about each of the eight possible cases (true, true and false, and so on) and evaluate what the outcome should be. SymPy offers a function to generate a compact logic expression that satisfies our truth table.

How to do it...

1. Let's import SymPy:

```
In [1]: from sympy import *
        init_printing()
```

2. Let's define a few symbols:

```
In [2]: var('x y z')
```

3. We can define propositional formulas with symbols and a few operators:

```
In [3]: P = x & (y | ~z); P
Out[3]: And(Or(Not(z), y), x)
```

4. We can use `subs()` to evaluate a formula on actual Boolean values:

```
In [4]: P.subs({x: True, y: False, z: True})
Out[4]: False
```

5. Now, we want to find a propositional formula depending on x, y, and z, with the following truth table:

x	y	z	??
T	T	T	*
T	T	F	*
T	F	T	T
T	F	F	T
F	T	T	F
F	T	F	F
F	F	T	F
F	F	F	T

A truth table

6. Let's write down all combinations that we want to evaluate to `True`, and those for which the outcome does not matter:

```
In [6]: minterms = [[1,0,1], [1,0,0], [0,0,0]]
        dontcare = [[1,1,1], [1,1,0]]
```

7. Now, we use the `SOPform()` function to derive an adequate formula:

```
In [7]: Q = SOPform(['x', 'y', 'z'], minterms, dontcare); Q
Out[7]: Or(And(Not(y), Not(z)), x)
```

8. Let's test that this proposition works:

```
In [8]: Q.subs({x: True, y: False, z: False}),
        Q.subs({x: False, y: True, z: True})
Out[8]: (True, False)
```

How it works...

The `SOPform()` function generates a full expression corresponding to a truth table and simplifies it using the **Quine-McCluskey algorithm**. It returns the smallest *Sum of Products* form (or disjunction of conjunctions). Similarly, the `POSform()` function returns a Product of Sums.

The given truth table can occur in this case: suppose that we want to write a file if it doesn't already exist (z), or if the user wants to force the writing (x). In addition, the user can prevent the writing (y). The expression evaluates to True if the file is to be written. The resulting SOP formula works if we explicitly forbid x and y in the first place (forcing and preventing the writing at the same time is forbidden).

There's more...

Here are a few references:

▶ The propositional formula on Wikipedia, at http://en.wikipedia.org/wiki/Propositional_formula

▶ Sum of Products on Wikipedia, at http://en.wikipedia.org/wiki/Canonical_normal_form

▶ The Quine–McCluskey algorithm on Wikipedia, at http://en.wikipedia.org/wiki/Quine%E2%80%93McCluskey_algorithm

Analyzing a nonlinear differential system – Lotka-Volterra (predator-prey) equations

Here, we will conduct a brief analytical study of a famous nonlinear differential system: the **Lotka-Volterra equations**, also known as predator-prey equations. These equations are first-order differential equations that describe the evolution of two interacting populations (for example, sharks and sardines), where the predators eat the prey. This example illustrates how to obtain exact expressions and results about fixed points and their stability with SymPy.

Getting ready

For this recipe, knowing the basics of linear and nonlinear systems of differential equations is recommended.

How to do it...

1. Let's create some symbols:

```
In [1]: from sympy import *
        init_printing()
In [2]: var('x y')
        var('a b c d', positive=True)
Out[2]: (a, b, c, d)
```

2. The variables x and y represent the populations of the prey and predators, respectively. The parameters a, b, c, and d are strictly positive parameters (described more precisely in the *How it works...* section of this recipe). The equations are:

$$\frac{dx}{dt} = f(x) = x(a - by)$$

$$\frac{dy}{dt} = g(x) = -y(c - dx)$$

Lotka-Volterra equations

```
In [3]: f = x * (a - b*y)
        g = -y * (c - d*x)
```

3. Let's find the fixed points of the system (solving *f(x,y) = g(x,y) = 0*). We call them *(x_0, y_0)* and *(x_1, y_1)*:

```
In [4]: solve([f, g], (x, y))
Out[4]: [(0, 0), (c/d, a/b)]
In [5]: (x0, y0), (x1, y1) = _
```

4. Let's write the 2D vector with the two equations:

```
In [6]: M = Matrix((f, g)); M
Out[6]: Matrix([[ x*(a - b*y)],
                [-y*(c - d*x)]])
```

5. Now, we can compute the **Jacobian** of the system, as a function of (x, y):

```
In [7]: J = M.jacobian((x, y)); J
Out[7]: Matrix([
        [a - b*y,      -b*x],
        [    d*y, -c + d*x]])
```

6. Let's study the stability of the first fixed point by looking at the eigenvalues of the Jacobian at this point. The first fixed point corresponds to extinct populations:

```
In [8]: M0 = J.subs(x, x0).subs(y, y0); M0
Out[8]: Matrix([a,   0],
               [0, -c]])
In [9]: M0.eigenvals()
Out[9]: {a: 1, -c: 1}
```

The parameters a and c are strictly positive, so the eigenvalues are real and of opposite signs, and this fixed point is a **saddle point**. As this point is unstable, the extinction of both populations is unlikely in this model.

7. Let's consider the second fixed point now:

```
In [10]: M1 = J.subs(x, x1).subs(y, y1); M1
```

```
Out[10]: Matrix([[    0, -b*c/d],
                  [a*d/b,      0]])
In [11]: M1.eigenvals()
Out[11]: {-I*sqrt(a)*sqrt(c): 1, I*sqrt(a)*sqrt(c): 1}
```

The eigenvalues are purely imaginary; thus, this fixed point is not hyperbolic. Therefore, we cannot draw conclusions from this linear analysis about the qualitative behavior of the system around this fixed point. However, we could show with other methods that oscillations occur around this point.

How it works...

The Lotka-Volterra equations model the growth of the predator and prey populations, taking into account their interactions. In the first equation, the *ax* term represents the exponential growth of the prey, and *-bxy* represents death by predators. Similarly, in the second equation, *-yc* represents the natural death of the predators, and *dxy* represents their growth as they eat more and more prey.

To find the **equilibrium points** of the system, we need to find the values *x, y* such that *dx/dt* = *dy/dt* = 0, that is, *f(x, y)* = *g(x, y)* = 0, so that the variables do not evolve anymore. Here, we were able to obtain analytical values for these equilibrium points with the `solve()` function.

To analyze their stability, we need to perform a linear analysis of the nonlinear equations, by taking the **Jacobian matrix** at these equilibrium points. This matrix represents the linearized system, and its eigenvalues tell us about the stability of the system near the equilibrium point. The **Hartman–Grobman theorem** states that the behavior of the original system qualitatively matches the behavior of the linearized system around an equilibrium point if this point is **hyperbolic** (meaning that no eigenvalues of the matrix have a real part equal to 0). Here, the first equilibrium point is hyperbolic as *a, c* > 0, but the second is not.

Here, we were able to compute symbolic expressions for the Jacobian matrix and its eigenvalues at the equilibrium points.

There's more...

Even when a differential system is not solvable analytically (as is the case here), a mathematical analysis can still give us qualitative information about the behavior of the system's solutions. A purely numerical analysis is not always relevant when we are interested in qualitative results, as numerical errors and approximations can lead to wrong conclusions about the system's behavior.

Here are a few references:

- ▶ Matrix documentation in SymPy, available at `http://docs.sympy.org/dev/modules/matrices/matrices.html`
- ▶ Dynamical systems on Wikipedia, at `http://en.wikipedia.org/wiki/Dynamical_system`
- ▶ Equilibrium points on Scholarpedia, at `www.scholarpedia.org/article/Equilibrium`
- ▶ Bifurcation theory on Wikipedia, at `http://en.wikipedia.org/wiki/Bifurcation_theory`
- ▶ Chaos theory on Wikipedia, at `http://en.wikipedia.org/wiki/Chaos_theory`
- ▶ Further reading on dynamical systems, at `http://en.wikipedia.org/wiki/Dynamical_system#Further_reading`

Getting started with Sage

Sage (`www.sagemath.org`) is a standalone mathematics software based on Python. It is an open source alternative to commercial products such as Mathematica, Maple, or MATLAB. Sage provides a unified interface to many open source mathematical libraries. These libraries include SciPy, SymPy, NetworkX, and other Python scientific packages, but also non-Python libraries such as ATLAS, BLAS, GSL, LAPACK, Singular, and many others.

In this recipe, we will give a brief introduction to Sage.

Getting ready

You can either:

- ▶ Install Sage on your local computer (`www.sagemath.org/doc/installation/`)
- ▶ Create Sage notebooks remotely in the cloud (`https://cloud.sagemath.com/`)

Being based on so many libraries, Sage is heavy and hard to compile from source. Binaries exist for most systems except Windows, where you generally have to use VirtualBox (a virtualization solution: `www.virtualbox.org`).

Alternatively, you can use Sage in a browser with an IPython notebook running on the cloud.

Note that Sage is not compatible with Python 3 at the time of this writing.

Typically, Sage is used interactively with the built-in notebook (which resembles the IPython notebook). If you want to use Sage in a Python program (that is, importing Sage from Python), you need to run Sage's built-in Python interpreter (`www.sagemath.org/doc/faq/faq-usage.html#how-do-i-import-sage-into-a-python-script`).

How to do it...

Here, we will create a new Sage notebook and introduce the most basic features:

1. Sage accepts mathematical expressions as we would expect:

   ```
   sage: 3*4
   12
   ```

2. Being based on Python, Sage's syntax is almost Python, but there are a few differences. For example, the power exponent is the more classical ^ symbol:

   ```
   sage: 2^3
   8
   ```

3. Like in SymPy, symbolic variables need to be declared beforehand with the `var()` function. However, the x variable is always predefined. Here, we define a new mathematical function:

   ```
   sage: f=1-sin(x)^2
   ```

4. Let's simplify the expression of `f`:

   ```
   sage: f.simplify_trig()
   cos(x)^2
   ```

5. Let's evaluate `f` on a given point:

   ```
   sage: f(x=pi)
   1
   ```

6. Functions can be differentiated and integrated:

   ```
   sage: f.diff(x)
   -2*cos(x)*sin(x)
   sage: f.integrate(x)
   1/2*x + 1/4*sin(2*x)
   ```

7. Sage also supports numerical computations in addition to symbolic computations:

   ```
   sage: find_root(f-x, 0, 2)
   0.6417143708729723
   ```

8. Sage also comes with rich plotting capabilities (including interactive plotting widgets):

```
sage: f.plot((x, -2*pi, 2*pi))
```

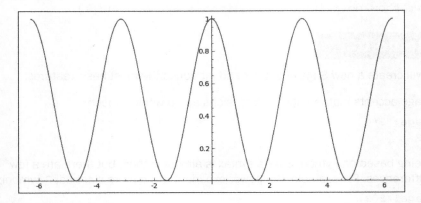

There's more...

This (too) short recipe cannot do justice to the huge list of possibilities offered by Sage. Many aspects of mathematics are covered: algebra, combinatorics, numerical mathematics, number theory, calculus, geometry, graph theory, and many others. Here are a few references:

▸ An in-depth tutorial on Sage, available at `www.sagemath.org/doc/tutorial/`

▸ The Sage reference manual, available at `www.sagemath.org/doc/reference/`

▸ Videos on Sage, available at `www.sagemath.org/help-video.html`

See also

▸ The *Diving into symbolic computing with SymPy* recipe

Index

G

Gaussian filter
about 358
reference link 361
Gaussian kernel 254
GCC (GNU Compiler Collection) 152
GDAL/OGR
reference link 442
General Purpose Programming on Graphics
Processing Units. *See* **GPGPU**
geographical distances
reference link 452
Geographic Information Systems
(GIS) 418, 420
geometry
references 420
GeoPandas
about 420
reference link 421
geospatial data
manipulating, with basemap 443-445
manipulating, with Shapely 443-445
ggplot2
reference link 208
ggplot, for Python
reference link 208
GIL
reference link 151
Git
about 53, 56
references 56
git branch command 57
Git branching
workflow 56-58
git diff command 57
git-flow 58
GitHub 53
git log command 57
Gitorious 53
git remote add command 55
git status command 57
Global Interpreter Lock (GIL)
about 151
reference link 151
glue language 10

Google code 53
GPGPU 176
gradient
reference link, for definition 322
gradient descent 321
graph coloring
reference link 418
graph dependency 187
Graphics Processing Units (GPUs) 150, 175
graphs
about 417, 418
edges 418
manipulating, with NetworkX 421-423
nodes 418
references 420
vertices 418
visualizing, with NetworkX 421, 423
graph theory
reference link 420
graph-tool package
about 419
reference link 420
graph traversal
reference link 418
GraphViz
reference link 260
grayscale image 354
great-circle distance 451
grid 179
grid search
about 280, 281
performing, with cross-validation 281-284
reference link 280
Gross Domestic Product (GDP) 442
groups. *See* **clusters**
GUI debuggers 77
GUI on Mac OS X 54
GUI on Windows 54
Guppy-PE
reference link 126

H

h5py
about 142
references 145, 146

reference links 195, 200
strengths 199
trying, in notebook 195-198
Jupyter
about 80
reference link 80
Just-In-Time compilation (JIT)
about 150
Python code, accelerating with 154-156

K

Kaggle
about 281
references 281, 289
Kartograph
about 420
reference link 421
KDE implementations, scikit-learn
reference link 254
KDE implementations, statsmodels
reference link 254
K-D trees 288
kernel
about 10, 179, 254, 296
creating, for IPython 39-44
multiple clients, connecting to 82
KernelBase API
reference link 44
kernel density estimation (KDE)
about 251-253
reference link 254
used, for estimating probability distribution
    nonparametrically 251-254
kernel spec 43
kernel trick 297
kernprof file
reference link, for downloading 123
Khronos Group 181
K-means algorithm
about 307
reference link 310
K-nearest neighbors (K-NN) classifier
about 285
handwritten digits, recognizing with 285-288
references 289

Kolmogorov-Smirnov test
about 249
reference link 250

L

L2 norm 278
Langevin equation
about 412
reference link 416
LAPACK 130
Laplacian matrix 424
LaTeX
about 17, 454
references 454
LaTeX equations 18
L-BFGS-B algorithm
about 329
reference link 330
least squares method
references 265, 280
Leave-One-Out cross-validation 280
left singular vectors 305
Levenberg-Marquardt algorithm
about 325
reference link 326
Lévi function 320
linear algebra
references 458
linear combination 134
linear filters
about 343, 346
and convolutions 346
applying, to digital signal 343-346
references 348
linear system 383
Linear Time-Invariant (LTI) 346
line_profiler
reference link 121
used, for profiling code 121-123
Linux 152
Lloyd's algorithm 309
LLVM (Low Level Virtual Machine) 156
load-balanced interface 186
locality of reference
about 130
reference link 132

local minimum 312, 313
local repository
  creating 54
logistic map
  about 384
  reference link 387
logistic regression
  about 281
  references 285
Lotka-Volterra equations 467, 469
low-pass filter
  about 348
  reference link 349
Lyapunov exponent
  about 384, 385
  reference link 387

M

machine learning
  about 267
  references 267, 272
magic commands
  about 16
  cythonmagic 35
  octavemagic 35
  reference link 35
  rmagic 35
Magics class 39
mandelbrot() function
  about 160, 164
  iterations argument 162, 177
  pointer argument 162, 177
  size argument 162, 177
manually-vectorized code
  Numba, comparing with 157
manual testing 67
MAP
  reference link 240
Maple 11
Markdown
  about 17
  reference link 60
Markdown cell 17
Markov chain Monte Carlo (MCMC)
  about 261

Bayesian model, fitting by sampling from
    posterior distribution 255-261
  reference link 261
Markov chains
  about 401
  references 406
Markov property
  about 401
  reference link 402
Mathematica 11
mathematical function
  minimizing 317-322
  root, finding of 314-316
mathematical morphology
  about 365
  reference link 366
mathematical optimization
  about 311
  reference link 314
MathJax
  about 454
  reference link 454
matplotlib
  about 10, 202
  dataset, exploring with 229-232
  reference link, for installation instructions 14
  references, for improving styling 205
matplotlib figures
  converting, to D3.js visualizations 215-217
  improving, with prettyplotlib 202-205
matrix
  about 30
  reference link 458, 470
maxima
  reference link 314
maximum a posteriori (MAP) 240
maximum likelihood estimate
  about 247
  reference link 250
maximum likelihood method
  about 245
  used for fitting, probability distribution
    to data 246-250
memoize pattern 61
memory mapping
  about 140, 142
  NumPy arrays, processing with 140, 141

W

Wakari 188
warps 179
wavelet transform 342
weave module 163
webcam images
  processing, from notebook 108-113
WebCL 184
WebGL 221
white box model 301
white noise
  about 415
  reference link 416
widget
  references 102
widget architecture, IPython notebook 2.0+
  references 108
Wiener process. *See* Brownian motion
Windows
  about 152
  DLL Hell 153
  Python 32-bit 152
  Python 64-bit 152

Winpdb 77
Wolfram's code
  about 388
  reference link 390
workflow, Git branching 56-58
workflows
  references 59
workflows, unit testing 73
wrapper kernels
  about 44
  reference link 44

Z

Zachary's Karate Club graph 212
ZeroMQ (ZMQ)
  reference link 81
z-test
  performing 233-236

Thank you for buying
IPython Interactive Computing and Visualization Cookbook

About Packt Publishing

Packt, pronounced 'packed', published its first book "*Mastering phpMyAdmin for Effective MySQL Management*" in April 2004 and subsequently continued to specialize in publishing highly focused books on specific technologies and solutions.

Our books and publications share the experiences of your fellow IT professionals in adapting and customizing today's systems, applications, and frameworks. Our solution based books give you the knowledge and power to customize the software and technologies you're using to get the job done. Packt books are more specific and less general than the IT books you have seen in the past. Our unique business model allows us to bring you more focused information, giving you more of what you need to know, and less of what you don't.

Packt is a modern, yet unique publishing company, which focuses on producing quality, cutting-edge books for communities of developers, administrators, and newbies alike. For more information, please visit our website: www.packtpub.com.

About Packt Open Source

In 2010, Packt launched two new brands, Packt Open Source and Packt Enterprise, in order to continue its focus on specialization. This book is part of the Packt Open Source brand, home to books published on software built around Open Source licenses, and offering information to anybody from advanced developers to budding web designers. The Open Source brand also runs Packt's Open Source Royalty Scheme, by which Packt gives a royalty to each Open Source project about whose software a book is sold.

Writing for Packt

We welcome all inquiries from people who are interested in authoring. Book proposals should be sent to author@packtpub.com. If your book idea is still at an early stage and you would like to discuss it first before writing a formal book proposal, contact us; one of our commissioning editors will get in touch with you.

We're not just looking for published authors; if you have strong technical skills but no writing experience, our experienced editors can help you develop a writing career, or simply get some additional reward for your expertise.

Learning IPython for Interactive Computing and Data Visualization

ISBN: 978-1-78216-993-2   Paperback: 138 pages

Learn IPython for interactive Python programming, high-performance numerical computing, and data visualization

1. A practical step-by-step tutorial which will help you to replace the Python console with the powerful IPython command-line interface.

2. Use the IPython notebook to modernize the way you interact with Python.

3. Perform highly efficient computations with NumPy and Pandas.

Python Data Visualization Cookbook

ISBN: 978-1-78216-336-7   Paperback: 280 pages

Over 60 recipes that will enable you to learn how to create attractive visualizations using Python's most popular libraries

1. Learn how to set up an optimal Python environment for data visualization.

2. Understand the topics such as importing data for visualization and formatting data for visualization.

3. Understand the underlying data and how to use the right visualizations.

Please check **www.PacktPub.com** for information on our titles

NumPy Cookbook

ISBN: 978-1-84951-892-5   Paperback: 226 pages

Over 70 interesting recipes for learning the Python open source mathematical library, NumPy

1. Do high performance calculations with clean and efficient NumPy code.

2. Analyze large sets of data with statistical functions.

3. Execute complex linear algebra and mathematical computations.

Matplotlib for Python Developers

ISBN: 978-1-84719-790-0   Paperback: 308 pages

Build remarkable publication-quality plots the easy way

1. Create high quality 2D plots by using Matplotlib productively.

2. Incremental introduction to Matplotlib, from the ground up to advanced levels.

3. Embed Matplotlib in GTK+, Qt, and wxWidgets applications as well as websites to utilize them in Python applications.

Please check **www.PacktPub.com** for information on our titles

Lightning Source UK Ltd.
Milton Keynes UK
UKOW06f1125091014

239806UK00001B/53/P